DOCTRINE AND COVENANTS

GUIDEBOOK

DOCTRINE AND COVENANTS

GUIDEBOOK

Conrad Knudson

CORNERSTONE

Published by:
Cornerstone Publishing & Distribution, Inc.
(also dba HORIZON PUBLISHERS)
PO Box 490
Bountiful, UT 84011-0490
800-453-0812

www.horizonpublishers.com
Email: horizonp@burgoyne.com

First Printing: August 1996

Printed in the United States of America
05 04 03 02 01   10 9 8 7 6 5 4 3 2

ISBN 0-88290-580-5

CONTENTS

ABBREVIATIONS

AGQ	*Answers to Gospel Questions*
AoF	*The Articles of Faith*
BOM	*Book of Mormon*
CHC	*Comprehensive History of the Church*
CHMR	*Church History and Modern Revelation*
Comp.	*A Companion to Your Study of the Doctrine and Covenants*
CR	*Conference Report*
D&C	*Doctrine and Covenants*
DBY	*Discourses of Brigham Young*
DCC	*Doctrine and Covenants Commentary*
DCSM	*The Doctrine and Covenants Student Manual*
DNTC	*Doctrinal New Testament Commentary*
DS	*Doctrines of Salvation*
DWW	*Discourses of Wilford Woodruff*
HC	*History of the Church*
GD	*Gospel Doctrine*
IE	*Improvement Era*
JD	*Journal of Discourses*
LDSBE	*L.D.S. Biographical Encyclopedia*
LHCK	*Life of Heber C. Kimball*
MD	*Mormon Doctrine*
MDC	*The Message of the Doctrine and Covenants*
MF	*The Miracle of Forgiveness*
MS	*Millennial Star*
PGP	*Pearl of Great Price*
ST	*Sacred Truths of the Doctrine and Covenants*
TETB	*Teachings of Ezra Taft Benson*
TPJS	*Teachings of the Prophet Joseph Smith*
TSWK	*Teachings of Spencer W. Kimball*
v.	Verse(s)

INTRODUCTION

What You Need To Know To Use This Guidebook

Warning: this guidebook will not make sense unless you read the Doctrine and Covenants along with it. Guidebooks are valuable, but they are no substitute for the real thing.

When sight-seeing, I have a more enjoyable and educational experience when I have a guidebook that gives good suggestions of where to go and what to see and provides information about the history, the people, and the language that will help it all mean something to me. However, while guidebooks can be beneficial, reading a guidebook about a foreign country and claiming you know that country is absurd.

It is also impossible to know the scriptures by only reading about them. I want you to understand and know the Doctrine and Covenants. I want you to see its revelations, hear the voice of the Lord, taste of His goodness, and feel the Spirit. To do this, you need to go there. Just reading a guidebook about that place will not do.

As the subtitle states, this book is intended to be a comprehensive, yet clear and concise study guide to the Doctrine and Covenants.

Comprehensive

By "comprehensive," I do not mean that this guidebook attempts to define every word used or give the biography of every person mentioned in the Doctrine and Covenants. Nor does it attempt to give a minute-to-minute account of Church history.

What I do mean by "comprehensive" is that an attempt is made to explain anything that is not plainly obvious and to give additional insight to things that very well may be "plainly obvious." "Comprehensive" also means that some biographical and historical information is presented. Often, it is the historical context or biographical information that is the key to unlocking a passage of scripture. Joseph Fielding Smith said:

> You may take it up if you want to by topics, or doctrines, that is good; but you are not going to understand the Doctrine and Covenants, you are not going to get out of it all there is in it unless you take it up section by section; and then when you do that, you will have to study it with its setting, as you get it in the history of the Church (*DS*, 3:199).

Clear

"For behold, my soul delighteth in plainness unto my people, that they may learn" (Nephi, 2 Ne. 25:4).

Every attempt has been made to write clearly. Although I expect even the most intelligent and knowledgeable reader will glean further insight into the Doctrine and Covenants by using this guidebook, I hope it is written clearly enough for the beginning Seminary student to understand.

I have also attempted to clearly document all quotes and other sources of information. Who said what and with what authority they said it makes a big difference (as will be taught over and over again in the *D&C*). When I use a title in front of a person's name, it means that person held that position when he or she made that statement or gave that explanation. Otherwise, I will not put the title in front of the person's name. For example, Gordon B. Hinckley may have said one thing, Elder Gordon B. Hinckley another, and President Gordon B. Hinckley another. Also note that I use the title of President (unless otherwise explained) only when speaking of the President of the Church and not when referring to presidents of other quorums or to other members of the First Presidency. This way, it should be very clear who said what and by what authority.

Concise

I repeat: you can't read this guidebook without reading the Doctrine and Covenants—it won't make sense. I purposely left out hundreds of pages of beautiful quotes from various passages of scripture. Instead, I wrote, "Read John 5:39 . . . " or "See 3 Ne. 23:1 for additional insight." I also narrowed down hundreds of pages of quotes by General Authorities to give you the essential teaching pertinent to the subject at hand. And I spared you hundreds of additional pages by not repeating the same lesson every section it comes up. Instead, I wrote, "Wait until we get to . . ." or "See . . ." or "Remember the material for . . ." or "Review the material for 1:37-39, 'The Challenge and Promises of the Doctrine and Covenants.'"

Personal Statement

I accept full responsibility for any mistaken conclusions or errors in this book. I have made every effort to present the truth. Like you, I hope to continue to learn truth from the Lord and His servants.

KEY QUOTES ABOUT THE DOCTRINE AND COVENANTS

"The book of Doctrine and Covenants is given for the Latter-day saints expressly for their everyday walk and actions" (Brigham Young, *DBY*, p. 128).

"The Book of Mormon and the Doctrine and Covenants are bound together as revelations from Israel's God to gather and prepare His people for the second coming of the Lord. . . .

"The Book of Mormon and the Doctrine and Covenants testify of each other. You cannot believe one and not the other. . . .

"The Doctrine and Covenants is the binding link between the Book of Mormon and the continuing work of the Restoration through the Prophet Joseph Smith and his successors. . . .

"The Book of Mormon brings men to Christ. The Doctrine and Covenants brings men to Christ's kingdom. . . .

"The Book of Mormon is the 'keystone of our religion,' and the Doctrine and Covenants is the capstone, with continuing latter-day revelation. The Lord has placed His stamp of approval on both the keystone and the capstone" (President Ezra Taft Benson, *Ensign*, May 1987, p. 83).

1

THE LORD'S PREFACE
PURPOSES OF THE DOCTRINE AND COVENANTS

Historical Context

Read the section heading.

Elder Joseph Fielding Smith further explained:

> Section one in the Doctrine and Covenants is not the first revelation received, but it is so placed in the book because the Lord gave it as the preface to the book of his commandments. The Doctrine and Covenants is . . . the only book in existence which bears the honor of a preface given by the Lord himself (*CHMR*, 1:251-252).

The Doctrine and Covenants Is for All (1:1-7, 34-36)

The Lord makes clear that His book is for all people (v. 4). As a good preface should do, Section 1 states the purposes of the Doctrine and Covenants and gives a summary of what will be encountered in it.

Why We Need the Doctrine and Covenants (1:8-33)

The Lord gives five purposes of His book:
1. To bring us to an understanding (v. 24).
2. To make known our errors (v. 25).
3. To instruct and give us wisdom (v. 26).
4. To chasten us that we might repent (v. 27).
5. To make us strong, bless us from on high, and give us knowledge from time to time (v. 28).

As we follow the teachings of the Lord's book, these five things will happen in our lives. As you read the Doctrine and Covenants and this guidebook, look for these five things happening in each section and in your life.

Given unto My Servants in Their Weakness (1:24)

Wait until we get to Section 67: "The Language of Scripture."

The Only True Church (1:30)

The Lord states that The Church of Jesus Christ of Latter-day Saints is the only true church (v. 30). The Lord also makes it clear that no individual member of the Church is perfect. (See the material for *D&C* 50:4-9, "Hypocrites in the Church.")

The Challenge and Promises
of the Doctrine and Covenants (1:37-39)

The Lord challenges us to search His book (v. 37) and promises us three things:

1. The prophecies and promises in His book will all be fulfilled (v. 37).
2. He will direct the Church (v. 38). (This will be further discussed in the material for 50:4-9, "Hypocrites in the Church.")
3. We can gain a testimony by the Spirit that the Doctrine and Covenants is true (v. 39).

I hope this guidebook will help you take on the Lord's challenge and receive these promises.

2

HEART TO HEART

Historical Context

The message of the restoration of the sealing powers is so important that it is repeated in each of the standard works (Mal. 4:5-6; 3 Ne. 25:5-6; *D&C* 2; 27:9; 128:17; J.S.—H. 1:37-39). In this section, Moroni gives additional insights into this message. In the material for 110:13-16 we will learn how this prophecy was fulfilled.

The Promises (2:2)

The promises referred to are promises made to people that all can receive gospel ordinances even though they may live while the gospel is not on the earth (Joseph Fielding Smith, *Improvement Era*, July 22, p. 829).

The Earth Would Be Utterly Wasted (2:3)

The reason the earth exists—its purpose—is to turn the hearts of the children to the fathers and the hearts of the fathers to the children. In other words, the purpose of the earth is to provide for the sealing together of families (*D&C* 49:15-17; 1 Ne. 17:36). Therefore, if we did not have the priesthood—the sealing power—the earth would have no reason to exist and would be "utterly wasted."

Applies to the Living

President Harold B. Lee said that turning the hearts of the children to the fathers and the fathers to the children

> applies just as much on this side of the veil as it does on the other side of the veil. If we neglect our families here . . . how could we feel that we are doing our full duty in turning the hearts of our children to their fathers (Priesthood Genealogy Seminar, 1973 in *ST*, 1:16).

3, 10

THE LOST 116 PAGES

3. *The Real Problem*   **10.** *Satan Works Hard, But the Lord Will Keep His Promises*

Historical Context

After Joseph Smith translated the first 116 pages of the Book of Mormon (called the "Book of Lehi"), Martin Harris wanted to show the pages to his family. Joseph Smith asked the Lord if Martin could take the pages. Joseph Smith said:

> The answer was that he must not [take the pages]. However, he was not satisfied with this answer, and desired that I should inquire again. I did so, and the answer was as before. Still he could not be contented, but insisted that I should inquire once more. After much solicitation I again inquired of the Lord, and permission was granted him to have the writings on certain conditions; which were, that he show them only to his brother Preserved Harris, his own wife, his father and his mother, and a Mrs. Cobb, a sister to his wife. In accordance with this last answer, I required of him that he should bind himself in a covenant to me in a most solemn manner that he would not do otherwise than had been directed. He did so. He bound himself as I required of him, took the writings, and went his way. Notwithstanding, however, the great restrictions which he had been laid under, and the solemnity of the covenants which he had made with me, he did

show them to others, and by stratagem they got them away from him, and they never have been recovered unto this day (*HC*, 1:20-22).

The Real Problems (3:4-15)

The lost pages were not a problem to the Lord. The Lord had already taken care of this problem about 2,400 years earlier (1 Ne. 9:5-6). The Lord uses this occasion to make known the errors of Joseph and Martin in order to make them stronger (3:9-11). The real problems were:

1. trusting in man instead of God (3:4,7);
2. giving sacred things to the wicked (3:12); and
3. breaking promises with the Lord (3:13).

The Lord explains that even though we may perform miracles, receive wonderful revelations, and have mighty spiritual experiences; if we do not remain humble, we will fall (3:4).

Satan Works Hard But
The Lord Will Keep His Promises (3:1-3, 16-20; 10:5-70)

Satan made a plan that would get people to think that Joseph Smith was a false prophet (10:5- 29). But the wisdom of the Lord is greater than the cunning of the devil (10:43). The Work of the Lord cannot be frustrated (3:1-3). The Lord made several promises to different Book of Mormon prophets that their writings would be preserved and taught to their descendants (3 Ne. 5:14). Some of these prophets are:

1. Lehi and Joseph (2 Ne. 3:6-23)
2. Nephi (1 Ne. 9:1-6; 13:35-41; 19:1-6, 18; 2 Ne. 11:2-3; 25:7-8; 26:16-17; 28:1-2; 29:11; 33:10-15)
3. Jacob (Jacob 1:1-8; 4:1-4)
4. Enos (Enos 1:12-18)
5. Jarom (Jarom 1:1-2)
6. Mormon (W of M 1:1-6; Morm. 5:8-13; 7:9)
7. Moroni (Morm. 8:14-16, 25-35; 9:36-37; Moro. 10:24, 27-29)

The Lord told Joseph Smith that He would keep these promises (3:16-20; 10:46-70). The Lord told Joseph Smith not to retranslate the lost pages, and showed him what to do instead (10:30- 45).

But Be Diligent (10:4)

Some quote the first half of this verse (or Mosiah 4:27) to justify their laziness and lack of progress; they forget that the verse also says to "be diligent unto the end." Neal A. Maxwell said:

> The scriptural advice, "Do not run faster or labor more than you have strength" (*D&C* 10:4) suggests paced progress. . . . There is a difference, therefore, between

being "anxiously engaged" and being over-anxious and thus underengaged (*Ensign*, Nov. 1976, 12-13).

Satan works hard to frustrate the plans of the Lord and our progress, but as we "pray always" and are "diligent unto the end" we will "come off conqueror" (3:5; 10:4).

You may wish to cross reference the material for 10:4 with that for 63:24, "Haste —> Confusion —> Pestilence."

4, 11, 12, 14, 15, 16
CALLED TO THE WORK

4.	**Joseph Smith, Sr.**	**14.**	**David Whitmer**
11.	**Hyrum Smith**	**15.**	**John Whitmer**
12.	**Joseph Knight, Sr.**	**16.**	**Peter Whitmer, Jun.**

Historical Context

Each of the men mentioned in the titles came to Joseph to find out what the Lord wanted them to do. Each of the men were called to the work of proclaiming the gospel.

Section 4 Applies to All Members

Joseph Fielding Smith said that Section 4

was not intended as a personal revelation to Joseph Smith, [Sr.] but to be of benefit to all who desire to embark in the service of God. It is a revelation to each member of the church, especially to all who hold the Priesthood. . . . No elder of the Church is qualified to teach in the Church, or carry the message of Salvation to the world, until he has absorbed, in part at least, this heaven-sent instruction (*CHMR* 1:32-33).

Qualifications of a Servant of Jesus Christ

The Lord taught each of the men in these sections that to serve God they needed certain tools. The Lord said these things also apply to everybody who desires to serve God (11:27). Some of the needed tools that qualify us for serving the Lord are:

1. **Christ-like attributes (4:2-6, 12:8).** When we are called to serve the Lord we are actually called to be His representative to others. To be a representative of Jesus Christ we must come to know Him. He said that coming to know Him is eternal life (John 17:3). To know Him is to be like Him (1 John 3:2). Peter understood this, and told the early saints that in order to "be partakers of the divine nature" they needed to take on almost the exact same attributes as listed in these sections of the Doctrine and Covenants (2 Pet. 1:4-9).

2. **An eye single to the glory of God (4:5).** The glory of God is "to bring to pass the immortality and eternal life of man" (Moses 1:39). As His servants, our eye must be single to this glory. Servants of Christ are called to love people by inviting them to come unto Christ through obedience to the principles and ordinances of eternal life (*D&C* 39:1- 6).

3. **Declare nothing but repentance (11:9; 15:6; 16:6).** Joseph Fielding Smith said:

> When the Lord calls upon his servants to cry nothing but repentance, he does not mean that they may not cry baptism, and call upon the people to obey the commandments of the Lord, but he wishes that all that they say and do be in the spirit of bringing the people to repentance. Any missionary who fails to do this in his ministry is derelict in his duty (*CHMR* 1:52).

The goal of missionary teaching is not just to share knowledge, but to help others make and keep commitments to come unto Christ. The most important part of any teaching experience is extending an invitation to obey what is taught. By extending this invitation we are following the Lord's instruction to "declare nothing but repentance."

4. **The proper authority (11:15-17).** This will be further discussed in the material for 36:5-7, "Must be Called of God by His Representatives."

5. **A knowledge of gospel truths (11:21-22).** The Lord told Hyrum Smith to gain this knowledge by studying the Bible and the Book of Mormon (11:22). (At this time there was no Doctrine and Covenants or Pearl of Great price.)

6. **Obedience to the commandments (11:18-20).**

Convincing Power (11:21)

Powerful missionaries throughout the scriptures have sought after and been blessed with "the power of God unto the convincing of men" (v. 21). Members and missionaries today, as they gain the tools and qualifications mentioned above, can also be blessed with this convincing power. But, some ask, is it right to *convince* people to repent and be baptized? Ponder *JST* Gen. 50:30; Acts 18:28; Titus 1:9; Jude 1:15; 1 Ne. 13:39; 14:7; 2 Ne. 3:1; 25:18; Mosiah 27:14; 28:2; Alma 21:17; 26:24; 37:8-9; 62:45; 3 Ne. 28:29; *D&C* 6:11; and 18:44. Are you convinced?

Convincing power will be further discussed in the material for 42:4-17, "Laws on Teaching;" 50:10-22, "Preach by the Spirit;" 100:5-8, "Teaching with Power;" and *Convincing (Converting) Power* in Appendix 3: "Blessings and Laws Upon Which they are Predicated."

Thrust in Your Sickle with Your Might (4:4)

The Lord needs people who are willing to work hard to help bring souls unto Him. On missionary work, President Kimball said:

> You are going out on your mission, not merely to make friends for the Church, though that is important, but to properly convert and baptize the numerous people who are anxious and ready for the gospel. Brethren, the spirit of our work must be urgency, and we must imbue our missionaries and saints with this spirit of "Now." We are not justified in waiting for the natural, slow growth which would come with natural and easy proselyting. . . . We believe that we must put our shoulder to the wheel, lengthen our stride, heighten our reach, increase our devotion so that we can do the work to which we have been assigned (quoted by Bruce R. McConkie, Mission Presidents' Seminar, June 21, 1976).

The Lord does not call missionaries to "plant seeds." Members plant the seeds. Missionaries are called to mightily reap the harvest. Missionaries, however, do plant seeds in the process of reaping. Vaughn J. Featherstone said: "Let's not use a sickle. Let's use a combine" (quoted by David B. Haight, *Ensign*, Nov. 1977, 58).

Missionary Work by Non-members

It is interesting to note that at the time the Lord called these men to be missionaries, they were not members of the Church. All people should be invited to be "missionaries." Even people who are about to slam the door in a missionary's face should be asked, "Out of the people you know, who is the most spiritually prepared to listen to our message?"

The Greatest Gift (14:7)

The Lord promises eternal life to all who become members of His Church and endure to the end. He says that this gift "is the greatest of all the gifts of God" (14:7).

5, 17
THE BOOK OF MORMON

5. *Witnesses*	17. *The Three Witnesses*

Historical Context

The Prophet Moroni wrote Joseph Smith a message in the Book of Mormon. The message told Joseph that he would be allowed to show the plates of the Book of Mormon to a few people. Moroni also said there would be three "special" witnesses (Ether 5:1-4). After Joseph Smith translated Moroni's message, Martin Harris pleaded with Joseph to let him be one of those three special witnesses. So Joseph asked the Lord about it and received the revelation in Section 5. Then Oliver Cowdery and David Whitmer pleaded with Joseph to let them be the other two special witnesses. Joseph asked the Lord and received the revelation in Section 17.

Why Both the Three Witnesses and the Eight Witnesses?

The Lord knew people would say that Joseph hypnotized the three witnesses or that they were on drugs. So the Lord provided a physical witness to eight men. These men could only claim that they knew Joseph had the plates and that they looked like ancient writings. This witness would be the same as if I brought this book over to your house and asked you to look through it and then write something down so that others would know that I had the book and that it looked real.

But the Lord also knew that there would be people who would say that Joseph tricked these men by making some plates himself. So the Lord provided a special witness to three other men. The Lord Himself would testify to these three men and also send them an angel to show them the plates.

A Physical Witness

Moroni wrote that Joseph Smith would be allowed to show the plates to some people (Ether 5:2). "The Testimony of Eight Witnesses" tells about when Joseph Smith showed the plates to eight men. There are two keys to this testimony:

1. It was Joseph Smith who showed them the plates—not the Lord.
2. They testify that the plates *appear* to be what Joseph told them they were.

This was a physical witness. These men could not say that they knew the plates were what Joseph said they were, they could only say that they *appeared* to be what he said and that they knew Joseph had them.

But the Lord knew that this kind of physical witness is not a strong enough foundation on which to build His church—people could still deny the truthfulness of the Book of Mormon (*D&C* 5:7). One example is Martin Harris:

> Martin Harris had already received a remarkable proof of the truth of the claims made by the Prophet Joseph regarding the Book of Mormon, when he carried a facsimile of the engravings to New York scientists. Professor Anthon had told him . . . that the "hieroglyphics were true characters." He had also, through the Prophet, received revelations (Sec. 3:12). But he was not yet satisfied (Smith and Sjodahl in *Comp.*, 1:74).

A Spiritual Witness

If Joseph Smith were not a prophet, and if he were only making up the Book of Mormon story himself, then he made a big mistake. In Ether 5:3 it says that three men will be shown the plates "by the power of God." Now how is Joseph Smith going to get God to come down and tell three people that the Book of Mormon is true unless he really is a prophet? If this witness did not happen, Joseph would be proven to be a false prophet—he would be destroyed (*D&C* 17:3-4). For this reason, the Lord called the Three Witnesses.

The keys to "The Testimony of Three Witnesses" are:
  1. "we . . . know."
  2. "by the power of God, and *not of man*" (emphasis added).
The Lord takes Joseph Smith completely out of the picture. Joseph Smith did not show the Three Witnesses the plates—an angel did. Joseph Smith did not tell them that the Book of Mormon is the word of God—the Lord did. These three men did not have to say the Book of Mormon *appeared* to be an ancient work; they could say that they *knew* it was true because God told them so.

Powerful Testimony

Neither the Three nor the Eight Witnesses were members of the Church at the time they wrote their testimonies. Although some of these men would fall away from the Church, none ever denied his testimony. Nearly 50 years after his experience, David Whitmer (who was excommunicated at the time) said:

> There appeared as it were a table with many records of plates upon it, besides the plates of the Book of Mormon, also the sword of Laban, the directors and the interpreters. I saw them just as plain as I see this bed, and I heard the voice of the Lord, as distinctly as I ever heard anything in my life, declaring that the records of the plates of the Book of Mormon were translated by the gift and power of God (*Life of Joseph F. Smith*, 242-243).

Jesus Christ added His testimony of the truthfulness of the Book of Mormon to the testimony of the Three and the Eight Witnesses when He said: "as your Lord and your God liveth it is true" (*D&C* 17:6).

Resolving Concerns with the Book of Mormon— The Keystone of Our Religion

Joseph Smith said that the Book of Mormon is "the keystone of our religion" (see the introduction to the Book of Mormon). President Benson wrote:

> Just as the arch crumbles if the keystone is removed, so does all the Church stand or fall with the truthfulness of the Book of Mormon. The enemies of the Church understand this clearly. This is why they go to such great lengths to try to disprove the Book of Mormon, for if it can be discredited, the Prophet Joseph Smith goes with it. So does our claim to priesthood keys, and revelation, and the restored Church. But in like manner, if the Book of Mormon be true . . . then one must accept the claims of the Restoration and all that accompanies it.
>
> Yes, the Book of Mormon is the keystone of our religion—the keystone of our testimony, the keystone of our doctrine, and the keystone in the witness of our Lord and Savior (*A Witness and A Warning*, p. 19).

President Benson explains how to use "the keystone of our religion" to resolve concerns people may have about Church doctrine. He wrote:

> All objections, whether they be on abortion, plural marriage, seventh-day worship, etc., basically hinge on whether Joseph Smith and his successors were and are prophets of God receiving divine revelation. Here, then is a procedure to handle most objections through the use of the Book of Mormon.
>
> *First,* understand the objection.
>
> *Second,* give the answer from revelation.
>
> *Third,* show how the correctness of the answer really depends on whether or not we have modern revelation through modern prophets.
>
> *Fourth,* explain that whether or not we have modern prophets and revelation really depends on whether the Book of Mormon is true.
>
> Therefore, the only problem the objector has to resolve for himself is whether the Book of Mormon is true. For if the Book of Mormon is true, then Jesus is the Christ, Joseph Smith was his prophet, The Church of Jesus Christ of Latter-day Saints is true, and it is being led today by a prophet receiving revelation (*A Witness and A Warning*, pp. 4-5; emphasis added).

These steps do not have to be followed in the order given. Here's an example of using President Benson's "procedure to handle most objections through the use of the Book of Mormon:"

Investigator: I would get baptized if I didn't have to stop drinking alcohol. I mean, all things in moderation can't be bad.

Step 1 - Understand the Objection

Missionary: Let me ask you a question. If God came down and personally asked you to stand on your head every day at six o'clock, would you do it?

Investigator: Sounds silly, but I guess so. (If the answer is no then you might as well stop here.)

Missionary: Why would you do it?

Investigator: I guess because God said so. And if God says to do something, you'd better do it.

Missionary: I'm glad to hear that you are willing to follow the Lord. I wish more people today were willing to follow Him. Now then, if you knew that the Lord told us not to drink alcohol, would you be willing to stop drinking and be baptized?

Investigator: I guess—if I really could know that it came from God and isn't just something the leaders of your church made up—I guess I would do as God commands.

Step 2 - Give the Answer from Revelation

Missionary: Now that we understand your concern, we would like to help you to know that drinking alcoholic beverages is prohibited by God Himself. Joseph Smith received a revelation in which God prohibited drinking alcohol. (One could, though it is unnecessary, turn to *D&C* 89.)

Step 3 - Show how the Correctness of the Answer Depends on Whether or Not We Have Modern Revelation through Modern Prophets

Missionary: Now then, if you knew for sure that Joseph Smith was a true prophet of God like Moses, you could be confident that God Himself has commanded us not to drink alcohol.

Investigator: But how can I know?

Step 4 - Explain that Whether or Not We Have Modern Prophets and Revelation Depends on Whether the Book of Mormon is True

Missionary: Remember us teaching you about the Book of Mormon?

Investigator: Sure. But what has that got to do with knowing that this alcohol business really comes from God?

Missionary: What you need to do is find out if the Book of Mormon is true. For if the Book of Mormon is true, then Joseph Smith was a true prophet of God. You can know for sure that he received revelation from God. You can also know that The Church of Jesus Christ of Latter-day Saints is true, and it is being led today by a prophet receiving revelation. Do you see how knowing the Book of Mormon is true can help resolve most of your concerns?

Investigator: I guess I need to find out more about the Book of Mormon.

Missionary: Let's start by reviewing what we talked about before. Let's turn to Moroni 10:3-5. It's on page 529. . . .

For more information on the Book of Mormon, see the material for 84:43-62, "Remember the New Covenant, Even the Book of Mormon."[1]

6, 8, 9

REVELATION

6. *Peace of Mind*	**9. *Study it Out***
8. *In Your Mind and In Your Heart*	

Historical Context

While Oliver Cowdery was living at the home of Joseph Smith's father, Oliver learned about the Prophet Joseph Smith's vision and the Book of Mormon. Oliver then prayed to find out if what he learned was true. Then Oliver traveled down to where Joseph Smith lived to find out more about the Book of Mormon.

Oliver began to help Joseph translate the Book of Mormon. Joseph had never seen Oliver before, so he asked the Lord why Oliver had come to help him (*HC* 1:32-35).

Quick and Powerful, Sharper Than a Two-edged Sword (6:2)

In the Bible, "quick" means "living" (Acts 10:42). The Lord's word is "quick" because it gives life when we obey it. But when we do not obey the word of the Lord, it kills us spiritually like a two-edged sword can kill physically.

Only God Knows our Thoughts—A Witness (6:14-17, 22-24)

The key verse to unlock Section 6 is verse 16. Nobody except God knows our thoughts and our hearts—this includes Satan (see also 1 Kings 8:39; Moses 4:6). Only Oliver Cowdery and the Lord knew that Oliver had prayed to know the truth (*HC* 1:35; *D&C* 6:24). Joseph Smith's revealing that Oliver Cowdery had not only prayed, but also felt peace was a witness to Oliver that Joseph Smith

---

1. For a more extensive discussion of resolving concerns with the Book of Mormon, including many more examples, I suggest reading *The Book of Mormon: Key to Conversion* by Glenn L. Pearson (Bookcraft, Salt Lake City, Utah, 1963).

was a true prophet (v. 14, 22-23). The only way Joseph could have known these things was to have received revelation from God (v. 17, 24).

The Gift of Aaron (8:6-9)

Just like Aaron went before his younger brother Moses as a spokesman, Oliver Cowdery was to be a spokesman for Joseph Smith (*CHMR*, 1:52).

Asking for, and Receiving Revelation

In Sections 8 and 9 the Lord teaches us what revelation is and how to ask for it. How to ask for revelation:

1. Study it out in your mind (9:7-8).
2. Ask in faith (8:1).
3. Ask with an honest heart (8:1).
4. Believe that you will receive it (8:1).

Asking with an honest heart—or with "real intent" (Moroni 10:4)—means that we are willing to believe the answer and follow the instruction that comes. If we are not going to do what the Lord says, then why should He even bother to tell us what to do?

Revelation is God speaking to our mind and heart (*D&C* 8:2-3). In other words, the answer will be:

1. Thoughts.
2. Feelings.

Not all answers come as the "burning in the bosom." Most come as an impression to do something or as a feeling of hope that everything will work out. This hope leads us to faith. As we act upon our faith, we will have even more hope, which in turn will lead us to greater faith, which in turn leads us to feel the sweet peace of charity (see Moroni 7:40-48). There is no greater witness that we can have than to feel peace about something (*D&C* 6:23). Not even seeing with our eyes is greater than the small impression of peace that we receive from the Lord. Laman and Lemuel never let themselves feel the Spirit, so even when they saw an angel they did not believe (1 Ne. 17:45). And Jesus said that those who do not let themselves believe in the prophets' words would still not believe even if they saw the miracle of the raising of the dead (Luke 16:31).

Commenting on *D&C* 9:8-9, President Joseph Fielding Smith said that "A similar privilege is given to any member of the Church" (*CHMR*, 1:51). And Melvin J. Ballard said:

> I know of nothing today that the Latter-day saints need more than the guidance of the Holy Spirit in the solution of the problems of life (*CR*, April 1931, 37-38).

The Lord Sometimes Withholds Answers to Prayers

If the Lord gave us the answer to every one of our questions, we would not mature spiritually. He wants us to do many good things on our own. This is how we progress and grow (*D&C* 58:26-28). Elder Richard G. Scott of the Quorum of the Twelve put it this way:

> When [Heavenly Father] answers yes, it is to give us confidence.
>
> When He answers no, it is to prevent error.
>
> When he *withholds an answer*, it is to have us grow through faith in Him. . . . We are expected to assume accountability by acting on a decision that is consistent with His teachings without prior confirmation. We are not to sit passively waiting or to murmur because the Lord has not spoken. We are to act.
>
> Most often what we have chosen to do is right. He will confirm the correctness of our choices His way. That confirmation generally comes through packets of help found along the way. We discover them by being spiritually sensitive. . . . If, in trust, we begin something which is not right, He will let us know before we have gone too far (*Ensign*, Nov. 1989, 32).

Sometimes the Lord lets us make a decision on our own, then after we do what we decided to do, we can receive a witness that we did the right thing (Ether 12:6). Many times, people who are investigating the church feel uncomfortable about being baptized because they feel that the Lord has not answered their prayers. They need to ask themselves, "Do I think this is the right thing to do?" and then do it. Only then will they receive the witness that they are looking for. Jesus said that only when we *do* what God asks, will we know that it is right (John 7:17).

For a good example of God withholding an answer to prayer to allow His children to mature spiritually, read 1 Nephi chapters 3-4.

Other Scriptures

1. **1 Kings 19:11-12.** A still small voice.
2. **Luke 24:32.** Did not our hearts burn within us?
3. **Galatians 5:22.** The fruits of the Spirit.
4. **Enos 1:10.** The voice of Lord came into my mind.

7

JOHN—A GREATER WORK

Historical Context

When the Apostle Peter asked Jesus what the Apostle John should do, Jesus said, "If I will that he tarry till I come, what is that to thee?" (John 21:22). Joseph Smith and Oliver Cowdery did not know what this meant. Joseph Smith asked the Lord about this. The Lord revealed to Joseph what the Apostle John wrote on a piece of parchment. *The Doctrine and Covenants Student Manual* states:

> It is not known whether Joseph saw the parchment referred to and was given power to translate it, or if its contents were revealed to Joseph without his seeing the original source. It makes no difference, since the material was given by revelation to the Prophet (p. 17).

John Did Not Die but Will Die

Otten and Caldwell state:

> John has a body of flesh and bones that has been changed in such a way that death is postponed for a period of time. Such a condition is described as a state of being translated (*ST*, 1:56).

Although John's death has been postponed, he will die in order that he may receive a resurrected body. Joseph Smith said:

> Translated bodies cannot enter into rest until they have undergone a change equivalent to death. Translated bodies are designed for future missions (*HC*, 4:425).

A Greater Work (7:5-6)

The Apostle Peter said to Jesus, "Lord, I am ready to go with thee, both into prison, and to death" (Luke 22:33). Peter was ready to die for the Lord and desired to live with Him after death. Jesus said that "this was a good desire" (*D&C* 7:5). John desired to live for the Lord and bring souls to Him. Jesus said that this was a "greater" work (*D&C* 7:5-6). Some people have interpreted this as meaning that John's desire was more mature or more righteous than Peter's. However, note that the term "greater," here, does not mean "better" or "more righteous." Peter and John had different talents, personalities, and callings to fulfill both in mortality and in the spirit world. Both Peter's and John's requests were righteous and fulfilled the Lord's plan perfectly. When the Lord said that John had a "greater" work, He only meant that John had "more" or "further" work to do in mortality.

A Ministering Angel (7:6)

"The word angel means messenger" (*DCC*, p. 41). An angel's calling, or job, is summed up in Moroni 7:29-31. Joseph Smith explained the difference between ministering angels and ministering spirits:

> the one a resurrected or translated body, with its spirit ministering to embodied spirits—the other a disembodied spirit, visiting and ministering to disembodied spirits (*HC*, 4:425).

Therefore, Jesus was a ministering spirit for three days in the spirit world, and then, upon His resurrection, He became a ministering angel and appeared to His disciples. For more information on translated beings see 3 Ne. 28:9, 19-22.

Some Places John Has Been

1. 1829 In New York to restore the Melchizedek priesthood (*D&C* 27:12).
2. 1831 Joseph Smith said John was:

> among the Ten Tribes of Israel who had been led away by Shalmaneser, king of Assyria, to prepare them for their return from their long dispersion (*HC*, 1:176).

3. 1836 At the Kirtland Temple (*LHCK*, pp. 91-92).

13

JOHN THE BAPTIST RESTORES THE AARONIC PRIESTHOOD

Historical Context

Read Joseph Smith—History 1:66-73 (in the Pearl of Great Price).

Why the Lesser Priesthood Is Called the Aaronic Priesthood

Read *D&C* 84:26-27 and 107:13-14.

Three Keys

1. **Ministering of angels.** To "minister" basically means to serve. The Lord promises that angels will serve those who are in His labor (*D&C* 84:88). This is not the same as praying to see an angel. President Wilford Woodruff said:

> One of the Apostles said to me years ago, "Brother Woodruff, I have prayed for a long time for the Lord to send the administration of an angel to me . . . but I have never had my prayer answered. . . ." I told him that the Lord never did nor never will send an angel to anybody merely to gratify the desire of the individual to see an angel. If the Lord sends an angel to anyone, He sends him to perform a work that cannot be performed only by the administration of an angel (*Deseret Weekly News* Vol. 55, No. 21, Nov. 7, 1896 in *ST*, 1:63).

John the Baptist had to come to restore the priesthood as an angel because Joseph Smith could not go to any mortal man to receive it.

2. **Gospel of repentance.** Aaronic priesthood holders use this key when home teaching, bearing testimony, and inviting friends to hear the missionaries.

3. **Baptism.** An Aaronic priesthood holder can be asked by the bishop to baptize somebody in order to have that Aaronic priesthood holder more fully appreciate and gain experience in his calling.

The Sons of Levi and Their Offering

People who can be called "sons of Levi" include:

1. **Melchizedek Priesthood holders (84:32).** Those that hold the Melchizedek priesthood "become the sons of Moses" (*D&C* 84:31-34). Moses is a descendant of Levi. Therefore, "the sons of Levi" are Melchizedek priesthood holders (*DS* 3:93).

2. **Aaronic Priesthood holders (13; 84:32),** using the same reasoning as above.

3. **All Latter-day Saints (128:24).** This obviously includes sisters.

The offering that the sons of Levi will make will take place in the temple and mainly concerns doing work for the dead (*D&C* 128:24). The sacrifice of animals as in the time of Adam (Moses 5:5) will also be restored as part of the restoration of all things, but will be done "apparently on a one-time basis" (McConkie, *MD*, p. 666). Joseph Fielding Smith said:

> The sacrifice of animals will be done to complete the restoration when the temple spoken of is built [the temple in Zion which will actually be twelve temples, some of which will be for the Aaronic Priesthood]; at the beginning of the millennium, or in the restoration, blood sacrifices will be performed long enough to

complete the fullness of the restoration in this dispensation. Afterwards sacrifice will be of some other character (*DS* 3:94).

Aaronic Priesthood Will Never Be Taken "Until. . . ."
Daniel H. Ludlow wrote:

> The use of the word until in this prayer of ordination does not mean that the Priesthood of Aaron will be taken from the earth once the sons of Levi "offer again an offering unto the Lord in righteousness." It is used in a continuing sense, much as in the expression "God be with you until we meet again" (*Comp.*, 1:115).

18

HOW GREAT SHALL BE YOUR JOY

Great Joy (18:13)
The Lord esteems all people, yet the righteous are favored (1 Ne. 17:35). The angels rejoice over a person who repents (Luke 15:10).

One and Many (18:15-16)
The Apostle Rudger Clawson said:

> And if one of these men should labor all his days, and bring save it be but one soul unto Christ, and that one should be his wife, what great joy he would have with his wife in heaven. Then if he should labor all his days and bring unto Christ the souls of his wife and his children, and none else perchance, how great would be his joy in heaven with his wife and children (*CR*, April 1901, 7-8).

To be powerful tools in the hands of the Lord we must first be willing to work our hardest even when we do not see the rewards of our work. Only after we have this kind of humble attitude will we be able to effectively help the Lord to save many souls. Ammon was willing to work with all his might just to save one soul. This humble attitude made him a tool in the hands of the Lord to save thousands of souls (Alma 26:30-31). After baptizing thousands of people, Ammon told us how we could become a tool in the hands of the Lord to bring thousands of souls unto Christ (Alma 26:22):

    1. We must repent, or change to become a better person each day.

2. We must exercise our faith by working hard.

3. We must pray always, or in other words, we must have our eye single to the glory of God.

Spencer W. Kimball prayed:

> Oh, our beloved Father in heaven, bring about the day when we may be able to bring in large numbers as Ammon and his brethren did, thousands of conversions, not dozens, not tens or fives or ones, thousands of conversions. The Lord promised it; He fulfills his promises.
>
> Our Father, may we move forward with Jesus Christ as our advocate to establish the Church among the inhabitants of the earth. . . . May we merit the promise that the Lord will do things that we can hardly believe. May we improve the efficiency of our missionaries, *each bringing thousands of converts into the Church* (Regional Representatives Seminar, April 3, 1975, emphasis added).

Contending Against the Church of the Devil (18:20)

In this verse, "church" may mean philosophy, doctrine, or teaching. To "contend against" means to make war upon. We make war upon false teachings simply by teaching the truth by the power of the Spirit. Joseph Fielding Smith said:

> When we are commanded to "contend against no church save it be the church of the devil," we must understand that this is instruction to us to contend against all evil. . . . All who go forth to teach should do so in wisdom and not contend with the churches or engage in profitless debates, but teach in the Spirit of kindness and try to persuade people to receive the truth" (*CHMR*, 1:83).

And Smith and Sjodahl wrote: "A minister of the Lord makes war upon the domain of the adversary by the sword of the Spirit; not by persecution" (*DCC*, p. 86).

For more information about the church of the devil, see the material for 29:21, "The Great and Abominable Church."

The Calling of the Twelve Apostles (18:26-47)

An apostle takes upon himself the name of Christ and is commissioned to bear witness of His name to the whole world and teach the world that salvation only comes by accepting Jesus Christ (*D&C* 18:14, 21-28, 41; 107:23, 35).

The Lord told the Three Witnesses of the Book of Mormon to choose the members of the first Quorum of Twelve Apostles (v. 37 and see *CHMR*, 1:75, 77). This was appropriate because both the Book of Mormon and the Twelve were to be witnesses of Christ in all the world (*HC* 2:187).

Our Apostolic Calling (18:24)

Otten and Caldwell state:

> Once we have a covenant relationship with Jesus Christ by taking upon us His
> name, we also have a responsibility. And what is that responsibility? To see as the
> Savior has declared—the value of each soul. . . . This is a universal apostolic call-
> ing (*ST*, 1:23, emphasis added).

Our apostolic calling is to take upon us the name of Christ just as the Twelve
Apostles have (*D&C* 18:24). We do this by keeping covenants such as baptism
(*D&C* 27:37).

Preach My Gospel Unto Every Creature (18:28)

Boyd K. Packer said:

> We accept the responsibility to preach the gospel to every person on earth. And
> if the question is asked, "You mean you are out to convert the entire world?" the
> answer is, "Yes. We will try to reach every living soul."
> Some who measure that challenge quickly say, "Why that's impossible! It can-
> not be done!"
> To that we simply say, "Perhaps, but we shall do it anyway" (*Ensign*, Nov.
> 1975, 97).

You Have Heard the Voice of the Lord (18:33-36)

After reading verses 33-36, Harold B. Lee said:

> I wish that our faith was sufficiently simple that we could read what I have just
> read to you, and . . . think about it again. The words that are in these scriptures are
> the words of the Lord, and when one like these authorized servants read them to
> you by the power and authority they possess and by the Spirit, you, all of you, all
> of us, can say, I have now heard His words, and I have heard His voice. Because
> whether it be "by His own voice or by the voice of his servants, it is the same"
> (*Church News*, Dec. 3, 1960, p. 14).

19
REPENT OR SUFFER—ETERNAL PUNISHMENT

A Commandment of God (Section Heading)

Joseph Smith usually introduced each section as "a revelation of God." But he introduced this section as "a commandment of God" (section heading). This section contains the "great and the last commandment," which is to repent (v. 32).

Other Names of Jesus (19:1)

Jesus is the Greek word for the Hebrew, *Joshua*. These names mean "savior." Other symbolic names of Jesus that He gives in this verse are:

1. **Alpha and Omega or The Beginning and the End.** These are the first and last letters of the Greek alphabet. This name symbolizes the eternal nature of the Lord.
2. **Christ the Lord.** *Christ* is the Greek word for the Hebrew, *Messiah*. These terms mean "anointed."
3. **I am He.** This is the name of Jehovah. For more information, see Appendix 1: "Jesus Christ is Jehovah."
4. **The Redeemer of the world.** Jesus has bought us and redeemed our souls from hell (1 Cor. 6:20; 7:23; 2 Pet. 2:1).

Repent or Suffer (19:4)

Everybody on this earth except Jesus has sinned. Therefore, we only have two choices—we can repent, or we can suffer in mind and spirit as Jesus suffered for our sins. (*D&C* 19:4, 16-20; also *JD*, 3:206).

God's Punishment (19:5-13)

Endless, Eternal, Everlasting, etc., are other names for God. So Endless punishment is just another name for God's punishment—the punishment that God gives. This does not mean that people will never come out of Hell. Elder James E. Talmage taught that Hell

> is a place prepared for the teaching, the disciplining of those who failed to learn here upon the earth what they would have learned. . . . No man will be kept in hell longer than is necessary to bring him to a fitness for something better (*CR*, April 1930, 97).

Revelation 20:13 shows that people will eventually come out of Hell.

Withdrawal of the Spirit (19:20)

When we sin we cannot have the Spirit with us. Without the strength of the Spirit we suffer. Brigham Young said:

> At the hour when the crisis came for him [Jesus] to offer up his life, the Father withdrew Himself, withdrew His Spirit, and cast a veil over him. That is what made him sweat blood (*JD* 3:206).

Teach Everyone You See (19:26-41)

Sometimes missionaries walk past 25 people on their way to go knock on the door of strangers. But the Lord may have put those people there so that the missionaries could see and talk to them. We should "speak freely to all" and among "every people that thou shalt be permitted to see" (*D&C* 19:37, 29). You may wish to cross reference these verses with 61:3.

Cry Hosanna (19:37)

Hosanna comes from the Hebrew language and could be translated "grant us salvation" (*Comp.*, 2:136). We are to declare unto all people that God will grant us salvation upon obedience to His gospel.

20

CHURCH GOVERNMENT

April Sixth (20:1)

The Lord said that the year we know as 1830 really was 1,830 years after the birth of Jesus Christ (A.D.) (v. 1). Talmage wrote: "We believe that Jesus Christ was born in Bethlehem of Judea, April 6, B.C. 1" (*Jesus the Christ*, 104).[2] Joseph Smith indicated that Jesus also died on April 6th:

> On the 6th of April, in the land of Zion . . . met for instruction and the service of God. . . .
>
> The day was spent in a very agreeable manner, in giving and receiving knowledge which appertained to this last kingdom—it being just 1,800 years since the Savior laid down his life (*Comp.*, 1:151).

2. For a detailed review of our current calendar, read pages 102-104 of *Jesus the Christ*.

The Name of the Church (20:1)

Wait until we get to Section 115: "For thus shall My Church be Called."

The Fullness of the Gospel (20:8-10)

Why did the Lord say the Book of Mormon contains the fullness of the gospel (v. 9) even though it does not contain anything about baptism for the dead, celestial marriage, and many other principles of the gospel? What is "the fullness of the gospel?" The Lord defined His gospel this way:

> And this is my gospel—repentance and baptism by water, and then cometh the baptism of fire and the Holy Ghost, even the Comforter, which showeth all things, and teacheth the peaceable things of the kingdom (*D&C* 39:6).

The Book of Mormon therefore contains the fullness of the gospel. It teaches that all must have faith, be baptized, receive the gift of the Holy Ghost, and continue to walk the path that leads to eternal life. In fact, by the fifth book of the Book of Mormon, we find Jarom saying: "For what could I write more than my fathers have written? For have not they revealed the plan of salvation?" (Jarom 1:2).

President Benson wrote:

> The Lord Himself has stated that the Book of Mormon contains the "fullness of the gospel of Jesus Christ." (*D&C* 20:9.) That does not mean it contains every teaching, every doctrine ever revealed. Rather, it means that in the Book of Mormon we will find the fullness of those doctrines required for our salvation (*A Witness and A Warning*, p. 18).

Joseph Fielding Smith said: "The meaning of the word 'fullness' as used in these scriptures is 'abundance,' or sufficient for the purposes intended" (*CHMR*, 1:81-82). And the prophet Mormon taught that what he included in the Book of Mormon is sufficient for us to learn the entire gospel. He wrote:

> When they shall have received this, which is expedient that they should have first, to try their faith, and if it shall so be that they shall believe these things then shall the greater things be made manifest unto them (3 Ne. 26:6-9).

And Charles W. Penrose further explained:

> You get the fullness of the gospel for this reason: if you really believe so as to have faith in our Eternal Father and in his Son, Jesus Christ, the Redeemer, and will hear him, you will learn all about what is needed to be done for the salvation of the living and the redemption of the dead (*CR*, April 1922, 27-28).

Doctrinal Foundation (20:11-35)

The Lord knew that Joseph Smith needed a lot of preparation before the Church could be restored. One way the Lord taught Joseph Smith the basic doctrines of the Gospel and helped him to grow spiritually was by having Joseph translate the Book of Mormon. By translating the Book of Mormon, Joseph came to know:

1. There is a God in heaven (v. 17-19).
2. All people have sins and need Jesus Christ (v. 20-25).
3. Jesus Christ did not sin (v. 22).
4. We can know God and His Son through the Holy Ghost (v. 26-27).
5. We all need to repent (v. 29).
6. We can be justified and sanctified through Jesus Christ (v. 30-31).
7. We must keep the commandments our whole life (v. 25, 29, 32-34).
8. The scriptures are true and we will be judged by what is in them (v. 11-15).

These truths form the doctrinal foundation of the Church. Searching the scriptures was a key to Joseph's spiritual preparation and growth. Searching the scriptures is also a key to our spiritual preparation and growth.

The Father, Son, and Holy Ghost Are One God (20:28)

Jesus taught that we should be one just like He and His Father are one (John 17:21-23). Obviously Jesus did not teach us to mash together into the same body. So to be one as He and His Father are one means we must become united in our efforts to help others receive eternal life just like Heavenly Father and Jesus Christ are one in helping us to receive eternal life (Moses 1:39). The Father, Son, and Holy Ghost being one God is the same as us being one people.

Jesus taught this same principle when He said: "No man can serve two masters; for either he will hate the one and love the other, or else he will hold to the one and despise the other" (Matt. 6:24; 3 Ne. 13:24). If Jesus Christ and our Heavenly Father were two different gods with two different plans, how could we follow one without disobeying the other? But they are one God with one master plan for our happiness. President Joseph Fielding Smith explained:

> It is perfectly true . . . that to us there is but one God. Correctly interpreted God in this sense means Godhead, for it is composed of Father, Son, and Holy Spirit. This Godhead presides over us, and to us, the inhabitants of this world, they constitute the only God, or Godhead (*AGQ*, 2:142).

Jesus Christ is the Son of God but is also called the Father. This will be further explained in the material for 93:3-4, "Jesus Christ as the Father."

Justification (20:30)

To justify means to pardon, to sanction, to authorize, to cleanse, and to approve. We cannot enter the Celestial Kingdom until we have been justified through Jesus Christ. In other words, until we have been cleaned of all our sins and have received His authorization and approval to enter His Kingdom. We receive this authorization by receiving the ordinances of the gospel and obeying the covenants we have entered into. Bruce R. McConkie wrote:

> An act that is justified by the Spirit is one that is sealed by the Holy Spirit of promise, or in other words, ratified and approved by the Holy Ghost (*MD*, p. 408).

Note that Jesus is the only one who has ever been justified by the law in His own right. All others have sinned against the laws of God and can only be justified by the law of mercy through Jesus Christ (Rom. 3:23-24). To be justified by mercy, we must seek to abide by God's laws. Those who will not do so cannot be justified and "must remain filthy still" (88:35).

Sanctification (20:31)

To sanctify means to cleanse, to purify, to forgive, to anoint, and to bless. When we love and serve God with all our might, mind, and strength, we become sanctified (v. 31). In other words, our sins are forgiven, we are made pure, and we are anointed to have eternal life. This anointing must be sealed through the law of justification as explained above.

Duties of the Saints (20:38-84)

Section 20 used to be called "The Articles and Covenants of the Church." Verses 68-84 would be read at general conferences of the Church to remind all the members of their duties in the Lord's church (*DCSM*, p. 39). Verses 38-84 should be studied so that each of us can do our duty as the Lord has required. For example, all home teachers should apply verses 47, 51, and 53; parents should apply verse 70; and all members should apply verse 75.

Duties of Church Officers

Wait until Section 107: "Priesthood Organization."

The Witness Before the Church (20:37)

Before people can be baptized they must have an interview. The Elder (or Bishop, etc.) doing the interview makes sure that the people who want to be baptized are willing to follow the example of Jesus Christ. This is the way people witness that they are worthy to be baptized.

General Conference (20:60-62)

David O. McKay said:

Reference to the Doctrine and Covenants will disclose the fact that there are four principal purposes of holding conferences of the Church: First, to transact current Church business [20:62]. Second, to hear reports and general Church statistics [73:2]. Third, to "approve those names which I (the Lord) have appointed, or to disapprove of them." [124:144.] Fourth, to worship the Lord in sincerity and reverence, and to give and to receive encouragement, exhortation, and instruction [58:56; 72:7] (*CR*, Oct. 1938, pp. 130-31).

The Sacrament (20:75-79)

Wait until we get to Section 27: "The Sacrament—The Armor of God—The Melchizedek Priesthood."

21

FOLLOW THE PROPHET

Gifts of the Lord's Prophet (21:1)

1. **A seer.** Elder John A. Widtsoe said a seer is

   one who sees with spiritual eyes. He perceives the meaning of that which seems obscure to others; therefore he is an interpreter and clarifier of eternal truth (*Evidences and Reconciliations*, 1:205-206).

2. **A translator**. A translator can translate from one language to another. For example, Joseph translated the Book of Mormon into English. A translator can also clarify what has been written or spoken in a given language. For example, Joseph Smith translated the Bible by clarifying what had already been written in English (*DCSM*, p. 44).

3. **A prophet.** A prophet of God is anybody who teaches revealed truth by the Spirit (Ex. 4:15-16; 7:1-2; Num. 11:25-29; Rev. 19:10; *D&C* 133:26).

4. **An apostle.** Apostle means "one sent forth." Apostles are sent forth to testify to the world that Jesus physically resurrected from the dead and is the Savior of all people (Acts 1:22; *D&C* 107:23).

5. **An elder.** An elder is a representative of Jesus Christ. Bruce R. McConkie said: "What is an elder? An elder is a minister of the Lord Jesus Christ" (*Ensign*, June 1975, p. 66).

6. **A prophet, seer, and revelator.** The term revelator is not mentioned in
this verse. A revelator is one who reveals truth that was not previously
known by man on the earth. A prophet, seer, and revelator, then, is a
person who teaches revealed truth, clarifies revealed truth, and reveals
more truth.

Faith in the Lord

The key to Section 21 is Article of Faith 4. It is important to stress that the
first principle of our religion is not just faith, but faith *in the Lord Jesus Christ*.
We do not put our faith in the prophet because he is not a perfect man (*D&C*
64:5-7)—we put our faith in Jesus Christ. Now then, the question is: Do we have
faith *in the Lord Jesus Christ* that He is telling us the truth in verses 4 and 5 of
this Section?

Obey *All* the Prophet's Words (21:4-5)

The prophet (the senior apostle—see the material for Section 43:7, "The
Gate"), is going to speak on many different subjects. Sometimes he will speak
about spiritual things and sometimes he will speak about things that will just help
us live from day to day. Brigham Young said:

> Some of the leading men in Kirtland were much opposed to Joseph the
> Prophet, meddling with temporal affairs. . . .
> I said, "Ye Elders of Israel, . . . will some of you draw the line of demarcation,
> between the spiritual and temporal in the Kingdom of God, so that I may under-
> stand it?" Not one of them could do it (*JD* 10:363-4).

And Ezra Taft Benson said:

> The prophet may be involved in civic matters. When a people are righteous
> they want the best to lead them in government. . . . Those who would remove
> prophets from politics would take God out of government (*TETB*, p. 138).

The Lord said to obey *all* the prophet's words (v. 4-5). This means that even
when the prophet does not say "Thus saith the Lord," we must still obey his
words. President J. Reuben Clark said:

> There are those who insist that unless the prophet of the Lord declares,
> "thus saith the Lord," the message may not be taken as a revelation. This is a
> false testing standard. For while many of our modern revelations as contained
> in the Doctrine and Covenants do contain these words, there are many that do
> not (*ST*, 1:91-92).

In Patience and Faith (21:5)

President Harold B. Lee said:

There will be some things that take patience and faith. You may not like what comes from the authority of the Church. It may contradict your political views. It may interfere with some of your social life. But if you listen to these things, as if from the mouth of the Lord himself, with patience and faith, the promise is that "the gates of hell shall not prevail against you" (*CR*, Oct. 1970, 152-153).

We can put our trust in the Lord and follow His words that He gives to us through His prophet even when we do not understand why the Lord gave them. President Wilford Woodruff said: "The Lord will never permit me or any other man who stands as President of this Church to lead you astray" ("Official Declaration—1," *D&C*, p. 292).

Blessings for Our Obedience (21:6-9)

As we put our trust in the Lord, and obey the words of the prophet, the Lord promises us that:

1. the gates of Hell will not prevail against us (v. 6);
2. the powers of darkness will be dispersed from before us (v. 6);
3. the heavens will shake for our good (v. 6); and
4. we can gain a testimony by the Spirit that the prophet's words really are the Lord's words (v. 8-9).

22

BAPTISM BY AUTHORITY

A New and Everlasting Covenant (22:1)

The new and everlasting covenant is the Gospel (*D&C* 66:2). Elder Bruce R. McConkie said:

> The gospel is the *everlasting* covenant because it is ordained by Him who is Everlasting. . . . Each time this everlasting covenant is revealed it is *new* to those of that dispensation. Hence the gospel is the *new and everlasting covenant* (*MD*, pp. 529-30).

Thus baptism is *a* new and everlasting covenant (*D&C* 22:1). Elder Joseph Fielding Smith said:

This covenant [baptism] was given in the beginning and was lost to men through apostasy, therefore, when it was revealed again, it became to man a *new covenant*, although it was from the beginning, and it is everlasting since its *effects* upon the individual endure forever. Then again, whenever there is need for repentance, baptism is the method, or law given of the Lord by which the remission of sins shall come, and so *this law is everlasting* (*DS*, 1:152).

Celestial marriage is also *a* new and everlasting covenant (*D&C* 132:4).

Dead Works (22:2)

It is the Spirit that gives life (2 Cor. 3:6). The Holy Ghost has to approve, or "seal" every ordinance in order for it to count (*D&C* 132:7). Without the Spirit, an ordinance is dead, or in other words, it does not count. Two reasons why the Spirit would not "seal" an ordinance are:

1. The person preforming the ordinance does not have the proper authority.
2. The person receiving the ordinance is not worthy.

If the person preforming the ordinance does not have the proper authority, it must be repeated by somebody who has the proper authority. But if the ordinance was not sealed because the person receiving the ordinance was unworthy, it does not have to be done again—the Holy Ghost can seal the ordinance when the person repents.

"But I've Already Been Baptized."

Missionaries: Will you be baptized?

Investigator: I've already been baptized.

Missionaries: That's great that you've been baptized because that shows that you are dedicated to following the example of Jesus Christ. We wish we could talk with more people like you. In fact, in the Bible, the apostle Paul spoke with a group of people just like you. . .

. . . Explain Acts 19:1-6 . . .

. . . Now that you've been baptized, would you like to receive the Gift of the Holy Ghost?

Investigator: Of course. Who wouldn't want a gift like that?

Missionaries: How long did the people Paul talked to wait to get this gift?

Investigator: Looks like they got it right then.

Missionaries: You could also receive this gift right now. May we call up our leader so that he can interview you? Then we can go fill up the font so that you can be baptized by the authority of God so that you can receive the Gift of the Holy Ghost.

23

GET BAPTIZED AND STRENGTHEN THE CHURCH

Historical Context

Four members and one non-member of the Church came to Joseph to find out what the Lord wanted them to do.

Hyrum Smith (23:3)

In *D&C* 11:21, Hyrum Smith was told that his tongue would be loosed after he obtained the word of God. Because Hyrum did what he was told, he could now preach the gospel effectively (*D&C* 23:3). Hyrum is a perfect example of blessings obtained through obedience to the Lord's commandments.

Joseph Knight, Sr. (23:6-7)

Joseph Knight was told to take up his cross. Jesus said: "And now for a man to take up his cross, is to deny himself all ungodliness, and every worldly lust, and keep my commandments" (*JST* Mat. 16:26).

When somebody who has not been baptized asks the Lord what to do, the Lord simply answers, "it is your duty to unite with the true church" (v. 7). Here are some other examples:

1. When the people asked Peter what to do he also told them that they needed to be baptized (Acts 2:37-38).
2. When the eunuch asked Philip for guidance Philip baptized him (Acts 8:26-38).
3. When the prison guard asked Paul and Silas what he should do they baptized him and his family that night (Acts 16:30-33).
4. When the people asked Alma what they should do he told them to get baptized (Alma 32:9-16).
5. W. W. Phelps is commanded by the Lord to get baptized and preach as an Elder in the Church (*D&C* 55).

When people ask in their heart, "What does the Lord want me to do?" they should be invited to be baptized and serve the Lord by bringing others into the Church.

24

JOSEPH SMITH TO DEVOTE ALL HIS SERVICE TO ZION

Historical Context—Joseph Smith's Calling

Joseph Smith was busy trying to run his farm as well as the Church. Because of this, he could not magnify his office. In this revelation, the Lord calls Joseph to work full-time for the Church (v. 3, 7). The Lord explains that the members should support Joseph. In Section 42, the Lord reveals more about when people can be supported by the church for their services.

Casting Off the Dust of Your Feet (24:15)

Wait until we come to the material for 60:15, "Shake Off the Dust of Thy Feet."

25

EMMA SMITH—MUSIC

Historical Context

Joseph Smith and his wife, Emma, had been staying at the house of Emma's parents. Emma's parents were not as fond of Joseph as she was, so she was not only under a lot of pressure from the persecution of the mobs, but also from her own parents. In section 25, the Lord speaks to Emma, giving her comfort and counsel.

Counsel (25:4-14)

1. **Murmur not because of the things which thou hast not seen (v. 4).**
   Even though many other people had seen the plates of the Book of Mormon, Emma had never seen them. Often, a bishop or other Church leader will need to keep sacred information confidential.

2. **Go with husband (v. 6).** One of the greatest purposes of life is to become one in all we do as husband and wife. This can only be done, of course, when the husband and wife are together. This does not mean that if a man is going to hell, that his wife should go with him. President Harold B. Lee said:

> The wife is to obey the law of her husband only as he obeys the laws of God. No woman is expected to follow her husband in disobedience to the commandments of the Lord (*Ensign*, Feb. 1972, 50).

3. **Lay aside the things of the world (v. 10).** Things of the world that should be laid aside are teachings that contradict the Lord's teachings. This includes what the world teaches about immodest fashions, sexual immorality, and abortion.

4. **Seek for the things of a better world (v. 10).** This includes setting and reaching goals to keep the commandments, to go on a mission, to do Church assignments, to only marry in the temple, to help children grow spiritually, and to help others to receive the Gift of the Holy Ghost.

5. **Let thy soul delight in thy husband (v. 14).** The soul includes the spirit and the body (*D&C* 88:15). Husbands and wives grow closer as they delight in each other's spirit and body. A righteous sexual relationship not only allows for procreation (Gen. 1:28), but also lets husbands and wives delight in each other and grow closer together (Gen. 2:24).

A Comforter (25:5)

This is the same as one of the callings of the Holy Ghost (John 14:26).

Thou Shalt be Ordained (25:7)

John Taylor said:

> The term "ordain" was used generally in the early days of the Church in reference to both ordination and setting apart, and, too, correctly according to the meaning of the word. . . . This saying that Emma Smith was "ordained" to expound scripture, does not mean that she had conferred upon her the Priesthood, but that she was set apart to this calling [in the Relief Society] (*JD* 21:367-68).

Music (25:11-12)

Harold B. Lee said:

> My experience of a lifetime and particularly the last thirty-two years as a General Authority, convinces me that the most effective preaching of the gospel is when it is accompanied by beautiful, appropriate music (*CR*, April 1973, 181).

Playing or singing uplifting music is one way we can invite the Spirit of the Lord into our meetings. For example, home teachers or missionaries can sing a hymn to the people they are teaching. While singing, they can ask in their hearts that the Lord soften the hearts of the people that they are going to teach and help them accept the challenge to keep the commandments. The Lord promises to answer this "prayer" (*D&C* 25:12). When Brigham Young talked about teaching families the gospel, he said: "I could make the acquaintance of the family, and sit and sing to them and chat with them, and they would be friendly" (*JD* 4:34). And Elder Boyd K. Packer said:

> Our people ought to be surrounded by good music of all kinds . . . we encourage parents to include musical training in the lives of their children (*CR*, Oct. 1973, 21-23).

Other Scriptures:
1. **1 Samuel 16:23.** David plays uplifting music to help Saul feel the peaceful Spirit of the Lord.
2. **Matt. 26:30.** The Lord and His disciples sing a hymn at the last supper just before He goes to Gethsemane.
3. **Colos. 3:16.** We are told to teach by using songs. (Also read Exodus 32:18 and 2 Chronicles 20:22.)

A Revelation to All (25:16)
In verse 16 the Lord says: "this is my voice unto all." Although some parts of this Section are specifically for Emma, most parts apply to everyone. Just as the Lord called Emma "an elect lady" (v. 3), He will also call us "elect" as we follow His words to us.

26

ALL THINGS BY COMMON CONSENT IN THE CHURCH

Historical Context
Joseph Smith already knew common consent was an important principle. The Lord told Joseph and Oliver Cowdery that they needed the approval of the people to be ordained their leaders. Joseph Smith said: "We were, however, commanded to . . . have them decide by vote whether they were willing to

accept us as spiritual teachers or not" (*HC*, 1:60-61). Even though they had received the authority from God to lead the people, they still needed the consent of the people.

When people do not accept the leaders that God gives them it does not mean the leaders are not called by God—it means that the people do not want to be led by God's leader. God will never force people to accept His leaders. When we are asked to vote on or sustain our leaders, we are not normally voting whether or not that person is worthy to be our leader, we are voting whether or not we desire to follow the leader that God gives us. The Lord has given the Church a form of government that gives us the chance to use our agency:

> In the Church of Christ where the government is that of the Kingdom of Heaven, neither autocracy nor democracy obtains, but government by Common Consent. . . . Obedience must be voluntary. The government of the Church has been called a Theo-democracy. It is the form of government that will be general during the Millennium (*DCC*, p. 131-132).

When Should We Cast a Vote of Opposition?

Joseph Fielding Smith said:

> I have no right to raise my hand in opposition to a man who is appointed to any position in this Church, simply because I may not like him, or because of some personal disagreement or feeling I may have, but only on the grounds that he is guilty of wrong doing, of transgression of the laws of the Church which would disqualify him for the position which he is called to hold (*DS*, 3:124).

Protection Against Deception

Sometimes anti-Mormons say, "Did you know that so and so was ordained in a *secret* meeting and given the keys and authority to hold such and such calling in the Church? And did you know that the General Authorities of the Church do not accept so and so's calling? Therefore the church is false." The Lord has given us the law of common consent to protect us from this kind of deception. He made it clear that nothing is done in secret in His church: "*All* things shall be done by common consent *in the church*" (*D&C* 26:2; emphasis added). The Lord also said:

> It shall not be given to any one to go forth to preach my gospel, or to build up my church, except he be ordained by some one who has authority, and *it is known to the church* that he has authority and has been regularly ordained by the heads of the church (*D&C* 42:11; emphasis added).

27

THE SACRAMENT—THE ARMOR OF GOD THE MELCHIZEDEK PRIESTHOOD

Emblems (27:2-4)

An emblem is a symbol. Bread and water are symbols that represent the body and blood of Christ. Except for alcoholic beverages (see *D&C* 27:3-4 and the material for *D&C* 89:6), it does not matter what we use to represent the body and blood of Christ, as long as we do it reverently (v. 2). The First Presidency has instructed us to use bread and water whenever possible (*ST,* 1:126).

Covenants

When we take the sacrament we renew our baptismal covenants. This means that we make the same promises that we made when we were baptized. We promise to be willing to:

1. Take upon us the name of Christ.
2. Always remember Christ.
3. Do what we have been commanded.

When we are willing to do these things, God promises us that we will have His Spirit, which means that He will forgive us (*D&C* 20:77, 79).

We take upon us the name of Jesus Christ by becoming His disciples. When Jesus administered the sacrament to the Twelve Apostles during the Last Supper, He told them how people would know that they were His disciples: "By this shall all men know that ye are my disciples, if ye love one another (John 13:35). To take upon us the name of Christ, we must love each soul as the Lord does. (Also see the material under "Our Apostolic Calling" for Section 18.)

Two Events (27:2, 5-14)

When we take the sacrament we should remember two events:

1. The atonement (v. 2).
2. The second coming (v. 5-14).

When the Savior comes again, He will hold a sacrament meeting with many of the prophets and also with worthy members of His church (*D&C* 27:5-14; *ST,* 1:128-129). Otten and Caldwell state:

Every Latter-day Saint has the potential opportunity to meet with the Savior in a sacrament meeting experience at the time of His coming (*ST*, 1:129).

The Hymn "In Remembrance of Thy Suffering" beautifully expresses the idea of using emblems to remember both the atonement and the second coming:

> In remembrance of thy suff'ring, Lord,
> These emblems we partake,
> When thyself thou gav'st an off'ring,
> Dying for the sinner's sake (v. 1).
>
> When thou comest in thy glory
> To this earth to rule and reign,
> And with faithful ones partakest
> Of the bread and wine again,
> May we be among the number
> Worthy to surround the board,
> And partake anew the emblems
> Of the suff'rings of our Lord (v. 3).

Armor (27:15-18)

In order to attend this sacrament meeting with Christ at His coming, we must remain worthy. To help protect us in our fight against evil, the Lord has given us some armor (*D&C* 27:16-18, also Eph. 6:14-17). The following ideas about the armor of God come from a talk given by Elder Harold B. Lee (*Speeches of the Year*, B.Y.U., Nov. 9, 1954):

1. **Loins Girt About With Truth (27:16).** When we know the truth we have a standard of morality—a guide—that we can base our decisions on to protect our virtue. For example, when we know the truth, we know that sexual relations are approved of only in marriage. We symbolically protect our loins with truth by protecting our virtue and chastity by basing our decisions on the true standard of morality.

2. **The Breastplate of Righteousness (27:16).** The breastplate covers the heart—the symbolic place of our testimony. When we know the true standard, we need to follow it. This will protect our testimony and help it to grow.

3. **Feet Shod with the Preparation of the Gospel of Peace (27:16).** We say, "I would do this if I were in your shoes." When we walk through life in the "shoes" of Jesus, we know what path to follow and what are the most important goals in life.

4. **The Helmet of Salvation (27:18).** We need to protect and purify our minds in order to be saved.

5. There Is No Armor for the Back. We have to be brave in our fight against sin; if we turn our backs, the enemy will be able to hurt us with a fiery dart (v. 17). In other words, if we are weak Satan will tempt us and we will sin.

We must put on the armor of God and be strong and brave in our fight against sin so that we will be worthy to attend the great sacrament meeting with the Savior when He comes again.

Restoration of the Melchizedek Priesthood (27:12)

We know the exact date that the Aaronic Priesthood was restored, but because many early events did not get written down as they occurred, we do not know the exact date of the restoration of the Melchizedek Priesthood (see the material for Section 47: "Church Records").

28

THE LAW OF REVELATION

Historical Context

Satan tries to destroy the church any way he can. He once tricked one of the Eight Witnesses of the Book of Mormon, Hyrum Page, into believing that he was receiving revelation from the Lord through a small stone. Because the members of the Church did not understand that only the prophet could receive revelation for the Church, many members of the church began to believe Hyrum's revelations. Even Oliver Cowdery became upset with Joseph Smith when Joseph said Hyrum's revelations were not from God (see the section heading and *CHMR*, 1:125).

Satanic Revelation (28:11)

Hyrum was receiving revelation but it was from Satan and not God (v. 11). In Section 10 we learned that Satan is real and works hard to deceive people. Satan will deceive those who play around with spiritual things or play with Ouija boards, seances, or witchcraft—even if they mean no harm. Otten and Caldwell state:

One of the lessons we learn from this section is that sincere people can be misled and misguided if they interpret satanic promptings as being revelation from the Lord (*ST*, 1:35).

Revelation from the Lord (28:2, 12-13)

The Lord protects His church from being deceived by false revelation by having a pattern for giving revelation that Satan cannot copy. The Lord's pattern is:

1. **The revelation is given to the prophet (D&C 28:2).** The prophet (the senior apostle—see material for *D&C* 43:7) is the only one who can receive revelation for the Church. Other members of the church (including general authorities) can only teach as doctrine what the prophet has taught. Satan cannot copy this pattern because the Lord will never permit Satan to deceive the prophet. The prophet cannot lead the Church astray by receiving false revelation (remember the material for *D&C* 21:4-9).

2. **The revelation is presented to the members of the Church (D&C 28:13; 26:2).** Remember the material for Section 26: "All Things by Common Consent in the church."

The Law of Revelation

After even more problems with members receiving satanic revelations and thinking that they were from the Lord, the Lord laid down a law about how revelation is received for the Church in Section 43.

29

GATHERING THE ELECT

Jesus Christ Is Jehovah (29:1)

Jehovah told Moses that His name is "I Am" (Exodus 3:14, 6:2-3). Jesus also said that His name is "I Am" (*D&C* 29:1). In fact, when Jesus told the Jews that He was the same person as Jehovah, they tried to kill Him (John 8:57-59). For more scriptures about Jesus Christ being Jehovah, read Appendix 1: "Jesus Christ is Jehovah."

Three Steps to Be Gathered (29:2)

The purpose of the Church is to bring people to Christ. In other words, gather the Lord's children so that they are under His wing of protection (read *D&C* 29:2, 8). There are three things that people need to do in order to be gathered (*D&C* 29:2):

1. Hear the voice of the Lord.
2. Be humble enough to do what the Lord says.
3. Pray.

This is a pattern that must be used to bring people unto Christ. The sooner people pray, the sooner they will come unto Christ. For example, in missionary work, the person being taught by the missionaries should be taught how to pray and say a prayer by the end of the first discussion.

Unity (29:6)

Separation is death. Unity gives life. Jesus prayed that we would be one in purpose even as He and His Father are one in purpose (John 17:21-22). And He said that if we are not unified, we cannot have the Spirit (*D&C* 38:27). The Lord promises that when we are united and ask Him for something, He will give it to us. One of the great revelations we have was given because six Elders were united in prayer (*D&C* 84:1). When missionary companionships, districts, marriages, ward leaders, etc. are unified, they can receive revelation just like the six Elders in section 84 did. Elder Harold B. Lee said:

> If we would be united in love and fellowship and harmony, this Church would convert the world. . . . Likewise, if in that Latter-day Saint home the husband and wife are in disharmony, bickering, and divorce is threatened, there is evidence that one or both are not keeping the commandments of God (*CR*, April 1950, 97-100).

Only Teach the Elect (29:7)

When missionaries do not work with elect people, it slows down the work. The Lord said to speak to all people (*D&C* 19:29), but to gather the elect (*D&C* 29:7). Elect people listen to missionaries who teach by the Spirit and do what the missionaries tell them to do. In other words, they keep their commitments (*D&C* 29:7). When the missionaries have done everything to help people keep their commitments, and the people still do not keep them, the missionaries need not spend more time with those people. Joseph Smith said: "Remember that 'it is a day of warning, and not a day of many words.' If they receive not your testimony in one place, flee to another" (*HC*, 1:468).

Speaking and Hearing the Voice of the Lord (29:7)

Elect people hear the voice of the Lord only when they are taught by the Spirit. When we speak by the Spirit, we speak with the voice of the Lord (*D&C* 68:4). Also, when we read the scriptures one to another with the Spirit we can say that we have spoken and heard the voice of the Lord (remember *D&C* 18:36). It is our duty to speak with the voice of the Lord, and it is the duty of the person being taught to hear it (*D&C* 50:13-23). This is why we are commanded not to teach without the presence of the Spirit (*D&C* 42:14).

The Second Coming (29:9-11, 14-21)

Signs and events surrounding the Second Coming will be discussed when we get to Section 45: "The Second Coming."

The Great and Abominable Church (29:21)

Any person that fights against the Lord's church (no matter to which religion that person belongs) may be regarded as being a member of "the great and abominable church" (2 Ne. 10:16). The members of this abominable church will destroy themselves in the last days (1 Ne. 22:13).

After the Millennium (29:22-29)

Wait until we come to the material for Section 101: "They Must Need be Chastened and Tried—The Millennium."

All Laws Are Spiritual (29:29-35)— Overcoming Spiritual Death (29:40-45)

Death is separation. Physical death is the separation of our spirit from our body. Spiritual death is the separation of our spirit from God. Depending on the context, spiritual death can be called the "first" or the "second" death. When used to mean "sin" (sin separates our spirit from God), spiritual death is called the "first" death. This is how it is used in verse 41. Adam died spiritually (sinned) before he died physically (*D&C* 29:41). When spiritual death is used to refer to the state of the wicked after this life, it is called the "second death" (*D&C* 63:17; Alma 12:12-18; Helaman 14:12-19).

Since all the Lord's laws are spiritual, when we break them (sin) we die spiritually. Part of overcoming spiritual death is obedience to the commandments. However, we cannot just obey the "letter" of the commandment; we must discover and obey the spirit of the commandment. We must find the spiritual aspect of the commandment that will help bring us unto Christ. For example, it is a commandment to study the scriptures. Just reading them will not help us overcome spiritual death. We must obey the spirit of the law and use the scriptures to grow spiritually by searching them for meaning and applying them to our lives.

Adam (29:34)

God the Father created Adam (Luke 3:38). In this verse, Jesus is speaking as if He were the Father. God the Father has given Jesus the authority to speak as if Jesus were the Father. This is called "divine investiture of authority." In this same section, Jesus talks about His Only Begotten (v. 1, 46). Here, again, Jesus is speaking as if He were His Father. Jesus does the same thing throughout the scriptures. (For example, see Moses 1:6.) Other people have been given authority to speak as if they were Jesus Christ. This is also "divine investiture of authority." (For example, see Ex. 23:21; Rev. 22:7-13; and 3 Ne. 1:13-14.) For more information read "The Father and The Son: A Doctrinal Exposition by The First Presidency and The Twelve," in *The Articles of Faith* by James E. Talmage, pp. 471-473; and *MD*, p. 130.

Mine Only Begotten Son (29:42, 46)

Here, Jesus Christ is speaking as if He were Heavenly Father. This will be explained in the material for 93:3-4, "Jesus Christ as the Father."

Little Children and the Mentally Handicapped (29:46-50)

Their salvation will be discussed in the material for *D&C* 137:5-10, "Heirs of the Celestial Kingdom."

They Cannot Sin (29:47)

This will be discussed in the material for *D&C* 68:27, "Children Shall Be Baptized When Eight Years Old."

30

DISOBEDIENCE

David Whitmer Is Disobedient (30:1-2)

Even though David Whitmer was one of the Three Witnesses, he believed very strongly in the false revelations that Hiram Page had received (remember the material for Section 28) (*HC* 1:109-110). The Lord pointed out four steps that led up to David's act of disobedience:

1. His fear of what others thought of him (v. 1).
2. Worrying about worldly things more than spiritual things (v. 2).
3. Not listening to the Spirit (v. 2).
4. Not following his authorized leaders (v. 2).

Let us learn a lesson and not go down this path of disobedience.

David Whitmer Is Punished (30:3-4)

The Lord sent David Whitmer to "his room" to think about how to change his behavior (see v. 3-4).

Peter and John Whitmer (30:5-11)

Peter Whitmer, Jun. is called to go on the first mission to the Lamanites which we will talk about in Section 32. John Whitmer is also called to be a missionary.

31

THRUST IN YOUR SICKLE AND YOUR SINS ARE FORGIVEN—GOVERN YOUR HOUSE IN MEEKNESS

Church Duties (31:3-8, 10)

Thomas B. Marsh's duty in the Church is summed up in verse four.

Forgiveness, the Greatest Sheave (31:5)

Another word for "sheaves" is "rewards" (Alma 26:5, footnote c). The Lord promised Thomas Marsh the greatest reward—forgiveness—as he worked with all his soul to bring people unto Christ.

Personal Duties (31:9, 11-13)

The Lord also gave Thomas Marsh seven personal duties:
1. Be patient in afflictions (v. 9).
2. Don't fight back (v.9).
3. Govern house in meekness (v. 9).
4. Be steadfast (v. 9).
5. Heed the Spirit (v. 11).
6. Pray always (v. 12).
7. Endure to the end (v. 13).

Five years after the Lord gave this revelation of counsel to Thomas Marsh, he was called to be the president of the Quorum of the Twelve. But four years after becoming the president of the Quorum of the Twelve, he apostatized over a petty situation which would have been avoided if he had followed the counsel of the Lord to govern his house in meekness. Elder George A. Smith told the sad story of Thomas Marsh:

> When the Saints were living in Far West, the wife of Marsh and Sister Harris agreed to exchange milk in order to enable each of them to make a larger cheese than they could do separately. Each was to take the other the "strippings" as well as the rest of the milk. . . . But Mrs. Marsh kept a pint of "strippings" from each cow. When this became known the matter was brought before the Teachers, and these decided against Mrs. Marsh. An appeal was taken to the Bishop. He sustained the Teachers. If Marsh had obeyed the Revelation and governed his house in humility with steadfastness, he would have righted the wrong done, but, instead of doing so, he appealed to the High Council. Marsh, who at the time was President of the Twelve, possibly thought that the Council would favor him, but that body confirmed the Bishop's decision. He was not yet satisfied, but appealed to the First Presidency. . . . They approved the finding of the High Council. Was Marsh satisfied then? No. With the persistency of Lucifer himself, he declared that he would uphold the character of his wife, "even if he had to go to hell for it." Elder George A. Smith observes:
>
> "The then President of the Twelve Apostles, the man who should have been the first to do justice and cause reparation to be made for wrong, committed by any member of his family, took that position, and what next? He went before a magistrate and swore that the "Mormons" were hostile to the State of Missouri. That affidavit brought from the government of Missouri an exterminating order, which drove some 15,000 Saints from their homes and habitations, and some thousands perished through suffering the exposure consequent to this state of affairs" (*JD*, Vol. 3, p. 284 [Apr. 6, 1856]) (*DCC*, p. 167).

Following this, Thomas Marsh was excommunicated in 1839. He then led a miserable and pitiful existence. As an old man on his deathbed, he acknowledged his folly and decided to return to the Church. He partially recovered, was rebaptized in 1857, and died in Ogden, Utah.

Let Thomas Marsh's experience serve as an example of the importance of governing our house in meekness.

32

FIRST MISSION TO THE LAMANITES

The Lord had already called Oliver Cowdery and Peter Whitmer, Jr. to serve missions to the Lamanites (*D&C* 28:8; 30:5). In this section, the Lord calls two more people to go on this first mission to the Lamanites.

These missionaries did not have much success among the Lamanite people (especially because other Christian missionaries got the government to ban the Mormon missionaries from Indian territories). However, their mission brought great blessings to the Church in the following ways:

1. Sidney Rigdon, Frederick G. Williams, Edward Partridge, and many others who would become leaders in the Church were converted by these missionaries.
2. It prepared the Church for its move to Ohio. 130 People were baptized in the Kirtland, Ohio area. This made Kirtland the area with the largest group of members of the Church at that time (*DCSM*, p. 66). Beginning with Section 37, we will read how the Lord gathered His church to Kirtland, Ohio.
3. It prepared the Church for its eventual gathering in Missouri. These missionaries traveled through Missouri and brought back information that would help Joseph Smith know about that area. Beginning with section 48 we will read how the Lord gathered His church to Missouri.

For more information about these missionaries' travels, read the *Autobiography of Parley P. Pratt*, pages 47-62.

33

THE TEN VIRGINS

Working at 11:00 (33:1-16)

In this section, the Lord calls two men on a mission (v. 1). He tells them that it is the eleventh hour and they need to warn people that the Lord is coming soon. People need to get ready for the Lord's coming by being baptized and receiving the gift of the Holy Ghost (v. 3, 10-11).

All Having Corrupt Minds (33:4)

The word "corrupt," here, means impure, not evil.

Called Forth out of the Wilderness (33:5)

In the book of Revelation we read about a woman (who symbolizes the Church of Christ) who is driven into the wilderness (which symbolizes apostasy) by the dragon (which symbolizes Satan) (Rev. 12:1-17, note the *JST* of v. 7). The woman has been "called forth out of the wilderness," symbolizing that after centuries of apostasy, the Lord restored His church upon the earth.

Spiritual Oil Cannot Be Shared (33:17)

The parable of the ten virgins (Mat. 25:1-13) is going to be fulfilled at the second coming of the Lord (*D&C* 45:56). "The Ten Virgins represent the people of the Church of Jesus Christ" (Kimball, *Faith Precedes the Miracle*, 254). To be worthy at His second coming we must keep our lamps burning, which means we need oil (*D&C* 33:17). The oil represents spiritual preparedness. But when the Lord comes, half the members of the Church will not be prepared and will want to buy or borrow oil from others (Mat. 25:2). The problem is that this kind of oil cannot be shared. Spencer W. Kimball said:

> The foolish [virgins] asked the others to share their oil, but spiritual prepared-ness cannot be shared in an instant. The wise had to go, else the bridegroom would have gone unwelcomed. They needed all their oil for themselves; they could not save the foolish. The responsibility was each for himself.
>
> This was not selfishness or unkindness. The kind of oil that is needed . . . is not shareable. How can one share obedience to the principle of tithing; a mind at peace from righteous living; an accumulation of knowledge? How can one share faith or testimony? How can one share attitudes or chastity, or the experience of a mission? How can one share temple privileges? Each must obtain that kind of oil for himself.

*   *   *   *   *

In the parable, oil can be purchased at the market. In our lives the oil of preparedness is accumulated drop by drop in righteous living. Attendance at sacrament meetings adds oil to our lamps, drop by drop over the years. Fasting, family prayer, home teaching, control of bodily appetites, preaching the gospel, studying the scriptures—each act of dedication and obedience is a drop added to our
store. Deeds of kindness, payment of offerings and tithes, chaste thoughts and
actions, marriage in the covenant for eternity—these, too, contribute importantly
to the oil with which we can at midnight refuel our exhausted lamps.

Midnight is so late for those who have procrastinated (*Faith Precedes the
Miracle*, pp. 255- 256).

I come quickly (33:18)

For nearly 2,000 years, the Lord has been saying that He will come quickly
(Rev. 3:11; 22:20). He is not referring to when He will come, but *how* He will
come. The parable of the ten virgins emphasizes the fact that there will not be
enough time to prepare once we see the bridegroom. We must be prepared prior
to that time because he will come quickly.

34

SERVICE AND SACRIFICE—ORSON PRATT

Historical Context

Orson Pratt is the younger brother of Parley P. Pratt. Orson was baptized on
his nineteenth birthday, after being taught by Parley. About six weeks later,
Orson traveled two hundred miles to ask the Prophet Joseph what the Lord
would have him do (*HC*, 1:127-28). The Lord called Orson on a mission.

Loving Is Giving (34:3)

Jesus said that we should love one another in the same way that He loved us
(John 15:12). Jesus loved us by giving His life (*D&C* 34:3). God also loved us
so much that He gave His Son (John 3:16). God-like love is to serve, to sacrifice
for, and to give to others.

In this section, the Lord calls Orson Pratt on his first mission. By serving and
sacrificing in this way, Orson would learn about the Lord's love. After serving
several more missions and fully developing Christ-like love, Orson not only ful-

filled the universal apostolic calling (remember what we talked about in Section 18), but was also ordained an Apostle. He was also a renowned mathematician and a great help to the saints when they crossed the plains (*CHMR*, 1:143-144).

35

Elect Non-member Leaders

Sidney Rigdon

When Sidney Rigdon was about 27 years old he became a Baptist minister. Later, Sidney realized that some of the Baptist doctrines are not true. Then Sidney met Alexander Campbell and Walter Scott, and they started the religion known as the "Campbellites," or "Disciples."

One day, Sidney Rigdon met Parley Pratt and the other Mormon missionaries who were called on the first Lamanite mission (remember Section 32). Sidney learned of the restored gospel and was baptized. Sidney then went to visit the prophet Joseph Smith. On this visit, Joseph Smith received the revelation given in Section 35.

That We May Be One (35:2)

Remember the material for 20:28, "The Father, Son, and Holy Ghost are One God."

Elect Non-member Leaders (35:3-6)

When Sidney was a preacher in other religions, he taught people that they needed to have faith, repent, and be baptized by immersion. Because these people now believed in these teachings, it was very easy for many of them to accept the fullness of the gospel and the true church. Even though Sidney was not a member of the true church, the Lord used him to prepare others to accept the truth in the same way that he used John the Baptist to prepare people to accept Jesus Christ (v. 4).

Alma taught that the Lord uses many people, whether they are members of His church or not, to help others accept truth (Alma 29:8).[3] An example is the

---

3. For an interesting (and fairly short and simple) side-by-side and topic-by-topic comparison of truths from sources from Ancient Egyptians, Babylonian, Chinese, Hindu, Greek and other writings, see C. S. Lewis, *The Abolition of Man*, "Appendix: Illustrations of the Tao," (pp. 97-101).

Islamic prophet, Muhammad. Because of his teachings, the entire Middle East gave up its idolatry, began to worship the One True God, and accepted Jesus as a great prophet born of a virgin. The Apostle George A. Smith said: "Now this man [Muhammad] descended from Abraham and was no doubt raised up by God on purpose" (*JD*, 3:32). And Elder Orson F. Whitney taught:

> Great men, not bearing the Priesthood, but possessing profundity of thought, great wisdom, and a desire to uplift their fellows, have been sent by the Almighty into many nations, to give them, not the fullness of the Gospel, but that portion of truth that they were able to receive and wisely use. Such men as Confucius, the Chinese philosopher; Zoroaster, the Persian sage; Guatama or Buddha, of the Hindus; Socrates and Plato, of the Greeks. . . . They were servants of the Lord in a lesser sense. . . .
>
> And not only teachers—not poets and philosophers alone; but inventors, discoverers, warriors, statesmen, rulers, et al. These also have been used from the beginning to help along the Lord's work . . . carrying out his purposes, consciously or unconsciously. (*CR*, April 1921, 32-33).

Sidney Rigdon's Call (35:6, 20)

Now that Sidney Rigdon had authority from God to do so, he was commanded to bless other people's lives with the gift of the Holy Ghost (v. 6). Sidney was also called to be a scribe to help Joseph translate the Bible (v. 20). The Joseph Smith Translation of the Bible will be discussed in the material for Section 91.

Thrashing the Nations (35:13)

Thrashing is what is done to separate the grain from the chaff. To thrash the nations means to find the elect and separate them from the world. This is done by bringing them unto Christ through repentance and the ordinances of baptism and confirmation.

36

I HAVE CHOSEN YOU

Historical Context

Edward Partridge was converted by the "Lamanite" missionaries along with Sidney Rigdon (remember section 35). Joseph Smith baptized Edward Partridge and said that he was "one of the Lord's great men" (section heading). Edward Partridge went along with Sidney Rigdon to visit Joseph Smith (remember Section 35). While there, Joseph Smith received the revelation given in Section 36 (*HC*, 1:31; *CHMR*, 1:150; heading to Section 36).

The Peaceable Things of the Kingdom (36:2)

David O. McKay said that the "'peaceable things of the kingdom' are the basic principles of the gospel, for their observance will lead to peace" (*CR*, October 1938, 133).

Must Be Called of God by His Representatives (36:5-7)

Just because people want to serve in the Lord's church does not mean that they can. Edward Partridge was told that everybody must receive authority from their priesthood leaders in order to serve (v. 5-7, *AoF* 5). The Lord Himself chooses who will serve in His church. The Lord said to His disciples: "Ye have not chosen me, but I have chosen you, and ordained you" (John 15:16).

Often, when Church ward or stake callings are in the process of being reorganized, several members may feel the promptings of the Holy Ghost telling them they may receive a new calling. Occasionally these inspired members, after not receiving a new calling, begin to worry about being proud and seeking after callings. Most of the time, however, these members were indeed inspired. They can feel grateful for the Lord's acknowledgment of their abilities and worthiness to receive the calling. They can also feel comforted that, for the moment anyway, they have not been called to act in the calling.

These verses do not mean that we should not seek after nor aspire to serving the Lord. Abraham sought after the priesthood and the right to administer in the priesthood (Abr. 1:2-4). We believe in seeking after good things (*AoF* 13) and in preparing ourselves to receive whatever calling may be extended to us by the Lord (see also 1 Tim. 3). The desire is not wrong (*D&C* 4:3); acting without authority is.

Gird Up Your Loins (36:8)

The Hebrews wore loose clothing that hung around their legs. When they needed to travel or work hard, they would tuck the lower part of their clothing into their sash so they could move their legs freely. In other words, they would "gird up their loins." When the Lord tells us to gird up our loins, He means that we need to prepare ourselves to go and work hard in the calling He gives us. When we "gird up our loins," we will not be stumbling over worldly things.

I Will Suddenly Come to My Temple (36:8)

Edward Partridge witnessed the fulfillment of the Lord's promise to come to His temple. He was at the dedication of the Kirtland Temple when the Lord came there (*CHMR*, 1:163). We will read about this in Section 109: "Dedicatory Prayer of the Kirtland Temple."

37

MOVE TO OHIO

Historical Context

A little while after Section 37 was given, the Church held a conference. The revelation contained in section 38 was given at this conference. In it, the Lord gives more information about the move to Ohio.

The Joseph Smith Translation (37:1)

This will be discussed in the material for Section 91: "The Apocrypha."

38

TRUSTING THE LORD

Historical Context

This is the first time (in this dispensation) that the Lord asked everybody in the Church to move to one place. Because the Lord knew that it was going to be hard for the church members to just up and move to Ohio, He showed them that He can be trusted and that people can have enough faith in Him to do whatever He commands.

See the map on page 296 of the *D&C* to become acquainted with the geography of the New York/Ohio area.

Seraphs (38:1)

Bruce R. McConkie said:

> Seraphs are angels who reside in the presence of God, giving continual glory honor, and adoration to him. . . . It is clear that seraphs include the unembodied spirits of pre-existence . . . (D. & C. 38:1). Whether the name seraphs also applies to perfected and resurrected angels is not clear (*MD*, 702).

We Can Trust the Lord Because He Knows Everything (38:1-8)

The Lord gives several reasons why we can completely trust Him:

1. He is Jehovah, the Great I AM (v. 1, 4; also see Appendix 1: "Jesus is Jehovah").
2. He knows everything (v. 2).
3. He created the world (v. 3).
4. He sees us, is with us, and we will eventually see Him (v. 7-8).

We could not put our complete trust in the Lord if there were something that He did not know. (For example, what if the only thing that the Lord did not know was that He did not exist?) But we do not have to worry about that. God does not progress by learning truth that He does not already know—He already knows everything (2 Ne. 9:20; Ether Chapter 3; Moses 1:8-28; *D&C* 88:41). And His perfect knowledge is not relative, but truly is a perfect knowledge of everything there is to know (*DS*, 1:8).

God does not progress in knowledge, but does progress through His creations. When a man has children he becomes a father. When his children have children he becomes a *grand*father. When his children's children have children he becomes a *great grand*father. Then he will become a *great great grand*father, and so on. God is glorified and made greater by His children becoming parents as He is.[4]

We Can Trust the Lord Because
He Wants the Best for Us (38:16-30, 34-39)

The Lord gives two reasons for the move to Ohio: "because of the enemy and for your sakes" (*D&C* 37:1). Enemies of the Church were already planning to kill some of the members (*D&C* 38:13, 28, 31-32). The Church also needed to stay a step ahead of the future U. S. Civil War (v. 29).

To help the members trust in Him enough to make the move to Ohio, the Lord showed them that He wanted the best for them. It would be hard to trust in the Lord without knowing that He cares for us very much and always wants the best for us. The Lord wants us to have:

1. the physical necessities of life (v. 16-20, 34-39);
2. freedom (v. 21-22);
3. unity (v. 23-27) (remember Section 27:6); and
4. safety from war and persecution (v. 29-30).

The Lord knew that the Church needed to move to Ohio in order to have these things.

If Ye Are Prepared Ye Shall Not Fear (38:30)

Ezra Taft Benson said:

> What are some of the calamities for which we are to prepare? In section 29 the Lord warns us of "a great hailstorm sent forth to destroy the crops of the earth." (*D&C* 29:16.) In section 45 we read of "an overflowing scourge; for a desolating sickness shall cover the land." (*D&C* 45:31.) In section 63 the Lord declares he has "decreed wars upon the face of the earth. . . ." (*D&C* 63:33.)
>
> In Matthew, chapter 24, we learn of "famines, and pestilences, and earthquakes. . . ." (Mat. 24:7.) The Lord declared that these and other calamities shall occur. . . . Prophecy is but history in reverse—a divine disclosure of future events.
>
> Yet, through all of this, the Lord Jesus Christ has said: ". . . if ye are prepared ye shall not fear." (*D&C* 38:30.)
>
> What, then, is the Lord's way to help us prepare for these calamities? The answer is also found in section 1 of the Doctrine and Covenants, wherein he says: [*D&C* 1:17-18, 37 quoted—read it now].
>
> Here then is the key—look to the prophets for the words of God, that will show us how to prepare for the calamities which are to come (*Ensign*, Jan. 1974, 68-69).

---

4. For further discussion of God's progression, see *Lectures on Faith*, "Lecture Fourth," Paragraph 11; and *DS*, 1:7-10.

Blessings For Obedience (38:31-32)

To help the members of the Church make the move to Ohio, the Lord promised them some blessings that they would receive for their obedience:

1. they would escape their enemies (v. 31);
2. be given the Lord's law (v. 32);
3. and be endowed with power (v. 32).

The Lord's promise to give the saints His law was fulfilled in Ohio, and will be discussed in the material for Section 42: "The Lord's Law." Some of the ways that the Lord's promise to endow the saints with power in Ohio was fulfilled are:

1. The first temple of this dispensation was built in Ohio.
2. Keys of the priesthood were restored by angelic messengers in the temple.
3. The Savior appeared to many of the saints.
4. The offices of Bishop, Quorum of Twelve Apostles, First Presidency, etc. were restored to the Church (ST, 1:185).

Be Ye Clean That Bear the Vessels of the Lord (38:42)

Only authorized priesthood holders were permitted to handle vessels used in the temple in ancient Israel. The phrase "vessels of the Lord" has come to mean priesthood blessings such as the gift of the Holy Ghost or the priesthood itself. The Lord commands all those who bear these "vessels" to be clean from sin.

39

ACCEPTING THE LORD

Historical Context

As a Baptist minister, James Covill knew that he needed to accept Jesus into his life. James Covill committed to do whatever the Lord told him through the Prophet Joseph Smith (section heading).

Accepting The Lord (39:1-6)

The Lord told James that to accept Jesus Christ, people *must* be baptized and receive the Holy Ghost (v. 1-6).

Get Baptized (39:7-10)

The Lord simply and boldly tells James Covill that he must be baptized (v. 10).

James Covill To Be a "Stake Missionary" (39:11-24)

The first thing James Covill was to do after his baptism was to help others accept Jesus Christ by baptizing them and giving them the gift of the Holy Ghost (v. 20, 23). Now is a good time to review the material for *D&C* 23:6-7.

40

REJECTING THE LORD

Satan works hard to keep us from doing the will of the Lord (remember Section 10). Satan does everything possible to get us to change our minds about our testimonies. Satan tries to make us feel that things we have prayed about and promised the Lord were never the will of the Lord to begin with. This is what happened to James Covill. The Lord told him that his day of deliverance had come (*D&C* 39:10). But he began to worry about what others would think of him. Then he began to think about how much he would have to give up when he joined the Church. Then he rejected his day of deliverance.

When we are tempted to not go through with promises we have made with the Lord, we should ask ourselves, "Why am I giving up my day of deliverance? Why am I giving up the great blessings the Lord has promised me?"

41

DISCIPLESHIP—CALLINGS

Historical Setting—Strange Notions and False Spirits (Heading to Section 41)

Another term for "false spirits" is "false doctrines" (*D&C* 50:2, footnote *a*). The Saints in Kirtland were "striving to do the will of God, so far as they knew it" but they believed and practiced some false doctrines (section heading). The Lord would soon give his law which would show the Saints how to correct these false beliefs.

The Lord's Law (41:1-4, 12)

In Section 38 (v. 32), the Lord promised the saints His law when they moved to Ohio. In Section 41, the Lord makes this same promise (v. 3). The Lord gives the saints His law in Section 42.

Discipleship (41:5-6)

Some of the things we must do to be disciples of Jesus Christ are:
1. follow the Lord at all costs (Mat. 8:21-22);
2. take up our cross (which means to deny ourselves all ungodliness and every worldly lust and keep the commandments) (Mat. 16:24, *JST* Mat. 16:24);
3. have no hypocrisy (Luke 12:1, 1 Cor. 5:7-8);
4. lay our treasures up in heaven (Luke 12:19);
5. prepare for the Second coming (Luke 12:36-39);
6. be willing to forsake all we have, including our family and our life (Luke 14:26, 33; *D&C* 103:27-28);
7. love one another (John 13:34-35);
8. keep the commandments (John 14:15, 21);
9. take upon us the name of Jesus Christ with full purpose of heart (*D&C* 18:27, remember the universal apostolic calling discussed in Section 18);
10. stand in holy places (*D&C* 45:32);
11. remember the poor, sick, and afflicted (*D&C* 52:40);
12. receive the Lord's representatives (*D&C* 84:89-91); and
13. have faith in God and not man (*D&C* 99:13-14).

The Lord sums these things up by saying: "He that receiveth my law *and doeth it*, the same is my disciple" (*D&C* 41:5, emphasis added).

The disciples that Jesus called in the New Testament are good examples of receiving Jesus's law and following it. When Jesus called Peter and Andrew to be His disciples, He said to them, "Follow me" (Mat. 4:19). They "*straightway* left their nets, and followed him" (Mat. 4:20, emphasis added). Then, when Jesus called James and John, "they *immediately* left the ship and their father, and followed him" (Mat. 4:22, emphasis added). For more information on being a disciple of Christ, see the material for Section 52: "A Pattern of Discipleship."

Callings (41:9-11)

In Section 36 we learned about Edward Partridge. In Section 41, Edward Partridge is called to be the first bishop of the Church in this dispensation (v. 9). His calling shows how all callings to serve the Lord are made. Verse 9 shows the three-part process:

1. The Lord calls a person through His representatives.
2. The people that the person will lead have the opportunity to accept or reject the Lord's choice (remember the material for Section 26).
3. The person is ordained or given the necessary authority (remember the material for Section 36).

42

THE LORD'S LAW

Historical Context

The Lord promised the saints that He would give them His law when they moved to Ohio (remember Section 38). About a month later, the Lord told them that they would receive it by the prayer of faith (remember Section 41). Five days after this, when twelve Elders were united in worship, the Lord finally revealed His law. Section 42 contains this law.

The Lord's Law Affects Our Life

The Lord's law governs all people whether they know it or not. William R. Bradford said:

Does the law of gravity exist? Does it have effect in your life? If you jump from a high place, will your body not fall? Can you defy gravity? Can you step outside of its control?

Does the law of the gospel of Jesus Christ exist? Does it have effect in your life? If you disobey its limits and conditions, will your spirit not fall? Can you defy the law of the gospel of Jesus Christ? Can you step outside its control? (*Ensign*, Nov. 1977, 65-66).

Why the Lord Gives Laws

The Lord said: "Thus I grant unto this people a privilege of organizing themselves according to my laws" (*D&C* 51:15). It is indeed a privilege to live under the Lord's law. The Lord gives His true law in order to show us the path to freedom and joy.

1. **Freedom.** The producer of the movie *The Ten Commandments*, Cecil B. DeMille, said:

> We cannot break the Ten Commandments. We can only break ourselves against them—or else, by keeping them, rise through them to the fullness of freedom under God. God means us to be free (*Commencement Address*, Brigham Young University Speeches of the Year, Provo, May 31, 1957).

God's law makes us free. Jesus said, "And ye shall know the truth, and the truth shall make you free," and "I, the Lord God, make you free, therefore ye are free indeed; and the law also maketh you free" (John 8:32; *D&C* 98:8).

The freedom that obedience to the laws of God brings is a societal, as well as personal issue. The societal implications of the Lord's law are addressed more fully in Appendix 5: "The Rock of Liberty."

2. **Joy.** The Lord knows everything about life. He knows what kind of lifestyle will bring the most joy. He wants us to have the kind of joy He has. So the answer to the question "Why did the Lord command us to do this?" is: "Because it will make us happy." Joseph Smith said that God

> never will institute an ordinance or give a commandment to his people that is not calculated in its nature to promote that happiness which he has designed, and which will not end in the greatest amount of good and glory to those who become the recipients of his law (*TPJS*, p. 256).

And Marion G. Romney said:

> It has always seemed somewhat paradoxical to me that we must constantly have the Lord command us to do those things which are for our own good (*Ensign*, Nov. 1982, 93).

The Lord gives us laws to guide us towards a happy life and greater freedom, "for the commandment is a lamp; and the law is light; and reproofs of instruction are the way of life" (Prov. 6:23).

Laws on Teaching (42:4-17)

David O. McKay said, "no greater responsibility can rest upon any man, than to be a teacher of God's children" (*CR*, Oct. 1916, 57). Just one teacher can lead many people to Christ, or can lead many *away from* Christ. For this reason, the Lord gave several laws concerning teaching. Some of these laws are:

1. People must be given authority before they can teach (v. 11, also *AoF* 5).
2. Teachers must teach true principles of the gospel as found in the scriptures (v. 12; note that the *D&C* and *PGP* had not been published yet).
3. Teachers must live what they teach (v. 13).
4. Teachers must only teach when the Spirit is present (v. 14).

The Lord emphasizes the importance of the Spirit in our teaching and learning. Study without the Spirit can only take us so far. Paul warns us of those who are "ever learning, and never able to come to the knowledge of the truth" (2 Tim. 3:7). And the Lord said that we should "seek learning, even by study *and also by faith*" (*D&C* 88:118, emphasis added). Otten and Caldwell state:

> The purpose of teaching the Savior's gospel is to change lives of people and bring them to the Lord. Teaching facts and presenting information only will never accomplish such purposes. People don't make changes in their lives based solely on what they know. They change because of what they feel. It has been said that religion is not taught, but caught. People must catch a feeling for truth as it is presented to them. It is the Holy Ghost that bears witness of truth and provides the necessary feeling (*ST* 1:198).

For information on inviting the Spirit into our teaching, see Appendix 2: "Inviting in the Spirit." And for the Lord's lesson on teaching with power, see the material for 100:5-8, "Teaching with Power."

Laws on Moral Issues (42:18-29, 42-79)

1. **Thou Shalt Not Kill (42:18-19, 79).** Murderers must suffer even as Jesus suffered in order to pay for their sin (D&C 19:4, 17; 42:18). They cannot pay for their sin in this life. The Lord commands that they be

dealt with according to the laws of the land and killed (v. 19, 79). Wilford Woodruff said:

> We regard the killing of a human being, except in conformity with the civil law, as a capital crime which should be punished by shedding the blood of the criminal, after a public trial before a legally constituted court of the land (*Deseret Weekly*, 39:809).

The Lord said that murderers cannot be forgiven after this life either. This means that they cannot live with God in His celestial kingdom. Murderers must spend time suffering in hell until they are clean, then they will be resurrected (after the millennium is over) and enter the telestial (the lowest) kingdom (Rev. 22:15; *D&C* 76:85).

The Lord also warned us against doing anything "like unto" murder (*D&C* 59:6). He declared that "the laws and constitution . . . should be maintained for the rights and protection of *all flesh*" (101:77; emphasis added). In 1973, the First Presidency issued this statement on abortion:

> The church opposes abortion and counsels its members not to submit to or perform an abortion except in the rare cases where, in the opinion of competent medical counsel, the life or good health of the mother is seriously endangered or where the pregnancy was caused by rape and produces serious emotional trauma in the mother. Even then it should be done only after counseling with the local presiding priesthood authority and after receiving divine confirmation through prayer.
>
> Abortion must be considered one of the most revolting and sinful practices in this day. . . .
>
> Members of the church guilty of being parties to the sin of abortion must be subjected to the disciplinary action of the councils of the church as circumstances warrant. In dealing with this serious matter, it would be well to keep in mind the word of the Lord stated in the 59th section of the Doctrine and Covenants, verse 6, "Thou shalt not steal; neither commit adultery, nor kill, nor do anything like unto it."
>
> As to the amenability of the sin of abortion to the laws of repentance and forgiveness, we quote the following statement made by President David O. McKay and his counselors, Stephen L. Richards and J. Reuben Clark Jr., which continues to represent the attitude and position of the church:
>
> As the matter stands today, no definite statement has been made by the Lord one way or another regarding the crime of abortion. So far as is known, He has not listed it alongside the crime of the unpardonable sin and shedding of innocent human blood. That He has not done so would

suggest that it is not in that class of crime and therefore that it will be amenable to the laws of repentance and forgiveness.

This quoted statement, however, should not, in any sense, be construed to minimize the seriousness of this revolting sin (*Church News*, Jan. 27, 1973, p. 7).

For further discussion, see Appendix 5: "The Rock of Liberty."

2. **Thou Shalt Not Steal (42:20, 54).** Members of the church carried over many of the beliefs from their previous religions, so many false doctrines were being taught in the Lord's church (remember the historical setting for section 41). One of the beliefs that was carried over was the plan of "common stock" (*HC*, 1:145-147). An organization called "the Family" (started before the people converted to the Church) believed that whatever belonged to one of them, belonged to all of them. Many people would take other members' things without paying for them. Although their motives may have been righteous, the results of the flawed system brought about dissent, excommunication, and hard feelings. The flawed economic doctrine of "the Family" is corrected when the Lord gives His law in verses 20 and 54. The Lord also introduces the saints to the economic portion of the law of consecration and stewardship in verses 30-41.

3. **Thou Shalt Not Lie (42:21).** The Lord commands that members of the Church who do not repent of stealing or lying should be excommunicated ("cast out") from His church and should be dealt with by the law of the land. If these people never change their ways, they will go to the telestial kingdom (*D&C* 76:103).

4. **Thou Shalt Love Thy Wife (42:22).** The only two commandments in the scriptures that tell us to love with all our heart are the commands to love God and to love our spouse (Mat. 22:35; *D&C* 42:22). The Lord said that we should cleave unto our spouse and none else (v. 22). Spencer W. Kimball said:

> The words *none else* eliminate everyone and everything. The spouse then becomes preeminent in the life of the husband and wife, and neither social life nor occupational life nor political life nor any other interest nor person nor thing shall ever take precedence over the companion spouse (*CR*, Oct. 1962, pp. 57-60).

5. **Thou Shalt Not Commit Adultery (42:23-26).** As with murder, the Lord commanded us not to commit adultery or anything like unto it (*D&C* 59:6). This includes premarital sex, petting, masturbation, homosexual activities, and pornography (*MF*, 65-81). Elder Richard G. Scott of the Quorum of the Twelve Apostles said:

Any sexual intimacy outside of the bonds of marriage—I mean any intentional contact with the sacred, private parts of another's body, with or without clothing— is a sin and is forbidden by God. It is also a transgression to intentionally stimulate these emotions within your own body (*Ensign*, Nov. 1994, p. 38).

The Lord puts lust in the same category as adultery (*D&C* 42:23; Mat. 5:28). Even if nobody else knows that we are doing these kinds of things, God does, and when we do them we loose the Spirit (*D&C* 42:23). Our actions and our thoughts can bring us closer to the Lord, or drive us away from Him. President David O. McKay liked to quote:

> Sow a thought, reap an act;
> Sow an act, reap a habit;
> Sow a habit, reap a character;
> Sow a character, reap an eternal destiny.
> (E. D. Boardman; in *CR*, April 1962, pg. 7).

And Elder Richard G. Scott said:

> **Question:** How do we keep bad thoughts from entering our minds, and what do we do when they come?
> **Answer:** Some bad thoughts come by themselves. Others come because we invite them by what we look at and listen to. Talking about or looking at immodest pictures . . . can stimulate powerful emotions. It will tempt you to watch improper vidocassettes or movies. These things surround you, but you must not participate in them. Work at keeping your thoughts clean by thinking of something good. . . . Above all, don't feed thoughts by reading or watching things that are wrong. If you don't control your thoughts, Satan will keep tempting you until you eventually act them out (*Ensign*, Nov. 1994, p. 37).

We have all been given different weaknesses. God may give us these weaknesses by way of our genes or by way of our life situation. Some people are predisposed to alcoholism, others are predisposed to homosexuality or other sexual activities. Our natural tendencies do not give us permission to break the laws of God. He knows our weaknesses and He will be our judge. He said:

> I give unto men weakness that they may be humble; and my grace is sufficient for all men that humble themselves before me; for if they humble themselves before me, and have faith in me, then will I make weak things become strong unto them (Ether 12:17).

With patience, faith in the Lord, and faith in ourselves, we can overcome our weaknesses. Jesus died for us to give us the chance to change ourselves. We can change our lives and be forgiven for any of these sins.

The Lord's hand is outstretched to all of us, even though our sins "be as scarlet" (Isa. 1:18) and have serious consequences. The Lord has called people and established programs to help us repent. All of the sexual sins just discussed require confession to the Bishop. Elder Scott said the Bishop "may seem to be busy or unavailable. Tell him you are in trouble and need help. He will listen" (*Ensign*, Nov. 1994, p. 38). For a further discussion on confessing sins to the Bishop, see the material for 58:43, "By This Ye may Know if a Man Repenteth of his Sins."

No matter how serious the sin, the Lord wants us to seek His love and forgiveness. A letter by the First Presidency dated February 1, 1994 stated:

> Every effort should be made in helping whose who conceive out of wedlock to establish an eternal family relationship. When the unwed parents are unable or unwilling to marry, they should be encouraged to place the child for adoption, preferable through LDS Social Services. . . . Unwed parents who do not marry should not be counseled to keep the infant as a condition of repentance or out of an obligation to care for one's own. . . . When deciding to place the baby for adoption, the best interests of the child should be the paramount consideration (in *Ensign*, Monte Brough, "Guidance for Unwed Parents, Sep. 1994, p. 19).

6. Thou Shalt Not Speak Evil of Thy Neighbor (42:27).
Someone wrote:

> There is so much good in the worst of us,
> And so much bad in the best of us,
> That it ill behooves any of us
> To find fault with the rest of us.

Controlling our speech is a key to overcoming all forms of sin: "If any man offend not in word, the same is a perfect man, and able also to bridle the whole body" (James 3:2).

7. Thou Shalt Not be Idle (42:42). We are told: "work out your own salvation with fear and trembling" (Philip. 2:12, emphasis added). The Lord has stressed our duty to work (Gen. 3:19; Ex. 20:9; *D&C* 42:42; 68:30; 75:29; 88:24). Besides, when we have nothing better to do, or when we are too lazy to work, we tend to gossip, lie, steal, lust, and commit adultery.

Law of Consecration (42:30-41)

See the material for Section 51: "The Law of Consecration and Stewardship."

Laws on Sickness and Death (42:43-52)

The Lord teaches that when we are sick:

1. we should seek medical help (v. 43);
2. we should receive a priesthood blessing (v. 44) (see also James 5:13-15); and
3. we need to have faith that the Lord can heal the sick (v. 48-52).

President Brigham Young said:

> I have no confidence in faith without works.
>
> You may go to some people here, and ask what ails them, and they answer, "I don't know, but . . . we wish you to lay hands upon us." "Have you used any remedies?" "No. We wish the Elders to lay hands upon us, and we have faith that we shall be healed." That is very inconsistent according to my faith. If we are sick, and ask the Lord to heal us, and to do all for us that is necessary to be done, according to my understanding of the Gospel of salvation, I might as well ask the Lord to cause my wheat and corn to grow, without my plowing the ground and casting in the seed. It appears consistent to me to apply every remedy that comes within the range of my knowledge, and to ask my Father in heaven, in the name of Jesus Christ, to sanctify that application to the healing of my body; to another this may appear inconsistent.
>
> But supposing we were traveling in the mountains . . . and one or two were taken sick, without anything in the world in the shape of healing medicine within our reach, what should we do? According to my faith, ask the Lord Almighty to send an angel to heal the sick. This is our privilege, when so situated that we cannot get anything to help ourselves (*JD* 4:24-25).

However, the Lord also explained that sometimes a person is going to die no matter what we do because it is that person's appointed time to die (v. 48). Harold B. Lee said:

> Death of a loved one is the most severe test that you will ever face, and if you can rise above your griefs and if you will trust in God, then you will be able to surmount any other difficulty with which you may be faced (*New Era*, Aug. 1971, 4-9).

When loved ones die, we miss them. The Lord said that it is alright to be sad and cry (v. 45). We can be comforted through our hope in the resurrection. The prophet Abinadi said: "There is a resurrection, therefore the grave hath no victory, and the sting of death is swallowed up in Christ" (Mosiah 16:8). The converted Lamanites understood this and

> never did look upon death with any degree of terror, for their hope and views of Christ and the resurrection; therefore, death was swallowed up to them by the victory of Christ over it (Alma 27:18).

And when thousands of these Christian Lamanites were killed, we read:

> While many thousands of others truly mourn for the loss of their kindred, yet they rejoice and exult in the hope, and even know, according to the promises of the Lord, that they are raised to dwell at the right hand of God (Alma 28:12).

Shall Not Taste of Death (42:46)

This does not mean that righteous people will not feel physical pain. It means they will not feel spiritual pain because they will know they are worthy to return to the Lord (see John 11:26).

A Just Remuneration (42:53, 55, 70-73)

During His mortal ministry, the Lord explained to the newly formed Quorum of the Seventy that "the labourer is worthy of his hire" (Luke 10:7). This applies to both physical and spiritual laborers. In Section 24, the Lord restored this principle when He commanded that the members of the Church should support the Prophet Joseph Smith (v. 3). Otten and Caldwell state:

> When the Lord calls certain people to fulltime service in His kingdom, He provides for their physical needs while so engaged in His work. This principle is of the Lord and makes it possible for His servants to accomplish what the Lord calls them to do (*ST* 1:107).

However, this only applies to certain people whom the Lord has called and designated. It is not based on the position the person holds, but on family need. It is clear that there is to be no paid ministry in the Lord's church (Isa. 45:13; 1 Cor. 9:18; 1 Pet. 5:2; Mosiah 27:5; etc.).

Joseph Smith's Translation of the Bible (42:56-60)

Wait until we come to Section 91.

The New Jerusalem (42:61-69)

Wait until we come to Section 57: "Zion: Independence is the Center Place."

Laws on What To Do with People Who Break the Lord's Law (42:74-93)

Church courts will be covered in Section 102. But the Lord also tells us what to do on a more personal level, before a case goes to a Church court. When someone's actions offend us, we should first try to resolve the matter with that person ourselves (v. 88). Then, if the situation warrants, we may go to the Bishop (v. 89). These guidelines help those who need to repent come unto Christ. When we do not follow these guidelines in the proper order, or when we gossip about the person, we drive that person and ourselves away from Christ.

43

THE GATE—OUR DUTIES

Historical Context

About six months after the problem with Hyrum Page claiming to be receiving revelation (remember Section 28), a Sister Hubble began telling people that she was a prophetess (*HC* 1:154, footnote). She claimed to be receiving revelation to direct the Church. Many people were deceived by Sister Hubble even though the Lord had already said that nobody except Joseph Smith could receive revelations for the Church (*D&C* 28:2). So in Section 43, the Lord lays down a law about who will be able to receive revelation for the Church.

The Law of Revelation For the Church (43:1-7)

The Lord gives this law to protect His church from being deceived by Satanic revelation. To understand how this protects the Church, review the material for Section 28: "The Law of Revelation."

The Gate (43:7)

"The gate" is to be the senior apostle. When the president of the Church dies, 14 apostles are left (two that were in the First Presidency and the twelve of the Quorum of the Twelve). Whichever of these 14 apostles has been an apostle longest is the new leader of the Church. Elder Boyd K. Packer, Acting President of the Quorum of the Twelve, said:

Some suppose that the keys of presidency pass from one man to another much like a baton in a relay. Some believe that the Prophet Joseph Smith secretly or privately conferred the keys of presidency upon a successor.

But that is not the order of things. President Ezra Taft Benson did not ordain Howard W. Hunter as President of the Church, nor did President Howard W. Hunter ordain Gordon B. Hinckley as President of the Church.

The Twelve bridge the line of authority from one administration to another and keep the line unbroken (*Ensign*, May 1995, p. 7).

And Joseph Fielding Smith said:

The senior apostle automatically becomes the presiding officer of the Church on the death of the President. If some other man were to be chosen, then the senior would have to receive the revelation setting himself aside (*CHMR* 1:172-173).

Nobody except the senior apostle can receive revelation for the Church. By establishing this, the Lord has protected His church from Satanic revelation. We know exactly who should be our leader and our leader cannot lead the Church astray (remember the material for Section 28).

Duties (43:8-28, 34-35)

In these verses, the Lord gives us commandments that will prepare us for His second coming and keep us from being deceived. Some of these duties are to:

1. instruct and edify each other about the laws of God (v. 8-10);
2. sanctify ourselves (v. 11);
3. uphold the prophet by praying for him and sustaining him (v. 12-14);
4. be taught from on high (v. 15-16);
5. prepare others for the Second Coming (v. 17-28);
6. ponder the word of God (v. 34); and to
7. be sober and keep the commandments (v. 35).

When we do these things, we will be taught by the Lord, come to know Him, be prepared for His second coming, and not be deceived by the philosophies of man (v. 8-10, 12-13). The prophet Mormon's experience is an example of being taught by the Lord. He wrote: "I, being fifteen years of age and being somewhat of a sober mind, therefore I was visited of the Lord, and tasted and knew of the goodness of Jesus" (Morm. 1:15).

Ye Saints Arise and Live; Ye Sinners Stay and Sleep (43:18)

See the material for *D&C* 88:96-102, "The First and Second Resurrections."

The Millennium and After (43:29-33)

See the material for 101:26-34, "The Millennium."

44

GATHER TO KIRTLAND

Historical Context—
The Elders Should Be Called Together (44:1-3)

In this revelation, the term "the elders" means "the missionaries" (v. 1). The Lord wanted everybody to meet for a conference. This conference was held about three-and-a-half months later. It was the fourth General Conference of the Church. Verse 2 was fulfilled at this conference. The day after the conference, Section 52 was given.

Refer to the map on page 296 of the *D&C* to become acquainted with the location of Kirtland, Ohio.

Why Gather (44:4-6)

At times, the Lord has asked His people to gather to a certain place. One of the reasons He does this is so the saints have the power to organize themselves according to the laws of man. When gathered as a group, the saints' votes become significant, and they have a voice in the local government. In this way, they can protect themselves from unjust laws that would allow enemies to "legally" destroy the Church. For example, the executive order of Governor Lilburn Boggs calling for the extermination or expulsion of the Mormons from the state of Missouri was legally in effect until 1976 (see *Ensign*, Nov. 1976, 4).

45

THE SECOND COMING

Historical Context

After the Lord called all the missionaries to the conference in Kirtland (remember Section 44), Satan began to cause as much trouble in the area as he could. Joseph Smith said:

Many false reports, lies, and foolish stories, were published in the newspapers, and circulated in every direction, to prevent people from investigating the work or embracing the faith. . . . But to the joy of the saints who had to struggle against every thing that prejudice and wickedness could invent, I received the following [Section 45] (*HC*, 1:158).

Hearken (45:1-15)

The Lord counsels us to hear Him at least ten times in the first fifteen verses of this Section. He makes it clear that it is important to understand and prepare for His second coming.

In an Hour Ye Think Not (45:2)

The Second Coming has not yet occurred (49:6). Nobody knows the hour and the day Christ will come again (49:7). When Christ does come again, He will come with His own resurrected body in glory and power (49:22-23). Everyone will see Him and know that He has come again (45:74-75; Mat. 24:26-27). He will come quickly (remember the material for 33:17-18, "Spiritual Oil Cannot be Shared" and "I Come Quickly").

As I Showed It Unto My Disciples (45:16-17)

During Jesus Christ's mortal life, His disciples asked Him how they could know when to expect His second coming. They knew that by His second coming, the righteous would be resurrected. Because not having a body (even in paradise) is "bondage" (v. 17), they wanted to know how long they would have to suffer before being resurrected. Melvin J. Ballard said:

> When we go out of this life, leave this body, we will desire to do many things that we cannot do at all without the body. We will be seriously handicapped, and we will long for the body; we will pray for the early reunion with our bodies (*Melvin J. Ballard—Crusader for Righteousness*, p. 213).

The Lord shared with His disciples some of the signs they could look forward to (Mat. 24; Mark 13; Luke 21; J.S.—Mat.). And in this section, the Lord shares with us the conversation He had with His disciples (v. 16-60).

Signs Fulfilled During the Savior's Generation (45:18-24)

Jesus told His disciples about three signs that would happen in their own generation (v. 21):

1. the Jewish nation would be destroyed (v. 19);
2. a remnant of the Jews would be scattered among all nations (v. 19, 24); and
3. the Jerusalem Temple would be destroyed (v. 20).

In A.D. 66, the Romans made war on Jerusalem. They burned the temple and leveled it to the ground. Over a million Jews were killed, and 97,000 were made prisoners. Many more died by starvation and disease until there were only about 8,000 Jews left in Palestine (Benson, *CR*, April 1950, 74-75).

Signs For Our Generation (45:25-43)

The fact that the signs that Jesus told the disciples of His day to look for came to pass in such a devastating manner should motivate us to learn and be prepared for the signs that will come to pass in our generation. The Lord has revealed many signs that will come to pass during our generation—the generation of the fullness of times. Here are a few of these signs:

1. **Weeping and wailing among the hosts of men (D&C 29:15).**
2. **A great hailstorm will destroy the crops of the earth (D&C 29:16).**
3. **Flies and other animals will eat the flesh of the inhabitants of the earth (D&C 29:18- 20).**
4. **Those who fight against Zion will be cast down (D&C 29:21).**
5. **A remnant of the Jews will be gathered at Jerusalem (45:24-25, 43).** All the Jews are not going to return to Jerusalem. This sign has been fulfilled—there is already a remnant of the Jews at Jerusalem.
6. **Men's hearts shall fail them (45:26).** Ezra Taft Benson said:

   > Many are giving up heart for the battle of life. Suicide ranks as a major cause of the deaths to college students. As the showdown between good and evil approaches with its accompanying trails and tribulation, Satan is increasingly striving to overcome the saints with despair, discouragement, despondency, and depression.
   >
   > Yet, of all people, we as Latter-day saints should be the most optimistic and the least pessimistic. For while we know that "peace shall be taken from the earth, and the devil shall have power over his own dominion," we are also assured that "the Lord shall have power over his saints, and shall reign in their midst" (*D&C* 1:35-36) (*Comp.*, 1:265).

7. **Some shall say that Christ delayeth his coming (45:26).**
8. **Wars and rumors of war (45:26).**
9. **The love of men shall wax cold, and iniquity shall abound (45:27).**
10. **The Gospel will be restored (45:28).**
11. **Many will reject the gospel because of the philosophies of men (45:29).**
12. **The times of the Gentiles shall be fulfilled (45:30).**
13. **A desolating sickness shall cover the land (45:31).** Bruce R. McConkie wrote: "New and unheard of diseases will attack the human system" (*MD*, p. 725). And Daniel H. Ludlow wrote: "The following will result from at least one of these afflictions: 'their flesh shall fall

from off their bones, and their eyes from their sockets.' (*D&C* 29:18-19)" (*Comp.*, p. 266).

14. **Some righteous disciples of Christ will stand in holy places (45:32).** The "holy places" are the stakes of the Lord's church (*D&C* 101: 21-22).

15. **Signs in the heavens and in the earth (45:40-42).**

16. **Jacob (the Twelve Tribes of Israel) shall flourish in the wilderness (49:24).**

17. **The Lamanites shall blossom as the rose (49:24).**

18. **Zion shall flourish upon the hills and rejoice upon the mountains (49:25).** Wilford Woodruff said:

> On Sunday night the Prophet called on all who held the Priesthood to gather into the little log school house they had there. It was a small house, perhaps 14 feet square. But it held the whole of the Priesthood of The Church of Jesus Christ of Latter-day saints who were then in the town of Kirtland. . . .
>
> When we got together the Prophet called upon the Elders of Israel with him to bear testimony of this work. When they got through the Prophet said, 'Brethren . . . I want to say to you before the Lord, that you know no more concerning the destinies of this Church and kingdom than a babe upon its mother's lap. You don't comprehend it.' I was rather surprised. He said, 'It is only a little handful of Priesthood you see here tonight, but this Church will fill North and South America—it will fill the world.' Among other things he said, 'It will fill the Rocky Mountains. There will be tens of thousands of Latter-day saints who will be gathered in the Rocky Mountains, and there they will open the door for the establishing of the Gospel among the Lamanites, who will receive the Gospel and their endowments and the blessings of God. This people will go into the Rocky Mountains; they will there build temples to the Most High. . . .' (*CR*, April 1898, p. 57).

And President Joseph F. Smith said:

> Who, let me ask, unless he was inspired of the Lord, speaking by the gift and power of God, at that remote period of the Church's history, when our numbers were few, when we had no influence, name or standing in the world— who, I would ask, under the circumstances in which we were placed when this prediction was made, could have uttered such words unless God inspired him? Zion is, indeed, flourishing on the hills, and it is rejoicing on the mountains, and we who compose it are gathering and assembling together unto the place appointed. . . . If there were no other prophecy uttered by Joseph Smith, fulfillment of which could

be pointed to, this alone would be sufficient to entitle him to the claim of being a true prophet (*GD*, p. 486-487).

19. **Zion shall be assembled together unto the place which I have appointed (49:25).**
20. **The waves of the sea will heave themselves beyond their bounds (D&C 88:90).**
21. **The waters of the Dead Sea will be healed (Ezek. 47:8-12).**

Only a few of the signs have been included in this list. It is not my purpose to discuss each sign, but to stress why the signs have been given. This will be done in the material for 63:6-12, "Faith Cometh Not by Signs."

If you would like to know more about the signs of the Lord's second coming, read *MD*, pp. 687-698; and *TPJS*, pp. 286-287, 305.

The Son of Man (45:39)

Other names for God the Father are "Man of Holiness" and "Man of Counsel" (Moses 6:57; 7:35). Therefore, Jesus Christ can be called the "Son of Man" (Moses 6:57).

Events At the Second Coming (45:44-54, 56-57, 74-75)

1. **Appearances of the Lord (29:11; 45:44-54, 74-75).** The Lord will appear to at least three different groups of people at different times during His second coming. These groups, in order, are:
    1. the righteous members of His church (*D&C* 45:44-46, 56-57; 133:18; 77:11);
    2. the Jews at Jerusalem (*D&C* 45:47-53); and
    3. everyone in the world (*D&C* 45:74-75; Mat. 24:26-27).
2. **The saints "shall come forth to meet me in the cloud" (45:45-46).**
3. **"The arm of the Lord [shall] fall upon the nations" (45:47, 50) and "every corruptible thing shall be consumed" (29:9; 101:24).** Bruce R. McConkie wrote:

> With the return of our Lord in the clouds of heaven in all the glory of his Father's kingdom, to usher in the millennial era of peace, will come the first great formal day of judgment. At that day shall be gathered before him all the nations of the living, and he shall separate the sheep from the goats, rewarding the righteous with an inheritance in his Father's kingdom and cursing the wicked with everlasting punishment. (Matt. 25:31-46.)

Anything that cannot be part of a terrestrial (at least) world will be destroyed (*D&C* 29:9; 63:54; 64:23-25; 101:24; 133:63-64; Isa. 13:9-14; Mal. 4:1).

Characteristics of the earth during the Millennium (a terrestrial world) will be discussed in the material for 101:26-34, "The Millennium." Characteristics of telestial, terrestrial, and celestial beings will be discussed in the material for 76:20-88, "The Vision" and Section 137: "The Celestial Kingdom."

4. **"The great and abominable church ... shall be cast down" (29:21).** Remember the material for 29:21, "The Great and Abominable Church."
5. **"The Lord [shall] set his foot upon this mount" (45:48).**
6. **"All the ends of the earth shall hear" the voice of the Lord (45:49).**
7. **The parable of the ten virgins will be fulfilled (45:56-57).** Remember the material for 33:17-18, "Spiritual Oil Cannot Be Shared" and "I Come Quickly."
8. **The earth shall be transfigured (63:49-51; 101:25).** The earth will go through two changes—one at the beginning of the Millennium and one at the end. Both of these changes are referred to as transfigurations. About the time the Second Coming ushers in the Millennium, the earth will be transfigured from a telestial to a terrestrial world. As discussed above, things belonging to a telestial order will be destroyed. In Section 101, we will learn more about the conditions that will exist during the Millennium on the terrestrialized earth. We will also wait until we get to Section 101 to discuss the second change the earth will go through at the end of the Millennium when it will be transfigured to a celestial world.

The First and Second Resurrections (45:54)

Wait until we come to 88:96-102, "The First and Second Resurrections."

The Millennium (45:55-59)

Wait until we come to 101:26-34, "The Millennium."

The Joseph Smith Translation of the Bible (45:60-61)

Wait until we come to Section 91: "The Apocrypha."

Wars in Your Own Lands (45:62-64)

Wait until we come to Section 87: "Prophecy On War."

The New Jerusalem (45:64-73)

Wait until we come to Section 57: "Zion: Independence, Missouri is the Center Place."

46

GIFTS OF THE SPIRIT

Historical Context—
Notwithstanding Those Things Which Are Written (46:1-7)

The Book of Mormon teaches that people may come to general Church meetings whether they are members of the Church or not (3. Ne. 18:22). But the members in the time of Joseph Smith were not sure if this teaching still applied. They were right to wonder about this. The Lord's church is not based on ancient scripture—not even the Book of Mormon. The Lord's church is a living church, based on modern revelation. Although we are told to liken the scriptures unto ourselves, it is sometimes difficult to know how to apply ancient scripture to our current situation. The Lord tells us to ask Him and then do as directed by the Spirit. He gives us gifts of the Spirit to help us do this.

Gifts of the Spirit—
Remember For What They Are Given (46:8-12)

Every one of us has been given a gift of the Spirit (even if it does not specifically mention it in our patriarchal blessing). We do not have to be perfect to use our gift, but we must be trying to live worthily (v. 9). We have been given these gifts to:

1. help us be guided by the Spirit in our specific situation (remember what we talked about for verses 1-7)—in this way we will not be deceived (v. 8);
2. benefit ourselves (v. 9); and
3. help others (v. 12).

We must remember to use our gifts for these righteous purposes. Joseph Smith said:

> The gifts of God are all useful in their place, but when they are applied to that which God does not intend, they prove an injury, a snare and a curse instead of a blessing (*HC*, 5:31-32).

Seek Ye Earnestly the Best Gifts (46:8, 28-33)

To receive the gifts of the Spirit we must do the following:

1. ask for them (v. 8,28-30);
2. use them to help ourselves and others come unto Christ (v. 31);

3. thank God for them (v. 32); and

4. live righteously (v. 33).

George Q. Cannon said:

> How many of you . . . are seeking for these gifts that God has promised to bestow? How many of you, when you bow before your Heavenly Father in your family circle or in your secret places, contend for these gifts to be bestowed upon you? How many of you ask the Father, in the name of Jesus, to manifest Himself to you through these powers and these gifts?. . .
>
> If any of us are imperfect, it is our duty to pray for the gift that will make us perfect. Have I imperfections? I am full of them. What is my duty? To pray to God to give me the gifts that will correct these imperfections. If I am an angry man, it is my duty to pray for charity, which suffereth long and is kind. Am I an envious man? It is my duty to seek for charity, which envieth not (*MS*, 56:260-61).

Because we have more than one imperfection, we must pray for more than one gift. The gifts we need right now are "the best gifts" (v. 8). Otten and Caldwell state:

> What makes a gift "best"? Simply stated, it is that gift which best satisfies the need and provides the desired spiritual assistance at a given time and according to the circumstances at that time (*ST*, 1:224).

Gifts of the Spirit—Remember What They Are (46:13-27)

Gifts of the Spirit are reviewed in 1 Cor. 12-14; Moroni 10; and *D&C* 46. Some of them are:

1. **The gift to know that Jesus Christ is the Son of God and that He was crucified for the sins of the world (46:13).**

2. **The gift to believe other people's testimony (46:14).** President Harold B. Lee said:

> Some of you may not have that testimony as firmly rooted as you would like to. May I ask you then, if you don't have, to cling to my testimony tonight, until you can develop one for yourselves. Say that you believe in one who holds the holy apostleship, that you believe what I said and then you start now to so search . . . until you too can say, as I say tonight, yes I know, by a witness that is more powerful than sight, I know that Jesus is the Savior of the world (LDSSA Fireside, Utah State University, Oct. 1971, in *ST*, 1:225).

3. **The gift to know the differences of administration (46:15).** This gift may refer to knowing the different responsibilities of the Aaronic and Melchizedek priesthood (*DCC*, p. 274).

4. **The gift to know the diversities of operations, whether they be of God (46:16).** Smith and Sjodahl wrote:

> This refers to various spiritual influences at work, for instance such as are manifested in Spiritism, anarchism, and the numerous other "isms." To know whether an influence with a professedly moral, or reformatory, aim is from the Holy Spirit, or from another source (*DCC*, p. 274).

5. **The gift of wisdom (46:17); 6. The gift of knowledge (46:18); and 7. The gift of the ability to teach (46:18).** Smith and Sjodahl wrote:

> There is a difference between wisdom, knowledge, and ability to instruct. According to Coleridge, "common sense in an uncommon degree: is what men call wisdom. . . . Knowledge is a carefully stored-up supply of facts. . . . The ability to instruct is the gift to impart of this supply to others (*DCC*, p. 274).

Wisdom is the ability to apply knowledge righteously.

8. **The gift of the faith to be healed (46:19); and**
9. **The gift of the faith to heal (46:20).** Remember the material for 42:43-52, "Laws on Sickness and Death."
10. **The gift of the working of miracles (46:21).** Remember what Brigham Young said about how to heal the sick in the material for *D&C* 42:43-52.
11. **The gift of prophecy (46:22).** As we study the scriptures, listen in church, or go to the temple, we should ask for this gift. Joseph Fielding Smith said:

> All members of the church should seek for the gift of prophecy, for their own guidance, which is the spirit by which the word of the Lord is understood and his purposes made known (*CHMR*, 1:184).

12. **The gift of the discerning of spirits (46:23).** We can use this gift to tell if a person or doctrine is of God. This will be discussed in detail in the material for Section 50: "Hypocrites—Preach by the Spirit—Deciding what is of God."
13. **The gift of tongues (46:24); and**
14. **The gift of the interpretation of tongues (46:25).** These gifts are given so that all people can be taught the gospel. Communicating in tongues is communicating by the Spirit. When tongues are given from God, both the one speaking and those hearing understand what is being said, and they are all edified by the Spirit (*D&C* 50:17-23).

People can also speak in tongues by the power of the Devil, for Satan can speak and tempt people in every language. Therefore, the Lord has set down some rules on speaking in tongues. You can read them in *D&C* 50:17-23 and 1 Cor. 14:6, 8-9, 13, 18-19, 26-28, 33, 39-40.

15. The gift of faith (Moro. 10:11).

16. The gift of the beholding of angels (Moro. 10:14). Remember what President Wilford Woodruff said about praying to see angels in the material for Section 13.

These are not all the gifts of the Spirit. Elder Bruce R. McConkie said: "In the fullest sense, they are infinite in number and endless in their manifestations" (*MD*, p. 315). And Elder Marvin J. Ashton said:

> Let us review some of the less-conspicuous gifts: the gift of asking; the gift of listening; the gift of hearing and using a still, small voice; the gift of being able to weep; the gift of avoiding contention; the gift of being agreeable; the gift of avoiding vain repetition; the gift of seeking that which is righteous; the gift of not passing judgement; the gift of looking to God for guidance; the gift of being a disciple; the gift of caring for others; the gift of being able to ponder; the gift of offering prayer; the gift of bearing a mighty testimony; and the gift of receiving the Holy Ghost (*Ensign*, Nov. 1987, p. 20).

47

CHURCH RECORDS

Some of the reasons that the Lord commands us to keep records are:

1. "to show . . . what great things the Lord hath done" (title page to the Book of Mormon);
2. to convince all people that Jesus is the Savior (title page to the Book of Mormon; Jacob 4:4);
3. to teach us how to properly follow the example of Jesus Christ and return to the presence of the Father (2 Ne. 25:26-27; Alma 37:8-9); and
4. because the dead will be judged according to what is written in the books. (One of the books that the dead are judged from will show whether or not they have received the proper ordinances—see the material for Section 128:6-14, "The Books were Opened.")

The Lord commanded Adam (Moses 6:5), Enoch (6:46), Lehi (1 Ne. 3:2-4), and Nephi (1 Ne. 9:1-6) to keep records. The first day the Church was organized, the Lord told Joseph Smith to keep a history of the Church (*D&C* 21:1). Oliver Cowdery kept this history for a while before John Whitmer was called to take Oliver's place. John Whitmer kept a record of the history of the Church for seven years but did not do a good job. When he was excommunicated, he would not give the record back to Joseph Smith, so Joseph then dictated a history of the Church. Joseph Smith said:

> If I now had in my possession, every decision which had been had upon impor-
> tant items of doctrine and duties since the commencement of this work [such as
> the date of the restoration of the Melchizedek priesthood], I would not part with
> them for any sum of money; we have neglected to take minutes of such things,
> thinking, perhaps, that they would never benefit us afterwards; which, if we had
> them now, would decide almost every point of doctrine which might be agitated.
> But this has been neglected, and now we cannot bear record to the Church and to
> the world, of the great and glorious manifestations which have been made to us
> with that degree of power and authority we otherwise could (*HC*, 2:198).

The book, *History of the Church*, is from the record dictated by Joseph Smith. (Many years later, the Church obtained a copy of the record that John Whitmer kept.)

48

PREPARE TO INHERIT ZION

Historical Context

About two months after the Lord commanded the saints to gather to Ohio (remember Sections 37 and 38), the members who were already there were get-ting ready for the rest to come. They needed to know how they could help the members who were still coming from the East, and the members who were mov-ing from the East needed to know where they should make their homes and for how long they would be likely to live there.

The key phrase of Section 48 is: "for the present time" (v. 3). Ohio was only to be a temporary gathering place. While in Ohio, the saints were counseled to save money and prepare to inherit Zion. They would then be called to move to "the city" (v. 4). They did not know where "the city"—meaning Zion—was going to be. We will find out in 57:1-3.

49

THE SHAKERS

Historical Context

The section heading summarizes some of the Shaker beliefs and explains why this revelation was given.

The Second Coming—Be Not Deceived (49:6-7, 22-25)

These verses were discussed in the material for 45:2, "In an Hour ye Think Not" and 45:25-43, "Signs for Our Generation."

Mine Only Begotten (49:5)

Here, the Lord is speaking as if He were Heavenly Father. This will be explained in the material for 93:3-4, "Jesus Christ as the Father."

Those Which I Have Reserved unto Myself (49:8)

The Shakers believed that they were nearly perfect because they never had sexual relationships. But the Lord commanded them to repent. (Remember that this revelation was read to them—see the section heading.) The Lord told them that everybody needs to repent except some people that the Lord has reserved unto Himself. These people who the Lord has reserved unto Himself include:

> Translated persons such as John the Revelator and the Three Nephites, who do not belong to this generation and yet are in the flesh in the earth performing a special ministry [remember the material for Section 7: "John—A Greater Work"] (Joseph Fielding Smith, *CHMR*, 1:191).

The Everlasting Covenant (49:9)

Remember the material for 22:1, "A New and Everlasting Covenant."

Marriage (49:15-17)

The purpose of the earth is to provide for the sealing together of families (v. 15-17, remember Section 2). This cannot happen without marriage. "Neither is the man without the woman, neither the woman without the man, in the Lord" (1 Cor. 11:11). God Himself performed the marriage (sealing) ceremony for the first couple, Adam and Eve (Gen. 2:24).

He Should Have One Wife (49:16)

See the material for Section 132: "The Law of Celestial Marriage."

Animals (49:18-21)

After the flood, the Lord told Noah to use animals as food (Gen. 9:3). But the apostle Paul taught that in the last days some would say that it was evil to eat meats. He said that this was a doctrine of the devil and that we could eat meats with thanksgiving (1 Tim. 4:1-4).

We have been given stewardship for the earth and all of the life on it (Gen. 1:28; *D&C* 59:16). The Lord has said that it is all right to use animals for food and clothing, but we will be held accountable for our stewardship over the earth (Gen. 9:3-5; *D&C* 49:21; 59:17-20). Smith and Sjodahl wrote:

> Man has been entrusted with sovereignty over the animal kingdom . . . that he may learn to govern, as God rules, by the power of love and justice, and become fit for his eternal destiny as a ruler of worlds. A tyrant who has learned nothing but selfishness and cruelty can hope for no position of trust hereafter in the kingdom of the Father (*DCC*, p. 286).

"A righteous man regardeth the life of his beast" (Prov. 12:10). For further discussion on eating meats, see the material for Section 89:12-13, "Meats."

Not Given That One Man Should Possess That Which Is Above Another (49:20)

See the material for 78:5-7, "That you May be Equal in the Bonds of Heavenly Things."

50
HYPOCRITES—PREACH BY THE SPIRIT DECIDING WHAT IS OF GOD

Historical Context

As Parley P. Pratt and his missionary companions visited the branches of the Church, they saw many of the members doing things like shaking, jumping up and down, clapping their hands, dancing, running around, babbling in strange tongues, and yelling during Church meetings. The members felt that it was the Spirit of God in them that was making them do these kind of things. Elder Pratt and his companions were not sure whether this was from the Spirit of God or not. When they asked Joseph Smith about it, he received the revelation in Section 50 (*CHMR*, 1:183- 184).

False Spirits (50:1-3)

There are many kinds of "spirits." At sports events we cheer for our team and yell: "We got spirit! Yes we do! We got spirit! How 'bout you?" This is the "spirit" of the game. Some people are fooled into thinking that this is how the Spirit of the Lord should feel. "False spirits" can also be doctrines, teachings, beliefs, practices, or ideas that keep us from growing closer to God. In verses 23-36 and 40-46, the Lord teaches us how we can decide if something is of God or not.

Hypocrites in the Church (50:4-9)

In the Old Testament we read about a man named Uzza. Uzza did not have the authority to touch the ark of the Covenant. One time while the ark was being carried, it looked like it might fall. Uzza reached out to steady the ark and was struck dead (1 Chron. 13:9-10).

There are hypocrites in the Lord's Church. The Lord knows it (v. 4, 7). Sometimes these hypocrites offend many good people in the Lord's Church. Sometimes the Lord even calls hypocrites to be leaders in His church. Sometimes it may look like the hypocrite is going to make an area of the Church fall. Many people have left the Church because they are offended by the hypocrites they find in it. These people have been deceived.

The Lord is in charge of His Church. We can trust Him to steady His own ark. We do not have the authority to steady the Lord's ark. When we start trying to steady it, we will find ourselves dying spiritually as Uzza did physically. Even though hypocrites may go unpunished their whole lives, the Lord will cut them off from His church and from the Celestial Kingdom (v. 8). It is our job, in the mean time, to act truthfully and righteously (v. 9). When those that have left the Church because they were offended by a hypocrite understand this principle, "behold such shall be reclaimed" (v. 7).

My Brigham Young University Doctrine and Covenants class instructor, L. G. Otten, gave us something to think about when he said: "When we allow a hypocrite to stand between us and the Lord, we are actually standing farther away from the Lord than the hypocrite is."

Preach by the Spirit (50:10-22)

Remember the material for *D&C* 42:4-17, "Laws on Teaching."

Deciding What Is of God (50:23-36, 40-46)

The Lord said: "Put your trust in that Spirit which leadeth to do good—yea, to do justly, to walk humbly, to judge righteously; and this is my Spirit" (*D&C* 11:12). He also said: "That which doth not edify is not of God" (*D&C* 50:23). When trying to decide whether something is of God, we should ask ourselves: "Is this edifying? Does this uplift me spiritually and morally? Does this make me want to do good, to be humble, and to be a better child of God?" (*D&C* 45:23; *ST*, 1:224). We can ask these questions about something somebody teaches, literature, art, music, television shows, movies, our relationships, and anything else that we face from day to day.

Five teachings of Christ and His prophets that we can use to decide if a person is using true gifts of the Spirit for the right reasons (using the priesthood and not priestcraft) are:

1. The person seeks to build up the Church and not to build up themselves (2 Ne. 26:29).
2. The person only teaches what the prophet has revealed (remember Section 21).
3. What the person is doing is edifying and uplifting (*D&C* 50:23).
4. The person uses the proper manner to preform ordinances (such as laying on of hands for spiritual healings (Mark 6:5)).
5. The person has received the gift of the Holy Ghost by an authorized priesthood holder (Marion G. Romney, *CR*, April 1956, p. 68-73).

However, sometimes, because we do not know everything, it is difficult to decide if something is of God or not. When we are living worthily, we can ask Him to help us in our decision (v. 28-31). However, God doesn't always just give us an answer (remember the material for Sections 6, 8, and 9), and there are some things that we will not find out about until the Lord comes again

(*D&C* 101:32-34). Until that time, the key is to build upon the rock of Christ and His teachings as given to His prophet (*D&C* 50:44; 21:4-6).

You may want to cross reference this material with that for 52:14-21, "A Pattern of Discipleship."

The Father and I Are One (50:43)

Review the material for 20:28, "The Father, Son, and Holy Ghost are One God."

51

THE LAW OF CONSECRATION AND STEWARDSHIP

Historical Background

Read the section heading.

Bishop Edward Partridge needed to know how to organize the many saints who were beginning to settle in Ohio. The revelation given in this section gave the bishop further instruction on the law of consecration and stewardship.

The law of consecration and stewardship is part of the "Lord's law" laid down in section 42 (v. 30-41). Ezra Taft Benson said:

> We covenant to live the law of consecration. This law is that we consecrate our time, talents, strength, property, and money for the upbuilding of the kingdom of God on this earth and the establishment of Zion (*Teachings of Ezra Taft Benson*, p. 121).

This law has never been revoked. The saints are still expected to obey the law of consecration. However, the way the saints have practiced the law of consecration has "developed and changed over several years" (Cook, viii).

1831-1833: All Properties Deeded to the Church

The way the law of consecration and stewardship was practiced from 1831-1833 is mainly spelled out in this section (Section 51) and in *D&C* 42:30-31. Both the rich and the poor legally turned over—deeded—all their possessions to the Bishop's Storehouse. Then the members were given "stewardships." A member's stewardship would come from the original property that the member had turned over to the Church. If the bishop determined that a member had excess or "surplus" property, the surplus would be kept in the Bishop's Storehouse and not given back to the member. The bishop could take the surplus from the Storehouse and add it to the stewardship of a poorer member. Any profits made by a member's wise use of his (only males participated—Cook, pp. 94-5) stewardship would be reconsecrated and redistributed yearly.

There were three major difficulties in the way the economic portion of the law of consecration and stewardship was practiced from 1831 to 1833:

1. **No private ownership of property.** This included turning over all profits made from the wise use of a member's stewardship. This did not help motivate members to increase their wealth.

2. **"Surplus" was determined primarily by bishop.** Feelings were hurt, and some members lied about how much they owned.

3. **"Members were by and large poor.** . . . Redistribution . . . thus resulted in a leveling down rather than a leveling up of the stewards' living standard" (Cook, p. 21).

In 1833, a member named Bates wanted his property back. Bates sued Bishop Partridge (*HC* 1:380). Even though Bates had legally given up his property, the court ruled in favor of Bates. The court also decided it was not fair for the Church to require its members to give up their property (Cook, pp. 20-21). Thus, the court obstructed the system the Church was using to practice the economic portion of the law of consecration and stewardship. However, this did not put an end to the law of consecration itself.

1833-1838: Individual Accountability and Ownership of Property

In May of 1833, Joseph Smith wrote to Bishop Partridge about the new system the Church would use to obey the economic portion of the law of consecration and stewardship. There were two main changes.

1. **Private ownership of property.** Joseph Smith wrote Bishop Partridge:

> Give a deed, securing to him who receives inheritances, his inheritance for an everlasting inheritance, or in other words to be his individual property, his private stewardship (Joseph Smith to Edward Partridge, 2 May 1833, Joseph Smith Collection, Church Archives; in Cook, pp. 29-30).

Members still entered a covenant to consecrate all their possessions to the Lord and His purposes, but (on paper) they only turned over their surplus property to the Bishop's storehouse. The bishop was to make sure all transfers of property were done legally. If a member left the Church or was excommunicated, he would keep his own property but the property he had legally given to the Church would not be given back (just like members today cannot get back tithing and other donations they have legally given to the Church). The surplus properties given to the Church could still be used to supplement other members' stewardships.

2. **Individual accountability for determining and consecrating surplus.** In 1833, the presidency of the Church (Joseph Smith, Jun., Sidney Rigdon, and F. G. Williams—*D&C* 90:6) wrote to Bishop Partridge concerning the consecration of property. They wrote:

> It is not right to condescend to very great particulars in taking inventories. . . . Every man must be his own judge how much he should receive and how much he should suffer to remain in the hands of the Bishop. . . .
>
> The matter of consecration must be done by the mutual consent of both parties; for to give the Bishop power to say how much every man shall have, and he be obliged to comply with the Bishop's judgement, is giving to the Bishop more power than a king has; and upon the other hand, to let every man say how much he needs, and the Bishop be obliged to comply with his judgement, is to throw Zion into confusion, and make a slave of the Bishop. . . .
>
> But in the case the two parties cannot come to a mutual agreement, the Bishop is to have nothing to do about receiving such consecrations; and the case must be laid before a council of twelve High Priests" (*HC*, 1:364-5).

After reaching an agreement, the Church member and the Bishop signed legal documents describing the agreement. (For an example of these documents, see *HC*, 1:365-6.)

1838—: Tithing

In July of 1838, the Lord revealed a new means of practicing the economic portion of the Law of Consecration and Stewardship. The revelation is contained in Section 119 and speaks about the "tithing of my people" (119:4). Refer to the material for section 119 for more information about this part of the practice of the economic portion of the law of consecration and stewardship.

Hundreds of families were driven out of Missouri during 1838-39. Many of these families settled in Iowa. Temporary welfare programs were put in place to help these poor Iowa Saints. These programs, the saints' hardships, and the fact that members themselves were to be the judges of what their surplus was, created some confusion in the minds of some of the Saints. On March 6, 1840 Joseph Smith told the Iowa High Council that

> the law of consecration could not be kept here, and that it was the will of the Lord that we should desist from trying to keep it; and if persisted in, it would

produce a perfect defeat of its object, and that he assumed the whole responsibility of not keeping it until proposed by himself (*HC* 4:93; see also *D&C* 56:4 and 124:49-50).

However, members were still encouraged to be charitable, and in October 1841 "scores of brethren" were "giving one-tenth part of their time, or one-tenth part or [sic] their income" to help build the Nauvoo Temple (*HC*, 4:434).

1842—: The Temple Endowment

Early in 1842, Joseph Smith emphasized the importance of receiving the temple endowment in order to enter into the covenant of the law of consecration and stewardship (*HC*, 4:492; 5:2; and 6:319). Under this system, Saints— both rich and poor—verbally consecrate all their "time, talents, strength, property, and money for the upbuilding of the kingdom of God on this earth and the establishment of Zion" (*Teachings of Ezra Taft Benson*, p. 121). In return, the endowed Saint receives a stewardship consisting of himself or herself,[5] his or her family, fellowman, vocation, and church responsibilities (Cook, p. 91). God promises that those who are wise stewards will be joint heirs with Christ (Rom. 8:17).

Lyndon W. Cook states:

> This then was the last, and perhaps the most lofty, phase of consecration outlined by Joseph Smith. It elevated the concept of consecration from the agrarianism and legalism of western Missouri to the free agency and deep spiritual commitment of a mature, endowed steward (p. 92).

The law of consecration and stewardship is in force today. All Saints are invited to enter into and obey the law of consecration and stewardship.

The "United Order"

For information on how the "United Order" fits into the practice of the law of consecration and stewardship, refer to the material for sections 78 and 104.

The "Privilege of Organizing . . . According to My Laws" (51:1-2, 15)

It is indeed a privilege to be organized according to the Lord's law. Remember the material for Section 42 under the heading "Why the Lord gives laws."

----

5. "There is no evidence that Mormon women were appointed as stewards in any of the previous economic programs established by the Prophet Joseph Smith. However, in the temple, the sisters, like the brethren, accepted and pledged to obey the covenants of consecration and therefore took on explicit stewardship responsibilities" (Cook, pp. 94-5).

Equality (51:3)

The definition of equality, especially as it is used to describe the economic portion of the law of consecration and stewardship, will be discussed in the material for 78:5-7, "That you May be Equal in the Bonds of Heavenly Things."

Churches (51:10-11, 18)

The word "Church" in these verses refers to branches of the church (as in D&C 20:81; 45:64; etc.). The properties of the Colesville Branch were to belong to that branch and not to the Church at large or to other branches (v. 10-11). Each branch was to be its own provider. The instructions given to the Colesville Branch were to serve as a pattern for other branches of the Church (v. 18).

Act Upon this Land as for Years (51:16-17)

Ohio was only to be a temporary gathering place before the righteous would be called to gather in Zion (v. 16). However, the saints were promised blessings if they behaved as if they would be living in Ohio "for years" (v. 17). Smith and Sjodahl note that this "is always a good rule, 'Whatsoever thy hand findeth to do, do it with thy might' (Ecclesiastes 9:10)" (p. 300). You may also want to cross reference this verse to D&C 64:25, "Wherefore, if ye believe me, ye will labor while it is called today."

52

A PATTERN OF DISCIPLESHIP

Historical Context

The revelation in this section was given the day after the conference in Kirtland (remember the historical setting of section 44).

Another Conference (52:1-13, 22-34)

The Lord tells the Elders that the place of their inheritance, Zion, is in Missouri (v. 2, 42) and that He would reveal the exact location of the city Zion during the next conference which was to be held in Missouri (v. 1-5). Then He designates missionary companionships and tells them to spread out ("and one man shall not build upon another's foundation") and preach the gospel as they traveled to Missouri (v. 6-13, 22-34).

A Pattern of Discipleship (52:14-21)

The Lord gave us a pattern to follow to be accepted of Him. He also gave us this pattern so that we could know—or discern—the spirits of other people (v. 19). An acceptable disciple of Christ is one who:

1. prays (v. 15);
2. is humble (v. 15);
3. obeys the covenants of the Lord's ordinances (v. 15);
4. uses language that is meek and edifying (v. 16);
5. understands the Lord's power (v. 17); and
6. lives and teaches by the Spirit what the prophets and apostles have written (v. 17, 9).

We should ask ourselves if we are living by this pattern and change our lives where necessary.

Now is a good time to review the material for 41:5-6, Discipleship" and 50:23-36, 40-46, "Deciding What Is of God."

53

FORSAKE THE WORLD—ENDURE TO THE END

Forsake the World (53:2)

Otten and Caldwell state: "A person forsakes the world when he becomes a member of the Lord's Church by entering into and keeping a covenant relationship with the Savior" (*ST*, 1:260). M. Russell Ballard said:

I like this little poem:

> All the water in the world
> No matter how it tried
> Could never sink the smallest ship
> Unless it got inside.
> All the evil of the world
> And every kind of sin
> Could never damn a human soul
> Unless we let it in.

We can live in the world, . . . without letting the world into us. We have the gospel message that can carry men and women buoyantly through the "mist of darkness" (1 Ne. 8:23) to the source of all light (*Ensign*, May 1989, p. 80)

The responsibility of an Elder in the Church is to declare this message of forsaking the world by entering into and keeping church covenants. The Lord called Sidney Gilbert to take upon him this responsibility (v. 3).

Be an Agent Unto this Church (53:4)

Smith and Sjodahl wrote:

> Sidney Gilbert was an able business man. The crucified Redeemer asks him to give his business talents to the Church. The Lord was about to gather His saints in a new locality, even in Missouri, and they needed men like Sidney Gilbert to transact business for them. Business talents, when consecrated to the service of mankind, are just as good and necessary as so-called spiritual gifts. . . . As an agent he could help in building up the Church (*DCC*, p. 313).

Endure to the End (53:7)

Neal A. Maxwell said:

> When in situations of stress we wonder if there is any more in us to give. We can be comforted to know that God, who knows our capacity perfectly, placed us here to succeed. No one was foreordained to fail or to be wicked. When we have been weighed and found wanting, let us remember that we were measured before and we were found equal to our tasks; and, therefore, let us continue, but with a more determined discipleship. When we feel overwhelmed, let us recall the assurance that God will not over-program us; he will not press upon us more than we can bear (*Speeches of the Year*, 1978, p. 156).

And Otten and Caldwell state:

> What we are at the end of our probation is what determines our eternal destiny. Our past, whatever mistakes it contained, becomes insignificant if we have come to the truth, repented of our sins, and are living in harmony with Jesus Christ (*ST*, 1:261).

No matter how hard life gets, we must endure to the end by continuing to obey the Lord's will. Bruce R. McConkie wrote:

> [Mortal life] is the probationary state or time during which man is tried and tested physically, spiritually, and mentally. No man has the right to run away from these tests, no matter how severe they may be, by taking his own life. Obviously persons subject to great stresses may lose control of themselves and become mentally clouded to the point that they are no longer accountable for their acts. Such are not to be condemned for taking their own lives. It should also be remembered that judgment is the Lord's; he knows the thoughts, intents, and abilities of men; and he in his infinite wisdom will make all things right in due course (*MD*, p. 771).

President Howard W. Hunter's life was a lesson in enduring to the end. No one example can do justice to the lessons from his life; however, the following highlights his determination to keep going. Elder Boyd K. Packer said:

> I once asked President Hunter if he had a doctor's book, and if so I wanted to borrow it. He asked why. I said, "I want to keep it. It seems to me you read through it looking for some major affliction you haven't had, wonder what it would be like, and decide to try it."
>
> When he was unable to walk or even stand, arrangements were made for him to speak in general conference from a sitting position. He quipped to the congregation, "You seem to enjoy conference so much sitting down, I thought I would do the same."
>
> After many months of agonizing therapy . . . he was able to stand at the pulpit to speak. He lost his balance and fell over backward. We helped him up. He matter-of-factly continued his speech without missing a word. . . . He had broken three ribs in that fall ("President Howard W. Hunter—He Endured to the End," *Ensign*, Apr. 1995, pp. 28-29).[6]

54

STAND FAST IN THE OFFICE WHEREUNTO I HAVE APPOINTED YOU

Historical Context—The Covenant Has Been Broken (54:2-6)

The Saints in New York were commanded to gather to Ohio (remember Sections 37 and 38). The Saints in Ohio were shown how to prepare to help the Saints coming from New York (remember Section 48: "Prepare to Inherit Zion"). However, soon after the Saints from New York had arrived, some of the members in Ohio broke their covenant to share their lands. Read the section heading for the rest of the story. (And wait until Section 56: "I, the Lord, Command and Revoke" to find out more about broken covenants.)

---

6. For a short overview of President Howard W. Hunter's life, see *Ensign*, Apr. 1995. For a more detailed biography, see *Howard W. Hunter* (Eleanor Knowles, Salt Lake City: Deseret Book Co., 1994).

Thus You Shall Take Your Journey to Missouri (54:7-9)

Joseph Smith asked the Lord what the Saints from New York should do now that their land was taken away. The Lord instructed these saints to go to Missouri (v. 8).

Be Patient in Tribulation (54:10)

Wait until we come to the material for 122:5-8, "If Thou Art Called To Pass Through Tribulation."

I Come Quickly (54:10)

Remember the material for 33:18, "I Come Quickly."

Shall Find Rest (54:10)

What kind of rest? Read *D&C* 84:24.

55

GET BAPTIZED AND PREACH—W. W. PHELPS

After Thou Hast Been Baptized (55:1-3)

The Lord told Brother Phelps that he needed to get baptized so that he could be made a stake missionary (v. 1-3). When people ask in their hearts, "What should I do now that I know about the gospel?" they should be told exactly what the Lord would say to them: "You need to be baptized and then help others to be baptized so that they can also have the wonderful gift of the Holy Ghost." Now is a good time to review the material for 23:6-7, "Joseph Knight, Sr."

Writing Books for Schools in This Church (55:4)

Brother Phelps not only wrote many of our hymns, but had experience in state politics and was an editor. Just as Sidney Gilbert's business talents were called upon by the Lord (remember Section 53), Bother Phelps was called to use his talents for the building up of the kingdom of God.

56

I, THE LORD, COMMAND AND REVOKE

I, the Lord, Command and Revoke (56:1-4)

The reason the Lord gives us commandments is to help us gain freedom and joy (remember the material for Section 42). As our conditions change, the Lord may need to give us new and sometimes different guidelines. This is why a "living" church—a church guided by revelation from the Lord to His authorized representatives—is so important.

Another reason for the Lord to revoke one of His commandments is rebellion (v. 1-4). There are two different cases of rebellion:

1. **The people who are commanded to do something rebel and do not do it.** In this case, the blessing that the people could have received for their obedience to the commandment is replaced by a cursing (*D&C* 58:30-33; 124:48). It would be better if they "had been drowned in the depth of the sea" (*D&C* 54:4-5).

2. **The people do their best to keep a commandment but are stopped by the rebelliousness of others.** In this case, the people still receive blessings for their attempt to be obedient. But those that kept them from keeping the Lord's commandment receive a cursing (*D&C* 124:49-51).

Take Up His Cross (56:2)

Remember the material for 23:6-7.

The Lord Makes Changes
in His Commandments to Some of the Brethren (56:5-13)

The key to understanding Section 56 is *D&C* 52:2. In this verse, the Lord commanded that Thomas B. Marsh and Ezra Thayre be missionary companions. Ezra Thayre, because of his pride, could not keep this commandment (v. 8 and remember the historical context of section 54). But Elder Marsh still needed a companion. Therefore, the Lord revoked His command to go with Ezra Thayre and gave Elder Marsh a new companion (v. 5).

You Have Many Things to Repent Of (56:14-20)

In these verses, the Lord told His people that they needed to repent because they had not followed the Lord's commandment to organize under the law of consecration. The Lord warned them that to live the law of consecration they must be willing to follow His will more than their own unrighteous desires (v. 14-15). Verses 16 and 17 sum up the reason the people were not living the law of consecration at that time—pride. Rich or poor, we can be prideful; rich or poor, we can be humble. Melvin J. Ballard said:

> I am sure that in perfect harmony with this revelation [*D&C* 56:18] I could add "and blessed are the rich, too, who are pure in heart, whose hearts are broken, whose spirits are contrite, for they shall see the kingdom of God (*CR*, April 1937, p. 89-90).

57

ZION: INDEPENDENCE IS THE CENTER PLACE

Historical Context

Joseph Smith said:

> The building up of Zion is a cause that has interested the people of God in every age; it is a theme upon which prophets, priests and kings have dwelt with peculiar delight; they have looked forward with joyful anticipation to the day in which we live; and fired with heavenly and joyful anticipations they have sung and written and prophesied of this our day (*HC*, 4:609-610).

The Latter-day saints were also eager to know the location of Zion. Smith and Sjodahl wrote:

> In the Book of Mormon the saints were told (Ether 13:1-13), that the new Jerusalem . . . should be located in America (Comp. III Nephi 20:22; 21:23), and they were anxious to know where the site for the City was. In September, 1830, the Lord gave them to understand that the City should be erected "on the borders by the Lamanites" (Sec. 28:9). In February, 1831, they were promised that a Revelation should be given on that subject, if they would pray for it (Sec. 42:62). On the 7th of March, the same year, they were given to understand that the gathering from the eastern States and the sending out of Elders on the mission to the West were preparatory steps to the establishment of that City, wherefore the saints should gather up their riches and purchase an inheritance in the place to be indicated, which would be a place of refuge for the saints of the most High

God (Sec. 45:64-66). The time had now come for the fulfillment of the promise referred to (Sec. 42:62) (*DCC*, p. 327-328).

Now that Joseph Smith and the other missionaries were in Missouri for the conference of the Church (remember the historical context of section 52), they were anxious to find out the exact location of the city Zion.

Zion

For information on different uses of the word "Zion," see the material for Section 97:21, "Meanings of the Term Zion."

Independence Is the Center Place (57:1-3)

See the map on page 297 of the *D&C* for the location of Independence and Jackson County, Missouri. Smith and Sjodahl wrote:

> The city of Independence is situated in one of the most attractive and healthful parts of Missouri, 338 feet above the level of the Missouri River, and 1,075 feet above sea level. It is an old town. It was laid out in 1827, but in 1831 it was only a village. It is now a suburb of Kansas City (*DCC*, p. 331).

Saints from the Colesville Branch began to buy the lands around Zion. On August 2, 1831, Joseph Smith presided over the dedication of the land:

> On the second day of August, I assisted the Colesville branch of the Church to lay the first log, for a house, as a foundation of Zion in Kaw township, twelve miles west of Independence. The log was carried and placed by twelve men, in honor of the twelve tribes of Israel. At the same time, through prayer, the land of Zion was consecrated and dedicated by Elder Sidney Rigdon for the gathering of the Saints. It was a season of joy to those present, and afforded a glimpse of the future, which time will yet unfold to the satisfaction of the faithful (*HC*, 1:196).
>
> On the third day of August, I proceeded to dedicate the spot for the Temple, a little west of Independence, and there were also present Sidney Rigdon, Edward Partridge, W. W. Phelps, Oliver Cowdery, Martin Harris and Joseph Coe.
>
> The 87th Psalm was read [I suggest you read it now]. . . .
>
> The scene was solemn and impressive (*HC*, 1:199).

The Line Running Between Jew and Gentile (57:4-5)

The saints were instructed to buy all the land around Zion and to the West that they could. At the time, "there was a great deal of unoccupied land, and this could be secured at the price of $1.25 an acre" (*DCC*, p. 329). The "line" was the Missouri river. At the time, it was the border between Lamanite Indian territory and U. S. Government territory. Joseph Fielding Smith explained: "The Lamanites, who are Israelites, were referred to as Jews, and the Gentiles were the people . . . living east of the [Missouri] river (*CHMR*, 1:188).

However, not only did the saints at this time not buy all the designated property, the property that was purchased was lost after the saints were driven out of Zion. Since that time, other organizations as well as the Church have purchased some of the dedicated properties. Refer to the following map:

Independence Temple Area

1. Church of Christ (Temple Lot)
2. Reorganized LDS Auditorium
3. LDS Visitors' Center
4. Proposed RLDS temple site
5. New Independence, MO Stake Center
6. Mission Home Residence
7. LDS Chapel (Dedicated 1914)
8. Mission Office
9. RLDS "The Campus" Property
10. LDS-owned lot

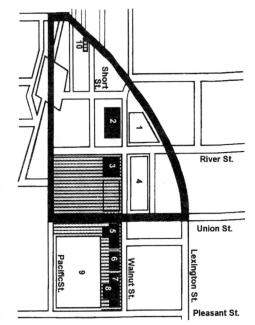

[Shaded area is owned by The Church of Jesus Christ of Latter-day Saints and the bolded line indicates the borders of the original property purchased by Bishop Edward Partridge on Dec. 19, 1832] *(DCSM, p. 119)*

> The . . . map shows the original temple site in Independence (shaded area) and the present ownership of significant sites within the original parcel of more than sixty-three acres and in adjoining areas (see Cowan, *Doctrine and Covenants*, p. 93, and warranty deeds, Real Estate Department, Central File 510-8578, The Church of Jesus Christ of Latter-day Saints, Salt Lake City, Utah) *(DCSM, pp. 118-119)*.

The key is that the Church presently owns land that has already been dedicated for the building of the temple of Zion. When the saints get prepared, the Lord will lead them in fulfilling His command

> that the city New Jerusalem shall be built by the gathering of the saints, beginning at this place, even the place of the temple, which temple shall be reared in this generation. For verily this generation shall not all pass away until an house shall

be built unto the Lord, and a cloud shall rest upon it, which cloud shall be even the glory of the Lord, which shall fill the house (*D&C* 84:4-5).

What the saints will need to do to be prepared to redeem Zion will be discussed in Section 105 (see the material under the heading "Requirements for the Eventual Redemption of Zion").

Instructions for Some of the Elders and the Members (57:6-16)

In these verses we see how the Lord calls people to positions where they can use their individual talents to help build up Zion. The following four Elders are specifically mentioned:

1. **Sidney Gilbert (6, 8-10, 15).** Sidney Gilbert was a good business man and called to be an agent unto the Church (remember Section 53).
2. **Edward Partridge (7, 15).** Edward Partridge was "one of the Lord's great men" and called to be a bishop (remember Sections 36 and 41).
3. **William W. Phelps;** and
4. **Oliver Cowdery (11-13).** Brother Phelps was an editor and Brother Cowdery was a school teacher. They were called to select, write, and print books for the schools in the Church (remember Section 55).

58

CONFESS AND FORSAKE

Historical Context

Now that the members knew where the city Zion was going to be built (remember Section 57), they wanted to know more about it. In Section 58, the Lord teaches more about Zion and how one must live to be worthy of inheriting a place in Zion (v. 1).

Zion Not To Be Redeemed in 1831 (58:1-7, 44-45)

Many of the saints believed they were going to finish building Zion at that time (1831). But the Lord warned them that this would not happen. Zion would only be redeemed after many years of tribulation (v. 1-7, 44-45). For more information about when Zion will be redeemed, refer to the material for Sections 101, 103, and 105.

After Much Tribulation Come the Blessings (58:4)

Wait until we come to Section 122: "If Thou Art Called To Pass Through Tribulation."

For This Cause Have I Sent You (58:6-14)

Although Zion was not to be completely built at that time (1831), the saints were called to live in Zion. Some of the reasons the Lord sent them to live in Zion are:

1. **To learn obedience (58:4, 6).** We learn obedience the same way Jesus did—by remaining obedient despite tribulations (Heb. 5:8).
2. **To prepare to bear testimony (58:6-7).** Just like a baby is born after its mother passes through much tribulation, a testimony can only be born after we pass through tribulation and trials (Ether 12:6).
3. **To lay the foundation of Zion (58:7).** One way the saints did this is discussed in verse 57. Although the Lord called Sidney Rigdon to consecrate and dedicate the land of Zion, which included the land for the temple, Joseph Smith dedicated the actual temple lot (*HC*, 1:199).
4. **To prepare a feast (58:8-11).** "Fat things" refers to flavorful meat, and "wine upon the lees" refers to good jellies or preserves (*DCSM*, pp. 120-121). The rich and the poor in Zion will be able to enjoy the good things in life. This will come through living the law of consecration. Smith and Sjodahl wrote:

> One great purpose of God in establishing Zion is to save the world, through its laws and institutions, from the curse of poverty and destitution. The object is to give to the world an entirely new social order, to establish a community in which even the poor would share the "fat things" with "the rich and the learned, the wise and the noble" (*DCC*, p. 336).

A Judge in Israel (58:14-20)

Duties of Bishops will be discussed in Section 72.

Obedience to Law (58:21-23)

This will be discussed in Section 134: "Church and State."

It Is Not Meet that I Should Command in All Things (58:26-33)

Here, the word "meet" means fitting, proper, or desirable. Now is a good time to review the material under "The Lord Sometimes Withholds Answers to Prayers" for Sections 6, 8 and 9.

I, the Lord, Remember Them No More (58:42)

Here, to "remember" could be interpreted as to "harbor," "hold," "carry," or "keep." God knows everything. His memory is perfect. However, He will not hold us accountable if we repent. He will not harbor bad feelings towards us. Ezekiel taught:

> If the wicked will turn from all his sins that he hath committed, and keep all my statutes, and do that which is lawful and right, he shall surely live, he shall not die. All his transgressions that he hath committed, they shall not be mentioned unto him (Ezekiel 18:21-22).

It is wonderful to know that even though the Lord knows everything about us—even our most ugly secrets—He still loves us. If we will turn to Him, He will accept us for who we are and who we can become. He will not resent us for who we were before we repented. Our confidence can "wax strong in the presence of God" (121:45).

We should follow the Lord's example. We should "remember" others' sins no more. This is not to say that we will forget, or in some cases that we should forget, others' actions. However, it does mean that we should not hold grudges or harbor bad feelings towards another.

This lesson applies to ourselves also. Even after we have fully repented and been forgiven for our sins, we will probably still remember them. This does not mean that we have not repented properly. We most likely will need to remember our sins for at least two reasons. First, so we will not do the same dumb thing again. And second, so we can teach others who may find themselves in a similar circumstance. As we turn fully to the Lord, Paul's testimony will be born in us: "We know that all things work together for good to them that love God" (Romans 8:28; see also *D&C* 100:15). However, Satan does not want us to believe that the Lord can truly forgive us. He wants us to feel that the Lord will always hold a grudge against us. He wants us to feel that we should hold a grudge against ourselves. He wants us to harbor self hatred. He does not care if we believe in Christ as long as we do not believe Christ's teachings.[7] But we can believe Jesus when He says:

> Come now, and let us reason together, saith the Lord: though your sins be as scarlet, they shall be as white as snow; though they be red like crimson, they shall be as wool (Isaiah 1:18).

By This Ye May Know If a Man Repenteth of His Sins (58:43)

Depending on the circumstances, we are to confess our sins to:
1. ourselves;
2. the Lord;

---

7. If you struggle believing Christ can or has forgiven you, reread Isa. 1:18. I also suggest you read *Believing Christ* by Stephen E. Robinson (Salt Lake City: Deseret Book Co., 1992).

3. the person whom we sinned against; and/or
4. an authorized representative of the Church.

Elder Marion G. Romney said:

> We are to confess all our sins unto the Lord. For transgressions which are wholly personal, affecting none but ourselves and the Lord, such confession would seem to be sufficient.
>
> For misconduct which offends another, confession should also be made to the offended one, and his forgiveness sought (*CR*, Oct. 1955, pp. 124-125).

And President Benson said:

> Certain sins are of such gravity that they put our standing in the church in jeopardy. Sexual sins are among those of such seriousness (see *D&C* 42:24).
>
> Full repentance of such sins requires that we not only confess our sins and resolve them with the Lord, but that we also do so with the Church. This is done though appropriate priesthood leaders (*Ensign*, Jan. 1988, p. 7).

The terms *guilt* and *shame* are often used interchangeably in the scriptures. However, for the purposes of the following discussion, I am going to give each a distinct definition.

The Lord teaches us *guilt*. The Lord teaches us to think: "I have *done* badly." Every single one of us has sinned. But Satan teaches us *shame*. Satan teaches us to think: "I *am* bad." Satan gets people to say to us, "Shame on you!" and call us a "bad boy" or a "naughty girl." Satan teaches us to feel that if people *really* knew us, they would not love us. He teaches us that we are not worth while—that we are not worthy of being loved—that we are not worthy of God's love—that we are not worthy of God's forgiveness. When we feel that we are not worthy of God's love or forgiveness, we feel that there is no use in trying to repent. When we feel this way, Satan has caught us.

Satan gets us to hide our sins. He has done this since the days of Adam (Moses 4:13-14). Satan knows that when we hide our sins, we can never come to know that we are worthy of God's love and forgiveness. When we hide our sins, we deny who we are. We cannot maintain our integrity—meaning we cannot be whole. Hiding our sins makes us feel even worse because even when people show us that they love us, we say to ourselves, "But if you *really* knew me, you wouldn't love me."

Confessing one's sins to the Lord's trustworthy servants is a most powerful way to learn that although we are guilty of committing sin, we are still worthy of God's love and forgiveness. The person to whom we confess will *really* know us. This person will know the rotten things that we have done in our lives. Then we can know that somebody loves us even when they know who we *really* are.

This knowledge helps us to know that even though we have made serious mistakes, we are still worthy of being loved by others and by God. When we know that the Lord truly loves us and that we are good people, we are motivated to change and become even better people. We will no longer feel like hiding from God and our confidence will "wax strong in the presence of God" (121:45).

Have I Been Forgiven?

It is sometimes difficult to feel that the Lord has truly forgiven us for past sins even though we have repented of them. We read 2 Ne. 25:23 and wonder if we have truly done "all we can do." Stephen E. Robinson wrote:

> I understand the preposition "after" in 2 Nephi 25:23 to be a preposition of separation rather than a preposition of time. It denotes logical separateness rather than temporal sequence. We are saved by grace "apart from all we can do," or "all we can do notwithstanding," or even "regardless of all we can do." Another acceptable paraphrase of the sense of the verse might read, "We are still saved by grace, after all is said and done."
>
> In addition, even the phrase "all we can do" is susceptible to a sinister interpretation as meaning every single good deed we could conceivably have ever done. This is nonsense. . . . It is precisely because we don't always do everything we could have done that we need a savior in the first place, so obviously we can't make doing everything we could have done a condition for receiving grace and being saved (*Believing Christ*, pp. 91-92).

And Harold B. Lee wrote:

> Some years ago, President Marion G. Romney and I were sitting in my office. The door opened and a fine young man came in with a troubled look on his face, and he said, "Brethren, I am going to the temple for the first time tomorrow. I have made some mistakes in the past, and I have gone to my bishop and my stake president, and I have made a clean disclosure of it all; and after a period of repentance and assurance that I have not returned again to those mistakes, they have now judged me ready to go to the temple. But, brethren, that is not enough. I want to know, and how can I know, that the Lord has forgiven me also."
>
> What would you answer one who might come to you asking that question? As we pondered for a moment, we remembered King Benjamin's address contained in the book of Mosiah. Here was a group of people asking for baptism, and they said they viewed themselves in their carnal state:
>
> > . . . And they all cried aloud with one voice, saying: O have mercy, and apply the atoning blood of Christ that we may receive forgiveness of our sins, and our hearts may be purified; . . .
> >
> > . . . after they had spoken these words the Spirit of the Lord came upon them, and they were filled with joy, having received a remission of their sins, and having peace of conscience. . . . (Mosiah 4:2-3.)

There was the answer.

If the time comes when you have done all that you can to repent of your sins, whoever you are, wherever you are, and have made amends and restitution to the best of your ability; if it be something that will affect your standing in the Church and you have gone to the proper authorities, then you will want that confirming answer as to whether or not the Lord has accepted of you. In your soul-searching, if you seek for and you find that peace of conscience, by that token you may know that the Lord has accepted of your repentance (*Stand Ye In Holy Places*, pp. 184-85).

Peace of conscience is indeed the greatest witness that we can have from God (*D&C* 6:23). Now is a good time to review the material for sections 6, 8, and 9 under the heading "Asking for, and Receiving Revelation."

59

THE LORD'S DAY

Those That Live Shall Inherit the Earth (59:2)

Those that live in Zion are meek—they are submissive to the Lord's teachings. Jesus said: "Blessed are the meek: for they shall inherit the earth" (Mat. 5:5). Since the earth will become the Celestial Kingdom, this means that those who are Zion-like people will inherit the Celestial Kingdom.

And Their Works Shall Follow Them (59:2)

This statement has two meanings. First, people die "but what good they have accomplished, remains. The architect may rest, but his house stands there" (*DCC*, p. 348). Second, our personalities are not changed when we die (Alma 34:34). If we have desired to do good works during mortality, we will continue to do good works after we die (*D&C* 138:57).

Crowned with Blessings and Commandments Not a Few (59:3-24)

In these verses the Lord teaches us what kinds of things He expects from a Zion people. Commandments really are blessings because they are instructions on how we can become free and have joy (remember the material for Section 42). They are the lights that guide our path to becoming a Zion people (Ps. 119:105). When we become a Zion people, we will have "peace in this world, and eternal life in the world to come" (v. 23). Some of the commandments that the Lord gives in this section to help us become a Zion people are:

1. **Love God with all thy heart, might, mind, and strength (59:5).** Smith and Sjodahl explained:

> 'Heart' stands for 'emotions,' 'sentiment.' 'Might' here stands for 'soul,' the term used in Matthew 22:37, and means the spiritual faculties. 'Mind' refers to the intellect, and 'strength' to the physical attributes. This commandment enjoins on us to love our heavenly Father so that our entire beings—our emotions, our spiritual faculties, our mental and physical activities are all devoted to Him and His service (*DCC*, p. 350).

2. **Love thy neighbor as thyself (59:6).** Loving our neighbor—which includes everybody in the world (Luke 10:25-37)—is the key to establishing a Zion society. Joseph Smith said: "Nothing is so much calculated to lead people to forsake sin as to take them by the hand, and watch over them with tenderness" (*HC*, 5:23). However, we must remember the counsel of Ezra Taft Benson:

> Only those who know and love God can best love and serve His children. . . . One needs to be in tune with God to best help His children. Therefore, if you desire to help your fellowmen the most, then you must put the first commandment first. When we fail to put the love of God first, we are easily deceived by crafty men who profess a great love of humanity (*CR*, Oct., 1967, p. 35).

3. **Thou shalt not steal; neither commit adultery, nor kill, nor do anything like unto it (59:6).** Remember the material for Section 42.

4. **Thank God in all things (59:7).** Everything we have is from God. There is nothing that upsets Him more than when we are ungrateful for what we have (v. 21). W. Eugene Hansen said: "The sin of ingratitude is more serious than the sin of revenge. With revenge, we return evil for evil, but with ingratitude, we return evil for good" (*Ensign*, Nov. 1989, 24).

   Remembering that all our blessings are from God is a key to receiving forgiveness of our sins and the gift of charity. After reading Mosiah 4:11-12 (read it now), Bishop Henry B. Eyring explained: "Remembrance is the seed of gratitude which is the seed of generosity. Gratitude for the remission of sins is the seed of charity, the pure love of Christ" (*Ensign*, Nov. 1989, 12, 13).

5. **Offer a sacrifice, even that of a broken heart and a contrite spirit (59:8).** After His death and resurrection, Jesus told the Nephites that they

should no longer sacrifice animals according to the Law of Moses, but they should offer a broken heart and a contrite spirit (3 Ne. 9:19-20). This same law of sacrifice is in effect today (*D&C* 59:8). J. Reuben Clark, Jr. explained how we offer this kind of sacrifice:

> Under the new covenant that came in with Christ, the sinner must offer the sacrifice out of his own life, not by offering the blood of some other creature; he must give up his sins, he must repent, he himself must make the sacrifice, and that sacrifice was calculated to reach out into the life of the sinner in the future so that he would become a better and changed man (*Behold the Lamb of God*, p. 107-108).

We must be willing to sacrifice the natural man within us. As Elder Neal A. Maxwell of the Twelve said, "So it is that real, personal sacrifice never was placing an animal on the altar. Instead, it is a willingness to put the animal in us upon the altar and letting it be consumed" (*Ensign*, May 1995, p. 68).

King Lamoni's father gave a perfect example of offering this kind of sacrifice when he said: "God, wilt thou make thyself known unto me, and I will give away all my sins to know thee" (see Alma 22 for the complete story). Those who will inherit Zion must offer this same sacrifice. Otten and Caldwell state:

> Zion's people not only sacrifice unrighteousness out of their lives, but willingly offer to be obedient and make whatever sacrifice the Lord may require of them. The condition of willingness is far more important than the sacrifice itself (*ST*, 1:291).

6. **Keep the Lord's day holy (59:9-15).** This will be discussed later in this section.
7. **Live righteously every day of the week (59:11).** To become a Zion people: "it is as necessary to be religious on Monday, Tuesday and every day of the week, as it is on the Sabbath day" (Joseph F. Smith, *JD*, 12:329).
8. **Use the earth's resources wisely (59:16-20).** Remember the material for 49:18-21, "Animals."

The Lord's Day (59:9-15)

Section 59 was given on Sunday, August 7, 1831 (section heading). The Lord said that this day—Sunday—is "the Lord's day" (v. 12). This day is also a day of rest (v. 10, 13). Because the word "sabbath" comes from the Hebrew word *shabbath* which means "day of rest," we can call Sunday "the sabbath day" (*MD*, p. 658). However, "the sabbath day" can refer to any day of the week, and the exact day of the observance of the sabbath has changed from time to time. Bruce R. McConkie wrote:

> Sabbath observance is an eternal principle, and the day itself . . . bears record of Christ by pointing particular attention to great works he has performed. From the day of Adam to the Exodus from Egypt, the Sabbath commemorated the fact that Christ rested from his creative labors on the 7th day. (Ex. 20:8-11.) From the Exodus to the day of his resurrection, the Sabbath commemorated the deliverance of Israel from Egyptian bondage. (Deut. 5:12-15.) . . . this necessarily means that the Sabbath was kept on a different day each year. From the days of the early apostles to the present, the Sabbath has been the first day of the week, the Lord's Day, in commemoration of the fact that Christ came forth from the grave on Sunday. (Acts 20:7.)

The Bible makes it clear that the early Christians observed the sabbath on the first day of the week, Sunday (Acts 20:7; 1 Cor. 16:1-2; Rev. 1:10). However, our sabbath day is not Sunday just because the early Christians' was (remember the material for *D&C* 46:1-7, "Notwithstanding Those Things Which Are Written"), but because the Lord told us to do it this way (*D&C* 59:12; 68:29).

To help us be a Zion people the Lord commands us to do the following things on His day:

1. **Go to church and renew our covenants with the Lord (59:9, 12).** One of the ways we do this is by partaking the sacrament (remember the material on the sacrament for Section 27).

2. **Rest from our temporal labors (59:10-11, 13).** This does not mean that we rest from all labor. On the Lord's day we have "His rest," "which rest is the fullness of his glory" (*D&C* 84:24). To have this kind of rest we must worship the Lord. In Hebrew "worship" means "to work" or "to serve." On the Lord's day we do His work and His glory— we work hard at serving others (Moses 1:39).

3. **Confess our sins (59:12).** Remember the material for *D&C* 58:42, "I, the Lord, Remember them No More" and 58:43, "By This Ye may Know if a Man Repenteth of his Sins."

The Law of the Fast (59:13-14)

Bruce R. McConkie wrote:

> Many specific reasons for fasting are found in the scriptures. It is a general obligation imposed by revelation upon church members in good standing. (D. & C. 59:13-14; 88:76; Luke 5:33-35; 2 Cor. 6:5; 11: 27.) It is itself a form of the true worship of God. (Luke 2:37; Acts 9:9; Alma 45:1; 4 Ne. 12.) It is proper to fast for the sick (2 Sam. 12:16); for special blessings (Mosiah 27:22-23); to gain a testimony (Alma 5:46); to gain revelation (Alma 17:3; 3 Ne. 27:1; Ex. 34:28; Deut.

9:9, 18); for the conversion of nonmembers to the truth, (Alma 6:6; 17:9); for guidance in the choice of church officers (Acts 13: 3); as an accompaniment of righteous mourning and sorrow (Alma 28:2-6; 30:2; Hela. 9:10); as a means of sanctifying one's soul (Hela. 3: 35); and for guidance along the path leading to salvation. (Omni 26.) Temples are houses of fasting. (D. & C. 88:119; 95:16; 109:8, 16.) To be acceptable fasting must conform to the Lord's law and not be done for hypocritical reasons. (Matt. 6:16-18; 3 Ne. 13:16-18.) (*MD*, p. 276).

And Joseph Fielding Smith stated:

Now, while the law requires the Saints in all the world to fast from "even to even" and to abstain both from food and drink, it can easily be seen from the Scriptures, and especially from the words of Jesus, that it is more important to obtain the true spirit of love for God and man, "purity of heart and simplicity of intention," than it is to carry out the cold letter of the law. The Lord has instituted the fast on a reasonable and intelligent basis. . . . Hence, those who can are required to comply thereto; it is a duty from which they cannot escape; but let it be remembered that the observance of the fast day by abstaining twenty-four hours from food and drink is not an absolute rule, it is no iron-clad law to us, but it is left with the people as a matter of conscience, to exercise wisdom and discretion. Many are subject to weakness, others are delicate in health, and others have nursing babies; of such it should not be required to fast. Neither should parents compel their little children to fast. I have known children to cry for something to eat on fast day. In such cases, going without food will do them no good. Instead, they dread the day to come, and in place of hailing it, dislike it; while the compulsion engenders a spirit of rebellion in them, rather than a love for the Lord and their fellows. Better teach them the principle, and let them observe it when they are old enough to choose intelligently, than to so compel them (*GD*, pp. 243-244).

As the Lord states in *D&C* 59:14, fasting truly is rejoicing. Why should we rejoice? One reason is because of the many blessings promised to us when we obey the law of the fast. The "true law of the fast" is contained in Isaiah 58:3-12. I suggest reading those verses now. Some of the blessings promised to us upon our obedience to the law of the fast are:
1. We will be magnified by the Spirit (Isa. 58:8).
2. Health (Isa. 58:8).
3. Divine protection (Isa. 58:8).
4. The continual guidance of the Lord (Isa. 58:9-11).
5. Productivity (Isa. 58:11-12).

Laughter (59:15)
Wait until we come to the material for 88:69, 121, "Cast Away Your Excess of Laughter."

60

YOUR TALENT

Historical Context

Now that the conference of the Church in Missouri was over (remember sections 52 and 57-59), the brethren wanted to know how they should return to Ohio.

Take Your Journey As Seemeth You Good (60:1, 5)

The Lord told the brethren that they should decide on their own how to return to Ohio. This is one of those times that the Lord expected His children to make a wise decision on their own (also read *D&C* 61:22, and remember the material under "The Lord Sometimes Withholds Answers to Prayers" for Sections 6, 8, and 9).

Share Your Talent (60:2-4, 13)

A *talent* is a weight of precious metal or a coin (see the Bible Dictionary, "Weights and Measures"). These verses make reference to the "Parable of the Talents" taught by Jesus in Matt. 25:14-30. Each servant was given a talent or talents. One servant did not use his talent wisely. Instead, he hid his talent in the earth because he was afraid. You can read what happened to this servant in Matt. 25:28-30.

A testimony of Jesus Christ and His true church is a gift given to us just as the talents were given to the servants in the parable. We are expected to use and share this talent wisely. Joseph Fielding Smith said:

> It is true that not every man is a natural missionary, and there are those who shrink from the responsibility of raising their voices in proclamation of the Gospel, and yet this is an obligation that we owe to this fallen world. . . . There are many who have been sent forth who have had a fear of man, yet the Lord has promised to support them in their labors if they will trust in him (*CHMR*, 1:203-4).

And Ezra Taft Benson said:

> The Lord has made it very clear that no man can assist with this work unless he is humble and full of love (see *D&C* 12:8). But humility does not mean timidity. Humility does not mean fear. Humility does not mean weakness. You can be

humble and still be courageous. You can be humble and still be vigorous and strong and fearless (*TETB*, p. 199).

In fact, the fear of man is not humility but pride. Who can forget President Benson's conference address on Pride? He said:

Pride is characterized by "What do I want out of life?" rather than by "What would God have me do with my life?" It is self-will as opposed to God's will. *It is the fear of man over the fear of God.* (*Ensign*, May 1986, pp. 6-7; emphasis added).

President Kimball said:

Seemingly small efforts in the life of each member could do so much to move the Church forward as never before. Think, brothers and sisters, what would happen if each active family were to bring another family or individual in to the Church before next April conference: We would be joined by several hundred thousand new members of the Church. Imagine, if only one additional mature couple were to be called on a full-time mission from each ward—our missionary force would go from 27,500 to over 40,000! Contemplate the results if each family were to assist—between now and next April conference—an inactive family or individual into full activity. How we would revel in the association of those tens of thousands!

Think of the blessings here and on the other side of the veil if each holder of a temple recommend were to do just one more endowment this next year! And how would our nonmember neighbors and friends feel if we were each to do just one more quiet act of Christian service for them before October conference—regardless of whether or not they are interested in the Church!

Imagine how much richer our family life would be if our spouses and children were to receive a few more minutes of individual attention each month! (*CR*, April 1979, p. 114).

Other scriptures on sharing our talent are: Mosiah 18:8-9; Alma 6:6; *D&C* 50:13-14; and 88:81. And for a "pick-me-up," read the great blessings given to those who share their talent—their testimony—in *D&C* 62:3 and Matt. 10:32.

My Jewels (60:4)

Daniel H. Ludlow wrote:

Jewels are precious things. Thus the jewels of the Lord are the things which are precious to him—his righteous (obedient) sons and daughters (*Comp.*, 1:324).

The Lord's glory is His righteous posterity (Moses 1:39). Smith and Sjodahl wrote:

This is an expression found in Malachi 3:17 [see also Isa. 62:3; Zech. 9:16; D&C 101:3], where "jewels" refers to the people of God, and where the meaning seems to be that when God segregates His people from the world, His power, as that of a monarch wearing a crown of jewels, will be made manifest to all men (*DCC*, p. 358).

Preach As You Journey
among the "Congregations of the Wicked" (60:6-14)

"Congregations of the wicked" refers to people who have not yet received the gospel (*CHMR*, 1:258). The Elders were to use their time effectively by preaching as they traveled to their destination. Remember the material for 19:26-41, "Teach Everyone You See."

Shake Off the Dust of Thy Feet (60:15)

The Doctrine and Covenants Student Manual explains:

> Cursings as well as blessings may be administered by the power and authority of the priesthood (see *D&C* 124:93) and include the sealing up of the unbelieving and rebellious to punishment (see *D&C* 1:8 9). The act of cleansing the feet as a testimony against those who reject the servants of the Lord is an ordinance of cursing and is not just a demonstration that a witness of the truth has been given and has been rejected. Through this cleansing ordinance, those who rejected the truth are on their own, and those who preached the gospel to them are no longer responsible for them before the Lord (see *D&C* 88:81-82). . . . *This ordinance is to be performed only when the Lord expressly commands it* (see also *D&C* 75:20-22; emphasis added).

This is a serious act. Jesus rebuked His disciples for not taking this kind of power seriously enough (Luke 9:53-56). Smith and Sjodahl wrote:

> The Elders of the Church were to perform this act *in secret* [*D&C* 84:92], as a testimony against scoffers and persecutors on the day of judgment, and *only when prompted by the Spirit*, lest they should make a serious mistake (*DCC*, p. 360; emphasis added).

61

LAND AND WATER

Historical Context

One of the fastest ways for the saints to travel from Kirtland, Ohio to Independence, Missouri was by boat. Satan—"the destroyer"—tried to stop the building up of Zion in Missouri by making these waterways unsafe for the saints to travel on (v. 5, 18-19). (You can see where McIlwaine's Bend is on the map on page 297 of the *D&C*.) By disturbing one little part of the route the saints were travelling, Satan could block the saints from reaching Zion.

However, today the Church is so big that it would be fruitless for Satan to try to destroy the Church in this same way. Section 61 is not the reason that missionaries are told not to go swimming. Missionaries are also told not to handle firearms or explosives, or play full-court basketball, and these are not mentioned in the scriptures. And neither the scriptures nor the *Missionary Handbook* tell missionaries that they should not jump off a cliff. Drowning is one of the most common causes of death for people under 25 years of age (Andreoli et. al., p. 176). Missionaries should not go swimming because it is much harder to drown on dry land.

The Inhabitants on Either Side Are Perishing (61:3)

Remember the material for 19:26-41, "Teach Everyone You See."

Satan Has Some Power Over the Elements But the Lord Has More (61:5-6, 21-29)

Satan could make the water ways (specifically, the part of the Missouri River that the saints traveled on at that time—see v. 5, 18-19) unsafe because he has some control over the earth's elements (Eph. 2:2). But the Lord will protect His saints when they use good judgement as they travel (v. 6, 22, 27-29).

Land and Water (61:13-19)

In the beginning, the water was blessed (Gen. 1:10, 20) and the land was cursed (Gen. 3:17- 19). But in these last days, the water is cursed (Rev. 8:10-11; 16:3-4; Moses 7:66) and the land is blessed (*D&C* 61:17). Elder Joseph Fielding Smith gave these insights:

> Some one may rise up and say that the soil in those days was just as produc-
> tive as now, and this may be the case. It is not a matter of dispute, but the manner

of cultivation did not lend itself to the abundant production which we are receiving today. It matters not what the causes were, in those early days of world history, there could not be the production, not the varieties of fruits coming from the earth, and the Lord can very properly speak of this as a curse, or the lack of blessing, upon the land (*CHMR*, 1:206).

And Smith and Sjodahl add:

Many have seen in the world war that broke out in 1914 a remarkable fulfillment of these predictions concerning troubles upon the waters. . . . More than 2,000 merchant vessels had been sunk by U-boats and mines. Submarine warfare is something new. It dates no farther back than 1885. Through the ingenuity of militarism the waters have been "cursed" by torpedoes and mines (*DCC*, p. 365).

I Was Angry with You (61:20; see also 1:13; 5:8; 19:15; 56:1; etc.)

It is not a sin to get angry. Anger is one of the passions we inherited from God. Like a knife, anger is not inherently good nor bad. In the hands of a murderer, a knife can be used to kill. In the hands of a skilled surgeon, a knife can be used to save a life. Anger is just an emotion the same as hurt, fear, sorrow, hope, and love. Our anger tells us that we have been physically, emotionally, or spiritually hurt. It tells us something needs to be fixed. When we harbor our anger and let it overcome our spirit, we become more like Satan. But when we let our spirit act upon our anger meekly, we become more like God.

62

YOUR TESTIMONY IS RECORDED IN HEAVEN AND YOUR SINS ARE FORGIVEN

Historical Context

Joseph Smith and some other men were returning home to Kirtland, Ohio from the conference in Independence, Missouri (remember Section 60). On the way, they met a group of elders who were heading to Independence. The revelation in this section was given to help this group of elders know what to do.

The Lord Knows How To Help Us Overcome Our Sins (62:1)

The word succor means "to go to the aid of one in want or distress" or "to relieve" (*Comp.*, 1:330). The Lord knows our weaknesses. As we desire to live righteously, He will come to our aid and forgive us for, or relieve us from, our sins. Read Ether 12:27 and remember the material for 42:23-26, "Thou shalt Not Commit Adultery."

Your Testimony Is Recorded in Heaven and Your Sins Are Forgiven You (62:3)

We bear testimony of Christ and His church by how we think, speak, and act. This testimony is recorded in heaven. Many people in heaven are interested in how we are doing. These people rejoice when they see that we are doing well. And as we continue to bear testimony to the world (especially of the restoration of the Lord's church and the Book of Mormon) our sins are forgiven us (*D&C* 84:57, 61).

63

FAITH COMETH NOT BY SIGNS

Historical Context

Now that Joseph Smith was back from Missouri (remember Sections 57-59), the saints desired to know even more about Zion. The revelation in this section taught the saints what they needed to do to live in Zion.

Faith Cometh Not by Signs (63:6-12)

The Lord taught the saints who wanted to live in Zion that they needed to truly live the first principle of the gospel first—they needed to have greater faith. Some of the saints would not trust the Lord until He gave them a personal sign (v. 8, 12). Their lack of faith was demonstrated by their immoral behavior (v. 13-17). If they were to live in Zion, they needed to repent and have faith (v. 15).

The Lord has already shown the world many signs of His existence, power, and promises (remember the material for *D&C* 45:16-43 about the signs of the Second Coming and the material about the witnesses of the Book of Mormon for Sections 5 and 17). However, signs are for the believers (v. 9). Signs will always be rationalized away by those unwilling to believe (v. 7, 10-11). Why should the Lord provide us with more personal signs when He has already given plenty of signs? LeGrand Richards gave the following example:

> While I was president of the Southern States Mission, one of our missionaries wrote in from Florida and said, "President Richards, I have been reading about the signs of the coming of the Lord." He said, "When the sun darkens and the moon ceases to give its light and the stars fall from heaven, everybody will know that he is coming."
>
> And I wrote back and said, "Probably they will know. The newspapers might announce some great phenomenon in the heavens, misplacement of planets, that have caused this consternation, and scientists will have their explanation to make of it, and unless they have faith in the Living God, unless as Jesus said, they can read the signs of the times, they may not know anything about what is going on in the world.
>
> "Why," I said, "if the inhabitants of this earth had the ability and the power to read the signs of the times, they would know that already the Lord has given far more than the darkening of the sun or obscuring the light of the moon or causing the stars to fall from heaven, for what he has accomplished in the establishment of his kingdom in the earth in these latter days, and the unseen power operating in the world for the accomplishment of his purposes, are greater signs than any of these phenomena that we read about the signs of his coming" (*CR*, April 1951, pp. 40-41).

Faith in Jesus Christ and His prophets is more powerful than any sign or miracle—even that of the raising of the dead (read Luke 16:19-31). Elder Spencer W. Kimball said:

> In faith we plant the seed, and soon we see the miracle of the blossoming. Men have often misunderstood and have reversed the process. They would have the harvest before the planting, the reward before the service, the miracle before the faith. . . . Many of us would have the vigor without the observance of the health laws, prosperity through the opened windows of heaven without the payment of our tithes. We would have the close communion with our Father without fasting and praying; we would have rain in due season and peace in the land without observing the Sabbath and keeping the other commandments of the Lord. We would pluck the rose before planting the roots; we would harvest the grain before its planting and cultivating.
>
> If we could only realize as Moroni writes:
>
> > For if there be no faith among the children of men, God can do no miracle among them. . . .
> >
> > And neither at any time hath any wrought miracles until after their faith; wherefore they first believed in the Son of God. (Ether 12:12, 18.)

The Master said:

> But, behold, faith cometh not by signs, but signs follow those that believe. (D. & C. 63:9.)
> And these signs shall follow them that believe. (Mark 16:17.)

To the scribes and Pharisees who demanded signs without the preliminary faith and works the Lord said:

> . . . An evil and adulterous generation seeketh after a sign. (Matt. 12:39.) (*CR*, Oct. 1952, pp. 47-48).

The Lord again links the sin of adultery with that of sign seeking in verses 14-17. Joseph Smith said:

> He who seeketh a sign is an adulterous person; and that principle is eternal, undeviating, and firm as the pillars of heaven; for whenever you see a man seeking after a sign, you may set it down that he is an adulterous man (*TPJS*, p.156).

And:

> When I was preaching in Philadelphia, a Quaker called out for a sign. . . . I told the congregation the man was an adulterer; that a wicked and adulterous generation seeketh after a sign; and that the Lord had said to me in a revelation, that any man who wanted a sign was an adulterous person. "It is true," cried one, "for I caught him in the very act," which the man afterwards confessed when he was baptized (*TPJS*, p. 278).

Elder Neal A. Maxwell explained:

> Sign seekers, like adulterers, often do have a clear preference for repeated sensation. Those who do not understand why adultery is intrinsically wrong will also fail to understand why faith is a justified requirement laid upon us by God. We are to walk by faith and to overcome by faith (see *D&C* 76:53) (*Sermons Not Spoken*, p. 58).

As we walk by faith, we will begin to understand signs that have been given and may receive personal signs. Signs "are given for the benefit of those who love me and keep all my commandments, and him that seeketh so to do" (*D&C* 46:9). For example, the young Joseph Smith was concerned about his sins. He prayed for forgiveness and for a "manifestation" to know how he stood before the Lord (JS—H 1:29). Some may say Joseph was seeking a sign. If one wishes to play a game of semantics, one might as well say that every time we pray for anything, we are seeking a sign. The key is faith. Have we had and will we have the faith to do the will of the Lord? Or do we seek a sign before we will believe or do anything? If we are waiting for the sign first, we will see a sign—our condemnation (*D&C* 63:6-7).

The important lessons to learn from these verses are the answers to the following questions:

1. **Why are signs given?** Reread the material for 46:8-12, "Gifts of the Spirit—Remember for what they are Given."
2. **What is the greatest sign and how can we receive it?** Reread the material for sections 6, 8-9 under the headings "Asking for, and Receiving Revelation" and "The Lord Sometimes Withholds Answers to Prayers."

Adultery and Lust (63:14-16)

Remember the material for 42:23-26, "Thou Shalt Not Commit Adultery."

The First and Second Death (63:17)

Death is separation. Physical death is the separation of our spirit from our body. Spiritual death is the separation of our spirit from God. Depending on the context, spiritual death can be called the "first" or the "second" death. When used to mean "sin" (sin separates our spirit from God), spiritual death is called the "first" death (remember the material for 29:29-35 "All Laws Are Spiritual"—29:40-45, "Overcoming Spiritual Death").

However, most of the time, spiritual death is used to refer to the state of the wicked after this mortal life. In this context, the "first death" is physical death—the separation of our spirit from our mortal body; the "second death" is spiritual death—the separation of our spirit from God. For more information on the "second death," read *D&C* 63:17; Alma 12:12-18; and Helaman 14:12-19.

The First Resurrection (63:18)

See the material for *D&C* 88:96-102, "The First and Second Resurrections."

The Earth Shall Be Transfigured (63:20-21, 49-51)

Wait until we come to the material for Section 101 under the heading "The End of the Millennium and of the Earth."

Haste —> Confusion —> Pestilence (63:24)

Otten and Caldwell wrote:

> There is a great principle taught in this verse. The fruits of doing things in haste are:
> a. Confusion
> b. Pestilence
> Note the sequence. Haste produces confusion and confusion results in pestilence, or in other words misery and suffering. The Lord does not direct His church to act in haste. All things therein are done only after there has been thorough thinking and evaluation of proper courses of action. Inspired decisions are made

based on proper preparation. Well might we apply this principle as we anticipate marriage, buying a home, choosing careers, etc. (*ST*, 1:308).

Elder Neal A. Maxwell of the Quorum of the Twelve wrote:

> The "take charge" mentality is out of alignment with the meekness of Jesus. The divine counsel "Be still, and know that I am God" (Psalm 46:10) is a required basic lesson not only in self-restraint but also in deference. "Stop, and stand still until I command thee, and I will provide means whereby thou mayest accomplish the thing which I have commanded thee" (*D&C* 5:34) (*Men and Women of Christ*, pp. 28-29).

And:

> Looking to God . . . often involves waiting upon His timetable: "Stop, and stand still until I command thee, and I will provide means" (*D&C* 5:34). Waiting is difficult for children. We can accept His declarations more easily if we realize that God has told us "all things must come to pass in their time" (*D&C* 64:32). Further, He will hasten His work (see *D&C* 88:73). On the one hand we must be very careful about trying to get ahead of His timetable; yet on the other, by its very nature, superficial discipleship is impatient (*Men and Women of Christ*, p. 38).

Haste does indeed make waste. Now is a good time to review the material for 10:4, "But Be Diligent."

Obtaining Zion (63:25-31)

The Lord states two ways that Zion could be obtained:
1. Purchase the land (v. 26-27, 29-30).
2. Fight a bloody battle for the land (v. 39, 31).

Even though the land belonged to the Lord (v. 25), He told the saints they would be blessed if they obeyed "Caesar"—the law of the land—and purchased the properties. Fighting for the land would not only be bloody, but was forbidden by the Lord (v. 31). The saints followed the instructions of the Lord and began buying up the land around Zion (remember the material for 57:4-5, "The line running Between Jew and Gentile").

Fear Shall Come Upon Every Man (63:32-37)

Although "the wicked shall slay the wicked," "the saints . . . shall hardly escape" the coming wars and fear (v. 33-35). To escape these fearful events, the saints must follow the Lord's instructions given in verses 36 and 37. If they do, they will receive the promise given in verse 34. Remember the material for 38:30, "If Ye are Prepared Ye Shall Not Fear."

Whitney's Store (63:42)

See footnote *b* (*D&C* 57:8).

Changed in the Twinkling of an Eye (63:50-51)

Wait until we come to 101:26-34, "The Millennium."

Foolish Virgins (63:54)

Remember the material for 33:17, "Spiritual Oil Cannot be Shared."

Sidney Rigdon's Writing (63:55-56)

See footnote *a* for verse 56 (*D&C* 58:50-51).

A Day of Warning and Not of Many Words (63:57-58)

What are we to warn others of? The destruction that awaits them at the Second Coming if they do not repent (see *D&C* 88:81-85). What are we to declare? Repentance. Remember the material for 11:9; 15:6; and 16:6, "Declare nothing but repentance."

That Which Cometh from Above Is Sacred (63:59-64)

The Lord warns against taking His name in vain. We do this in several ways.

1. **We take the Lord's name in vain when we use it without the Spirit (63:64).** We are to use the Lord's name with care. Unnecessary repetitions should be avoided. The key is to use it with the Spirit—"in this there is no condemnation" (v. 64).

2. **We take the Lord's name in vain when we use profane speech.** Elder Bruce R. McConkie states:

> Profanity embraces any language that shows contempt for holy things, that breathes a spirit of irreverence or blasphemy, or that is vulgar in nature, thus leaving a mental impression of unclean and unwholesome things. Profanity is an evidence of a diseased soul. "Out of the abundance of the heart the mouth speaketh." (Matt. 12:34; 15:10-20; Mark 7:1-23; Luke 6:45.) The most wicked of all profanity is that which blasphemes the name of Deity (*MD*, p. 602).

Ezra Taft Benson said: "One of the cardinal sins in our country is profanity" (*TETB*, p. 355). And Spencer W. Kimball adds:

> Profanity displays poverty of language. We note the increasing coarseness of language and understand how Lot must have felt when he was, according to Peter, "vexed with the filthy conversation of the wicked." (2 Peter 2:7. . . .) Language is like music; we rejoice in beauty, range, and quality in both, and we are demeaned by the repetition of a few sour notes (*TSWK*, p. 199).

While bad language is condemned by the Lord and we will be judged for it (Mosiah 4:30), we should keep in mind the following words of Joseph Smith:

> I love that man better who swears a stream as long as my arm yet deals justice to his neighbors and mercifully deals his substance to the poor, than the long, smooth-faced hypocrite (*TPJS*, p. 303).

3. **We take the Lord's name in vain when we speak or do things in His name without authority (63:62).** Meanings of vain include ineffectual and pointless. Things done in the name of the Lord without His authority are ineffectual and pointless.

4. **We take the Lord's name in vain whenever we sin.** Other terms for vain are: arrogant, conceited, egotistic, haughty, and futile. When we are baptized and when we take the sacrament, we show the Lord that we are willing to take His name upon us (remember the material for Section 27 under the heading "Covenants"). How would you feel about a man who says he's Christian, and even has the last name of Christ, who leads a wicked life? You would probably think that person is not only arrogant, conceited, egotistical, and haughty, but that his covenants are futile, ineffectual, and pointless. He has taken the Lord's name in vain.

The Lord also reminded the saints, "that which cometh from above is sacred" (v. 64). Life, family, church callings, spiritual gifts, scripture, and even our body (1 Cor. 6:19-20) are not our own but have been given to us from above. These things should be spoken of and treated with care (v. 64).

64

FORGIVE ALL MEN

Historical Context

In this section, the Lord teaches a group of brethren who had been commanded to go to Zion how to live to be worthy of living in a Zion society.

Receiving Forgiveness from the Lord (64:1-14)

We must receive forgiveness of our sins to be worthy of living in Zion, for Zion is "The Pure In Heart" (*D&C* 97:21). Three things we must do to receive forgiveness for our sins that the Lord mentions in this section are:

1. **Confess our sins (64:7, 12-14).** Remember the material for 58:42, "I, the Lord, Remember Them No More" and 58:43, "By This Ye May Know if a Man Repenteth of his Sins."

2. **Ask for forgiveness (64:7).** The Lord will not force us to receive His forgiveness. We must humble ourselves before Him and ask Him for that forgiveness.

3. **Forgive All Men (64:8-11).** The men that the Lord was talking to in this section wanted to receive the Lord's forgiveness and be worthy of living in Zion, but they were unwilling to forgive the Prophet Joseph for his sins (v. 6-7). The Lord explained to them that we cannot receive forgiveness for our sins until we forgive all others for their sins. In fact, until we forgive others, we are committing a grievous sin by putting ourselves in the place of Christ and attempting to keep others from coming unto Him (v. 9).

When Elder Heber J. Grant was in the Quorum of the Twelve Apostles, a certain prominent man who had been excommunicated desired to be rebaptized. President John Taylor told the quorum that if they so voted unanimously, this man could be rebaptized. Year after year the quorum voted on this issue until the only one against it was Elder Grant. President Taylor talked to Elder Grant about it. Elder Grant said:

> While I live I never expect to consent [to the man's baptism] if it is left to my judgement. That man was accused before the apostles several years ago and he stood up and lied and claimed that he was innocent, and the Lord gave to me a testimony that he lied, but I could not condemn him because of that. I got down on my knees that night and prayed God to give me the strength not to expose that man, seeing that he had lied but that we had no evidence except only the testimony of the girl that he had seduced. And I prayed the Lord that some day additional testimony might come, and it did come, and we then excommunicated him. And when a man can lie to the apostles, and when he can be guilty while proclaiming repentance of sin, I think this Church has been disgraced enough without ever letting him come back into the Church.

But later on that day, Elder Grant went to read from the Doctrine and Covenants. He said:

As I picked it up, instead of opening where the bookmark was, it opened to [D&C 64:9-10 quoted—read it now]. And I closed the book and said: "If the devil applies for baptism and claims that he has repented, I will baptized him" (CR, Oct. 1920, pp. 5-7).

Note that the commandment to forgive all people does not mean that we should let others abuse or continue to abuse us. This will be discussed more fully in the material for 98:23-32, "The Law of Retaliation and the Law of Forgiveness."

The Keys of the Mysteries of the Kingdom (64:5)

This will be discussed in the material for 84:19-29, "The Greater Priesthood."

Sin Unto Death (64:7)

This will be discussed in the material for 76:30-49, "A Vision of Sons of Perdition."

Retain a Strong Hold in ... Kirtland for ... Five Years (64:21)

The Lord knew that if the saints had all moved to Zion at the time this revelation was given, they would not have been able to build a temple for many years because of the persecution. About four-and-a-half years after this revelation was given, the first temple of this dispensation was built in Kirtland. Six months after this temple was built, the saints were forced to flee from Kirtland.

Tithing (64:23)

In this verse "tithing" means "sacrifice." To be worthy of living in a Zion society, we must be willing to sacrifice. At this point in time "tithing" only meant "free-will offering," and did not mean "one-tenth." This will be discussed further in the material for Section 119: "The Law of Tithing."

Ye Are On the Lord's Errand (64:29)

Daniel H. Ludlow wrote:

Those who are doing the official business of the Lord in his Church are on his errand; that is, they are (or should be) doing his work as he would if he were here (Comp., 1:346).

Be Not Weary in Laying
the Foundation of a Great Work (64:30-43)

The Lord again informs this company of brethren who were called to go to Zion that they were only laying its foundation (v. 32-33). But the Lord also told them that every nation would eventually respect their work (v. 41-43). Sometimes we may feel that our hard work goes unnoticed or that our Church calling is too small to matter. But President Gordon B. Hinckley said: "Your obligation is as serious in your sphere of responsibility as is my obligation in my sphere. No calling in this church is small or of little consequence" (*Ensign*, May 1995, p. 71).

Even when others do not notice our hard work, the Lord does, and he will reward us with great blessings (v. 33-34). I suggest also reading *D&C* 81:4-6.

The Rebellious Are Not of the Blood of Ephraim (64:36)

One of the stewardships of the tribe of Ephraim is to build up Zion. The Lord informed the company of brethren who were called to go to Zion that they must remain worthy of this stewardship. All things are spiritual to the Lord (*D&C* 29:34). Whether or not we are considered to be of a certain lineage depends just as much on spiritual characteristics as it does on physical characteristics. The apostle Paul taught this to the Jews when he told them that they would only be counted as true descendants of Israel if they lived righteously (Rom. 2:25-29).

65

THE KINGDOM OF GOD PREPARES FOR THE KINGDOM OF HEAVEN

Historical Context

This revelation helped to strengthen the Prophet Joseph, who in the near future would be severely persecuted. It can also strengthen our vision of, and commitment to, the Lord and His church.

The Kingdom of God and The Kingdom of Heaven (65:2, 6)

Both these terms can refer to the Church. Smith and Sjodahl wrote:

> The Prophet Joseph tells us that the kingdom of heaven is the Church. "The kingdom of heaven," he says, "is like unto a mustard seed. Behold, then, is not this the kingdom of heaven that is raising its head in the last days in the majesty of its God, even the Church of Latter-day Saints?" (*HC* 2:286.) He also states that, "Where there is a prophet, a priest, or a righteous man unto whom God gives His oracles, there is the kingdom of God" (*HC* 5:286). The Church, then, is also the Kingdom of God (*DCC*, p. 399).

However, these terms are given slightly different meanings in this section. The "kingdom of God" refers to the Church—God's kingdom on this side of the veil. The "kingdom of heaven" refers to God's kingdom on the other side of the veil. It is the kingdom of God that will prepare the earth to receive the kingdom of heaven which will rule the entire earth during the millennium.

The Church Will Fill the Earth As "The Stone" (65:2)

The Church was established by God and not by the hand of any man. The Church is the stone which is cut out of the mountain without hands that king Nebuchadnezzar saw in a dream (see Daniel 2 and *D&C* 138:44).

The Purpose of The Church (65:3-6)

The purpose of the Church (the kingdom of God) is to prepare all people to enter the kingdom of heaven. *Everything* we have and do in the Church (meetings, quorums, activities, etc.) should have the final goal of helping people to enter the kingdom of heaven. This will be further discussed in the material for Section 96: "The Purpose of All that is Done in the Church."

Gather the Elect through Prayer (65:4-5)

We often hear: "Bless the missionaries so they can find the elect." This is good, but we also need to follow the Lord's teaching in verse 5 by praying: "Bless the elect so they can find the Church and be baptized." And then we probably need to add: "Bless us and the missionaries so we will be prepared when the elect come to us."

66

THE EVERLASTING COVENANT

The Everlasting Covenant (66:2)

Review the material for 22:1, "A New and Everlasting Covenant."

Historical Context—
You Are Clean, But Not All—Repent (66:3-4, 10)

The Lord showed Brother McLellin (or M'Lellin) that he had some past sins that needed to be repented for and that he needed to notice his trouble with sexual temptations (v. 3, 10). Joseph Fielding Smith said:

> This was a wonderful revelation to William E. M'Lellin and should have been a great blessing and incentive to him to remain faithful. . . . He was not accused of committing such a sin, but was warned of dangers because of his failings, which lay in this direction (*CHMR*, 2:17).

And President Ezra Taft Benson said:

> I recognize that most people fall into sexual sin in a misguided attempt to fulfill basic human needs. We all have a need to feel loved and worthwhile. We all seek to have joy and happiness in our lives. Knowing this, Satan often lures people into immorality by playing on their basic needs. He promises pleasure, happiness, and fulfillment.
>
> But this is, of course, a deception (*Ensign*, Jan. 1988, p. 4-5).

We all get a little confused in life. We have all done things that at the time we did them we did not fully understand we were sinning. Sometimes we cover these things up and forget about them. Luckily, as we strive to follow the Lord's will, He will reveal to us the things about us that do not please Him. We can then change these things, and if we need to confess past transgressions to our authorized leader, we can do that. In this way, we can better ourselves each day.

Remember the five purposes of the Doctrine and Covenants that the Lord taught us in Section 1? They are:

1. To bring us to an understanding (1:24).
2. To make known our errors (1:25).
3. To instruct and give us wisdom (1:26).
4. To chasten us that we might repent (1:27).
5. To make us strong, bless us from on high, and give us knowledge from time to time (1:28).

Are these things happening in your life as you search the Doctrine and Covenants?

Seek Not To Be Cumbered (66:10)

Sometimes, just as "Martha was cumbered about much serving," we let ourselves get so cumbered—burdened—with doing all we do as faithful Latter-day Saints that we forget to be like Martha's sister, "Mary, which also sat at Jesus' feet, and heard his word" (Luke 10:38-42). Brother McLellin was told that if he did not concentrate on hearing the word of the Lord, he would be cumbered with the sin of adultery (*D&C* 66:9-10). When we stop hearing the Lord because we are too burdened with our Church "chores," we will also soon become burdened with sin.

So how can we "seek not to be cumbered" (66:10)? Stephen E. Robinson wrote:

In the New Testament the two means of justification, by law and by faith, are referred to as separate yokes or burdens. The obligation of the law with its demand for perfect obedience was compared to a heavy "yoke of bondage" (Gal. 5:1; see Acts 15:10), while the obligations of the gospel covenant with its repentance, forgiveness, and atonement are called "easy"and "light": "Come unto me, all ye that labour and are heavy laden, and I will give you rest. Take my yoke upon you, and learn of me; for I am meek and lowly in heart: and ye shall find rest unto your souls. For my yoke is easy, and my burden is light." (Matt. 11:28-30.)

There is no heavier yoke than the demand for perfection—the curse of the law. And many of the Saints still struggle under its lead. But the good news is that in Christ we are set free of that crushing burden. He bore that particular burden for us, and his perfect performance extended and applied to us frees us from a similar requirement at this time. In the gospel covenant, we exchange the burden of sin for the obligation to love him and each other and to do the very best we can (*Believing Christ*, p. 44).

When we yoke ourselves to Christ we are spared the burden that He bore for us. What is the "burden" that Christ bore for us? Death and sin. How do we take His yoke upon us? Hear His voice and repent.

67

THE LANGUAGE OF SCRIPTURE

The Language of Scripture

The Lord gives revelation to His servants "in their weakness, after the manner of their language, that they might come to understanding" (*D&C* 1:24). The Lord speaks to His prophets in a way that they will understand His will. The prophets must then communicate the will of the Lord to others. Thus, the language used by the prophets when writing scripture is their own language. For example, the Lord did not write the Book of Isaiah, Isaiah did; and the Lord did not write the Doctrine and Covenants, Joseph Smith did (at least most sections). Joseph Smith used the best language he knew to effectively communicate the mind and will of the Lord.

Historical Context—
But There Were Fears in Your Hearts (67:1-5)

A conference was held to act on the commandment to publish the "Book of Commandments" (the Doctrine and Covenants). The Elders at the conference accepted the revelations contained in the "Book of Commandments" as scripture. They testified that there was no unrighteousness (false doctrine) in the revelations (v. 9). However, some of the Elders were ashamed of the language used by Joseph Smith to write the revelations. (For an example of some of the language used by Joseph Smith, see *D&C* 123:5-6.) These Elders feared the criticism of the world (v. 3). They wanted to rewrite the revelations to improve the language used in them (v. 5).

A Challenge (67:5-9)

The Lord challenged the proud Elders to improve upon the language that Joseph Smith had used in the revelations. Joseph Smith said:

> After the foregoing was received, William E. M'Lellin, as the wisest man, in his own estimation, having more learning than sense, endeavored to write a commandment like unto one of the least of the Lord's, but failed (*HC* 1:226).

And Orson F. Whitney said:

> One of them, who thought himself the wisest, and who possessed some learning [William E. McLellin], took up the challenge and actually attempted to frame a revelation; but it was a flat failure. He could utter, of course, certain words, and roll our a mass of rhetoric; but the divine spirit was lacking, and he had to acknowledge himself beaten. . . .
>
> Man cannot breathe into the body of things the breath of life; that is a function and prerogative of Deity. It is not so easy to frame revelations from God. A vain boaster making ridicule of the proverbs of Solomon, said: "Anybody can make proverbs." His friend answered, "Try a few," and the conversation ended (CR, Apr. 1917, p. 42).

William E. McLellin and the other proud Elders failed to understand that it is not the language used, but the Spirit that qualifies writing as scripture.

Promises and Counsel to the Elders (67:10-14)

The Lord counselled the Elders to humble themselves (v. 10) and to not let their minds "turn back"—or go back to their proud ways (v. 14). Now that they had accepted the "Book of Commandments" as the word of God, they were to move forward to publish it to the world without fear or regret in their hearts. If they followed this counsel, they would see the Lord (v. 10). Smith and Sjodahl wrote:

This is a promise which no man could have given with the hope of fulfilling it. But it was fulfilled. On the evening of the first day of the dedication of the Kirtland Temple, there was a gathering of Elders, numbering over four hundred, and many of them testified that they had visions. They heard a sound of a mighty wind. "Almost every man in the house," one report says, "arose, and hundreds of them were speaking in tongues, prophesying and declaring visions, almost with one voice" (*JD* 40:10). Frederick G. Williams testifies that he saw the Savior on that occasion (*DCC* 406).

It is hard to look at the sun with our natural eyes without hurting them. The Lord's countenance is even brighter than the sun (*D&C* 110:3; J.S.—H. 1:16-17). It would be impossible to look at Him with our natural eyes. Mortals can only look upon the Lord with transfigured—spiritual—eyes (v. 10-11).

The Lord also counseled the saints to "continue in patience until ye are per-fected" (v. 13). Elder Mark E. Petersen said:

> Paul tells us that the Church organization was given to us, among other reasons for the perfecting of the Saints [Eph. 4:11-12]. In spite of this commandment, and in spite of this statement of Paul, there are some people who believe that it is impossible for us to become perfect. Perfection is not for this life, they say, and so why try?
>
> I would like to say that I believe with all my heart that if the Lord had any idea that we could not begin in mortality on the march toward perfection, he would never have given us that commandment [Matt. 5:48]; neither would he have given us a Church organization for the perfecting of the Saints.
>
> I believe that in many ways, here and now in mortality, we can begin to per-fect ourselves. A certain degree of perfection is attainable in this life. I believe that we can be one hundred percent perfect, for instance, in abstaining from the use of tea and coffee. We can be one hundred percent perfect in abstaining from liquor and tobacco. We can be one hundred percent perfect in abstaining from eating two meals on fast day and giving to the bishop as fast offering the value of those two meals from which we abstain.
>
> We can be one hundred percent perfect in keeping the commandment which says that we shall not profane the name of God. We can be perfect in keeping the commandment which says, "Thou shalt not commit adultery." (Ex. 20:14.) We can be perfect in keeping the commandment which says, "Thou shalt not steal." (*Ibid.*, 15.) We can become perfect in keeping various others of the command-ments that the Lord has given us.
>
> I am confident that one of the great desires of the Lord our God is that we shall keep that great commandment which says, "Be ye therefore perfect." (Matt. 5:48.) (*CR*, Apr. 1950, 152- 3.)

68

SCRIPTURE—THE PRESIDING BISHOP
PARENTS AND CHILDREN

Historical Context

Read the section heading.

An Ensample (68:2)

Ensample means example.

Scripture (68:3-5)

In verse three, the Lord gives the definition of scripture. Otten and Caldwell wrote:

> It is a blessing to the Church to have a constant flow of scripture for the guidance and benefit of the membership. It is not to be understood that any one or all of the apostles in the Quorum of Twelve ever produce scripture that contains new doctrine. Such a responsibility belongs to the president of the Church only. He is the Lord's prophet, seer, and revelator, and has sole responsibility for the announcing of any new doctrine (*ST* 2:337).

The Presiding Bishop (68:15-21)

Verses 15-21 speak about the *presiding* bishop of the Church and not about bishops of wards (*DS*, 3:92). If a man can prove that he is a first born son and literal descendant of Aaron, he is entitled to claim the office of the presiding bishop (v. 18, 21). He must still be found worthy and be ordained by the First Presidency before he can hold the office (v. 20). When no man claims to be a literal descendant of Aaron, the First Presidency is free to consider any worthy male member of the Church. The man chosen must be ordained a high priest of the Melchizedek Priesthood before he can be ordained the presiding bishop of the Church (v. 19).

The First Presidency Tries the Presiding Bishop (68:22-24)

Joseph Fielding Smith said:

> In case of the transgression of the Presiding Bishop of the Church, he could not be tried by a high council in the stake in which he lives, but he would have to be tried by the First Presidency of the Church. The reason for this is that he holds

the keys of presidency of the Aaronic Priesthood and is not under the jurisdiction of any ward or stake in this capacity. This order given for the trial of the presiding bishop does not apply to a local bishop in a ward, who is under the jurisdiction of the presidency of the stake (*CHMR* 2:30-31).

Church courts will be more fully discussed in the material for Section 102: "Church Courts."

Stakes (68:25-26)

Wait until we come to the material for 82:13-14, "Stakes."

Parents (68:25-35)

Parents have the responsibility to teach their children the gospel—specifically:
1. repentance (v. 25);
2. faith in Christ (v. 25);
3. baptism when eight years old (v. 25);
4. the gift of the Holy Ghost (v. 25);
5. prayer (v. 28);
6. righteous living (v. 28);
7. keeping the sabbath day holy (v. 29);
8. labor (v. 30-31); and
9. charity (v. 31).

The Lord says, "The sin be upon the heads of the parents" if they do not teach their children the gospel. Note that it is "the sin," not "the sins." (v. 25). Parents will be punished for the sin of not teaching their children the gospel. If the parents have taught their children the gospel, they will not be punished for the sins of their children. Children have free agency and can choose to sin despite the teachings of their parents. Our Heavenly Parents taught their children perfectly in the pre-existence, yet a third chose to rebel before even coming to the earth. They felt pain and sorrow (*D&C* 76:26); however, the sins of their children will not be upon their heads.

Children Shall Be Baptized When Eight Years Old (68:27)

We know from the Joseph Smith Translation of the Bible that the Lord told Abraham: "children are not accountable before me until they are eight years old" (*JST* Gen. 17:11). However, the age at which children became accountable of their sins was not recorded in any ancient scripture. Some people speculated that 1 Pet. 3:20-21 meant the saints of the New Testament baptized children beginning at the age of eight. But the only doctrine the latter-day saints knew for sure was that little children should not be baptized until they reached the age of accountability (*D&C* 18:42; Moroni 8:8-23). The revelation in this section specifies that children reach the age of accountability at the age of eight. This is why we baptize children when they are eight years old.

Before children are eight years old, "they cannot sin, for power is not given unto Satan to tempt little children" (*D&C* 29:47). Why, then, do children younger than eight years sometimes act so cruelly, teasing and hitting others? One reason is that the fall of Adam and Eve caused all people (including children) to become carnal, sensual, and devilish (Mosiah 16:3-5). If it were not for the atonement of Christ, even children could not be saved (Mosiah 3:16-18). Children are fallen and natural just like adults are. Children can be "devilish" without being inspired by the devil. The "natural man" in children, just as in adults, acts contrary to the commandments. Without guidance, children will continue to act contrary to the will of God until they become responsible enough to yield to the enticing of the Holy Spirit, put off the natural person, and become a saint through the atonement of Christ the Lord (Mosiah 3:19). This is why the commandment given to parents to teach their children the gospel is so important to follow in both word and deed (*D&C* 68:25-35).

Observe the Sabbath Day (68:29)

Remember the material for *D&C* 59:9-15, "The Lord's Day."

69

ENTRUSTED WITH THE BOOK OF COMMANDMENTS

Historical Context

At the special conference to act on the publishing of the "Book of Commandments" (the Doctrine and Covenants), the saints had accepted the revelations it contained as the word of God (remember section 67). Now in section 69, the Lord gives instructions on how the "Book of Commandments" was to be transported from Ohio to Independence, Missouri for printing.

Entrusted With the Book of Commandments (69:1-8)

Verse 1 does not mean that Oliver Cowdery was untrustworthy. Oliver was going to have to cross lawless frontier country. He would not only be carrying the manuscript of the "Book of Commandments," but also a large sum of money.

For safety's sake, Oliver needed a traveling companion. John Whitmer was called to be that companion.

Oliver Cowdery and John Whitmer were entrusted with the "Book of Commandments." We are entrusted with the Doctrine and Covenants. We are entrusted to read and understand it by the Spirit. And just as Oliver Cowdery and John Whitmer were entrusted to carry the "Book of Commandments" to be published, we are entrusted to "publish"—meaning declare—the messages of the Doctrine and Covenants to the elect of the earth (1 Ne. 13:37).

Let My Servant John Whitmer
Travel from Church to Church (69:7)

Here, "church" means stake or ward. John Whitmer is reminded to continue in his calling as Church historian while journeying to Independence, Missouri with Oliver Cowdery (remember Section 47: "Church Records").

70

STEWARDSHIPS

Stewards Over the Revelations (70:1-3)

In Section 69, the Lord entrusted Oliver Cowdery and John Whitmer to transport the manuscript of the "Book of Commandments" to Independence, Missouri. Now in Section 70, the Lord calls certain brethren to be stewards over the publication and sale of the "Book of Commandments" (v. 1-3).

Stewardships (70:4, 14, 17-18)

In these verses, the Lord teaches two principles about stewardships:
1. An account of this stewardship will I require in the day of judgement (70:4).
2. Be ungrudging stewards (70:14, 17-18).

This means that we are to appreciate our stewardships. As we do this, the Lord will bless us with an "abundance of the manifestations of the Spirit" (v. 14). This means that we will be guided in our stewardships. When we give an account of our stewardships before the Lord in the day of judgement, we will be able to report that we were wise and faithful stewards over many things, and we will be given even greater, eternal stewardships (v. 17-18).

Instructions To the Stewards
Over the Book of Commandments (70:5-13, 15-16)

The profits from the sale of the Book of Commandments were not to be given "unto the church, neither unto the world" (v. 6). They were to be used to help support the men who had been appointed stewards over the publishing of the Book of Commandment and their families. If they had money left over after providing for the wants and needs of their families, they were to give it to the Bishop's storehouse to help the poor and needy (v. 7-8, 15-16).

See the material for 72:20-22, "Literary Concerns" for more information.

He Who Is Appointed To Administer Spiritual Things
Is Worthy of His Hire (70:12)

Remember the material for 42:53, 55, 70-73, "A Just Remuneration."

In Temporal Things You Shall Be Equal (70:14)

Wait until we come to 78:5-7, "Purposes of the Law of Consecration and Stewardship."

71

A SPECIAL MISSION
FOR JOSEPH SMITH AND SIDNEY RIGDON

Historical Context

It is important to note from the heading to this section that Ezra Booth (after returning from serving a mission) had published some articles that caused people to hate the Church. In this Section, the Lord calls Joseph Smith and Sidney Rigdon on a special mission.

Power in the Ministry (71:1-6)

The Lord gives steps that one must follow to receive power in teaching the gospel:

1. **Teach the gospel (71:1).**
2. **Teach the gospel out of the scriptures (71:1).** Otten and Caldwell state:

When the time comes for scriptural presentation, the time for scriptural preparation has passed for that presentation. It is one thing to know the gospel is true—it is quite another to know the gospel (*ST* 2:2).

3. **Teach the gospel by the power of the Spirit (71:1).**
4. **Continue to follow and receive the revelations of the Lord (71:4-6).** The Lord tells Joseph and Sidney to "prepare the way for the commandments and revelations which are to come" (v. 4). The Book of Commandments and Revelations (the Doctrine and Covenants) was about to be published and the Lord wanted people to be ready to accept modern revelation.

When a person follows these steps, that person "shall be given more abundantly, even power" (v. 6). For more on teaching, review the material for 42:4-17, "Laws on Teaching."

Enemies of the Church (71:7-11)

The Lord tells Joseph and Sidney to meet their enemies in public and in private and confound them. Remember that this is a *special* call to Joseph and Sidney to ease the hatred against the Church caused by Ezra Booth. The Lord did not tell Joseph and Sidney to debate, but to confound their enemies (v. 7). The Lord has made it perfectly clear that debating and causing contention is not the way to teach His gospel. (Read 3 Ne. 11:28-30 and review the material for 18:20, "Contending Against the Church of the Devil").

People who reason against the Church are reasoning against the Lord (v. 8). About these people, the Lord says:

1. "their shame shall be made manifest" (v. 7);
2. their cause shall not prosper (v. 9); and
3. they "shall be confounded in mine own due time" (v. 10).

Enemies of the Church are enemies of the Lord and He will confound them. Let us not contend with the Lord's enemies. Let us gather His elect.

72

SOME DUTIES OF A BISHOP

Historical Context

In *D&C* 41:9, the Lord called Edward Partridge to be the first bishop appointed in the latter-days. Now in Section 72, Newel K. Whitney is called to be the second bishop (v. 8) and some of the duties of a bishop are outlined.

Some Duties of a Bishop

1. **Receive an account of members' stewardships (72:3, 5).** As a bishop conducts temple recommend interviews or tithing settlements, he is actually receiving an accounting of the members' stewardships in time (in mortality).

2. **Keep the Lord's storehouse (72:10).** Bishops help manage Bishop's Storehouses in order to most effectively help Church welfare recipients.

3. **Receive funds of the church (72:10; 107:72).**

4. **Provide temporal assistance (72:11-13).**

5. **Provide certificates of verification (72:15-18, 25-26).** The certificate of verification entitled the worthy member to privileges and blessings from the Lord (such as financial assistance in times of need—see the material for 83:1-3, 6, "Faithful Widows Have Claim upon the Church"). Bishops continue to provide these certificates in the form of temple recommends. Only by showing a "certificate of verification" can a member receive the privilege and blessings of entering a temple.

6. **Be a judge in Israel (58:14-20; 107:72).** Old Testament judges over the Israelites were to hear the cases the people brought to them and then judge righteously (Deut. 1:16). Likewise, Bishops today are to judge the members of their ward. To help Bishops judge righteously, they have the right (based on their obedience) to the gift of discernment and the power to discern all other spiritual gifts (*D&C* 46:27).

   Elder Spencer W. Kimball further explained:

   > Although there are many ecclesiastical officers in the Church whose positions entitle and require them to be judges, the authority of those positions does not necessarily qualify them to forgive or remit sins. Those who can do that are extremely few in this world.

The bishop, and others in comparable positions, can forgive in the sense of waiving the penalties. In our loose connotation we sometimes call this forgiveness, but it is not forgiveness in the sense of "wiping out" or absolution. The waiver means, however, that the individual will not need to be tried again for the same error, and that he may become active and have fellowship with the people of the Church. . . .

It is the Lord, however, who forgives sin. This point, and the position of the bishop and comparable officers in the matter, was brought out in the following instruction given to bishops of the Church by President J. Reuben Clark on April 5, 1946:

*   *   *   *   *

There is in the Church . . . the power to remit sins, but I do not believe it resides in the bishops. That is a power that must be exercised under the proper authority of the priesthood and by those who hold the keys that pertain to that function. Woo back every sinner. Forgive them personally. The Lord has said that. Do all you can, but short of that formal remission the matter then rests between the transgressor and the Lord, who is merciful, who knows all of the circumstances, who has no disposition but to aid his children, give them comfort, guide them, and help them. . . .

Let it be said in emphasis that even the First Presidency and the Apostles do not make a practice of absolving sins (*MF*, p. 264).

For more information on judges in Israel, see the material for Section 102: "Church Courts."

7. **Preside over the Aaronic Priesthood (107:13-15).** Note that Bishops do not preside over quorums of the Melchizedek Priesthood.

Literary Concerns (72:20-22)

The Literary Firm was organized in November of 1831 to print church literature (remember the material for 70:5-13, 15-16, "Instructions to the Stewards Over the Book of Commandments"). Members of this firm practiced the law of consecration slightly differently from other members (remember the material for Section 51: "The Law of Consecration and Stewardship"). *D&C* 72:20-22 outlines their stewardship. They could receive funds from the Bishop's storehouse but in order to "be accounted as wise stewards" they were to raise money from the sale of Church literature (v. 21-22).

For more information on the Literary Firm and its relationship to the United Order, see the material for Section 78: "Purposes of the Law of Consecration and Stewardship."

73

WHAT TO DO WHILE WAITING

Historical Context—Continue Preaching (73:1, 5-6)

A conference at Amherst, Ohio was scheduled for January 25, 1832. Elders traveling from the mission field to the conference began arriving early. They wanted to know what they should do while waiting for the conference. The Lord basically tells them not to sit around (v. 1). President Joseph F. Smith said:

> I desire to say to this congregation at this time that I have felt very strongly of late a desire, a responsibility, I may say, resting upon me, to admonish the Latter-day saints every where to cease loitering away their precious time, to cease from all idleness . . . Read good books. Learn to sing and to recite, and to converse. . . . Read anything that is good (*GD*, p. 235).

And President Gordon B. Hinckley said:

> The Church needs your strength. It needs your love and loyalty and devotion. It needs a little more of your time and energy.
> I am not asking anyone to give more at the expense of his or her employer. We have an obligation to be men and women of absolute honesty and integrity in the service of those who employ us.
> I am not asking anyone to do so at the expense of your families. . . . But I am suggesting that we spend a little less time in idleness. . . . Time so utilized can be put to better advantage, and the consequences will be wonderful (*Ensign*, May 1995, p. 88).

Much can be accomplished in the time spent just waiting around.

It Shall Be Made Known unto Them (73:2)

See section 75 for the Elders' names and missions, and remember the material for 20:60-62, "General Conference."

It Is Expedient to Translate Again (73:3-4)

Joseph and Sidney had been busy serving their special mission call (remember Section 71). It was now time to resume the translation of the Bible they had been working on. The Joseph Smith Translation of the Bible will be discussed further in Section 91: "The Apocrypha."

74

MARRIAGE WITHIN THE CHURCH

Many scholars have wondered what Paul meant in 1 Corinthians 7:14. While translating the Bible, Joseph Smith received an explanation of this scripture. *D&C* 74:1 reviews what Paul stated in 1 Cor. 7:14.

Because the Church was so new in the days of Paul, he had to answer many questions. Apparently, some of the members of the Church in Corinth believed that when a husband or wife had been converted, he or she should leave the unconverted spouse because of his or her "uncleanliness." Paul makes the argument that if, for example, the wife had to leave her husband because he was "unclean," she would also have to leave her children because they would be "unclean," and says that this is not required.

Paul goes on to tell the Corinthian saints that problems of religious conflicts can be avoided by deciding to marry within the church. Spencer W. Kimball gave this same counsel:

> Clearly, right marriage begins with right dating. . . . Do not take the chance of dating non-members or members who are untrained and faithless. A girl may say, "Oh, I do not intend to marry this person. It is just a "fun date." But one cannot afford to take a chance on falling in love with someone who may never accept the gospel. True, a small percentage have finally been baptized after marrying Church members. Some good women and some good men have joined the Church after the mixed marriage and have remained devout and active. We are proud of them and grateful for them. They are our blessed minority. Others who did not join the Church were still kind and considerate and cooperative and permitted the member spouse to worship and serve according to the Church patterns. But the majority did not join the Church and, as indicated earlier, friction, frustration and divorce marked a great many of their marriages (*MF*, 241-242).

75

SOME MISSIONARY DUTIES

Historical Context

The revelation in this section was given at the conference that the missionaries had been waiting for (remember section 73). At this conference, the Lord calls the missionaries to their new fields of labor and instructs them in some of their duties.

Some Missionary Duties

1. **Proclaim truth as with the sound of a trump (75:1-4).** A trumpet has a strong and clear voice.
2. **Call on the Comforter (75:10-11).** Missionaries can overcome trials and sadness and be taught by the Spirit as they pray for it.
3. **Leave a blessing and testimony (75:18-22).** Missionaries are commanded to leave a blessing upon a home that accepts their message. This can be done simply by asking, "May we say a prayer and bless your home?" Missionaries are also commanded to leave their testimony in all homes that they enter whether or not the home has accepted the truth.

   See the material for 60:15 for information on verses 20-22.

Sheaves (75:5)

Remember the material for 31:5, "Forgiveness, the greatest Sheave."

The South Countries (75:8)

This refers to the southern states of the United States (*DCC*, 75:8).

76

THE VISION

Introduction and Background (76:1-19)

Joseph Smith and Sidney Rigdon received the six visions contained in this section after returning from the conference (remember Section 75). In the first ten verses of this section, the Lord tells us how we can prepare to receive and understand the things that Joseph and Sidney saw. The Lord promises many blessings to those who "fear"—in other words, respect and worship—Him (v. 5). The Lord promises that as we continue to worship Him, we will receive knowledge by the Spirit of all things. Knowledge that will not only help us understand the vision of Joseph and Sidney, but will also help us attain eternal (celestial) glory (v. 6).

The Joseph Smith Translation (76:15-18)

Wait until we come to Section 91: "The Apocrypha."

The Vision (76:20-88)

1. **A vision of Jesus Christ (76:20-24).** Compare verse 24 with Moses 1:32-33. Regarding the salvation of the sons and daughters of God who reside on other worlds, Joseph Smith said:

> By Him [Jesus Christ], of Him, and through Him the worlds were all made. Even all that career in the heavens so broad, whose inhabitants, too, from the first to the last, are saved by the very same Savior of ours (see *Times and Seasons*, Feb. 1, 1843, pp. 82-85).

2. **A vision of Lucifer (76:25-29).**

3. **A vision of sons of perdition (76:30-49).** Joseph Smith said:

> What must a man do to commit the unpardonable sin? He must receive the Holy Ghost, have the heavens opened unto him, and know God, and then sin against him. . . . He has got to say that the sun does not shine while he sees it; he has got to deny Jesus Christ when the heavens have been opened unto him, and to deny the plan of salvation with his eyes open to the truth of it; and from that time he begins to be an enemy (*HC*, 6:314-315).

Although sons of perdition will not be redeemed nor inherit a degree of glory, they will be resurrected (1 Cor. 15:22; *D&C* 29:26-27; 88:32; 2 Ne. 9:21-22; John 5:28-29). They will "reign" under the laws of the kingdom of the Devil (v. 44). Smith and Sjodahl state:

> They [the sons of perdition] will "reign", under such laws and rules as obtain in the kingdom of the Devil, and of which we have had numerous illustrations in human history, during the dark ages of ignorance, superstition, tyranny, and iniquity. Think of a place where the evil passions of human beings and evil spirits rage, unrestrained by the influence of the gospel! Such is the kingdom of the Devil, where the sons of Perdition will reign (*DCC*, pp. 454-55).

People who choose a path of wickedness foolishly believe:

> To reign is worth ambition though in hell:
> Better to reign in hell than serve in heav'n (Milton, *Paradise Lost*, 1:2:262).

4. **A vision of the celestial kingdom (76:50-70).** Those who are worthy to enter the highest degree of glory will receive "all things, whether life or death" (v. 59). They will receive ordinances and priesthood keys that cannot be received in this mortal life. For example, the keys of spirit creation (*D&C* 131:4) and the ordinance and keys of the resurrection (*D&C* 138:51). This will be further discussed in the material for 138:51, "The Lord Gave Them Power To Come Forth From the Dead."

5. **A vision of the terrestrial kingdom (76:71-80).** Verse 74 refers to those who had a chance to receive the gospel but did not.

6. **A vision of the telestial kingdom (76:81-88).** Even the lowest kingdom of glory "surpasses all understanding" (v. 89).

The Spirit World: Paradise, Prison, and Hell (76:73, 84)

There is a division of the spirit world called spirit prison. It is a prison because the people there cannot progress—they are trapped—until they accept gospel principles and ordinances. People who did not have the chance to accept the gospel in mortality will have the opportunity to escape from spirit prison to spirit paradise through obedience to the ordinances and covenants of the gospel (*D&C* 138:31-34). Those who remain in spirit prison will inherit the terrestrial kingdom (v. 73).

Sometimes the terms spirit prison and hell are used interchangeably in the scriptures. For the sake of illustrating the difference between terrestrial and telestial people, I will give each term a distinct meaning. I am going to use the term hell to describe another division of the spirit world—perhaps a subdivision of spirit prison (v. 84). Those that will eventually inherit the telestial kingdom and those that will not inherit a kingdom of glory at all are kept in hell until after the millennium (v. 85, 106-107; 88:100-101). Verses 81-83 and 103 describe the kind of people who will be in hell before going to the telestial kingdom.

Brigham Young taught that the spirit world is on this earth:

> Where Is the Spirit World—Is the spirit world here? It is . . . on this earth that was organized for the people that have lived and that do and will live upon it. No other people can have it. . . .
>
> Where is the spirit world? It is right here. Do the good and evil spirits go together? Yes, they do. Do they both inhabit one kingdom? Yes, they do. . . . Do they go beyond the boundaries of the organized earth? No, they do not (*Discourses of Brigham Young*, p. 376).

Whether or not paradise, spirit prison, and hell are separated geographically is not clear. It may be a state of being rather than a location. For example, you have probably been in a room together with people with celestial, terrestrial, and telestial characteristics. However, each of these people are separated by the covenants they have made and kept (see *D&C* 88:28-32). There are places (such as temples) where faithful saints are geographically separated from other people in the world. In these places, the Lord can go to the righteous without going to the wicked. He can then call these righteous people to teach others the gospel so they may also enter paradise (*D&C* 138:6-32).

Some quote scripture and interpret it as meaning that paradise, spirit prison, and hell are separated geographically. Others quote the same scriptures and interpret them as meaning they are only separated by degrees of righteousness. For now, it is not important to know which interpretation is correct (see the material for 101:32-34, "The Lord Shall Reveal All Things"). The key is to strive to be a celestial-type person.

Where God and Christ Dwell
They Cannot Come, Worlds Without End (76:112)

There is no progression between kingdoms (76:112). Spencer W. Kimball said: "After a person has been assigned his place in the kingdom, either in the telestial, the terrestrial or the celestial, or to his exaltation, he will never advance from his assigned glory to another glory. That is eternal!" (*MF*, pp. 243-244). And Joseph Fielding Smith said:

> The celestial and terrestrial and telestial glories, I have heard compared to the wheels on a train. The second and third may, and will, reach the place where the first was, but the first will have moved on and will still be just the same distance in advance of them. This illustration is not true! The wheels do not run on the same track, and do not go in the same direction. The terrestrial and the telestial

are limited in their powers of advancement [*D&C* 131:4], worlds without end (*DS*, 2:32).

Which Things He Commanded Us We Should Not Write (76:113-119)

Joseph Smith said: "I could explain a hundredfold more than I ever have of the glories of the kingdoms manifested to me in the vision, were I permitted, and were the people prepared to receive them" (*HC*, 5:402). We can prepare ourselves to see and understand all that Joseph Smith saw as we love God and purify ourselves before him (v. 116-118).

Degrees Within the Kingdoms of Glory

There are three degrees within the celestial kingdom (see *D&C* 131:1-4). It has not been revealed as doctrine to the Church how many degrees are within the terrestrial kingdom. The number of degrees within the telestial kingdom are as innumerable as the stars (v. 98, 109; 1 Cor. 15:41-42).

Jesus Christ Will Be Our Judge

It is important to remember that Jesus Christ will be our judge (John 5:22; Acts 10:42; 2 Cor. 5:10; 2 Tim. 4:1). He knows and understands our backgrounds, our weaknesses, the circumstances in which we make decisions, and our capacity to understand. He will judge everyone perfectly. Let us not feel that we have the capacity to assign people to their kingdoms of glory just because we have studied section 76 a little bit.

77

INSIGHTS TO THE BOOK OF REVELATION

This section provides some insights to the Book of Revelation. While some of the symbolism of the Book of Revelation is self-explanatory or has been explained by the Lord, some of the symbolism is difficult to interpret. Joseph Smith said:

> Whenever God gives a vision of an image, or beast, or figure of any kind, He always holds Himself responsible to give a revelation or interpretation of the meaning thereof, otherwise we are not responsible or accountable for our belief in it (*TPJS*, p. 291).

Joseph Smith also said: "We may spiritualize and express opinions to all eternity; but that is no authority," and, "Never meddle with the visions of beasts and subjects you do not understand" (*TPJS*, p. 292). Joseph Smith followed his own counsel. Instead of expressing his opinions about the Book of Revelation, Joseph asked the Lord for the true interpretation.

To learn more about the topics covered in section 77, see Appendix 4: "A Guide to the Book of Revelation."

78

PURPOSES OF THE LAW OF CONSECRATION AND STEWARDSHIP

Historical Background

In March 1832, a business known as the United Firm was set up in Kirtland, Ohio. The members of the firm were "a handful of Church leaders, never exceeding twelve in number" (Cook, p. 57). The members of the United firm covenanted to live the law of consecration by consecrating their lands, time, and business talents to make money to help the Literary Firm; provide for their own living; and contribute surplus funds to the Church (*D&C* 78:3, 14; *HC*, 1:165-66; and remember the material for 72:20-21, "Literary Concerns"). In this section, the Lord gives instructions to the Literary Firm and the United Firm.

Early manuscripts of section 78 make it clear that the Lord was speaking about the Literary and United business firms:

> For verily I say unto you the time has come, and is now at hand, and behold and lo it must needs be that there be an organization of the literary and mercantile establishments of my church both in this place and in the land of Zion for a permanent and everlasting establishment and firm unto my church to advance the cause which ye have espoused ("Kirtland Revelation Book," p. 16).

The verse which made explicit reference to these business concerns was deleted when the revelation was published in 1835 (Cook, p. 67). For more on the United Firm, see the material for section 104: "The United Order."

Purposes of the Law of Consecration
and Stewardship (78:1-7, 13-15)

In this section, the Lord gives two purposes for the law of consecration and stewardship:

1. **That you may be equal in the bonds of heavenly things (78:5-7).** Defining terms is important. For example:

> It has been said that Abraham Lincoln asked someone how many legs a dog would have if you called his tail a leg. The reply was five. He said, "No. He would have only four. Calling a dog's tail a leg doesn't make it a leg" (Pearson, p. 35).

The term *equal* can mean many things. Ezra Taft Benson taught:

> It has been erroneously concluded by some that the united order is both communal and communistic in theory and practice because the revelations speak of equality. Equality under the united order is not economic and social leveling as advocated by some today. Equality, as described by the Lord, is "equal[ity] according to [a man's] family, according to his circumstances and his wants and needs" (*D&C* 51:3) (*TETB*, p. 122).

In *D&C* 82:17-18, the Lord says:

> You are to be equal, or in other words, you are to have equal claims on the properties . . . every man according to his wants and his needs, inasmuch as his wants are just . . . that every man may improve upon his talent, that every man may gain other talents.

This is to be done while "seeking the interest of his neighbor, and doing all things with an eye single to the glory of God" (82:19). As far as seeking riches goes, Jacob gives the key in Jacob 2:18-21. Also see Appendix 3: "Blessings and Laws Upon Which They Are Predicated" under the heading "Riches."

Obviously, *equality*, as used in these verses, does not mean everybody must have the same of everything. It means that people, upon obedience to the pertinent principles, have the same claim to assistance and blessings. George Q. Cannon said:

> "Equality," as it is used in the revelation . . . means to have an equal claim on the blessings of our Heavenly Father—on the properties of the Lord's treasury, and the influences and gifts of His Holy Spirit. This is the equality meant in the revelations, and until we attain to this equality we cannot be equal in spiritual things, and the blessings of

God cannot be bestowed upon us until we attain to this as they otherwise would (*JD*, 13:99).

And Otten and Caldwell state:

> The term "equal", as used in this context, should not be understood to
> mean "dead-level equality." Or in other words, the Lord does not expect
> that all people will have the same quantity of the same things of the
> earth. Rather, in a subsequent revelation, the Lord explained equality as
> meaning that each person under the law should have equal claims or
> opportunities to obtain the necessary and desirable things of the earth.
> (See *D&C* 82:17)
>
> This desired equality is obtained under this law through the processes
> of consecrating of resources and the development of individual steward-
> ships. Each individual has opportunity to provide for his own needs and
> share his surplus with others who may be in need. Thus, the equality of
> the saints is assured and achieved when equal opportunity is afforded
> each individual (*ST*, 2:45-46).

Spencer W. Kimball also noted the use of the term *equality* when
speaking of the relationship of men and women. He taught:

> We had full equality as his spirit children. We have equality as recipi-
> ents of God's perfected love for each of us. . . . Within those great assur-
> ances, however, our roles and assignments differ. These are eternal dif-
> ferences—with women being given many tremendous responsibilities of
> motherhood and sisterhood and men being given the tremendous respon-
> sibilities of fatherhood and the priesthood—but the man is not without the
> woman nor the woman without the man in the Lord (see 1 Corinthians
> 11:11) (*TSWK*, p. 315).

Here, again, equality does not mean having the same of everything. The
key is equal opportunity or claim to promised blessings.

One of the reasons King Mosiah proposed setting up a system of
judges was to establish equality. He said:

> I desire that this inequality should be no more in this land . . . but I
> desire that this land be a land of liberty, and every man may enjoy his
> rights and privileges alike (Mosiah 29:32).

If all people do not have an equal opportunity to obey the necessary
principle to lay claim to earthly things, how will we ever become celestial—or Zion—people (*D&C* 78:5-7)? For God is no respecter of persons (*D&C* 1:35). He invites all:

to come unto him and partake of his goodness; and he denieth none that come unto him, black and white, bond and free, male and female; and he remembereth the heathen; and all are alike unto God, both Jew and Gentile (2 Ne. 26:33).

It is then up to the individual to act. Depending on the actions, equal opportunity may not mean equal outcome.

2. **That the Church may stand independent (78:14).** Another purpose of the law of consecration and stewardship is that the Church may stand independent. Otten and Caldwell state:

> The church's place is above all things that are not celestial. Latter-day Saints can see the hand of the Lord as He directs His church to purchase and operate production projects, printing presses, broadcasting facilities, etc. The church is developing independence.
>
> The concept of independence extends beyond the church as an organization and becomes a desirable and sought-for objective in the lives of the church members. The church is a vehicle whereby the members may be prepared to become rulers (*ST*, 2.47).

Adam-ondi-Ahman (78:15)

Wait until Section 116: "Adam-ondi-Ahman."

The Son Ahman (78:20)

This is a name of Jesus Christ (see the material for Section 116: "Adam-ondi-Ahman."

79

POWER IN OUR CALLINGS

In the Power of the Ordination (79:1-4)

In this section, Jared Carter is commanded to go preach "in the power of the ordination wherewith *he* has been ordained" (v. 1; emphasis added). To have power in our callings, we must work within the boundaries of our callings. As we perform our callings diligently and within the boundaries of our callings, the Lord will reward us with power and guidance (v. 2-3; remember the definition of "sheaves" is "rewards"). But the Lord will not reward us if we try to do something outside the boundaries of our callings. For example, an elder's quorum president will not be given power by the Lord to direct the entire ward—that is the bishop's calling.

I suggest reviewing the material for 64:30-43, "Be Not Weary in Laying the Foundation of a Great Work."

80
DECLARE WHAT YOU KNOW TO BE TRUE

Declare the Things Which Ye Have Heard, and Verily Believe, and Know to Be True (80:1-5)

To have power in our callings we must work within the boundaries of our callings (remember the material for Section 79). To have power in our callings we must also declare the things that we have heard and come to believe to be true. We can declare that we have heard the voice of the Lord (remember *D&C* 1:38 and 18:36). When we come to believe what we have been taught by the Lord, we must declare these teachings to others. By cultivating our *beliefs*, we will come to *know* that they are true (see Alma 32:26-43). Then our testimonies will be even more powerful because we will be testifying of what we know to be true.

Some reason that one can never know spiritual things and must settle on only believing them. The scriptures abundantly refute this philosophy. Just as we can feel, taste, hear, smell, and see things of this world, we can come to do the same for spiritual things. We can feel the Spirit (Alma 32:28; Gal. 5:22), taste the joy the Spirit gives (Alma 36:24; Ps. 34:8; 119:103), hear the voice of the Lord (remember the material for 18:33-36, "You Have Heard the Voice of the Lord;" and see Mark 8:18), smell the sweetness of the Spirit (Ps. 115:6; Isa. 3:24; Rev. 8:4), and see God and His works in our lives (Matt. 5:8). In fact, it is only by the power of the Spirit that we can truly know what is real, for our other senses can be deceived (1 Cor. 2:9-14). Now is a good time to review the material for Sections 6, 8, and 9 under the heading "Asking for, and Receiving Revelation;" and 46:13-14, "The Gift to Know that Jesus Christ is the Son of God."

81

Duties of a Counselor—The First Presidency

Duties of a Counselor (81:1, 3-7)

In this section, Frederick G. Williams is called to serve as a counselor in the First Presidency. The Lord outlines some of the duties of a counselor.

1. **Be faithful in counsel (81:3).** The Lord would not call counselors if He did not expect them to give counsel to their leader. After giving counsel, the counselor must then accept the decision of the leader.

2. **Pray always (81:3).** Jesus is called "counselor" by Isaiah (Isa. 9:6). By praying, a faithful counselor can receive counsel from the master counselor—Jesus Christ.

3. **Proclaim the gospel (81:3).** Review the material for 60:2-4, 13, "Share Your Talent."

4. **Succor, lift up, and strengthen (81:4).** It is the duty of counselors to not only strengthen those that they preside over, but also to strengthen their leader. In the Old Testament, Aaron and Hur held up the weary hands of their leader, Moses, while he stood on a hill watching the battle his people were waging. This helped the Israelites have faith in Moses and in the Lord and win the battle (read more of the story in Ex. 17:8-13). Counselors can strengthen their leaders in our day by lifting them up in the eyes of the people they preside over by speaking good things about their leader.

By doing these duties a counselor will "do the greatest good" (v. 4) and will receive eternal rewards (v. 6).

The First Presidency (81:2)

The First Presidency holds the keys of the kingdom of God (v. 2). Since the kingdom of God is the Church (remember the material for Section 65), the First Presidency is not only the presidency of the High Priesthood (v. 2), it is also the presidency over the entire Church. Joseph Fielding Smith said:

> There is a difference between the office of President of the Church and President of the High Priesthood; however these two offices cannot be separated and must be held by the same person duly appointed and sustained by proper vote. As President of the church the presiding officer presides over all the membership of the Church. As President of the High Priesthood he presides over all the Priesthood of the Church and has authority to regulate it, for he holds the keys of that priesthood (*CHMR*, 2:79-80).

82

UNTO WHOM MUCH IS GIVEN MUCH IS REQUIRED

Historical Context—Inasmuch as You Have Forgiven One Another, I Forgive You (82:1-2, 23)

The revelation in this section was given to Joseph Smith while he was in Missouri at a conference. Bishop Partridge and Elder Rigdon were also at this conference. They were having problems getting along together but were touched by the Spirit at this conference, forgave each other, and became friends again. The Lord reminds us that to receive forgiveness of our sins, we must forgive others (remember *D&C* 64:10).

The Former Sins Return (82:7)

Repentance brings us from a condition of wickedness to a condition of righteousness. When we sin again, our former condition of wickedness returns. Brigham Young taught about the condition of righteousness and the condition of wickedness. He said:

> If a person with an honest heart, a broken, contrite, and pure spirit, in all fervency and honesty of soul, presents himself and says that he wishes to be baptized for the remission of his sins, and the ordinance is administered by one having authority, is that man saved? Yes, to that period of time. . . .
>
> It is present salvation and the present influence of the Holy Ghost that we need every day to keep us on saving ground. When an individual refuses to comply with the further requirements of Heaven, then the sins he had formerly committed return upon his head; [in other words,] his former righteousness departs from him, and is not accounted to him for righteousness: but if he had continued in righteousness and obedience to the requirements of heaven, he is saved all the time (*JD*, 8:124).

Now would be a good time to review the material for Section 58 under the headings "I, the Lord Remember Them No More," "By This Ye May Know if a Man Repenteth of His Sins," and "Have I Been Forgiven?"

I Am Bound When Ye Do What I Say (82:8-10)

I suggest cross referencing these verses to "the law of blessings" given in *D&C* 130:20-21. Then see Appendix 3: "Blessings and Laws upon Which They Are Predicated."

The United Firm (82:11-21)

Remember the material for Sections 51: "The Law of Consecration and Stewardship;" 78: "Purposes of the Law of Consecration and Stewardship;" and wait until we get to Section 104: "The United Order."

Stakes (82:13-14)

Imagine a tent being set up. The material is lying on the ground. Now a pole is put under the center of the material and holds the material up. To spread the material out to form the tent, ropes are tied to the edges and then stretched out from the pole. To hold the ropes in place, they are tied to stakes which are driven into the ground. Now you have a well supported and strong tent that will protect those who enter it from rough weather.

This is the imagery Isaiah used to describe Zion when he said: "Enlarge the place of thy tent, and let them stretch forth the curtains of thine habitations: spare not, lengthen thy cords, and strengthen thy stakes" (Isa. 54:2). When the stakes are driven deep into firm ground, the tent will not fall. Isaiah saw the "tent" or "tabernacle" of Zion being so secure that it would be "a tabernacle that shall not be taken down; not one of the stakes thereof shall ever be removed, neither shall any of the cords thereof be broken" (Isa. 33:20). Bruce R. McConkie further explains:

> In keeping with this symbolism, the great areas of church population and strength, which sustain and uphold the restored Zion, are called stakes. They are the rallying points and the gathering centers for the remnants of scattered Israel. (D. & C. 68:25-26; 82:13-14; 101:17-21; 115:6, 18; 124:134; 133:9.) In area they cover from a few blocks to many miles; in membership they comprise from a few to several thousand saints; in organization they are divided into smaller units called wards and (in some instances) branches (*MD*, p. 764).

You Are to Be Equal (82:17-18)

Remember the material for 78:5-7, "That You May Be Equal in the Bonds of Heavenly Things."

Make unto Yourselves Friends with the Mammon (82:22)

Joseph Fielding Smith said:

> The commandment of the Lord that the Saints should make themselves "friends with the mammon of unrighteousness," seems to be a hard saying when not properly understood. It is not intended that in making friends of the "mammon of unrighteousness" that the brethren were to partake with them in their sins; to receive them to their bosoms, intermarry with them and otherwise come down to their level. They were to so live that peace with their enemies might be assured. They were to treat them kindly, be friendly with them as far as correct and virtuous principles would permit, but never to swear with them or drink or carouse with them. If they could allay prejudice and show a willingness to trade with and show a kindly spirit, it might help to turn them away from their bitterness. Judgement was to be left with the Lord (*CHMR*, 2:89).

83

LAWS CONCERNING WIDOWS AND ORPHANS

Women Have Claim upon Their Husband—
Children, upon Their Parents (83:2)

Otten and Caldwell wrote:

> The word *claim* means rights, privileges, and/or entitlements. A wife has a right before the Lord to expect her husband to provide for her temporal necessities of life. She should not have to feel that she is a recipient of charity. He is not giving charity, but rather he is honoring his marriage covenant responsibility before God. A righteous woman will be grateful for the labors of her husband in her behalf, but is not obligated to feel indebted to him for her maintenance (*ST* 2:64).

President Howard W. Hunter said:

> You who hold the priesthood have the responsibility, unless disabled, to provide temporal support for your wife and children. No man can shift the burden of responsibility to another, not even to his wife. The Lord has commanded that women and children have claim on their husbands and fathers for their maintenance (see *D&C* 83; 1 Tim. 5:8). President Ezra Taft Benson has stated that when a husband encourages or insists that his wife work out of the home for their convenience, "not only will the family suffer in such instances, . . . but [his] own spiritual growth and progression will be hampered" (*Ensign*, Nov. 1987, p. 49).
>
> We urge you to do all in your power to allow your wife to remain in the home, caring for the children while you provide for the family the best you can. We further emphasize that men who abandon their family and fail to meet their responsibility to care for those they have fathered may find their eligibility for a temple recommend and their standing in the Church in jeopardy. In cases of divorce or separation, men must demonstrate that they are meeting family support payments mandated by law and obligated by the principles of the Church in order to qualify for the blessings of the Lord (*Ensign*, Nov. 1994, p. 51).

And President Kimball said:

> Peter urged us to give honor unto our wives. (See 1 Pet. 3:7.) It seems to me we should be even more courteous to our wives and mothers, our sisters and our daughters, than we are to others. When Paul said that a man who did not provide

for his own and those of his own household was "worse than an infidel" (1 Tim. 5:8), I like to think of providing for our own as including providing them with affectional security as well as economic security. When the Lord told us in this dispensation that "women have claim on their husbands for their maintenance" (*D&C* 83:2), I like to think of maintenance as including our obligation to maintain loving affection and to provide consideration and thoughtfulness as well as food (*CR*, Oct. 1978, 62-63).

The counsel given by President Kimball above applies to the parent/child relationship as well. Children have claim upon their parents. In other words, they have the right to expect their parents to provide for them.

Faithful Widows Have Claim upon the Church (83:1-3, 6)

When a woman's husband dies and she cannot support herself, she has the right to receive support from the Church as long as she remains worthy. President Joseph F. Smith said:

When one comes to a bishop and asks for assistance because of his or her straitened circumstances, the first thing the bishop should do is to inquire if he or she is a tithe-payer. He should know whether the name is on the book of the law of the Lord [see the material for 85:1-5, 9-12], and if not on the book, if he or she has been derelict and negligent in relation to this principle of tithing, he or she has no claim upon the bishop, neither have their children; and if, under those circumstances, the bishop assists him, it will simply be out of pure charity and not because such have any claim upon the Church (*GD*, p. 231).

Orphans Shall Be Provided For, as Also the Poor (83:1, 4-6)

President Joseph F. Smith said:

Orphans shall be provided for from the funds of the Church; that they shall be clothed and fed, and shall have opportunity for education, the same as other children who have parents to look after them. When a child is fatherless and motherless the Church becomes the parent of the child, and it is obligatory upon the Church to take care of it, and to see that it has opportunities equal with the other children in the Church. This is a great responsibility. Have we ever seen the day since the Church was organized when we could carry out this purpose of the Lord fully, and to our heart's content? We have not, because we never have had the means to do it with. But if men will obey the laws of God so that there shall be abundance in the storehouse of the Lord, we will have wherewith to feed and clothe the poor and the orphan and to look after those who are in need in the Church (*CR*, Oct. 1899, pp. 39-40).

84

THE OATH AND COVENANT OF THE PRIESTHOOD

Historical Context

Elders serving missions in the eastern states were beginning to return home. They wanted to know more about Zion and how they could continue to fulfill their callings in the priesthood. See the heading to this section for more details.

Unity (84:1)

Review the material for 29:6, "Unity."

The New Jerusalem Temple
Shall Be Reared in this Generation (84:4-5)

Smith and Sjodahl wrote:

> This statement has been a stumbling block to some and there have been various interpretations of the meaning of a generation. It is held by some that a generation is one hundred years; by others that it is one hundred and twenty-years; by others that a generation as expressed in this and other scriptures has reference to a period of time which is indefinite. The Savior said: "An evil and adulterous generation seeketh after a sign." This did not have reference to a period of years, but to a period of wickedness. A generation may mean the time of the present dispensation (*DCC*, p. 497).

And Charles W. Penrose said:

> We understand that certain things predicted through the Prophet Joseph Smith are to take place before this generation shall pass away, and the Lord will see to it that the generation in which those things were predicted will not all pass away until all shall be fulfilled, but there is no fixed period for a generation, no set time in the revelations of God, no year or date given when these things shall take place, and it is folly for anybody to put a date to it. Leave that in the hands of the Lord and he will take care that his word is fulfilled (*CR*, Apr. 1918, p. 21).

By the Hand of Adam (84:16)

Joseph Smith said:

> The Priesthood was first given to Adam; he obtained the First Presidency, and held the keys of it from generation to generation. He obtained it in the creation, before the world was formed, as in Genesis 1:26-28. He had dominion given him

over every living creature. He is Michael, the archangel, spoken of in the Scriptures. Then to Noah who is Gabriel; he stands next in authority to Adam in the Priesthood; he was called of God to this office, and was the father of all living in his day, and to him was given the dominion. These men held keys first on earth, and then in heaven.

The Priesthood is an everlasting principle, and existed with God from eternity, and will to eternity, without beginning of days or end of years. The keys have to be brought from heaven whenever the gospel is sent. When they are revealed from heaven, it is by Adam's authority (*HC*, 3:385-86).

The Greater Priesthood (84:19-29)

Some keys and responsibilities of the greater priesthood (the Melchizedek priesthood) are listed in these verses. Some of the ordinances to which these verses refer take place in temples. The missionaries returning from the eastern states needed to understand that to magnify their callings and to inherit the blessings of Abraham (discussed later in this section), they needed to build and attend temples.

Without This No Man Can See the Face of the Father (84:22)

This is not to say that a person must hold the Melchizedek priesthood to see God the Father. Joseph Smith saw God the Father long before he held the priesthood. What this verse means is that it is through the power of the priesthood that God does things, including revealing himself to mortals (see *D&C* 88:13 and Heb. 11:3).

The Lesser Priesthood (84:26-28, 30)

Review the material for Section 13: "John the Baptist Restores the Aaronic Priesthood."

The Sons of Moses and Aaron
Shall Offer an Acceptable Offering (84:31)

This offering mainly concerns doing work for the dead. Review the material for Section 13 under the heading "The Sons of Levi and Their Offering."

Sons of Moses—Daughters of Sara—
The Seed of Abraham (84:32, 34)

In these verses the Lord refers to righteous men as "sons of Moses." In the Bible, Peter referred to righteous women as daughters of Sara (1 Pet. 3:6). As we keep our covenants we inherit the blessings promised to Abraham. These blessings will be further discussed in the material for 110:12, "Elias commits the keys of the dispensation of Abraham."

The Oath and Covenant of the Father (84:33-48)

God the Father makes an oath to every man who enters into the covenant of the Melchizedek priesthood. God the Father promises to give all that He has to the man who keeps the covenant of the priesthood. To keep the covenant, the man must be faithful and magnify his calling.

Whoso Breaketh this Covenant
Shall Not Have Forgiveness (84:41)

About this verse, Joseph Fielding Smith said:

> That does not mean that man is going to become a son of perdition, but the meaning is that he will never again have the opportunity of exercising the priesthood and reaching exaltation. That is where his forgiveness ends. He will not again have the priesthood conferred upon him . . . but as far as other things are concerned, he may be forgiven (*DS*, 3:141-142).

Remember the New Covenant,
Even the Book of Mormon (84:43-62)

Everyone who comes into the world is given the light of Christ (v. 45-46). Following this light leads us to God the Father (v. 47). When we do not follow the light, we are left in darkness.

The light is also the word of the Lord (v. 45). The Lord told the saints at that time (1832) that they were in darkness and under condemnation because they were treating the word of the Lord, specifically the Book of Mormon, carelessly (v. 54-57). President Ezra Taft Benson said that the saints are still under this condemnation. He said:

> In section 84 of the Doctrine and Covenants, the Lord declares that the whole Church and all the children of Zion are under condemnation because of the way we have treated the Book of Mormon. (Verses 54-58.) This condemnation has not been lifted, nor will it be until we repent.
>
> *   *   *   *   *
>
> The Lord inspired His servant Lorenzo Snow to reemphasize the principle of tithing to redeem the Church from financial bondage. . . . So too in our day the Lord has inspired His servant to reemphasize the Book of Mormon to get the Church out from under condemnation— the scourge and judgement.
>
> *   *   *   *   *
>
> I bless you with increased understanding of the Book of Mormon. I promise you that from this moment forward, if we will daily sup from its pages and abide by its precepts, God will pour out upon each child of Zion and the Church a blessing hitherto unknown—and we will plead to the Lord that He will begin to lift the condemnation—the scourge and judgement. Of this I bear solemn witness.
>
> I promise you that as you more diligently study modern revelation on gospel subjects, your power to teach and preach will be magnified and you will so move

the cause of Zion that added numbers will enter into the house of the Lord as well as the mission field (*A Witness and a Warning*, pp. vii-viii).

If we follow the light (the word of the Lord) contained in the Book of Mormon, we will receive more light. If we do not cherish the light, we will be left in darkness. This promise and warning has not only been given to us by latter-day prophets, but by the writers of the Book of Mormon themselves. I suggest reading what Mormon wrote in 3 Ne. 6-11 and what Moroni wrote in Morm. 8:12, 17. This is also a good time to review the material for sections 5 and 17, "The Book of Mormon."

(The light of Christ and how it relates to righteousness, revelation, spirit, truth, law, power, knowledge, intelligence, and glory will be discussed in the material for 88:7-13, "The Light of Christ" and 93:24-40, "The Light of Truth.")

Gifts of the Spirit (84:64-73)

Remember the material for Section 46: "Gifts of the Spirit."

Take No Purse or Script (84:78-86)

Bruce R. McConkie explained:

> Jesus sent his disciples out without purse or scrip. They were to dress modestly, carry no money, food, or extra clothing, have only one staff, and rely on the hospitality of the people for food, clothing, and shelter. Shoes (made in that day of soft leather) were forbidden as too luxurious; sandals (of more rugged construction) were approved. A purse was a girdle in which money was carried; scrip was a small bag or wallet used to carry provisions. Later Jesus revoked the requirement to rely on the hospitality of the people and commanded instead, "Now, he that hath a purse, let him take it, and likewise his scrip." (Luke 22:35-36.)
>
> Similar but not wholly identical divine direction was given to missionaries in the early days of this dispensation [*D&C* 24:18; 84:77-78, 86]. . . .
>
> Acting through his duly appointed representatives on earth, the Lord has now withdrawn this requirement that all modern missionary work should be done by laborers who go forth without purse or scrip. Legal requirements, and different social, economic, and industrial circumstances, have made such a change necessary—a fact which illustrates the need for continuous revelation so that the Lord's affairs on earth always may be conducted as befit the existing circumstances. Instead of relying for food, clothing, and shelter upon those to whom they are sent, missionaries are now expected to support themselves or be supported by their family or friends (*DNTC*, 1:325-26).

Neither Take Ye Thought Before Hand What Ye Shall Say (84:85)

Wait until we come to the material for 100:6, "It Shall Be Given in the Very Moment What to Say."

Angels Shall Be Round About You, to Bear You Up (84:88)

There are many people on the other side of the veil who are interested in our well being (for example, our friends and relatives, and the relatives of non-members with whom we may have the chance to share the gospel). These people, as well as others, may sometimes watch over and protect us.

Joseph Smith recorded a dream that he had in 1844. He wrote: "I was riding out in my carriage, and my guardian angel was along with me" (*TPJS*, p. 368). Whether every person has one or more guardian angels watching over him is a question which has not yet been resolved within the Church. Several general authorities have expressed varying viewpoints. For instance, John A. Widtsoe stated:

> Undoubtedly angels often guard us from accidents and harm, from temptation and sin. They may properly be spoken of as guardian angels. . . . Without the help that we receive from the constant presence of the Holy Spirit, and from possibly holy angels, the difficulties of life would be greatly multiplied. The common belief, however, that to every person born into the world is assigned a guardian angel to be with that person constantly, is not supported by available evidence. It is a very comforting thought, but at present without proof of its correctness. An angel may be a guardian angel though he come only as assigned to give us special help. In fact, the constant presence of the Holy Spirit would seem to make such a constant, angelic companionship unnecessary (Widtsoe, *Gospel Interpretations*, p. 28-29 in *Comp.*, 1:558).

And Joseph Fielding Smith stated his view that: "The true guardian angel given to every man who comes into the world is the Light of Truth or Spirit of Christ" (*DS*, 1:54). Bruce R. McConkie expressed his personal opinion that: "Expressions of patriarchs or others relative to guardian angels must be interpreted either as figurative statements or as utterances having reference to special instances of guarding care" (*MD*, p. 342). Although the scriptures do not tell us whether the concept that every person has a personal guardian angel, it is clear from *D&C* 84:88 that angels do watch over and protect those who serve the Lord. It is also clear that the ministration of angels is a key of the Aaronic priesthood (remember the material for Section 13: "John the Baptist Restores the Aaronic Priesthood").

Cleanse Your Feet (84:92)

Remember the material for 60:15, "Shake Off the Dust of Thy Feet."

85

THE BOOK OF THE LAW OF GOD

The Book of the Law of God (85:1-5, 9-12)

In the book of the law of God are recorded the names of worthy saints who have paid their tithing. After reading from the reference given in verse 12, President Joseph F. Smith said:

> This is the position the people will be in when they come to claim an inheritance in Zion, if their names are not found recorded in the book of the law of God. And I want to tell you that this refers directly to the law of tithing. . . .
>
> Some people may not care very much whether their names are recorded or not, but this comes from ignorance of the consequences. If their names are not recorded they will not only be cut off from the assistance which they would be entitled to from the Church if they needed it, but they will be cut off from the ordinances of the house of God (*CR*, Oct. 1899, 42).

Review the material for 83:1-3, 6, "Faithful Widows Have Claim upon the Church."

One Mighty and Strong (85:6-8)

At the time of the revelation in this section, William W. Phelps was helping Bishop Partridge to provide for the saints under the law of consecration. Joseph Smith had given Bishop Partridge instructions on how to do this, but Bishop Partridge was not following these instructions. William W. Phelps wrote Joseph Smith to find out what to do about the situation. The revelation in this section is taken from the inspired letter that Joseph Smith wrote in return to William W. Phelps.

The man referred to in verse 8 is Bishop Partridge. (See the material for 50:4-9 about "steadying the ark of God.") The Lord warned Bishop Partridge that if he did not repent, he would die and one mighty and strong would take his place as Bishop (v. 7-8). The revelation does not say who the one mighty and strong may have been. If this mighty and strong person had replaced Bishop Partridge, he would have been called according to the pattern discussed in Section 26: "All things by Common Consent in the Church." However, Bishop Partridge repented so there was no need for the one mighty and strong to take his place (*HC*, 2:302; *D&C* 124:19).[8]

---

8. For more information about the one mighty and strong see *IE*, Oct. 1907, pp. 929-943.

86

THE PARABLE OF THE WHEAT AND THE TARES

Parables

"The word *parable* is Greek in origin, and means a setting side by side, a comparison" (Bible Dictionary). A parable is usually based on real life experience. If it is fictitious, it is still consistent with real life experience. In this way it is different from an allegory and a fable.

Keys to Understanding Parables

1. **Understand the context.** Although many parables can be applied differently to different situations, their original interpretation can be understood only when set in its original context. Learn to whom Jesus was speaking, where, when, and why Jesus gave the parable. Joseph Smith said: "I have a key by which I understand the scriptures. I enquire, what was the question which drew out the answer, or caused Jesus to utter the parable?" (*TPJS*, pp. 276-7).

2. **Remember that a parable is based on real-life experience.** "The parable draws a picture of life as it is, not as it ought to be" (Bible Dictionary). Therefore, we cannot "force" doctrine from every little detail of a parable. For example, the parable of the unjust judge teaches us how we must pray. It does not teach that God is an unjust judge.

3. **"The same illustration does not always have the same significance**—leaven, [for example], signifies a principle of *good* as well as a principle of *evil"* (Bible Dictionary; emphasis added).

4. **Find out if Jesus Himself gives an interpretation of the parable somewhere else in the scriptures.**

Why Jesus Taught in Parables

Read why Jesus taught in parables in Matt. 13:10-17. It is unlawful (and useless) to teach people more than they are ready to understand (Alma 12:9). Jesus taught people with a wide range of spirituality at the same time. By teaching in parables, each person could receive light and truth in proportion to his or her spiritual preparedness and willingness to ponder and feast upon Christ's words. Note that Jesus spoke about 40 parables to the Jews but He spoke very plainly to the Nephites. Also note that after Jesus told the parable of the wheat and the tares, He had to interpret it to His disciples; even they were not ready to understand the full meaning of this parable. Christ gives an even more in-depth interpretation of this same parable to Joseph Smith in this section.

The Wheat and the Tares

Tares refer to bearded darnel plants. These plants intertwine their roots with the wheat and look just like wheat when they are young, but when they are grown they can easily be distinguished (*Jesus the Christ*, pp. 300-301). The Lord warns against trying to determine who is a wheat and who is a tare too early. Many changes occur as we mature. It is a mistake to judge people prematurely. We may think someone is a tare who will turn out to be a golden shaft of wheat.

The Priesthood Lineage (86:8-11)

Theodore M. Burton explained these verses this way:

> One thing we often fail to realize is that our priesthood comes to us through the lineage of our fathers and mothers. The Lord explained it in these words: "Therefore, thus saith the Lord unto you, with whom the priesthood hath continued through the lineage of your fathers. . . ." (*D&C* 86:8.)
>
> "Oh," I can hear some of you say, "there must be something wrong with that statement, for I am the only member of my family who has joined the Church. How could I have received the priesthood from my parents?"
>
> In this scripture the Lord was not talking about your priesthood line of authority. He was talking about your inherited right to receive and use priesthood power. This readiness to listen and believe is an inherited gift which enabled you to recognize and hear my voice, and I know them, and they follow me." (John 10:27.)
>
> That spirit of acceptance is a manifestation of your inherited right to priesthood blessings. Such willingness to believe does not represent predestination, but it does represent foreordination. The Lord continues the revelation: "For ye are lawful heirs, according to the flesh, and have been hid from the world with Christ in God." (*D&C* 86:9).
>
> This means we receive a right to priesthood blessings from our blood ancestry. I hope you can understand that priesthood with its accompanying blessings is dependent to a great degree on family relationship.
>
> What does the Lord mean by the expression "hid from the world with Christ in God"? He means that according to the plan of salvation you were reserved or held back in the heavens as special spirit children to be born in a time and at a place where you could perform a special mission in life (*CR*, Apr. 1975, p. 103).

87

PROPHECY ON WAR

Historical Context

Read the section heading.

Prophecy of the United States' Civil War (87:1-4, 6-7)

The Lord began warning the saints about the future United States' Civil War long before He gave the revelation in this section (see *D&C* 38:29; 45:63; 63:33). Joseph Fielding Smith said:

> Scoffers have said it was nothing remarkable for Joseph Smith in 1832, to predict the outbreak of the Civil War. . . . It was not, however, within the power of man to predict in the detail which the Lord revealed to Joseph Smith, what was shortly to come to pass as an outgrowth of the Civil War and the pouring out of war upon all nations (*CHMR*, 2:122-123).

The revelation in this section was not just a prophecy, but a warning. Charles A. Callis said:

> It is a part of a prophet's work not only to foretell and warn of impending conflicts and calamities, but also to show the means of escape. Joseph Smith was a prophet-statesman. He predicted the war which would terminate in the death and misery of many souls; but this great prophet had a peace offering to give to the people. He told them of ways and means to avoid war. . . .
>
> In 1844 the Prophet Joseph Smith gave the following counsel with respect to a coming event which was soon to cast its black shadow over the land, and which was of great and general concern. "Pray Congress to pay every man a reasonable price for his slaves out of the surplus revenue arising from the sale of public lands, and from deduction of pay from the members of Congress, break off the shackles from the poor black man, and hire him to labor with other human beings, for an hour of virtuous liberty on earth is worth a whole eternity of bondage. . . .
>
> Abraham Lincoln, the Great Emancipator, probably knew Joseph Smith very well. During a political campaign he wrote a letter in which "he gives a long list of names to which he wants documents to be sent," and in the same letter he tells a candidate "that Joseph Smith is an admirer of his, and that a few documents had better be mailed to the Mormon people." Abraham Lincoln was familiar with the prophetic message that Joseph Smith delivered and the means to escape that the

Prophet opened up to the nation to save the people from the dreadful calamity which bathed the land in the blood of human bodies. . . .

Lincoln wrote, in his own hand, the joint resolution to be presented to Congress, providing an appropriation of $400,000,000 to be paid to the owners of the slaves if war should cease immediately. He laid this proposition before his cabinet, but it was unanimously disapproved. The great and lonely Lincoln, the best friend the South had, turned away sadly. "I see," he said, "you are all against me. The war is costing us $3,000,000 a day, and think of the lives being lost." (*Abraham Lincoln, A History*, by John G. Nicolay and John Hay, 10:132-39.)

Oh, if the words of Joseph Smith, the prophet-statesman, had been heeded, what an effusion of blood would have been prevented! Those young men buried in soldiers' graves would have walked the earth in the full vigor of youth and splendid manhood if the nation had accepted the means of escape which Joseph Smith pointed out to them (*CR*, Oct. 1938, pp. 24-25).

The Lord's warning of conflict and means of escape were rejected along with His prophets. In *D&C* 101:81-95, the Lord told the prophet and the saints to "importune" the state and national leaders. If these leaders would not "heed" the saints, the Lord promised to "come forth out of his hiding place, and in his fury vex the nation" (101:89). The cold blooded murder of Joseph and Hyrum Smith sealed the revelations and warnings given to the nation (*D&C* 135:1, 4). "Their *innocent blood* on the banner of liberty, and on the *magna charta* of the United States . . . will cry unto the Lord of Hosts till he avenges that blood on the earth" (135:7). The U. S. Civil War that followed began to fulfill *D&C* 87:6-7. Otten and Caldwell wrote:

It is a serious thing to reject the message and testimony of the Lord's servants.

We recall that ancient Nephites rejected the testimonies of two of the Lord's servants in the city of Ammonihah. When the wicked drove the righteous from their midst, they lost the protecting blessings that had come through the prayers of the faithful. The ultimate result was the total destruction of the city. (See B of M, Alma 10:22-23; 16:1-11)

In this last dispensation, a nation rejected the testimony of the Lord's servants, killed the Lord's prophets, and drove out the Lord's people. For these acts of wickedness, the Lord forewarned that calamity would befall that nation if they did not repent. (See *D&C* 136:34-36) History provides the evidence of the fulfillment of the Lord's warning. The great civil war caused the death and misery of many thousands of citizens as a result of the rejection of the Lord's servants at that time (*ST*, 2:387).

Prophecies on War and Slaves (87:1-7)

This section is not just a prophecy about the U. S. Civil War. There are many prophecies in this section. Joseph Fielding Smith said:

The rising up of slaves, it is thought by many, was fulfilled in the Civil War when many of the negroes found their way into the armies of the north and fought against their former masters. Others think this is yet to come. The history of this American continent also gives evidence that the Lamanites have risen up in their anger and vexed the Gentiles. This warfare may not be over. It has been the fault of people in the United States to think that this prophetic saying has reference to the Indians in the United States, but we must remember that there are millions of the "remnant" in Mexico, Central and South America. It was during our Civil War that the Indians in Mexico rose up and gained their freedom from the tyranny which Napoleon endeavored to inflict upon them contrary to the prediction of Jacob in the Book of Mormon, that there should be no kings among the Gentiles on this land. The independence of Mexico and other nations to the south has been accomplished by the uprising of the "remnant" upon the land. However, let us not think that this prophecy has completely been fulfilled (*CHMR*, 2:127).

The Lord of Sabaoth (87:7)

Bruce R. McConkie explained:

Christ is the Lord of Sabaoth. (Isa. 1:9; Rom. 9:29; Jas. 5:4; D. & C. 87:7; 88:2; 98:2.) Sabaoth is a Hebrew word meaning hosts or armies; thus, Jehovah Sabaoth means the Lord of Hosts. Also, as revealed to the Prophet, "The Lord of Sabaoth, . . . is by interpretation the creator of the first day, the beginning and the end." (D. & C. 95:7.) (*MD*, pp. 451-52).

Stand in Holy Places (87:8)

To be saved from the wrath of God spoken of in verses 6-7, we are to stand "in holy places, and be not moved" (v. 8). These holy places are the stakes of Zion. Harold B. Lee said:

The Lord has told us where these "holy places" are:
And it shall come to pass among the wicked, that every man that will not take his sword against his neighbor must needs flee unto Zion for safety. (*D&C* 45:68.)
Where is Zion?
During the various periods of time or dispensations, and for specific reasons, the Lord's prophets, His "mouthpieces," as it were, have designated gathering places where the saints were to gather. After designating certain such places in our dispensation, the Lord then declared:
Until the day cometh when there is found no more room for them; and then I have other places which I will appoint unto them, and they shall be called stakes, for the curtains or the strength of Zion. (*D&C* 101:21.) (*Stand Ye In Holy Places*, p. 22.)

To "stand in holy places" is to be a faithful member of the Church. Only those with clean hands and a pure heart can stand in holy places (Ps. 24:3-4). After all, Zion is the pure in heart (*D&C* 97:21). Harold B. Lee said: "The all-important thing is not where we live but whether or not our hearts are pure" (*CR*, Oct. 1968, p. 62). And Daniel H. Ludlow further explains that the term *stand in holy places* also means "do what is right" (*Comp.*, 2:277). To be saved from the wrath of God, we must stand in holy places. In other words, we must do what is right.

88

THE OLIVE LEAF

Historical Context

Read verses 1-2 and the section heading.

Joseph Smith taught a conference of high priests held in Kirtland on December 27 and 28, 1832. The revelations contained in verses 1-126 of this section were received during this conference. The rest of the verses were received on January 3, 1833 and were added to the section in the 1835 edition of the Doctrine and Covenants ("Kirtland Revelation Book," pp. 47- 48).

The Lord of Sabaoth (88:2)

Remember the material for 87:7, "The Lord of Sabaoth."

The Book of the Names of the Sanctified (88:2)

See the material for 128:6-14, "The Books were Opened."

Another Comforter (88:3-5)

The First Comforter, Second or Other Comforter, Holy Spirit of Promise, and the promise of eternal life—having one's calling and election made sure— will be covered in the material for *D&C* 131:5, "The More Sure Word of Prophecy."

Kingdoms of Glory (88:4-5, 20-24, 28-32)

Remember the material for Section 76: "The Vision."

The Light of Christ (88:7-13)

Light, righteousness (1:33; 10:21), revelation (6:21; 50:24; 84:45; 93:28), spirit (84:85; 88:13), truth (84:45; 88:6; 93:24), law (88:13), power (88:13), knowledge (93:24), intelligence (93:29, 36), glory (93:36), and Jesus Christ

(84:45; 93:2, 9, 11, 17, 26, 40) are all closely related and sometimes used interchangeably in the scriptures. Other phrases to keep in mind when pondering the use of "light" in the scriptures are *to enlighten, to bring to light*, and to *shed (or shine or cast) light on* as in "We will be enlightened when the records we have are brought to light because it will shed further light on the case."

This section highlights the light of Christ as priesthood power. Four specific powers are reviewed:

1. **Power to Create (88:7-10).** Cross reference these verses to Hebrews 11:3. And cross reference verse 7 to Abraham, facsimile 2, figure 5.

2. **Power to Enlighten (88:11).** Everyone is blessed with a portion of this light to serve as a conscience to make righteous decisions and learn truth (84:46; 93:2; Moroni 7:19). We can receive a greater portion of this light as we seek it. How we can do this will be covered in the material for verses 77-80, "Of Things Both in Heaven and in the Earth;" verse 118, "Seek Learning, even by Study and also by Faith;" and 93:36, "The Glory of God is Intelligence."

3. **Power to Give Life (88:13).** This applies to mortal life as well as the resurrection and immortality.

4. **Power to Govern (88:13).** Cross reference this to 50:26-27. One can gain more of this power through righteous dominion. (This will be further discussed in the material for Section 121: "There Are Many Called, But Few Are Chosen.")

The fullness of some of these powers will only be gained after this life (see the quote by Brigham Young in the material for 76:50-70, "A Vision of the Celestial Kingdom").

The Spirit and the Body Are the Soul (88:15)

Cross reference this verse with verse 27 and 93:33.

Sanctification (88:20-21, 34, 68)

Remember the material for 20:31, "Sanctification."

The Earth Abideth the Law of a Celestial Kingdom (88:25-26)

The earth was created in a "week." It is now nearing the end of its "second week." It is near the end of the "sixth day" of her temporal existence and will soon enjoy a "sabbath day." Then its second week will end and it will start a glorious new existence. Elder Bruce R. McConkie wrote:

> As is the case with man, the earth itself is passing through a plan of salvation. It was created (the equivalent of birth); it fell to its present mortal or telestial state; it was baptized by immersion, when the universal flood swept over its entire surface (Ether 13:2-11); it will be baptized by fire (the equivalent of baptism of the Spirit) in the day when it is renewed and receives its paradisiacal glory; it will die;

and finally it will be quickened (or resurrected) and become a celestial sphere (*MD*, p. 251).

It is interesting to note that one of the often-repeated phrases the scriptures use to describe death, "having gone the way of all the earth," reflects this belief (Alma 1:1; Josh. 23:14; etc.)

How does the earth fill "the measure of its creation" (v. 25)? Review the material for 2:3, "The Earth Would Be Utterly Wasted."

A Spiritual Body (88:27)

Note the difference between a spirit body and a spiritual body. Only the spiritual body can receive a fullness of joy (93:33).

Your Glory Shall Be That Glory by Which Your Bodies Are Quickened (88:28-32)

To quicken is to give life. What is it that quickens—gives life to—the body? The spirit. Therefore, what these verses say is that a person with a celestial spirit will inherit the celestial kingdom (v. 29) and so forth. How can we attain a celestial spirit? We must "walk towards the light." We gain more light—we add more glory to that which quickens our bodies—as we follow light (truth) we have already learned (84:46), and as we follow the Lord's directions in verses 40, 62-69, and 121-126.

Conditions of Justification (88:34-41)

Review the material for 20:30, "Justification."

Who Hath Seen the Least of These Hath Seen God (88:42-50, 68)

Cross reference these verses with Alma 30:44 and see See God in Appendix 3: "Blessings and Laws Upon Which They are Predicated."

If Your Eye Be Single to My Glory (88:67-68)

Review the material for 4:5, "An Eye Single to the Glory of God."

Cast Away Your Excess of Laughter (88:69, 121)

This verse does not condemn all laughter, but specifies a time and a place for seriousness and reverence. Joseph Fielding Smith wrote:

> We should not get the idea from this scripture that the Lord is displeased with us when we laugh, when we have merriment, if it is on the right occasions. He has said, however, that in our solemn assemblies such things as light-mindedness, laughter, and merriment are out of order (*DS*, 3:303).

And Elder Hugh B. Brown said:

> We have often urged our young people to carry their laughter over into their mature years. A wholesome sense of humor will be a safety valve that will enable you to apply the lighter touch to heavy problems and to learn some lessons in problem solving that "sweat and tears" often fail to dissolve. A line from Proverbs advises us that "a merry heart doeth good like a medicine: but a broken spirit drieth the bones." (Prov. 17:22.) (*CR*, Apr. 1968, p. 100.)

Continue in Prayer and Fasting (88:76)

Review the material for 59:13-14, "The Law of the Fast."

Of Things Both in Heaven and in the Earth (88:77-80)

John A. Widtsoe wrote:

> These studies, the Lord considers necessary. God does not require all His servants to become doctors, or professors, or even profound students of these subjects, but to magnify their callings as His ambassadors to the world (*Priesthood and Church Government*, pp.55-56).

Note that to learn the truth of things "both in heaven and in the earth" we need God's grace (v. 78-79). We must "be taught from on high" to learn truth about things even though they be "under the earth" (43:16; 88:79). How can we receive this kind of teaching? "Even by study and also by faith" (v. 118).

Warning (88:81)

What are we to warn others of? The gist of verses 84-92.

The Second Coming and Beyond (88:87-116)

See the material for Section 45: "The Second Coming;" 101:26-34, "The Millennium;" and Appendix 4: "A Guide to the Book of Revelation."

A Great Sign in Heaven (88:93)

Joseph Smith taught:

> There will be wars and rumors of wars, signs in the heavens above and on the earth beneath, the sun turned into darkness and the moon to blood, earthquakes in divers places, the seas heaving beyond their bounds; then will appear one grand sign of the Son of Man in heaven. But what will the world do? They will say it is a planet, a comet, etc. (*TPJS*, pp. 286-87).

And Smith and Sjodahl further explain:

> A great sign will appear in heaven, which, like the sun, will be seen all round the world. Our Lord calls it the "Sign of the Son of Man" (Matt. 24:30). What this sign is has not been revealed, but there will be no uncertainty about it, when it

appears. In 1843 one Mr. Redding . . . claimed to have seen the sign. The Prophet Joseph then wrote to the *Times and Seasons*:

"Notwithstanding Mr. Redding may have seen a wonderful appearance in the clouds one morning about sunrise (which is not uncommon in the winter season), he has not seen the sign of the Son of Man, as foretold by Jesus [Matt. 24:30]; neither has any man, nor will any man, until after the sun shall have been darkened and the moon bathed in blood; for the Lord hath not shown me any such sign; and as the Prophet saith, so it must be—'Surely the Lord God will do nothing, but he revealeth his secret unto his servants the prophets' (Amos 3:7). . . . (*Hist. of the Church*, Vol. V, p. 291)."

It may be gathered from this that when the sign appears, God will make its meaning known to the Prophet, Seer and Revelator who at that time may be at the head of the Church, and through him to His people and the world in general (*DCC*, p. 560).

The Great and Abominable Church (88:94)

Remember the material for 29:21, "The Great and Abominable Church."

The First and Second Resurrections (88:96-102)

These verses divide the timing of the resurrection into two main phases, each having two parts (also see 45:45, 54; 76:15-17, 50, 64-65, 85; Acts 24:15).

1. **The First Resurrection or Resurrection of the Just (88:96-99).**
    A. *Celestial people (88:96-98).* These people are referred to as the "first fruits" (v. 98; also see 1 Cor. 15:20, 23; and Rev. 14:4). This phase of the resurrection is sometimes called the "morning of the first resurrection." This phase has been going on since the resurrection of Christ and will continue through the beginning of the Second Coming (also see 45:54; 63:18; 76:64; 132:19; Jacob 4:11; Mosiah 15:21-24; 18:9; and Rev. 20:5-6). No one was resurrected before Jesus Christ (1 Cor. 15:20, 23).
    B. *Terrestrial people (88:99).* This is sometimes referred to as the "evening of the first resurrection."
2. **The Second Resurrection or Resurrection of the Unjust (88:100-102;** also see 76:17 and *JST* John 5:29).
    A. *Telestial people (88:100-101).* This is sometimes referred to as the "morning of the second resurrection." It will not take place until after the Millennium.
    B. *Sons of Perdition (88:102).* This is sometimes referred to as the "evening of the second resurrection."

For more information on these types of people and their state after this life, review the material for 76:20-88, "The Vision."

What do resurrected beings look like? Read Alma 11:43-44; 40:23; John 20:19-27; Luke 24:36-43; and JS—H 1:17. What age do we look when we are resurrected? There is no definitive revelation on the subject, but consider the following description of heavenly beings by the protagonist of *The Great Divorce,* by C. S. Lewis:

> Some [of the heavenly beings] were bearded but no one in that company struck me as being of any particular age. One gets glimpses, even in our country [earth], of that which is ageless—heavy thought in the face of an infant, and frolic childhood in that of a very old man. Here it was all like that (p. 30).

Seek Learning, Even by Study and Also by Faith (88:118)

President Spencer W. Kimball taught:

> It takes more than a decade to get a high school diploma; it takes an additional four years for most people to get a college degree; it takes nearly a quarter-century to become a great physician. Why, oh, why do people think they can fathom the most complex spiritual depths without the necessary experimental and laboratory work accompanied by compliance with the laws that govern it? (see "Absolute Truth," *Ensign,* Sep. 1978, pp. 3-5).

How does one seek learning by faith? What is "the necessary experimental and laboratory work" that President Kimball referred to? Study *D&C* 84:46-48 and Alma 32:26-43.

Establish a House of . . . . (88:119-126)

Neal A. Maxwell wrote:

> Though this scripture referred to the School of the Prophets, every home ought to be a mini-school of the prophets, since so much learning can occur there. Indeed, so much learning (good or bad) does occur in a family whether we wish it to or not. It is simply a question of how righteously influential we want our family school to be. Family standards are the criteria by which we measure other important things too: " . . . only men to whom the family is sacred will ever have a standard or a status by which to criticize the state." (G. K. Chesterton, Everlasting Man, p. 146.) (*That My Family Should Partake*, pp. 97-98.)

The School of the Prophets (88:119-141)

To fulfill the commandments given in verses 74-81 and 118-122, the school of the prophets was set up in Kirtland (v. 122, 127-141). Elder Bruce R. McConkie notes that this school was

> also called "the school of mine apostles" (D. & C. 95:17), meaning apostles who were special witnesses of the name of Christ and not apostles ordained to that

office in the Melchizedek Priesthood, for at this time (1833) there were no ordained apostles (*MD*, p. 679).

Another school of the prophets was later set up in Zion and some were set up when the saints moved west. Elder McConkie explains:

> After a short period these schools in the west were discontinued, and gospel teaching today is done mainly through church schools, priesthood quorums, and the various auxiliary organizations [seminary and Sunday school, etc.] (*MD*, p. 681).

Our day's centers of higher learning that most resemble the old school of the prophets are missionary training centers and temples. For more about the school of the prophets, read *MD*, pp. 679-681.

That Your Bodies and Minds May Be Invigorated (88:124)

Cross reference this verse with 84:33.

I Come Quickly (88:126)

Remember the material for 33:18, "I Come Quickly."

The Ordinance of the Washing of Feet (88:139-141)

Read *JST* John 13:8-10 and then John 13:13-17.
Elder Bruce R. McConkie wrote:

> Our Lord did two things in the performance of this ordinance: 1. He fulfilled the old law given to Moses; and 2. He instituted a sacred ordinance which should be performed by legal administrators among his true disciples from that day forward.
>
> As part of the restoration of all things, the ordinance of washing of feet has been restored in the dispensation of the fullness of times. In keeping with the standard pattern of revealing principles and practices line upon line and precept upon precept, the Lord revealed his will concerning the washing of feet little by little until the full knowledge of the endowment and all temple ordinances had been given.

And Daniel H. Ludlow further explains: "The ordinance of washing of the feet has now been incorporated in the ordinances that are revealed to be administered in the Lord's house" (*Comp.*, 2:323).

Note that this ordinance is not the same as the act of cleansing the dust of the feet (review the material for 60:15, "Shake Off the Dust of Thy Feet"). For more on the ordinance of washing of feet, see *History of the Church*, Volume 2, pages 287, 308-310, and 428-430.

89

THE WORD OF WISDOM

Historical Context

The Section heading gives the historical background for this section. Brigham Young gave more detail when he said:

> The first school of the prophets was held in a small room situated over the Prophet Joseph's kitchen, in a house which belonged to Bishop Whitney, and which was attached to his store. . . . The brethren came to that place for hundreds of miles to attend school in a little room probably no larger than eleven by fourteen. When they assembled together in this room after breakfast, the first they did was to light their pipes, and, while smoking, talk about the great things of the kingdom, and spit all over the room, and as soon as the pipe was out of their mouths a large chew of tobacco would then be taken. Often when the Prophet entered the room to give the school instructions he would find himself in a cloud of tobacco smoke. This, and the complaints of his wife at having to clean so filthy a floor, made the Prophet think upon the matter, and he inquired of the Lord relating to the conduct of the Elders in using tobacco, and the revelation known as the Word of Wisdom was the result of his inquiry (*JD*, 12:158).

The Word of Wisdom Is a Commandment (89:1-2)

At the time this revelation was given (1833), it was not given as a commandment (v. 2). Joseph F. Smith explained:

> The reason undoubtedly why the Word of Wisdom was given—as not by "commandment or restraint" was that at that time, at least, if it had been given as a commandment it would have brought every man, addicted to the use of these noxious things, under condemnation; so the Lord was merciful and gave them a chance to overcome, before He brought them under the law. Later on, it was announced from this stand, by President Brigham Young, that the Word of Wisdom was a revelation and a command of the Lord (*CR*, Oct. 1913, p. 14).

The Word of Wisdom is now a commandment for all members of the Church. Joseph Fielding Smith wrote:

> Question: "Will you please tell me if the Word of Wisdom has ever been presented to the Church as a commandment making its observation obligatory upon the members of the Church?"

Answer: This question is one of a score that have been received in relation to the Word of Wisdom. Some of the questions are due to misunderstanding and others, apparently, seeking answers that will justify a violation or modification of the provisions enumerated in the revelation. The simple answer to this question is yes, such commandment has been given and repeated on several occasions. September 9, 1851, President Brigham Young stated that the members of the Church had had sufficient time to be taught the import of this revelation and that henceforth it was to be considered a divine commandment. This was first put to vote before the male members of the congregation and then before the women and by unanimous vote accepted. President Joseph F. Smith at a conference meeting in October 1908, made the same statement, and this has been repeated from time to time (*AGQ*, 1:197-198).

The Word of Wisdom Is for Saints in the Last Days (89:2-4)

The Word of Wisdom is specifically given for saints in the last days "in consequence of evils and designs which do and will exist in the hearts of conspiring men in the last days" (v. 4). It is obvious that evil designs do exist in the hearts of the conspiring people of our day who promote the use of alcohol and tobacco—just examine the advertisements they design. They would have us believe that money, power, looks, "coolness," and sex outside of marriage are the best things in life and that we can have these things by using their products. And they certainly do not promote humility, prayer, and families. John A. Widtsoe said that Section 89

> is prophetic. Throughout the ages the lust for gold has tempted men to place adulterated or dangerous foods upon the market. While pure food and drug laws now protect the people more than in the past, these "evils and designs," through excessive and misleading advertising, continue to appear in new and deceptive forms (Evidences and Reconciliations, 3:154 in *Comp.*, 1:466).

Pure Wine of the Grape (89:6)

Smith and Sjodahl wrote:

> The use of "pure wine" in the Sacrament is permitted. But what is "pure wine" if not the pure juice of the grape, before it has been adulterated by the process of germentation? No fewer than thirteen Hebrew and Greek terms are rendered in our Bible by the word "wine." There is the pure grape juice, and a kind of grape syrup, the thickness of which made it necessary to mingle water with it previously to drinking (Prov. 9:2, 5). There was a wine made strong and inebriating by the addition of drugs, such as myrrh, mandragora, and opiates (Prov. 23:30; Isa. 5:22). Of the pure wine which was diluted with water, or milk, Wisdom invites her friends to drink freely (Prov. 9:2, 5). There was also "wine on the lees," which is supposed to have been "preserves" or "jellies" (Isa. 25:6). The "pure wine" is not an intoxicating, but a harmless liquid (*DCC*, p. 572).

Hot Drinks (89:9)

"Hot drinks" does not refer to hot chocolate, soup, or many herbal teas. Joseph Smith said:

> I understand that some of the people are excusing themselves in using tea and coffee, because the Lord only said "hot drinks" in the revelation of the Word of Wisdom. Tea and coffee are what the Lord meant when he said "hot drinks" (Widtsoe, *The Word of Wisdom*, pp. 75-92 in *MD*, p. 368).

And again:

> There are many who wonder what this [hot drinks] can mean, whether it refers to tea or coffee, or not. I say it does refer to tea and coffee (*Times and Seasons*, 3:800 in *MD*, p. 368).

Cola Drinks and Other Items

When we commit to live the Word of Wisdom we commit to abstain from tobacco, alcohol, tea, coffee, and harmful drugs. Bruce R. McConkie states: "Obviously the standard of judgement must be uniform throughout the Church, and local officers are not at liberty to add other items to this list" (*MD*, p. 845). He also states: "There is no prohibition in Section 89, for instance, as to the eating of white bread, using white flour, white sugar, cocoa, chocolate, eggs, milk, [or] meat" (*MD*, p. 846). An official Church statement explains:

> With reference to cola drinks, the Church has never officially taken a position on this matter, but the leaders of the Church have advised, and we do now specifically advise, against the use of any drink containing harmful habit-forming drugs under circumstances that would result in acquiring the habit. Any beverage that contains ingredients harmful to the body should be avoided (*Priesthood Bulletin*, Feb. 1972, p. 4).

Every Herb and Fruit in the Season Thereof (89:11)

John A. Widtsoe said:

> The phrase "in the season thereof," referring to fruits and vegetables, has raised much speculation. It indicates simply the superior value of fresh foods as demonstrated by modern science, but does not necessarily prohibit the use of fruits or vegetables out of season if preserved by proper methods (*Evidences and Reconciliations*, 3:157 in *Comp.*, 1:469-70).

And Joseph Fielding Smith said:

> Some have stumbled over the meaning of the expression "in the season thereof," and have argued that grains and fruits should only be used in the season of their growth and when they have ripened. This is not the intent, but any grain or fruit is out of season no matter what part of the year it may be, if it is unfit for use.

The apple under the tree bruised and decaying is out of season while the good fruit is waiting to be plucked from the tree (*CHMR* 1:385).

Meats (89:12-13)

The *Doctrine and Covenants Student Manual* states:

This verse [verse 13] has caused some to ask if meat should be eaten in the summer. Meat is a very heavy food and provides warmth and energy, both of which are less needed in summer than in winter. When the Word of Wisdom was revealed, methods for preserving meat were still primitive. Spoiled meat can be fatal if eaten, but the chance of spoilage is not as great in winter as in summer. Modern methods of refrigeration now make it possible for meat to be frozen and thereby preserved for later use in any season. The key word with respect to the use of meat is "sparingly" (*D&C* 89:12) (p. 210).

We may also choose to not eat meats at all.[9]

A Principle with Promise (89:3, 18-21)

The Lord promises that as we obey the Word of Wisdom and live the commandments (v. 18), we will be blessed with the following:

1. **Health in the navel and marrow to the bones (89:18).** Otten and Caldwell state:

    This phrase appears but once in all of the revealed *latter-day* scripture in the standard works of the Church. The scriptures do not provide an explanation as to its meaning. To those who are worthy of this promise, the meaning will be manifest by the Lord in His own time and place (*ST*, 2:121; emphasis added).

    The phrase also appears in Prov. 3:8. Reading the context in which that verse is used may give you additional insights.

2. **Wisdom and hidden treasures of knowledge (89:19).** Knowledge that is "hidden" is spiritual knowledge. Great treasures of hidden knowledge include a testimony that Jesus is our savior, Joseph Smith is a prophet of God, the Book of Mormon is the word of God, and the president of the Church in our day is a prophet of God. These hidden treasures of knowledge can be found only by those who diligently seek for them. Heber J. Grant said:

---

9. Care must be used to supplement the diet with the needed nutrients that only meats provide. For more information on vegetarian diets, consult your local library or bookstore.

No man or woman in this Church who does not observe the Word of Wisdom can grow and increase in a knowledge and testimony of the gospel as he or she could otherwise do *(Gospel Standards*, p. 249).

And concerning the commandment of the Word of Wisdom, Brigham Young said:

What will be the consequence of their disobedience? Darkness and blindness of mind with regard to the things of God will be their lot; they will cease to have the spirit of prayer, and the spirit of the world will increase in them in proportion to their disobedience until they apostatize entirely from God and His ways *(JD*, 12:117).

Missionaries and home teachers need to help the people they teach to commit to live the Word of Wisdom. Then the people will be able to gain a testimony or have their testimony grow.

3. **Shall run and not be weary—physical and emotional strength (89:20).** We are all vulnerable to disease and illnesses. Individuals who have obeyed the Word of Wisdom their entire lives may live with terrible disease. However, collectively speaking, it is a well documented fact that Latter-day Saints are blessed with greater than average health and strength. But perhaps an even greater blessing than physical strength is the spiritual and emotional strength that comes from obeying the Word of Wisdom and living the commandments. Remember that the Word of Wisdom is a spiritual and not a temporal law *(D&C* 29:34). Even people with life-threatening or terminal illnesses or crippling handicaps can "run and not be weary." Although these people may be running the race of life in more physical pain or up a shorter yet steeper track, they can run with peace of mind and a strong spirit. "They shall mount up with wings as eagles; they shall run, and not be weary" (Isa. 40:31).

4. **The destroying angel shall pass by them (89:21).** The destroying angel passed by the children of Israel because they possessed a hidden treasure of knowledge. They received a commandment to put blood on their doors and not to leave their homes the night of the passover. Those that accepted this commandment as the word of God obeyed it and were saved (see Exodus 12 for the whole story). The destroying angel will pass by us— perhapsmeaning we will be saved in the celestial kingdom—as we act upon the hidden treasures of knowledge that we possess.

The Word of Wisdom Promotes the Well-Being of Families and Society

Ponder for a minute what it would be like to have such a strong emphasis on having children and raising families without the guidelines of the Word of Wisdom. In John 9:2-3, the disciples ask:

> Master, who did sin, this man, or his parents, that he was born blind?
>
> Jesus answered, Neither hath this man sinned, nor his parents: but that the works of God should be made manifest in him.

While this was the case for this man, there are thousands of children being born with devastating health problems directly related to the crimes of their parents. (Hopefully, the works of God shall be made manifest in these children also.) For example, in the U. S., 4 of every 1,000 newborns show features of fetal alcohol syndrome (Garber, Fox, and Tabsh, p. 104), 10%-20% of cases of mild to moderate mental retardation are due to the effects of alcohol in utero (Cassidy and Whiteman, p. 167), and 350,000-625,000 infants are drug exposed each year (Institute of Medicine, in *The President's Commission. . .*, p. 3-9). The cost to the children is inestimable; some of the direct costs to society have been studied.

Some Costs Due to Alcohol and Other Drug Problems		
Type of Cost	*Alcohol*	*Other Drugs of Abuse*
Criminal Justice System		
Police Protection	$1,338,000,000	$5,810,000,000
Legal and Adjudication	$274,000,000	$1,108,000,000
State and Federal Prisons	$884,000,000	$2,130,000,000
Local Jails	$1,238,000,000	$460,000,000
Other Legal Costs		
Private Legal Defense	$342,000,000	$1,381,000,000
Property Destruction	$175,000,000	$759,000,000
Other Direct Costs		
Motor Vehicle Accidents	$2,584,000,000	-
Fire Destruction	$457,000,000	-
Indirect Costs		
Victims of Crime	$465,000,000	$842,000,000
Incarceration	$2,701,000,000	$4,434,000,000
Crime Careers	-	$13,976,000,000

Note that this data does not include the cost of AIDS (about 20% attributed to intravenous drug abuse), other social diseases, and perinatal and pediatric morbidity caused by drug and alcohol abuse by the parent (Wright, 1988, in *The President's Commission. . .*, p. 3-8, 3-9).

The Word of Wisdom is also powerful in its prevention of unwittingly stepping beyond the bounds of the law of chastity. Here, the benefits to the family are obvious. The benefits to society will be discussed more fully in Appendix 5: "The Rock of Liberty."

The Word of Wisdom Hits the Mark

Why, some ask, can't you use alcohol, tobacco, coffee, and tea moderately? After all, just a little bit can't hurt. Two reasons are: one, the Word of Wisdom proves "even the weakest of all saints" (v. 3); and two, zero is an easy limit to understand.

Say the Lord said we could use alcohol with moderation. The first thing we would ask is how much does that mean. Say the Lord said one glass. We would then ask: how big a glass, how full, how often, and what kind of alcohol? To answer, more questions would have to be asked. How big are you? Are you pregnant? What are you going to be doing? What is your tolerance level?

In other words, the Lord's limit is so easy to understand that not even the "weakest of all saints" can look beyond the mark. Besides, "the mark" is not even the limitation, but the principle of obedience to, and respect for the Lord.

90

THE KEYS OF THE KINGDOM—ORACLES

Historical Context

Read the section heading.

The Oracles (90:1-5)

The term oracle can refer to a person who receives revelation or to the revelation itself. The president of the Church holds the keys of the kingdom—the authority to receive revelation for the Church and to confer all priesthood powers. Therefore, the president of the Church is an oracle. The revelations that come through the president of the Church are also oracles. The Lord promises to protect us as we receive and esteem His oracles—His prophets and the revelations given through them (v. 5). For more information on the Lord's oracles and how they provide protection, review the material for Section 21: "Follow the

Prophet;" 28:2, 12-13, "Revelation from the Lord;" 43:1-7, "The Law of Revelation for the Church;" and 43:7, "The Gate."

Counselors Are Accounted as Equal with the President (90:6)

The *Doctrine and Covenants Student Manual* explains: "Counselors can do everything their presiding officer directs them to do, as if the president were personally acting; however, they have no power to act independent of the president" (p. 213). The counselors can only act under the direction and permission of the president. Only the president is authorized to receive revelation for the Church and use all the keys of the kingdom (review the material for 43:7, "The Gate").

Now is a good time to review the material for 81:1, 3-7, "Duties of a Counselor."

The Joseph Smith Translation (90:13)

Wait one more section when we come to Section 91: "The Apocrypha."

Let Your Families Be Small (90:25)

This does not refer to immediate family. Ludlow explains:

> Both the Prophet Joseph Smith and his father had provided food and lodging for many visitors and members of the Church as they came to meet the Smith family. Here the Lord cautions them to be wise in these things so that "those things that are provided for you . . . be not taken from you and given to those that are not worthy." (*D&C* 90:26.) (*Comp.*, 1:479.)

Meet (90:30)

Meet means fitting, proper, or desirable.

91

THE APOCRYPHA

Historical Context

Read the section heading.

The Apocrypha (91:1-6)

The term *apocryphal* means "hidden" or "secret." The Apocrypha is a collection of books that some churches consider part of the Old Testament. These books were held sacred by the Jews but were not part of the Hebrew Bible. Nothing from the books of the Apocrypha is quoted elsewhere in the standard works. For more information, look under *Apocrypha* and *Canon* in the Bible Dictionary.

Although not specifically mentioned in this section, verse 5 can apply to the Pseudepigrapha as well as the Apocrypha. For more information, look under *Pseudepigrapha* in the Bible Dictionary.

The Joseph Smith Translation

The *JST* is spoken of in *D&C* 37:1; 45:60-61: 76:15-18; 90:13; 94:10; 104:58; and 124:89. Bruce R. McConkie wrote:

> At the command of the Lord and while acting under the spirit of revelation, the Prophet corrected, revised, altered, added to, and deleted from the King James Version of the Bible to form what is now commonly referred to as the *Inspired Version of the Bible. . . .*
>
> This inspired revision of the ancient scriptures was never completed by the Prophet, and up to the present time none of his successors have been directed by the Lord to carry the work forth to its final fruition. President George Q. Cannon has written: "On the 2nd day of February, 1833, the Prophet completed, *for the time being*, his inspired translation of the New Testament. No endeavor was made at that time to print the work. . . . Joseph did not live to give to the world an author-itative publication of these translations. . . ." (George Q. Cannon, *Life of Joseph Smith*, new ed., pp. 147-148; *History of the Church*, vol. 1, p. 324; Sidney B. Sperry, *Knowledge Is Power*, pp. 9-61.)
>
> Such changes as the Prophet made in the Bible were done, in the main, by *topics or subjects*. He did not go from Genesis to Revelation and make all needed corrections in every passage as he came to it. True, in many passages all neces-sary changes were made; in others he was "restrained" by the Spirit from giving the full and clear meaning. As with all revealed knowledge, the Lord was offer-ing new truths to the world, "line upon line, precept upon precept; here a little, and there a little." (*D&C* 128:21.) Neither the world nor the saints generally were then or are now prepared for the fullness of Biblical knowledge. The Lord was operating in conformity with the principle explained by Alma: "It is given unto many to know the mysteries of God; nevertheless they are laid under a strict com-mand that they shall not impart only according to the portion of his word which he doth grant unto the children of men, according to the heed and diligence which they give unto him." (Alma 12:9.)
>
> Such Biblical revisions as have been made may be used with safety, and parts of these are now published by the Church in its standard works. The first 151 verses of the Old Testament, down to Genesis 6:13, are published as the Book of Moses in the Pearl of Great Price. But as restored by the Prophet the true ren-dition contains about 400 verses and a wealth of new doctrinal knowledge and

historical data. The revised 24th chapter of Matthew is also found in the Pearl of Great Price.

*   *   *   *   *

The fact that some changes were made in a particular passage or chapter does not mean that all needed corrections were given even in that portion of the Bible. Important changes were made in several thousand verses, but there are yet thousands of passages to be revised, clarified, and perfected. . . .

There will be a not too distant day when all necessary changes shall be made in the Bible, and the Inspired Version—as then perfected—shall go forth to the world (*MD*, pp. 383-385).

For more information on the *JST*, see the Bible Dictionary under *Joseph Smith Translation*.

92

A LIVELY MEMBER

Historical Context

Joseph Smith introduced the revelation in this section as "a revelation given to Shederlaomach [a code name for Frederick G. Williams] . . . constituting him a member of the United *Firm*" (*HC* 1:340; emphasis added). Although the revelation in this section is speaking of membership in the United Firm, its teachings are important lessons to learn on membership in the Church.

For information on the United Firm, see the material for Section 78: "Purposes of the Law of Consecration and Stewardship" and Section 104: "The United Order."

Receive Him into the Order (92:1)

When new members join the church, we should receive them as equals, regardless of their background or past experiences. It is our responsibility to make them feel welcomed and appreciated.

A Lively Member (92:2)

We can be "lively" members as we attend and actively participate in our Church meetings and magnify our callings.

93

THE SPIRIT OF TRUTH

Shall See My Face (93:1)

See *See God* in Appendix 3: "Blessings and Laws Upon Which They Are Predicated."

I Am the True Light (93:2)

Remember the material for 88:7-13, "The Light of Christ."

Jesus Christ As the Father (93:3-4)

Read Mosiah 15:2-5 for further explanation of these verses.

Jesus Christ is the Son of our Heavenly Father. However, Jesus Christ can also be called the Father. Three explanations for this are:

1. **Jesus Christ is the Creator.** Mosiah 3:8 is a good example of this use of the term Father. "Jesus Christ, being the Creator, is consistently called the Father of heaven and earth . . . and since His creations are of eternal quality He is very properly called the Eternal Father of heaven and earth" ("The Father and The Son," p. 467).

2. **Jesus Christ is the Savior.** In this sense, Jesus is the Father of those who follow His teachings. For example, citizens often refer to their nation's founders as the "founding *fathers*." And great leaders are sometimes called the *father* of their cause. While these examples apply, the role of Jesus Christ as the Father of His people has even more significance. It is only by becoming a son or daughter of Christ that we can be saved. To do this we must be born again and become new creatures in Christ. It is Jesus Christ that makes it possible for the spirit and flesh to become inseparably connected and receive a fullness of joy (v. 33). Thus, Heavenly Father is the Father of our spirits, our earthly father is the father of our flesh, and Jesus Christ is the Father of our soul (see Heb. 12:19 and *D&C* 88:15). Other scriptures to ponder are Mosiah 15:10-13; John 17:6-12, 20-24; *D&C* 11:28-30; 25:1; 34:3; 39:1-4; 45:7-8; 50:41.

3. **Jesus Christ speaks on behalf of Heavenly Father.** Heavenly Father has given Jesus Christ the authority to speak for Him. This is often referred to as "divine investiture of authority." The Lord often speaks as if He were Heavenly Father and sometimes even refers to Himself as

His Only Begotten Son (for example, read Moses 1:1-6). Divine investiture of authority has also been granted at times to angels to speak in behalf of Jesus Christ (see Ex. 23:21 and Rev. 22:7-13). In a more general sense, divine investiture of authority has been given to all priesthood holders to represent and act in the name of Jesus Christ (see the material for 99:1-5, 7-8, "Who Receiveth You Receiveth Me").

Concerning Jesus Christ and Heavenly Father being one God, review the material for 20:28, "The Father, Son, and Holy Ghost are One God."

The Record of John (93:6-18)

The full record of John the Baptist has yet to be revealed to the Church. Pieces of the record are in these verses and in John 1:19-34.

He Received Not of the Fullness at the First (93:12-14)

President Lorenzo Snow said:

> When Jesus lay in the manger, a helpless infant, He knew not that He was the Son of God, and that formerly He created the earth. When the edict of Herod was issued, He knew nothing of it; He had not power to save Himself; and His father and mother had to take Him and fly into Egypt . . . . Well, He grew up to manhood, and during His progress it was revealed unto Him who He was, and for what purpose He was in the world (*CR*, Apr. 1901, p. 3).

The Sign of the Dove (93:15)

Joseph Smith said:

> [John the Baptist] had the privilege of beholding the Holy Ghost descend in the form of a dove, or rather in the sign of the dove . . . . The sign of the dove was instituted before the creation of the world, a witness for the Holy Ghost, and the devil cannot come in the sign of a dove. The Holy Ghost is a personage, and is in the form of a personage. It does not confine itself to the form of the dove, but in the sign of the dove. The Holy Ghost cannot be transformed into a dove; but the sign of a dove was given to John to signify the truth of the deed, as the dove is an emblem or token of truth and innocence (*HC*, 5:260).

Grace for Grace (93:19-20)

The Lord gave "these sayings that you may understand and know how to worship" (v. 19). Five ways to worship are given in verse 1. As we follow the Lord's instructions, we can receive the fullness of the Father the same way Jesus did—by receiving grace for grace (v. 12- 13, 19-20).

The Light of Truth (93:24-40)

Both sections 88 and 93 discuss the light of Christ. Section 88 concentrates on the power of the light, while section 93 focuses on the source of the light.

I suggest reviewing the material for 88:7-13, "The Light of Christ," to better understand the material in these verses of section 93.

This section was given that we may know what we worship (v. 19). So why does the Lord start talking about light, truth, and intelligence in these verses? The key to unlocking these verses is highlighted in verses 2, 9, 11, 17, 26, and 40. Christ is the Spirit of Truth. In Him is the fullness of truth, light, and intelligence. Understanding this sheds more light on what other verses teach about truth. For example:

- v. 24 The definition of truth. Emphasizes that Christ and truth are eternal.
- v. 28-29 We gain truth, light, and intelligence as we come unto Christ.
- v. 31-35 We are judged by Christ.
- v. 36 Intelligence is the wisdom of Christ.
- v. 37 We overcome the evil one through Christ.
- v. 39 We lose Christ's redeeming power through disobedience.
- v. 40-47 We are to bring up our children in Christ.

Intelligence (93:29)

Joseph Fielding Smith stated:

> Some of our writers have endeavored to explain what an intelligence is, but to do so is futile, for we have never been given any insight into this matter beyond what the Lord has fragmentarily revealed. We know, however, that there is something called intelligence which always existed. It is the real eternal part of man, which was not created or made. This intelligence combined with the spirit constitutes a spiritual identity or individual (*Progress of Man*, p. 11).

Spirit and Element (93:33-35)

Are we bodies of flesh and blood? No. We are more than tissues and the complex physiological processes that go on in them. We are spirits (who have bodies). We cannot receive a fullness of joy until we become like God, inseparably connected to the elements which make up our tabernacle (our body) (v. 33-35).

Man Is the Tabernacle of God (93:35)

Read 1 Corinthians 3:16-17 and the footnotes for those verses.

The Glory of God Is Intelligence (93:36)

Verse 29 uses the term *intelligence* to describe a being while verse 36 uses *intelligence* to describe a property of a being. Intelligence is more than knowledge. It is the wisdom of Jesus Christ (remember the material for verses 24-40, "The Light of Truth"). Elder Joseph Fielding Smith said:

> We very frequently quote from one of the revelations the words of the Lord to this effect, that "The glory of God is intelligence," and I wonder if we ourselves really comprehend what it means. We stop in the middle of a sentence. That is not

the end of the sentence, for the Lord says, "The glory of God is intelligence, or in other words light and truth." And then he adds that "light and truth forsaketh that evil one."

When we have the Spirit of the Lord we have intelligence—light and truth . . . . It is pure intelligence, if you please, and he who has it has the power to discern between right and wrong, truth and error, and he will follow righteousness (*CR*, Oct. 1933, p. 60).

The wisdom of Jesus Christ is not necessarily gained by going to school—not even a university. So how do we receive this intelligence? Read verses 27-28 and review the material for 88:77-80, "Of Things Both in Heaven and in the Earth" and 88:118, "Seek Learning, even by Study and also by Faith."

The Lord Rebukes His Friends (93:40-53)

What member of the family did the Lord hold accountable for the spiritual well being of that family? (See verses 41, 44, 47, and 50.)

Cross reference these verses with the material for 68:25-35, "Parents;" 68:27, "Children Shall Be Baptized when Eight Years Old;" 88:119-126, "Establish a House of . . . .;" and 95:1-2, 9-17, "Responsibilities of a Chastiser."

Translate My Scriptures and Obtain Knowledge (93:53)

Remember the material about the Joseph Smith Translation in Section 91: "The Apocrypha" and the material for 88:77-80, "Of Things Both in Heaven and in the Earth."

94

THE LORD'S BUILDINGS

Historical Context

Otten and Caldwell wrote: "The church did not own any buildings at that time [1833]. The church had reached a point in its growth where it was necessary to have facilities to carry out its programs, meetings, and activities" (*ST*, 2:146).

Stakes (94:1)

Remember the material for 82:13-14, "Stakes."

A House for the Lord (94:1-2)

In these verses, the Lord instructed the saints to begin building the city of Kirtland. The Lord desired to live among them. He instructed the saints to build the city around His house. It is wonderful that the Lord desires to have us as neighbors. He would love for us to come to His home to visit Him.

A House for the First Presidency (94:3-9)

The work of the First Presidency is to direct the Church—the kingdom of God. This, of course, requires guidance from the Lord. Therefore, the saints were commanded to build a special building, wholly dedicated to the Lord so His glory and presence would be there to direct the First Presidency (v. 3-9).

A House for the Work of the Printing (94:10-12)

The Church was not to depend on the world for the printing needs of the kingdom of God.

The Joseph Smith Translation (94:10)

Remember the material for Section 91: "The Apocrypha."

The Building Committee to Build the Lord's Houses (94:13-17)

The Lord told the members of the newly formed building committee where they would live. The Lord commanded this committee to "build mine houses" (v. 15). The Lord refers to buildings owned by the Church as belonging to Him. We ought to respect and maintain the Church's buildings, for they are the Lord's.

95

RESPONSIBILITIES OF A CHASTISER

Historical Context—Ye Have Sinned a Grievous Sin (95:3-8)

In December of 1832, the saints had been commanded to build a temple in Kirtland (*D&C* 88:119). It was now June of 1833 and the saints still had not begun to build the temple. The saints were failing to recognize the importance of the temple (v. 3-8). In this section, the Lord chastises the saints for delaying the building of the Kirtland temple.

Responsibilities of a Chastiser (95:1-2, 9-17)

We are sometimes placed in the position of chastiser. It is often a difficult position in which to be. We can look to the Lord's example. In this section, the Lord demonstrates three responsibilities of a chastiser.

1. **Express love (95:1).** The Lord first tells the saints that He loves them.
2. **Have the proper motive (95:1-2).** The Lord chastised the saints "that their sins may be forgiven" (v. 1). The Lord's motive is to help us come unto Him. He wants to help us correct our mistakes, not make us feel like we *are* mistakes (remember the material for 58:43, "By this ye may Know if a man Repenteth of his Sins"). He wants to build us up, not build Himself up by tearing us down. When we are in the position of chastiser, we should ask ourselves what our motive is. We should ask ourselves, "Why am I doing this? Is it to help the person correct a mistake? Is it to help the person come unto Christ? Is it to help the person be better and not to make me look better than that person? What is my motive?"
3. **Prepare a way for their deliverance (95:1, 9-17).** The Lord did not just tell the saints that they had made a mistake. He showed them how they could correct it. It is useless to chastise unless the one being chastised knows how to fix the situation or how to prevent it from happening again.

The Pattern of Zion (95:2)

The Lord gave detailed instructions to His prophets Moses and, later, Joshua on how the tabernacle should be built and how the Promised Land should be laid out (Ex. 25-30; Josh. 14-21). Similarly, the Lord gave Joseph Smith a pattern for the laying out of the city Zion and the building of her temples (there are to be more than one temple, each having a special purpose). The instructions are too long and detailed to include here (it would be like including Exodus chapters 25-30 and Joshua chapters 14-21 here). But you can read them in *History of the Church*, volume 1, pages 357-364.

My Strange Act (95:4)

Smith and Sjodahl wrote:

> The expression quoted is from the Prophet Isaiah (28:21), where it refers to the fact that God would fight against His own people, because of their apostate condition [Isa. 10:11]. . . . But in this dispensation our Lord was to perform an equally strange act, in revealing His marvelous plan of salvation and making war upon an apostate church which is boasting of its intimate relations with Deity. He was now waiting for the Saints to build that house, in which His messengers were to

be prepared for that strange war and endowed with power from on High (v. 8). No wonder that He rebuked them for their tardiness! (*DCC*, p. 603.)

Lord of Sabaoth (95:7)

Remember the material for 87:7, "The Lord of Sabaoth."

Son Ahman (95:17)

Ahman is a name for God the Father. Son Ahman is Jesus Christ. Ahman is similar in meaning to Man of Holiness. Review the material for 45:39, "Son of Man." For further commentary see "Ahman" in *Mormon Doctrine*.

96

THE PURPOSE OF ALL THAT IS DONE IN THE CHURCH

Historical Context

The Lord commanded the saints to build a city in Kirtland (*D&C* 94:1). The saints bought up land in response to this commandment. At the time this revelation was given, they were trying to figure out how to divide the land that now belonged to the Church and, in particular, how to divide the piece of land known as the French farm.

Stakes (96:1)

Remember the material for 82:13-14, "Stakes."

How to Divide the Farm and for What Purpose (96:1-5)

The Lord told the priesthood leaders to divide the property "according to wisdom . . . as it shall be determined in council among you" (v. 3). The Lord knew they were capable of making a wise decision. To guide them in their decision, the Lord told them for what purposes the property was being divided. All that we do in the Church should be based on the purposes the Lord gave. These purposes are:

1. **For the benefit of those who seek inheritances (96:3).** Every activity the Church sponsors, every decision its leaders make, and every meeting held should help people gain inheritances in the celestial kingdom. Review the material for 65:3-6, "The Purpose of the Church."
2. **To bring forth the Lord's word to the children of men (96:4).**

3.   To subdue the hearts of the children of men (96:5).

Sometimes we get so caught up in what we are doing that we forget for what purpose we are doing it. As we keep our minds focused on these purposes, we will have more power in our labors.

John Johnson Should Become a Member of the Order (96:6-9)

In these verses, John Johnson is called to be a member of the United Firm (remember the material for Section 92: "A Lively Member"). He is given the task of helping "to take away incumbrances that are upon the house named among you" (v. 9). In other words, he was to help the Firm get out of debt.

97

ZION: THE PURE IN HEART

Historical Context

Read the section heading.

The Pattern (97:10)

Remember the material for 95:2, "The Pattern of Zion."

Let the Temple Be Built Speedily (97:10-17)

The Lord had already shown the saints where to build the temple in Zion (*D&C* 57:1-3). In Section 97, the Lord told the saints to build the temple speedily because the salvation of Zion depended on it (v. 11-12). The Lord knew that the saints in Zion could not overcome the persecution they were facing without the blessings and strength they could receive in the temple. Smith and Sjodahl said:

> The history of Temples teaches us that the people of God have been strong, or weak, in proportion to the faithfulness with which they have attended to their sanctuaries. The history of the Temple of Jerusalem is, as Dr. Joseph Angus, in his *Bible Handbook*, notes, "an index to the history of the Jews. When it fell, they were scattered; as it rose from its ruins, they gathered round it again; and history dates the captivity, with equal accuracy, from the destruction of the Temple, or from the first capture of Jerusalem." Speaking of the Temples in this dispensation, someone has declared that the completion of the Nauvoo Temple was the

salvation of the Church from annihilation, although the saints were forced to flee into the desert. Since the completion of the Salt Lake Temple, the adversary has had less power to injure the Church than he had before. If we remember that the Temples are the palaces of God, where His Presence is manifested, we can understand why, when the adversary was marshalling his forces against the Church, our Lord urged the saints to build the Temple speedily. We can also understand why the evil one planned to have them scattered before they could rear that sacred edifice (*DCC*, p. 612).

In Section 101 we will find out what the saints did about building the temple speedily. In fact, the Lord will even tell the saints a parable about it (see the material for 101:43-62, "A Parable Concerning the Redemption of Zion").

The Pure in Heart Shall See God (97:16)

Look under *See God* in Appendix 3: "Blessings and Laws Upon Which they are Predicated."

Zion Shall Prosper (97:18-28)

Beginning in verse 18, the Lord pronounced many blessing on Zion. He said it would become "very great and very terrible" (v. 18). The word *terrible*, here, means terrifying and powerful. The nations of the earth will respect, admire, and fear the power of Zion (v. 19).

The blessings the Lord pronounced on Zion are based on the obedience of its people. Zion will prosper because its people will be pure in heart. When the people are pure in heart, they will be of one heart and one mind and they will dwell in righteousness; therefore, there will be no poor among them (Moses 7:18). In Section 101, we will see that Zion did not prosper at this time because the people were not obedient and did not have pure hearts.

Meanings of the Term Zion (97:21)

The term *Zion* is sometimes used to describe geographical locations. For examples, look up *Zion* in the Bible Dictionary. When used to speak of a geographical location in the Doctrine and Covenants, *Zion* most often refers to the center place of Zion—Jackson County, Missouri.

Zion also refers to the Church or its branches (wherever they may be located). However, the key meaning of *Zion* is "the pure in heart" (v. 21). This was the key that was disregarded by the early latter-day saints. They thought they could build the city Zion without first building a Zion people. The saints of our day have been warned not to make the same mistake. President Spencer W. Kimball said:

Zion can be built up only among those who are pure in heart, not a people torn by covetousness or greed, but a pure and selfless people. Not a people who are pure in appearance, rather a people who are pure in heart.

*   *   *   *   *

Defining and describing Zion will not bring it about. That can only be done through consistent and concerned daily effort by every single member of the Church. No matter what the cost in toil or sacrifice, we must do it. That is one of my favorite phrases: "Do It" (*Ensign*, May 1978, pp. 80-81).

The "it" that we need to "do" to build Zion will be discussed in the material for 105:4-37, "Requirements for the eventual redemption of Zion."

98

LAWS ON WAR, RETALIATION AND FORGIVENESS

Historical Context—Let Your Hearts Be Comforted (98:1-3)

Read the section heading.

The Lord comforts the saints by reassuring them that He is watching over them (v. 1- 3).

The Lord of Sabaoth (98:2)

Remember the material for 87:7, "The Lord of Sabaoth."

Constitutional Law of the Land—Seek Good and Wise Men (98:4-10)

Wait until we come to Section 134: "Church and State."

The Purpose of Law (98:8)

Remember the material for Section 42 under the subheading "Why the Lord Gives Laws."

Laws on War (98:16, 33-38)

The Lord's first law on war is: "Renounce war and proclaim peace" (v. 16). However, as long as lust exists in the world, there will be wars (James 4:1). Therefore, in verses 33-38, the Lord restates some of His laws regarding warfare. Harold B. Lee said:

What is the position of the Church with respect to war? A declaration of the First Presidency given during World War II is still applicable in our time. The statement said: ". . . the Church is and must be against war. The Church itself cannot wage war unless and until the Lord shall issue new commands. It cannot regard war as a righteous means of settling international disputes; these should and could be settled—the nations agreeing—by peaceful negotiations and Adjustments.

There is a scripture that has direct bearing there: [*D&C* 98:4-7 quoted]. . . .

Note particularly that the revelation [in *D&C* 98:4-7] is directed to members of the Church. Therefore, it is applicable to persons of all nations, not just those in the land we call America.

There are many who are troubled and their souls harrowed by the haunting question of the position of the soldier who in combat duty kills the enemy. Again, the First Presidency has commented:

"When, therefore, constitutional law, obedient to those principles, calls the manhood of the Church into the armed service of any country to which they owe allegiance, their highest civic duty requires that they meet that call. If, hearkening to that call and obeying those in command over them, they shall take the lives of those who fight against them, that will not make of them murderers, nor subject them to the penalty that God has prescribed for those who kill, beyond the principles to be mentioned shortly: for it would be a cruel God that would punish his children as moral sinners for acts done by them as the innocent instrumentalities of a sovereign whom he had told them to obey and whose will they were powerless to resist." God is at the helm (*The New Era*, Aug. 1971, pp. 4-5).

And David O. McKay said:

There are, however, two conditions which may justify a truly Christian man to enter—mind you, I say enter, not begin—a war: (1) An attempt to dominate and to deprive another of his free agency, and, (2) Loyalty to his country. Possibly there is a third, viz., Defense of a weak nation that is being unjustly crushed by a strong, ruthless one.

                    *   *   *   *   *

The greatest responsibility of the state is to guard the lives, and to protect the property and rights of its citizens; and if the state is obligated to protect its citizens from lawlessness within its boundaries, it is equally obligated to protect them from lawless encroachments from without—whether the attacking criminals be individuals or nations.

Does the Lord permit the shedding of blood and justify it? Yes, sometimes he does [see Ex. 15:3; Josh. 2:24; and *D&C* 98:36] (*CR*, Apr. 1942, pp. 72-73).

For more information, refer to the material under "War, Protection and Help in Time of" in Appendix 3: "Blessings and Laws upon Which They Are Predicated."

Turn the Hearts of the Children and Fathers (98:16)

Review the material for Section 2: "Heart to Heart."

Turn the Hearts of the Jews unto the Prophets (98:17)

Ezra Taft Benson said:

> In Jacob's blessing to Judah, he declared: "Judah is . . . as an old lion: *who shall rouse him up?* (Gen. 49:9; italics added.) We come as messengers bearing the legitimate authority to arouse Judah to her promises. We do not ask Judah to forsake her heritage. We are not asking her to leave father, mother or family. We bring a message that Judah does not possess (*Ensign*, Dec. 1976, p. 72).

And LeGrand Richards said:

> As I understand this command we the prophets must turn our hearts unto the Jews, and then we may hope that they will turn their hearts unto us because of the message that we shall bring unto them through the restoration of the gospel in this dispensation (*CR*, Oct. 1956, p. 24).

If this did not happen the whole earth would be smitten with a curse and all flesh would be consumed because many prophecies could not be fulfilled as a result of the disobedience of the saints to this commandment (v. 17).

The Law of Retaliation and
the Law of Forgiveness (98:23-32; 39-48)

Otten and Caldwell state:

> To teach the saints how to dispel their feelings of hate and revenge toward their persecutors, the Lord counselled the saints to seek redress, not revenge. (See *D&C* 98:23-24) If they did not obtain justice under the laws of the land, they were to bear their afflictions patiently before the Lord. Even if their enemies were to come upon them a second and third time, they still were not to revile. Instead, the saints were to warn their enemy. The Lord further stated, that after the third time, the Lord would give the saints power over their enemy. (See *D&C* 98:25-29)
>
> To illustrate the above principle, we recall that the saints were driven from Jackson County, Missouri in 1833. In 1838, they were also driven from the state of Missouri. In 1845, they were driven from Illinois. On each of these three occasions, the saints collectively followed the counsel of the Lord in this revelation. They did not retaliate. Thus, the blessings promised in this revelation have literally been fulfilled for the benefit of the church. There are many third and fourth generation descendants who are now reaping the blessings because of the obedience of their forefathers. (See *D&C* 98:30) (*ST*, 2:167-68).

It is important to understand that although "it is written, Vengeance is mine . . . saith the Lord" (Rom. 12:19), the Lord does counsel the saints to seek justice under the laws of the land. If you are being abused, get help! Sister Aileen H. Clyde, Second Counselor in the Relief Society General Presidency, said:

If charity is not always quick to our understanding, it may occasionally be quick to our misunderstanding. It is not charity or kindness to endure any type of abuse or unrighteousness that may be inflicted on us by others. God's commandment that as we love him, we must respect ourselves, suggests we must not accept disrespect from others. It is not charity to let another repeatedly deny our divine nature and agency. It is not charity to bow down in despair and helplessness. That kind of suffering should be ended, and that is very difficult to do alone. There are priesthood leaders and other loving servants who will give aid and strength when they *know* of the need. We must be willing to let others help us (*Ensign* (Report of General Conference), Nov. 1991, 77).

Jesus said: "Whosoever shall smite thee on thy *right* cheek, turn to him the other also" (Matt. 5:39; emphasis added). Since most people are right-handed, a blow to the *right* cheek would be a back-handed slap to the face. A "slap in the face" is a blow to our pride and not a threat to our physical, emotional, mental, or spiritual well being. In cases that threaten our well being, we are to seek help under the laws of the Church and the laws of the land (see *D&C* 101:81-95). Seeking help and redress is not in conflict with the counsel given in *D&C* 98:40. Yes, we must forgive all people (remember the material for *D&C* 64:8-11, "Forgive All Men"), but this does not mean we must let someone continue to abuse us.

99
WHO RECEIVETH YOU RECEIVETH ME

Who Receiveth You Receiveth Me (99:1-5, 7-8)

Authorized servants of the Lord acting within their calling represent the Lord (v. 2). We must receive them as we would the Lord. (This is something to put into practice the next time the home teachers come over.) Also, as we act within our callings, we should be conscious that we are representing the Lord. We should ask ourselves what He would do if He were in our place. (This is something to put into practice the next time you are out visiting or home teaching.)

It Is Not Expedient That You Should Go until Your Children Are Provided For (99:6).

About a year and a half before the revelation in this section was given, John Murdock's wife, Julia, died leaving five small children behind. John was not to go on his mission until his children were cared for. John's infant twins were taken by Emma Smith to raise as her own. His three older children were sent to Bishop Partridge (the Bishop of Zion referred to in v. 6), who was a friend of the family.

100

TEACHING WITH POWER

Historical Context—
Missionaries, Let Your Hearts Be Comforted (100:1-4, 15)

Joseph Smith and Sidney Rigdon were on a mission to Canada and the eastern United States. They had been away from their families for several days. Joseph Smith was homesick and worried about his family. He wrote in his journal: "The Lord is with us, but have much anxiety about my family" (*HC*, 1:419). It is normal for missionaries to get homesick and worried about their families while they are away. To these missionaries, the Lord would say the same words that he did to Joseph Smith: "Your families . . . are in mine hands. . . . Therefore, let your hearts be comforted" (v. 1, 15).

Teaching with Power (100:5-8)

To teach with power we must follow the guidelines set out in these verses. We must:

1. **Speak the thoughts that the Lord shall put into our hearts (100:5).** This will be discussed along with the material for verse 6.

2. **Declare in the Lord's name (100:7).** When we wish to bear powerful testimony, we may say, "I testify in the name of Jesus Christ that. . . ." Or a missionary may say, "As a representative of the Lord Jesus Christ, I testify that. . . ." Naturally, this manner of testifying is sacred, and should be used with respect.

3. **Declare in solemnity of heart (100:7).** *Solemnity* means serious or dignified. Otten and Caldwell state: "Solemnity does not eliminate

humor in good taste, but it does not allow for making light of sacred things" (*ST*, 2:179).

4. **Declare in the spirit of meekness (100:7).** To declare things in the Lord's name requires that we be humble yet strong like He is.

When we follow these guidelines the Lord promises that:

1. **We will not be confounded before men (100:5).** We will not be confounded because of the following promise in verse 6.

2. **It shall be given in the very moment what to say (100:6).** This promise is based on a commandment that the Lord gave in section 84. To be given what to say in the very moment, we must be continually studying the word of God (*D&C* 84:85). Therefore, this promise does not mean that we need not prepare before we give a talk or teach a lesson. Also see John 14:26.

3. **The Holy Ghost will bear record of what we say (100:8).** This is what gives power to our teaching. Effective teaching of the gospel requires that the lesson touch *the hearts* of the students, not just their minds. Nephi said: "when a man speaketh by the power of the Holy Ghost the power of the Holy Ghost carrieth it unto the hearts of the children of men" (2 Ne. 33:1). The Spirit will carry what we say to people's hearts if we have followed the guidelines given in *D&C* 100:5-8 *and* if the people will let that Spirit in. Now is a good time to review 50:10-22 and the material for 11:21, "Convincing Power" and 42:4-17, "Laws on Teaching."

Orson Hyde and John Gould (100:14)

While Joseph Smith and Sidney Rigdon were on their mission they not only worried about their families, but also about the management and membership of the Church. Joseph was obviously concerned about two people in particular— Orson Hyde and John Gould. They had been sent from Kirtland to deliver important instructions from the First Presidency to the leaders of the Church in Jackson County (*DCC*, p. 634). The Lord assured Joseph Smith that these two brethren were in His hand (v. 14).

101

THEY MUST NEED BE CHASTENED AND TRIED
THE MILLENNIUM

Historical Context

Read the section heading.

On December 10, 1833 Joseph Smith wrote a letter to the Saints who had been run out of Zion. He wrote:

> Now, there are two things of which I am ignorant; and the Lord will not show them unto me . . . —and they are these; Why God has suffered so great a calamity to come upon Zion and what the great moving cause of this great affliction is; and again, by what means He will return her back to her inheritance, with songs of everlasting joy upon her head. These two things, brethren, are in part kept back that they are not plainly shown unto me (*HC*, 1:454).

This is an example of the honesty and humility of Joseph Smith. When he did not know something, he did not make things up and claim they came from the Lord. Six days later, however, the Lord did show the prophet why the saints had been cast out of Zion. The revelation given to the prophet is contained in this section.

Why the Saints Were Cast Out of Zion (101:1-8, 35-36)

Smith and Sjodahl wrote:

> In his letter to the scatted saints in Missouri, dated December 10th, 1833, the Prophet [Joseph Smith] stated that the spirit withheld from him definite knowledge of the reason why the calamity had fallen upon Zion. . . . On the 16th of December, however, this Revelation [Section 101] was received concerning the saints in Zion (*DCC*, p. 637).

The Lord gave two reasons why the saints were cast out of Zion.

1. **In consequence of their transgressions (101:1-2, 6-8).** The Lord had told the saints that possession of Zion would be based upon their obedience (remember 58:4, 6). When the persecution started in Zion, the Lord told the saints that they must speedily build the temple (remember the material for 97:10-17, "Let the Temple Be Built Speedily"). But

many of the saints did not take the Lord's counsel seriously (v. 7-8). The Lord had also told the saints that they must be pure in heart for Zion to prosper (remember the material for 97:18-28, "Zion Shall Prosper"). But the saints had not become pure in heart (v. 6). In consequence of their transgressions, the saints were cast out of Zion (v. 1-2).

Let us learn a lesson from these saints—especially the one taught in verse 8. Let us not, in the day of our peace, "esteem lightly" the revelations the Lord gives through His prophets. This way, we will not be "cast out" but will be prepared to inherit Zion and the celestial kingdom.

2. **They must needs be chastened and tried (101:3-5, 35-36).** The saints at this time needed to grow spiritually if they were to become the Lord's jewels (v. 2). Trials present us with the opportunity to mature spiritually. When we pass through this "baptism by fire" and remain true to the Lord, we are sanctified and become worthy to inherit Zion and celestial glory (v. 4-5, 35-36).

Some reasons we are chastened are:
1. to become clean (90:36);
2. to be led to forgiveness (remember the material for 95:1-2, 9-17, "Responsibilities of a Chastiser");
3. to be sanctified (101:5);
4. to learn obedience (105:6); and
5. to be refined as gold (Job 23:10).

You can read about Abraham's trial in Gen. 22:1-19. Obviously, Abraham's test was not to prove to the Lord what Abraham could do— the Lord knows everything. Abraham's trial was to show Abraham what he could do. George Q. Cannon said:

> The purpose was to impress upon Abraham a lesson, and to enable him to attain unto knowledge that he could not obtain in any other way. That is why God tries all of us. . . . He tries us for our own good, that we may know ourselves; for it is most important that a man should know himself (*CR*, Apr. 1899, p. 66).

Each of us will face trials in life. Although we will probably not be called upon to sacrifice our only son as Abraham was, we will face trials that will be just as difficult for us to pass through as it was for Abraham to offer up his son for a sacrifice. For some, this trial may be the loss of a loved one. For others, it may be dealing with the effects of a debilitating disease. For others, it may be overcoming sexual temptations, obeying the Word of Wisdom, paying tithing, serving a mission,

overcoming a low self-esteem, or attending Church meetings. These trials will help us mature and become more patient, long-suffering, kind,
and charitable as we endure them maintaining the pure love of Christ—
which is to love Christ and love others as Christ does.

Trials will be discussed further in the material for 122:5-8, "If Thou
Art Called To Pass Through Tribulation."

I Shall Come To Make Up My Jewels (101:3)

Remember the material for 60:4, "My Jewels."

Sanctified (101:5)

Remember the material for 20:31, "Sanctification."

I Will Remember Mercy (101:9-21, 35-42, 63-68)

The Lord did not completely "cast off" the saints (v. 9). He promised them:
1. mercy (v. 9);
2. justice (v. 10-11) (remember the material for 87:1-4, 6-7, "Prophesy of
   the United States' Civil War");
3. Israel would be gathered and saved (v. 12-13);
4. comfort (v. 14);
5. martyrs would be crowned (v. 15);
6. Zion would not be moved to another location and was in His hand (v.
   16-17); and
7. the eventual redemption of Zion and fulfillment of all the prophets'
   words (v. 18- 19).

Stakes (101:21)

Remember the material for 82:13-14 under the heading "Stakes."

Stand in Holy Places (101:22)

Remember the material for 87:8, "Stand in Holy Places."

The Second Coming (101:23-25)

Remember the material for 45:44-54, 56-57, 74-75, "Events at the Second
Coming."

The Millennium (101:26-34)

Millennium refers to a period of 1,000 years. "The Millennium" refers to the
1,000 years that are ushered in by the second coming of Christ. Some events of
the Second Coming and Millennium overlap. Therefore, some events of the
Millennium have already been discussed along with the material for 45:44-54,
56-57, 74-75, "Events at the Second Coming." In Section 101 and elsewhere we
gain some insight into what the Millennium will be like.

1. **"The enmity of all flesh shall cease" (101:26).** *Enmity* means hatred, hostility, or antagonism. It is usually used to imply that two things are antagonists.

2. **"Whatsoever any man shall ask, it shall be given" (101:27).** The Lord promises that "Whatsoever thing ye shall ask the Father in my name, which is good, in faith believing that ye shall receive, behold, it shall be done unto you" (Moroni 7:26; see also Mosiah 4:21; 3 Ne. 18:20; and Morm. 9:21). People living during the millennium will meet these conditions. The Lord promises these people, as He did such prophets as Enos and Nephi, "that all things shall be done unto thee according to thy word, for thou shalt not ask that which is contrary to my will" (Helaman 10:5; see also Enos 1:15).

3. **"Satan shall not have power to tempt any man" (101:28;** see also 43:30-31; 45:55). Satan will be bound in two ways. First, Satan will have no power "because of the righteousness of his [the Lord's] people" (1 Ne. 22:26). People will be "like unto Moroni" and "if all . . . were . . . like unto Moroni, behold, the very powers of hell would have been shaken . . . ; yea, the devil would never have power over the hearts of the children of men" (Alma 48:17). But the righteousness of the people is not enough to bind Satan (*CHMR*, 1:192). Another power is necessary. Satan will be bound by the power of God (v. 28).

   Children will grow up without any sin. This is further discussed in the material for 137:5-10, "Heirs of the celestial kingdom."

4. **"There is no death" (101:29-31).** Death will not be a separation of the spirit from the body. In the time it takes to blink, the body will change from a mortal body to a resurrected, immortal body. At what age will this take place? At "the age of a tree" (v. 30). How old is "the age of a tree?" Old.

   Note that translated beings have not yet been changed in this way (remember the material for Section 7 under the heading "John Did Not Die, but Will Die").

5. **The Lord "shall reveal all things" (101:32-34).** The Lord has blessed his saints with an abundance of knowledge, but there is still much we do not know about history, science, philosophy, and religion (v. 33). Some of it will not be revealed until the Lord comes again.

   The learning of man can only take us so far in discovering truth. For example, fill in the blanks in the following series of numbers:

   _____, 1, 2, 3, 4, 5, 6, _____

The business of science is to fill in "the blanks." This is done by examining the available data. When enough data is gathered, a pattern generally emerges. Then, based on the pattern, the blanks can be filled in.

So, what did you put in the blanks? The point of this exercise is that if you really believe you're right, you must have a lot of faith in your method of figuring out the answer. In other words, your answer is based on faith.

The fact is, science is based on faith. To start doing science, one must lay down a rule. This rule is called the principle of uniformity. It is that the laws in action "here" and "now" explain events everywhere throughout time. Without establishing this rule, one can't even begin to do science. You might say that today we are held to the earth by gravity, but tomorrow, by little invisible men pushing down on our heads. This is just no way to do science.

However, the principle of uniformity that all science is based on is an axiom, a postulate—in other words, an assumption. It is not a fact that can be proved. Can it be proved that the law of gravity will exist tomorrow? No. But how can we "fill in the blanks" unless we assume it will.

To go back to the fill-in-the-blanks example above, one can look at the sequence of numbers and assume that what goes in the blanks follows the same sequence. But what if the rules—the "laws"—that the sequence is based on could not be learned from the amount of information given? Or what if the "laws" changed when it came to the blanks? Then, to fill in the blanks, one would need more information. As our information base grew, we might have to change our minds about the answer. As I was told on my first day of medical school: "Half of what we teach you will be proved wrong. The problem is, we don't know which half."

The Lord, through His prophets, has given us more information about the "things of the earth, by which it was made, and the purpose and the end thereof" (v. 33). He has expanded our data base. Based on this revealed data, we know that the principle of uniformity (as we define it) that all theory is based on is not a solid foundation. Some scientific "laws" are only temporary and in conflict with the idea of eternity. And we know some scientific "laws" (like death) were not in effect as they are today about 6,000 years ago, before the fall. We also know something about the purpose of the earth (remember the material for 2:3, "The Earth Would Be Utterly Wasted"). But we obviously do not know everything. There will be some things at the time of the Second Coming that "no man knew" (v. 33).

Now is a good time to review the material for 88:77-80, "Of Things Both in Heaven and in the Earth."

6. **The Lord "will be their king and their lawgiver" (45:59).** Bruce R. McConkie wrote:

> The Church of Jesus Christ of Latter-day Saints is the kingdom of God on earth [remember the material for Section 65: "The Kingdom of God Prepares for the Kingdom of Heaven"]. . . . But for the present it functions as an ecclesiastical kingdom only.
>
> With the millennial advent, the kingdom of God on earth will step forth and exercise political jurisdiction over all the earth as well as ecclesiastical jurisdiction over its own citizens. When the saints pray, according to the Lord's pattern, "Thy kingdom come. Thy will be done in earth, as it is in heaven" (Matt. 6:10), they are petitioning the Father to send the political or millennial kingdom so that complete righteousness, both civically and religiously, will prevail on earth. . . .
>
> Until that glorious day when the Lord shall make "a full end of all nations" (D&C 87:6), when he shall reign "whose right it is to reign," the saints are commanded to "be subject to the powers that be." (D&C 58:22.) But in that day the whole system of government will be changed. Christ having previously come in the clouds of heaven to Adam-ondi-Ahman where "there was given him dominion, and glory, and a kingdom, *that all people, nations, and languages, should serve him*" (Dan. 7:13-14)—shall then take over the reigns of government personally. "Ye shall have no laws but my laws when I come, for I am your lawgiver," he has said. (D&C 38:22. . . .)
>
> At the time there will be two world capitals, "for out of Zion shall go forth the law, and the word of the Lord from Jerusalem." (Isa. 2:3; *Doctrines of Salvation*, vol. 3, pp. 66-72.) That resurrected personages will have positions of power and responsibility in the kingdom is evident from John's millennial statement: "And hast made us unto our God kings and priests: and we shall reign on the earth." (Rev. 5:10; 20:4.) Of this the Prophet Joseph Smith said: "Christ and the resurrected saints will reign over the earth during the thousand years. They will not probably dwell upon the earth, but will visit it when they please, or when it is necessary to govern it." (Teachings, p. 68.) Obviously many governmental offices will be filled by mortal persons living on the earth (*MD*, pp. 499-500).

With Christ reigning upon the earth, all people will come to a knowledge of the truth, "for the earth shall be full of the knowledge of the Lord, as the waters cover the sea." (Isa. 11:9; Hab. 2:14.) "And they shall teach no more every man his neighbor, and every man his brother, saying, Know the Lord: for *they shall all know me*, from the least of them unto the greatest of them, saith the Lord: for I will forgive their iniquity, and I will remember their sin no more." (Jer. 31:34; emphasis added).

However, not all people will choose to become members of the Lord's church. Elder McConkie wrote:

> Since all who are living at least a terrestrial law—the law of honesty, uprightness, and integrity—will be able to abide the day of our Lord's coming, there will be nonmembers of the Church on earth during the millennium. (*Doctrines of Salvation*, vol. 1, pp. 86-87; vol 3, pp. 63-64.) Honest and upright people who have been deceived by the false religions and false philosophies of the world will not have their free agency abridged. They will continue to believe their false doctrines until they voluntarily elect to receive gospel light. Speaking of the millennial period, Micah said, "*All people will walk every one in the name of his god*, and we will walk in the name of the Lord our God for ever and ever." (Micah 4:5.) (*MD*, p. 498-99.)

7. **"Temple work will be the great work of the Millennium" (*MD*, p. 501).** Elder McConkie wrote:

> Obviously, due to the frailties, incapacities, and errors of mortal men, and because the records of past ages are often scanty and inaccurate, this great [temple] work cannot be completed for every worthy soul without assistance from on high. The millennial era is the time, primarily, when this assistance will be given by resurrected beings. Genealogical records unknown to us will then become available. Errors committed by us in sealings or other ordinances will be rectified, and all things will be arranged in proper order (*MD*, p. 501).

The End of the Millennium and of the Earth

We only know a little bit about the Millennium. We know even less about what happens towards the end of the Millennium and afterwards. Bruce R. McConkie wrote:

> When the thousand years are ended Satan shall be loosed, men again shall begin to deny their God, and rebellion shall well up in the hearts of many. For a little season the devil will be free to gather together his armies, even the hosts of hell; and then the final battle will be fought in which Satan (who is Perdition) together with all his sons shall be cast out forever. (*D&C* 29:22-29; 43:31; 88:110-115; Rev. 20:7-10; 2 Ne. 9:16.) Then will come the end of the earth as it is now constituted [*D&C* 29:23-24], for it will attain its final destiny as a celestial sphere, and the meek shall inherit it forever. (*D&C* 88:16-20.)

Recall from the material for 45:44-54, 56-57, 74-75, "Events at the Second Coming" that the earth will go through two changes—one at the beginning of the Millennium and one at the end. Both of these changes are referred to as transfigurations. At the beginning of the Millennium, the earth will be transfigured from a telestial to a terrestrial world. Some of the conditions of a terrestrial world were discussed above. At the end of the Millennium, the earth will be transfigured to a celestial world. It will become like the place where God resides—"a sea of glass and fire"—"a great Urim and Thummim" (130:6-9). Brigham Young said:

> When it (the Earth) becomes celestialized, it will be like the sun, and be prepared for the habitation of the saints, and be brought back into the presence of the Father and the Son. It will not then be an opaque body as it now is, but it will be like the stars of the firmament, full of light and glory; it will be a body of light (*JD*, 7:163).

And:

> This earth, when it becomes purified and sanctified, or celestialized, will become like a sea of glass; and a person, by looking into it, can know things past, present, and to come (*JD*, 9:87).

Care Not for the Body (101:35-38)

This verse, obviously, does not mean we should not maintain our physical health. Read carefully the context in which verse 37 lies (v. 35-38). Many saints had died or were about to die due to mob violence. They did not need a sermon on eating properly and exercising. They needed to know that their spiritual integrity was more important than their physical life; that even in physical death, they could have eternal life if they would be patient and not deny their testimonies because of the mobs (v. 38).

The Salt of the Earth (101:39-42)

Salt does not spoil with age. Salt loses its savor when it gets contaminated and mixed up with other elements. So too, the gift of the Holy Ghost and spiritual covenants do not spoil with age. They lose their savor when contaminated with impure thoughts and sin or mixed with the ways of the world. This is why we are counseled to be careful about the "little things" such as the music we listen to, the way we dress, and the entertainment we seek (see Elder Carlos E. Asay's talk in *Ensign*, May 1980, pp. 42-43).

A Parable Concerning the Redemption of Zion (101:43-62)

Now would be a good time to review the material for Section 86 about parables, keys to understanding parables, and why the Lord teaches in parables. The following interpretations will also help:

1. *The nobleman* is the Lord
2. *A very choice spot of land* is Jackson County
3. *The vineyard* is the earth
4. *The olive trees* are places where the saints lived
5. *The watchmen* are Church leaders
6. *The tower* is the temple commanded to be built in Zion
7. *The servants* are members of the Church
8. *One of the Lord's servants* is Joseph Smith

As you recall (remember the material for 97:10-17, "Let the Temple Be Built Speedily" and 101:1-2, 6-8, "In Consequence of Their Transgressions"), the saints "became very slothful" and did not build the Temple (v. 46-50). Then "the enemy [mobs] came by night . . . and destroyed" the works of the saints (v. 51). The saints "were affrighted, and fled" (v. 51). After rebuking the saints (v. 52-54), the Lord "said unto one of his servants," Joseph Smith: "Go and gather together the residue of my servants . . . and redeem my vineyard" (v. 55-56).

Joseph Smith did as the Lord commanded and called the brethren to join Zion's Camp. They were to redeem Zion not by force, but by buying up the land (103:23). We will learn more of the story in Section 103: "Zion's Camp." The moral of the story is that the redemption of Zion would occur "when I [the Lord] will" (v. 59-60). As we will see in the sections to follow, this was not to happen for "many days" (v. 62), but it will eventually happen (v. 56, 62).

Note that similar parables comparing the redemption of Zion to the Lord's vineyard are given in Isaiah 5:1-7; Matthew 21:33-46; and Jacob 5.

Wisdom Concerning Zion (101:63-75, 96-101)

In these verses, the Lord gives more instructions concerning Zion. He tells them that they already have enough to redeem Zion (v. 75) but it cannot be done "in haste, nor by flight" (v. 68).

The churches spoken of in these verses are the branches of the Church. The parable of the wheat and the tares spoken of in verses 64-66 is discussed in the material for Section 86: "The Parable of the Wheat and the Tares." The lands to be purchased spoken of in verses 70-74 are discussed in the material for Section 57: "Zion: Independence, Missouri Is the Center Place."

In verses 96-101, the saints are told not to sell their lands to their enemies. Their lands were actually the Lord's lands (v. 56). Although the enemy would pollute the land (v. 97), the Lord did not want the saints to consent to this pollution by selling their lands (v. 97). The Lord promised the saints that He would take care of the enemy and the saints would eventually inherit their lands (v. 98, 100-101).

The Constitution Should Be Maintained for the Rights of All Flesh (101:76-80)

The constitutional law of the land and its protection of "all flesh" (101:77) will be discussed in the material for Section 134: "Church and State."

I Established the Constitution by the Hands of Wise Men (101:80)

Ezra Taft Benson taught:

> The temple work for the fifty-six signers of the Declaration of Independence and other Founding Fathers has been done. All these appeared to Wilford Woodruff when he was president of the St. George Temple [*CR*, Apr. 1898, pp. 89-90]. President George Washington was ordained a high priest at that time. You will also be interested to know that, according to Wilford Woodruff's journal, John Wesley, Benjamin Franklin, and Christopher Columbus were also ordained high priests at that time (*TETB*, p. 604).

See Section 134: "Church and State" for further discussion of the Constitution.

Redeemed the Land by the Shedding of Blood (101:80)

See footnote *b* of this verse.

Obedience to Law (101:76-95)

Wait until we get to Section 134: "Church and State."

My Strange Act (101:95)

Remember the material for 95:4, "My Strange Act."

102

CHURCH COURTS

Historical Context

Read the section heading and verses 1-2.

Joseph Smith said:

> No man is capable of judging a matter, in council, unless his own heart is pure; and that we are frequently so filled with prejudice, or have a beam in our own eye, that we are not capable of passing right decisions.

Our acts are recorded, and at a future day they will be laid before us, and if we should fail to judge right and injure our fellow beings, they may there, perhaps, condemn us; there they are of great consequence, and to me the consequence appears to be of force, beyond anything which I am able to express. Ask yourselves, brethren, how much you have exercised yourselves in prayer since you heard of this council; and if you are now prepared to sit in council upon the soul of your brother (*HC*, 2:25-26).

To help the high councilors judge righteously, the Lord shows them how to organize their Church courts in this section.

Standing Councils (102:3)

"Standing," here, means open at all times. The high council is to be open at all times to conduct hearings. This ensures that the purposes of the high council are carried out in a timely manner.

The Purpose of Church Courts

The purpose of Church courts is to protect the Church, as well as the individual being tried, from insult and injustice (v. 15-17). For this reason the council is divided into two groups. One group has the responsibility to protect the Church, and the other, the individual being tried (v. 12-18). After the council has met, the president, assisted by his two counselors, makes a decision. The high council is then asked to sustain this decision. The president's decision is final unless:

1. **The councilors discover an error in the decision of the president.** When this occurs, the case shall have a rehearing (v. 20-23).
2. **Either party is dissatisfied with the decision.** When this occurs, an appeal is made to the First Presidency. The decision of the First Presidency is final (v. 27, 33).

Other Church Tribunals

1. **The Bishop's Court (107:68-72).** This court has jurisdiction over members within its ward boundaries. It cannot excommunicate a man who holds the Melchizedek priesthood.
2. **The Stake High Council Court (102:1-23).** This court consists of the stake presidency and twelve high councilors. A temporary councilor can be appointed in the absence of one of the regular high councilors.
3. **The First Presidency Court (68:22-24; 107:78-81).** This court consists of the First Presidency, their clerk, and the Quorum of Twelve Apostles. It has jurisdiction over the entire church. Like the above two courts, it can claim original jurisdiction. It is also a court of last appeal. (Also see the material for 68:22-24, "The First Presidency Tries the Presiding Bishop.")

There is no person or position in the Church above the Church court system. The Church can protect itself from the actions of any of its members and every member can be protected from insult and injustice (v. 15-17). For this reason, there are other Church tribunals which open when the need arises. These include the Presiding Bishop's Court (opened when a member of the First Presidency must be tried) and the Quorum of Twelve Apostle's Court (opened when a member of this quorum must be tried). The other court spoken of in this section is the Council of the High Priests When Abroad (102:24-26). It consisted of any 12 High Priests where a stake did not exist. It was only necessary in the early days of the Church.

Concerning the specifics of each court and how it functions, Priesthood leaders should follow the policies and procedures outlined in the Church's *General Handbook of Instructions.*

Results of Church Court Action

1. **Exoneration.** No action is necessary because the person is innocent.
2. **Probation.** The person is given goals to reach to demonstrate repentance. If the goals are not reached, a Church court can take further action.
3. **Disfellowship.** The person may attend Church meetings (except priesthood), pay tithes and offerings, and, if endowed, wear temple garments but cannot offer public prayer, partake of the sacrament, hold a temple recommend or Church calling, or exercise the priesthood (*DCSM*, p. 410).
4. **Excommunication.** Elder Spencer W. Kimball wrote:

> The scriptures speak of Church members being "cast out" [41:5; 42:21-37, 75] or "cut off," [1:14; 50:8; 56:10; 85:11; 104:9; 133:63] or having their names "blotted out." [20:83.] This means excommunication. This dread action means the total severance of the individual from the Church. The person who is excommunicated loses his membership in the Church and all attendant blessings. As an excommunicant, he is in a worse situation than he was before he joined the Church. He has lost the Holy Ghost, his priesthood, his endowments, his sealings, his privileges and his claim upon eternal life. . . .
>
> An excommunicant has no Church privileges. He may not attend priesthood meetings (since he has no priesthood); he may not partake of the sacrament, serve in Church positions, offer public prayers, or speak in meetings; he may not pay tithing except under certain conditions as determined by the bishop (*MF*, p. 329).

Concerning the forgiveness of sins, remember the material for Section 72 under the heading "Some Duties of a Bishop."

Let Accountability Rest with the Church Council

Elder Spencer W. Kimball wrote:

> Some people not only cannot or will not forgive and forget the transgressions of others, but go to the other extreme of hounding the alleged transgressor. Many letters and calls have come to me from individuals who are determined to take the sword of justice in their own hands and presume to see that a transgressor is punished. "That man should be excommunicated," a woman declared, "and I'm never going to rest till he has been properly dealt with." Another said, "I can never rest, so long as that person is a member of the Church." Still another said: "I will never enter the chapel so long as that person is permitted to enter. I want him tried for his membership." One man even made many trips to Salt Lake City and wrote several long letters to protest against the bishop and the stake president who did not take summary disciplinary action against a person who, he claimed, was breaking the laws of the Church.
>
> To such who would take the law into their own hands, we read again the positive declaration of the Lord: there remaineth in him the greater sin." (*D&C* 64:9.) The revelation continues: "And ye ought to say in your hearts—let God judge between me and thee, and reward thee according to thy deeds." (*D&C* 64:11.) When known transgressions have been duly reported to the proper ecclesiastical officers of the Church, the individual may rest the case and leave the responsibility with the Church officers. If those officers tolerate sin in the ranks, it is an awesome responsibility for them and they will be held accountable (*MF*, p.264).

Now is a good time to review the material for 50:4-9, "Hypocrites in the Church" and 64:8-11, "Forgive All Men."

103

ZION'S CAMP

Historical Context

The saints had been driven out of Jackson County, Missouri—the land of Zion (remember Section 101). They wanted to know how to get the land back in order to redeem Zion. In this section, the Lord showed the saints how they could do this.

Inasmuch as They Harken unto the Lord's Counsel, They Will Prevail (103:1-14)

In the first four verses of this section, the Lord reminds the saints of the reasons why they were cast out of Zion (remember Section 101). Then the Lord promises that they will prevail against His enemies and redeem Zion if they hearken unto His counsel (v. 5-14).

They Are as Salt (103:10)

Remember the material for 101:39-42, "The Salt of the Earth."

The Redemption of Zion must Needs Come by Power (103:15-20)

Zion will not be redeemed by human power, but by the power of the Lord. The Lord will direct the redemption of Zion through His prophet (v. 16). As the saints obey the prophet, they will receive power from the Lord and His angels (v. 17-20). In Section 105, we will read how the Lord taught the saints how to receive this power.

The Man like Moses (103:16)

This prophecy was partially fulfilled when the Prophet Joseph Smith led Zion's Camp to Missouri. The man like Moses not only refers to Joseph Smith, but to any president of the Church (*D&C* 107:91).

The Parable of the Vineyard (103:21)

Remember the material for 101:43-62, "A Parable Concerning the Redemption of Zion." Specifically note 101:55. In fulfillment of this parable, Joseph Smith organized and led Zion's Camp to Missouri.

The Lord's Counsel to Organize Zion's Camp (103:22-40)

The Lord commands that the saints in Ohio send a relief expedition to help the saints who had been cast out of Zion. This expedition came to be known as Zion's Camp. The Lord promised the saints would prevail against their enemies if they obeyed Him (v. 5-14). He told them that the blessing of victory was predicated upon their "diligence, faithfulness, and prayers" (v. 36). But the saints at this time did not obey the Lord's counsel; therefore, they had no promise. Zion would not be redeemed at that time. See the material for Section 105: "Zion: Requirements for the Redemption Of" for more information about the redemption of Zion.

Churches (103:23)

"Churches," here, refers to wards or stakes.

Ye Shall Curse Them (103:24-25)

Remember the material for 60:15, "Shake off the Dust of Thy Feet."

Unto the Third and Fourth Generation (103:26)
Wait until we come to the material for 124:50-52, "Unto the Third and Fourth Generation."

The Eastern Countries (103:29)
"The eastern countries," here, refers to the eastern states of the United States.

104

THE UNITED ORDER

Historical Background
The key to understanding section 104 is to remember that the United Firm was a business partnership of a few of the Church leaders and not the same thing as the law of consecration practiced by the entire Church. (Remember the material for sections 51: "The Law of Consecration and Stewardship" and 78: "Purposes of the Law of Consecration and Stewardship.")

The United Firm struggled to fulfill its purposes but suffered serious financial setbacks. Legal fees and travel expenses had to be paid to defend against a law suit brought by an apostate named Philastus Hurlburt (see *HC*, 1:355, 475); a vicious mob destroyed the Church printing press and Gilbert's store (see *HC*, 1:393, 411 and "Outrage in Jackson County," *Evening and Morning Star*, Dec. 1833, p. 118); and certain members of the Firm were not completely faithful (*D&C* 104:3). By late 1833, the members of the Firm knew they would not be able to pay back its loans without help from the Saints. And on April 23, 1834—not being able to come up with the needed funds—the United Firm was dissolved. On that day, Joseph Smith received a revelation (*D&C* 104) on how to go about dissolving the United Firm.

The second edition of the Doctrine and Covenants was being prepared in the summer of 1835. Revelations about the United Firm (now sections 78, 82, 92, 96, and 104) were to be included in this edition because they taught important principles about the gospel and consecration. However, some of the Firm's debts were still not paid (Cook, p. 65). To protect the Firm's members from persecution, code names were substituted for the members' names. Code names were also substituted for the name of the United Firm. These code names included "the United Order" and "the Order of Enoch" (Cook, p. 65). The code names of the Firm's members have since been changed back to their real names (see the heading to Section 78). However, the terms "United Order," "Order of Enoch," "law of consecration," and "law of consecration and stewardship" are now mostly used interchangeably. It must be clearly understood, though, that the United Order (Firm) was only one system used by no more than a dozen men to obey the law of consecration and stewardship. And, although the Order/Firm was dissolved, the law of consecration and stewardship was never revoked. Lyndon W. Cook states:

> Inasmuch as the members of the [United Firm] partnership were also presiding Church leaders, it is difficult to determine which of their financial transactions were purely personal and which were purely ecclesiastical. This dual relationship has led some writers to erroneously conclude that the United Firm directly administered the law of consecration. While it is true that these presiding officers had supervisory responsibilities over Church finances, including the program of consecration, at this particular time the church bishop administered the program of consecration. The United Firm was essentially a private business concern (p. 58).

Dissolving the Firm (104:1-11, 19-86)

In *D&C* 104:1-10 the Lord reviews the serious nature of the covenant the members of the Firm had made. Verses 11 and 19-46 detail how the properties of the Firm are to be divided up among its members. In verses 47-53, the Lord explains that each member—whether a member of the Kirtland, Ohio or the Zion, Missouri branch of the United Firm—was now to "do their business in their own name" (v. 49). In verses 54-77 the Lord emphasizes that even though each member of the Firm was now responsible for his own stewardship, the property and money was still the Lord's. To help the members of the now dissolved Firm be "wise and faithful" stewards—using their stewardship for the purposes the Lord outlines in these verses—a treasurer was to be appointed to guard the treasury (v. 60-61). Profits made from a member's stewardship were to be put in the treasury (v. 68). The contents of the treasury could only be withdrawn by the majority vote of the members of the Firm or by revelation from the Lord (v. 64, 70-71). Although the United Firm was now dissolved, its debts still needed to be paid. In verses 78-86, the Lord explains how the members of the Firm were to pay their debts.

Principles of the United Order for All To Live By (104:12-16, 18)

Why include a revelation given to members of the United (business) Firm in the Doctrine and Covenants? Because the overall principles of the Firm apply to all people. All of us will be asked to give an account of our stewardships to the Lord, "for it is expedient that I, the Lord, should make *every* man accountable" (v. 12-13; emphasis added). We must all learn the lesson that everything is the Lord's. If we are ever going to be like Him, we must learn how to provide for people the way He does (v. 14-16). Although the Lord is rich, He is humble. His lowliness can exalt us all (v. 16; Moses 1:39). One who will not follow the Lord's path, "shall, with the wicked, lift up his eyes in hell" (v. 18).

There Is Enough and to Spare (104:17)

Elder Ezra Taft Benson wrote:

> The precepts of men would have you believe that by limiting the population of the world, we can have peace and plenty. That is the doctrine of the devil. Small numbers do not insure peace; only righteousness does. After all, there were only a handful of men on the earth when Cain interrupted the peace of Adam's household by slaying Abel. On the other hand, the whole city of Enoch was peaceful; and it was taken into heaven because it was made up of righteous people.
>
> And so far as limiting the population in order to provide plenty is concerned, the Lord answered that falsehood in the Doctrine and Covenants when He said [*D&C* 104:17 quoted] (*God, Family, Country*, pp. 257-8).

Millions of starving people live in fertile lands. "Nevertheless, when the wicked rule the people mourn" (*D&C* 98:9; see also Prov. 29:2). As Margaret Thatcher, prime minister of Great Britain from 1979-1990, said:

> If resources were the key to wealth, the richest country in the world would be Russia, because it has abundant supplies of everything from oil, gas, platinum, gold, silver, aluminum, and copper to timber, water, wildlife, and fertile soil.
>
> Why isn't Russia the wealthiest country in the world? Why aren't other resource-rich countries in the Third World at the top of the list? It is because their governments deny citizens the liberty to use their God-given talents. Man's greatest resource is himself, but he must be free to use that resource (*Imprimis*, March 1995, p. 4).

Why cultivate the land if the ravages of war, civil unrest, or brutal taxation will eat up the crops before they can be harvested? However, given their freedom, productive citizens will find that indeed "the earth is full" (104:17). And upon obedience to the commandments, they will find "a blessing, that there shall not be room enough to receive it" (Malachi 3:10-12).

Think what would happen economically if the world were to live according to gospel principles. Just think of little things. For example, just insurance fraud costs us millions of dollars a year. Now think of bigger things. Crime costs the world trillions of dollars.[10] Now add in the cost of disobeying the Word of

---

10. One study estimated that the total cost (not including harder-to-estimate things such as lost sales and jobs when businesses must close) of crime in the United States in 1984 was $92.5 billion (Mark A. Cohen, "Pain, Suffering and Jury Awards: A Study of the Cost of Crime to Victims," *Law and Society Review*, Vol. 22, 1988, p. 539). And another study showed the cost of putting a criminal in jail in the U. S. is about $25,000 per year; but the cost to society of leaving the criminal loose on the streets is about $430,000 per year (National Center for Policy analysis, "1992 Update: Why Does Crime Pay?" Dec. 8, 1992).

Wisdom and law of chastity. What you come up with is trillions of dollars per year that could be used by people to cure disease, improve fuel and food production, provide jobs, and help people out of tragic circumstances. Yes, when the world does things the Lord's way, it will see that "the earth is full, and there is enough and to spare" (*D&C* 104:16-17).

Stakes (104:40, 48)
Remember the material for 82:13-14, "Stakes."

The Joseph Smith Translation (104:58)
Remember the material for Section 91: "The Apocrypha."

105

REQUIREMENTS FOR THE REDEMPTION OF ZION

Historical Context—
Wait for a Little Season for the Redemption of Zion
The saints in Zion had been forced off their land (remember Sections 98 and 101). The Lord commanded them to organize Zion's Camp to get back their land (remember Section 103). The Lord promised the saints that they would get back their land if they obeyed Him (*D&C* 103:1-14). He told them that Zion could only be redeemed by power—the power of the Lord (remember *D&C* 103:15-20). When the leaders of Zion's Camp arrived near Jackson county, they held negotiations with the governor, but the governor refused to help the saints. Because the saints had not been obedient to the word of the Lord, Zion's Camp did not have enough men or money to take back their land without the help of the governor and the state militia. Because of their disobedience, the saints did not have the Lord's power to help them redeem Zion.

The revelation in this section was given while Zion's Camp was stationed near Jackson County. The Lord reveals to them that because of disobedience, Zion could not be redeemed in 1834. The saints would have to wait a little season for the redemption of Zion (v. 9).

1. **The saints must be unified (105:4).** Remember the material for 29:6, "Unity."
2. **The saints must learn obedience (105:6).**

3. **The saints must be taught more perfectly (105:10).** Remember the material for 42:4-17, "Laws on Teaching;" 84:43-62, "Remember the New Covenant, Even the Book of Mormon;" and 100:5-8, "Teaching with Power."

4. **The saints must gain experience in and knowledge of their duties (105:10).**

5. **The saints must be endowed with power (105:11-12, 37).** The Lord said "the redemption of Zion must needs come by power" (*D&C* 103:15). In *D&C* 105:11-12, the Lord states that in order to redeem Zion, the saints must be endowed with power. *Endowment* means gift. The gift of righteous power comes from the Lord. Since the time this revelation was received, the Lord has given the saints many gifts of power. Otten and Caldwell note:

> The restoration of the Quorum of Twelve Apostles, temple ordi- nances and privileges, welfare programs, priesthood correlation, world- wide missionary efforts, and restoration of certain keys of priesthood are but a few of the many ways the Lord has endowed His church with power (*ST*, 2:213).

One of the gifts of power that the Lord has to offer us is called the endowment. This gift and covenant can only be received in the temple. The saints at the time this revelation was given had still not completed the Kirtland Temple (remember Section 95). The Lord again empha- sizes the importance of the temple as the center place of Zion. (Even after the saints completed the Kirtland Temple, they did not receive the full endowment that faithful members of the Church can receive today.)

6. **The saints must become sanctified (105:31).** Refer to the material for 20:30-31, "Justification" and "Sanctification."

Throw Down the Towers and Scatter the Watchmen (105:16)

Remember the material for *D&C* 101:43-62, "A Parable Concerning the Redemption of Zion."

Unto the Third and Fourth Generation (105:30)

See the material for 124:50-52, "Unto the Third and Fourth Generation."

Sue for Peace (105:38)

This phrase means to beg or plead for peace.

106

CHILDREN OF LIGHT

Warren Cowdery Called to Devote His Whole Time (106:1-3, 6-8)

In these verses, Warren Cowdery is given counsel, promised blessings, and called to work full-time for the Church. The Lord said that he should be compensated for this work (v. 3) (remember the material for *D&C* 42:53, 55, 70-73, "A Just Remuneration").

Children of Light (106:4-5)

Jesus is the light of the world (93:2). The Lord counsels the saints to "be the children of light" so that they will be prepared for His second coming. To be "children of light" means to accept Jesus as the father of our salvation and follow His teachings. In Section 95, the Lord chastised the saints for "walking in darkness at noon-day" (95:6). They were not yet "children of light." Therefore, they were not prepared for the redemption of Zion or the Lord's second coming.

Gird up Your Loins (106:5)

Remember the material for *D&C* 36:8, "Gird up Your Loins."

107

PRIESTHOOD ORGANIZATION

Historical Context

Read the section heading.

On February 14, 1835 the Quorum of Twelve Apostles was organized (*HC*, 2:181-91). It was now six weeks later. They were about to be separated to go on missions. In this section, the Lord teaches the Apostles more about their callings, the priesthood, and Church government.

The Priesthood Is Greater than its Appendages (107:5)

Elder Bruce R. McConkie illustrated this principle when he wrote:

The priesthood is greater than any of its offices. No office adds any power, dignity, or authority to the priesthood. All offices derive their rights, prerogatives, graces, and powers from the priesthood. This principle may be diagramed by dividing a circle into segments. The priesthood is the circle; the segments of the circle are the callings or offices in the priesthood. Anyone who serves in a segment of the circle must possess the power of the whole circle. No one can hold an office in the priesthood with out first holding the priesthood.

Thus it is that priesthood is *conferred* upon worthy individuals, and they are then *ordained* to offices in the priesthood; and thus it is that all offices in the priesthood and in the Church are specifically designated as *appendages* to the priesthood; that is, they grow out of the priesthood, they are supplemental to it, they are less than the priesthood in importance. (*D&C* 84:29-30; 107:5.) It follows that it is greater and more important to hold the Melchizedek Priesthood, for instance, than it is to hold any office in that priesthood. . . .

Further, there is no *advancement* from one office to another within the Melchizedek Priesthood. Every elder holds as much priesthood as an apostle or as the President of the Church, though these latter officers hold greater administrative assignments in the kingdom. It follows, also, that any holder of the Melchizedek Priesthood could perform any priestly function he was appointed to do by the one holding the keys of the kingdom. Normally a priesthood bearer works in the particular segment of the priesthood circle in which his primary responsibility lies. (*Gospel Doctrine*, 5th ed., pp. 148-149; Teachings, p. 112.) (*MD*, pp. 595-96).

The Power and Authority of the Melchizedek Priesthood (107:1-12, 14-19)

These verses speak mainly of two powers of the Melchizedek Priesthood.

1. **The right of presidency (v. 8-12, 14-17).** This includes serving as the president of the Aaronic Priesthood (v. 14-17).
2. **The keys of spiritual blessings (v. 18-19).** It is by the power of the Melchizedek Priesthood that one receives the gift of the Holy Ghost, a patriarchal blessing, and the endowment of knowledge and power that comes from making temple covenants.

The Power and Authority of the Aaronic Priesthood (107:13-17, 20)

Remember the material for Section 13: "John the Baptist Restores the Aaronic Priesthood."

The Office of a Bishop (107:13-15, 68-76)

Remember the material for Section 72 under the heading: "Some Duties of a Bishop."

A Literal Descendant of Aaron (107:15-17, 69-70, 73, 76)

Remember the material for *D&C* 68:15-21, "The Presiding Bishop."

Presiding Officers and Offices (107:21-41, 58-67, 85-98)

1. **The President of the Church (107:91-92).**
2. **The First Presidency (107:22).**
3. **The Quorum of Twelve Apostles (107:23-24, 33-35, 38-39, 58).** The first Quorum of Twelve Apostles of this dispensation had just been ordained (remember the historical context). In these verses, the Lord teaches them about three of the duties of their new calling:
    1. to be special witnesses of Christ in all the world (v. 23);
    2. to hold the keys of missionary work (v. 35); and
    3. to ordain and set in order other Church officers (v. 58).

    This quorum is also to be equal in authority and power to the First Presidency (v. 24). This is only true when there is no First Presidency and the conditions in verses 27-31 are met (see *CR*, Apr. 1970, pp. 117-124). Now is a good time to review the material for *D&C* 43:7, "The Gate."
4. **The Quorum of Seventy (107:25-26, 34, 38, 93-97).** The main responsibility of members of this quorum is missionary work, as directed by the Quorum of Twelve Apostles. The Quorum of Seventy's leadership is described in verses 93-95. The *Doctrine and Covenants Student Manual* explains:

    > Although the First Quorum of the Seventy was organized by Joseph Smith, it did not continue to function as a quorum after the exodus to Utah. After the colonization of the West, quorums of seventies were organized in each stake; but on a general authority level, there was just the First Council of Seventy, or the First Seven Presidents of the Seventy.
    >
    > Not until the time of President Spencer W. Kimball was the First Quorum of the Seventy organized again. . . . (*Ensign*, Nov. 1975, p. 4) (p. 286).

    In the Fall of 1986, the seventies quorums in the stakes of the Church were discontinued; however, the stakes were urged to emphasize missionary work by establishing stake mission presidencies and stake missionaries (statement approved by the First Presidency and Council of the Twelve Apostles announced by President Ezra Taft Benson in the priesthood session of General Conference; see *Ensign*,

Nov. 1986, pp. 48, 97-98). Then, in the Spring of 1989, a Second Quorum of Seventy was formed (see Ensign, May 1989, p. 17). Its members, like members of the First Quorum of Seventy, are general authorities of the Church. And "if the labor in the vineyard of necessity requires it," more Quorums of Seventy can be formed (v. 95-96).

The First Quorum of Seventy is to be equal in authority to the First Presidency and Quorum of Twelve Apostles (107:26). This is only true when there is no First Presidency, no Quorum of Twelve Apostles, and the conditions in verses 27-31 are met.

5. **The Standing High Councils, at the stakes of Zion (107:36-37).** The Quorum of Twelve Apostles are a "Traveling Presiding High Council" (v. 33). This means they have authority throughout the world—they have "general" authority. A "Standing" High Council, on the other hand, only "stands" with authority in its stake. Each stake high council is equal in authority to other stake high councils in the way each presides over their own stake (v. 37; HC 2:220).

The historical context of verse 36 must be understood. At the time this revelation was given there were only two Standing High Councils. One was in Kirtland, Ohio, the other in Clay County, Missouri. The Kirtland, Ohio council was the first High Council organized and was presided over by the First Presidency. This council had general authority over the entire Church (D&C 102:9-10; JD, 19:241). Because it was presided over by the First Presidency and had general authority, this council formed "a quorum equal in authority . . . to the quorum of the presidency, or to the traveling high council" (v. 36). However, as stated above, Standing High Councils now only have authority within their stake boundaries.

6. **The Patriarch (107:39-41).** An evangelist or evangelical minister is a patriarch (HC, 3:381). Bruce R. McConkie explains:

> The office of *patriarch to the Church* is conferred as a result of lineage and worthiness; *stake patriarchs* are chosen and ordained by the apostles without respect to lineage. Patriarchs are also high priests. (D&C 107:39-53) Their special priestly assignment is to give patriarchal blessings to members of the Church, but they can also perform any duty of a high priest. . . .
>
> . . . In addition to ordained patriarchs, there are also natural patriarchs. Every holder of the higher priesthood who has entered into the patriarchal order of celestial marriage—thereby receiving for himself the blessings of the patriarchs Abraham, Isaac, and Jacob—is a natural patriarch to his posterity (MD, p. 560).

And:

> In modern times it [the office of patriarch to the Church] descended from Joseph Smith, Sr., to his son, Hyrum Smith (*D&C* 124:91-96), and has continued on in that rightful lineage to the present time. . . .
>
> Of the patriarch to the Church the Lord says: "He shall hold the keys of the patriarchal blessings upon the heads of all my people." (*D&C* 124:92.) As one of the General Authorities, the patriarch to the Church stands next in order to the members of the Council of the Twelve (*MD*, p. 561).

That a literal descendant must still be worthy is discussed in the material for *D&C* 68:15-21, "The Presiding Bishop."

7. **The Elders' Quorum (107:60, 89-90).** Each quorum can be made up of up to 96 Elders. Some of an Elder's duties are discussed in *D&C* 20:45.

8. **The Priests' Quorum (107:61, 87-88).** The president of this quorum of up to 48 Priests is the ward's Bishop. Some of a Priest's duties are discussed in *D&C* 20:46-52.

9. **The Teachers' Quorum (107:62, 86).** A Teacher is president of a quorum of up to 24 Teachers. Some of a Teacher's duties are discussed in *D&C* 20:53-59.

10. **The Deacons' Quorum (107:62, 85).** A Deacon is president of a quorum of up to 12 Deacons. Some of a Deacon's duties are discussed in *D&C* 20:57-59.

11. **Other Officers of the Church (107:98).** President Gordon B. Hinckley explained:

> Now in the ongoing of this work, administrative changes sometimes occur. The doctrine remains constant. But from time to time there are organizational and administrative changes made under provisions set forth in the revelations (*Ensign*, May 1995, p. 51).

President Hinckley explained that "twenty-eight years ago the First Presidency was inspired to call men to serve as regional representatives of the Twelve" and that "more recently the Presidency were inspired to call men from the Seventy to serve in area presidencies." He then announced that the office of regional representative would be dissolved and a new office would be created "to be known as an area authority" (*Ensign*, May 1995, p. 52). President Hinckley explained that these kinds of administrative changes are provided for in *D&C* 107:98.

Duties of quorum presidents will be discussed in the material for Section 112: "Some Duties of Church Leaders."

Stakes (107:36-37, 74)

Remember the material for 82:13-14, "Stakes."

The Church Conference at Adam-ondi-Ahman (107:42-57)

Wait until we come to Section 116: "Adam-ondi-Ahman."

Church Courts (107:76-84)

Remember the material for Section 102: "Church Courts."

Let Every Man Learn His Duty (107:99-100)

Elder James E. Faust said: "President Lee placed the emphasis on let, in the sense of permitting or allowing those given responsibilities to function within their callings without unnecessary restrictions" (*CR*, Apr. 1973, p. 114).

Also, remember the material for 10:4, "But Be Diligent."

108

STRENGTHEN YOUR BRETHREN

Lyman Sherman (108:1-6, 8)

Lyman Sherman was a president of the First Quorum of Seventy. The Lord promised Elder Sherman that as he remained worthy, he would be called to be numbered among the "first" (presiding) Elders of the Church (v. 4). Elder Sherman was later called to the Quorum of Twelve Apostles, but he died before he was ordained an Apostle. His priesthood continues with him on the other side of the veil (*D&C* 124:130; 138:57).

Strengthen Your Brethren (108:7)

Lyman Sherman was counseled to strengthen his brethren in four ways.

1. In all your conversation (108:7). George F. Richards said:

> When we say anything bad about the leaders of the Church, whether true or false, we tend to impair their influence and their usefulness and are thus working against the Lord and his cause. When we speak well

of our leaders, we tend to increase their influence and usefulness in the service of the Lord (*CR*, Apr. 1947, p. 24).

2. **In all your prayers (108:7).** President Kimball said:

> I have all my life sustained my leaders, praying for their welfare, and I have in these past years felt a great power coming to me from similar prayers of the saints, raised to heaven on my behalf (BYU Speeches of the Year, 1979, p. 164).

3. **In all your exhortations (108:7).** We are to strengthen our brethren in our teachings. We should teach that we are to receive the prophet's words as if from the mouth of the Lord (remember the material for Section 21: "Follow the Prophet").

4. **In all your doings (108:7).** Our brethren are not perfect but we strengthen them by obeying their counsel. Joseph Smith said:

> I was but a man, and they must not expect me to be perfect; if they expected perfection from me, I should expect it from them; but if they would bear with my infirmities and the infirmities of the brethren, I would likewise bear with their infirmities (*TPJS*, p. 268).

109
DEDICATORY PRAYER OF THE KIRTLAND TEMPLE

Historical Context

In December of 1832, the saints were commanded to build a temple in Kirtland (*D&C* 88:119; also remember the material for Section 95: "Responsibilities of a Chastiser"). On March 27, 1836 Joseph Smith dedicated the Kirtland Temple. The dedicatory prayer was an inspired prayer. Joseph Smith wrote it out and then read it at the temple dedication. President Joseph Fielding Smith said:

> Dedicatory prayers for temples . . . are formal and long and cover many matters of doctrine and petition. This pattern was set by the Prophet Joseph Smith in the dedication of the Kirtland Temple. The prayer given on that occasion was

revealed to him by the Lord; all prayers used since then have been written by the spirit of inspiration and have been read by such of the Brethren as have been appointed to do so (*Church News*, Feb. 12, 1972 in *ST*, 2:240).

Dedicatory Prayers

President Joseph Fielding Smith taught: "When we dedicate a house to the Lord, what we really do is dedicate ourselves to the Lord's service, with a covenant that we shall use the house in the way He intends that it shall be used" (*Church News*, Feb. 12, 1972 in *ST* 2:240). How does the Lord intend that we shall use His buildings and homes? Review the material for 65:3-6, "The Purpose of the Church" and Section 94: "The Lord's Buildings."

The Son of Man (109:5)

Remember the material for 45:39, "The Son of Man."

Blessings Promised and Requested (109:6-80)

1. **Blessings promised for those who faithfully enter the Lord's house (109:6-21).** Those who faithfully enter the temple can feel the power of the Lord and come to know that the temple is truly the Lord's house (v. 12-13). In His house, the Lord will teach people how to proceed from day to day and how to become more like Him (v. 8, 14-16). Review verses 6-21 to appreciate the many blessings promised to those who faithfully enter the Lord's house. Now consider what Elder J. Ballard Washburn of the Seventy said about temple covenants and blessings: "We go to the temple to make covenants, but we go home to keep the covenants that we have made. The home is the testing ground" (*Ensign*, May 1995, p. 12).

2. **Blessings requested for the saints (109:22-49).** The main blessing that Joseph Smith requests for the saints in these verses is power. Why? Remember the material for 103:15-20, "The Redemption of Zion must needs come by Power" and 105:11-12, 37, "The Saints Must be Endowed with Power."

3. **Blessings requested for all people (109:50-58).** In these verses, Joseph Smith requests blessings for various groups of people. He asks the Lord to have mercy upon them and to soften their hearts so that the righteous can find and accept the true Church (v. 50, 54, 56-58). These groups of people include:

   a. *Enemies of the Church (109:50-53).* Read Matt. 5:43-47 and 3 Ne. 12:43-45.

   b. *The nations of the earth and their leaders (109:54-58).* Earthly governments and laws will be discussed in the material for Section 134: "Church and State."

   c. *All the churches of the earth (109:55-58).* Review the material for 35:3-6, "Elect Non-member Preachers."

    d. *The poor, the needy, and afflicted ones of the earth (109:55-58).*
    Read 3 Ne. 12:3-12 and Jacob 2:19.
    The prayer of Joseph Smith for these groups of people is a pattern we
can follow in our prayers.
    4. Blessings requested for the tribes of Israel (109:59-67). Compare
these verses with Mormon 7. Also remember the material for 45:25-43,
"Signs for Our Generation."
    5. Blessings requested that the Church might prosper (109:68-80).

Thine Angels Have Charge over Them (109:22)

    Remember the material for 84:88, "Angels Shall Be Round About You, To
Bear You Up."

Praying to Jesus Christ (Jehovah) (109:31-80)

    Beginning in verse 31, it appears that Joseph Smith is praying to Jesus Christ
(who is Jehovah—see Appendix 1: "Jesus Christ is Jehovah"). King Solomon
appears to have done the same in his dedicatory prayer (1 King. 8:22-54 and 2
Chron. 6:12-7:3). Both Joseph Smith and King Solomon knew that normally
prayers are to be directed towards God the Father in the name of Jesus Christ
(Moses 5:4; Jacob 4:5; 3 Ne. 13:9-12). However, because the House of Jesus
Christ was being dedicated, it seems natural and appropriate that Joseph Smith
and King Solomon directed part of their prayers to Jesus Christ Himself. Also
note that when Joseph Smith received the revealed dedicatory prayer and when
he was in the temple, it may have been an experience much like the one we read
about in 3 Ne. 19:17-23.

Stakes (109:39, 59)

    Remember the material for 82:13-14, "Stakes."

The Mountains and Valleys (109:74)

    Some say that after the second coming of the Lord, there will be no more
mountains and valleys. However, "the earth shall be like as it was in the days
before it was divided" (*D&C* 133:24). Therefore, there will be mountains and
valleys. Besides, without mountains and valleys, where would we ski?

We Shall Be Caught Up in the Cloud To Meet Thee (109:75)

    See *D&C* 88:96-102, "The First and Second Resurrections."

Seraphs (109:79)

    Remember the material for 38:1, "Seraphs."

Additional Insights

    Compare this section with the dedicatory prayer of King Solomon found in
1 King. 8:22-54 and 2 Chron. 6:12-7:3.

110

Keys Restored in the Kirtland Temple

Historical Context

Remember *D&C* 109:78 where Joseph Smith pleaded with the Lord to accept the dedication of the Kirtland Temple? One week later, the Lord appeared to Joseph Smith and Oliver Cowdery and accepted the dedication of the Kirtland Temple (v. 1-8).

Appearance of the Savior in His House (110:1-8)

Joseph Smith describes the countenance of Jesus Christ as being even brighter than the sun (v. 3; see also J.S.—History 1:16-17). Imagine staring at the bright noon-day sun and trying to describe it. No wonder it is difficult for mortal beings to describe eternal beings. Joseph Smith describes the Savior as having eyes like a "flame of fire" (v. 3). It is said that the eyes are the window to the soul. Fire often symbolizes passion. The passion of the Lord for His people is reflected in his eyes. Otten and Caldwell give further insight: "A flame of fire has an intensity about it that demands one's attention. To look into the Savior's eyes, would be an experience demanding one's total attention and respect" (*ST*, 2:247).

Blessings Shall Be Poured Out (110:9-10)

The promises contained in these verses would be fulfilled by the power of the keys restored in verses 11-16.

Keys Restored (110:11-16)

After the vision of Jesus Christ closed, three messengers came to restore more priesthood keys. Note that every time keys were restored in this dispensation, there were two witnesses present in accordance with divine law (2 Cor. 13:1).

1. **Moses commits the keys of the gathering of Israel and the leading of the ten tribes from the land of the north (110:11).** Moses was in charge of the gathering and the leading of the tribes of Israel in his day. He also predicted the scattering and eventual regathering of Israel (see Deut. 4). The keys that Moses restored are the authority to lead and gather all the people from the ten tribes of Israel (which includes all the people of the earth) into stakes of Zion.

Wait until we come to the material for 133:26-35, "The Restoration of the Ten Tribes" for further discussion of this topic.

2. **Elias commits the keys of the dispensation of Abraham (110:12).** Here, Elias refers to Noah (see Joseph Fielding Smith, *CR*, Apr. 1960, 71). Noah restored the keys that would allow us to enjoy all of the blessings given to Abraham. The greatest blessing given to Abraham was that of the eternal family (*D&C* 132:29-31). The keys that Noah restored are the keys to make eternal marriage vows in the Lord's temples.

3. **Elijah commits the keys of the sealing power (110:13-16).** Joseph Fielding Smith wrote:

> It is interesting to know that on the third day of April, 1836, the Jews were celebrating the feast of the Passover, and were leaving the doors of their homes open for the coming of Elijah. On that day Elijah came, but not to the Jewish homes, but to the Temple in the village of Kirtland near the banks of Lake Erie, to two humble servants of the Lord who were appointed by divine decree to receive him (*CHMR*, 3:84).

He also said:

> Elijah restored to this Church and, if they would receive it, to the world, the keys of the sealing power; and that sealing power puts the stamp of approval upon every ordinance that is done in this Church and more particularly those that are performed in the temples of the Lord (*CR*, Apr. 1948, p. 135).

Without the keys of the sealing power which Elijah restored, the other keys would be useless and the whole earth would be utterly wasted at the Lord's coming (see 132:7 and remember the material for 2:3, "The Earth Would Be Utterly Wasted").

111

FOLLIES

Follies (111:1-2)

A brother named Burgess came to Kirtland and told Church leaders that he knew where a large amount of money was hidden. He said that it was in the basement of a house that had been owned by a widow who was now dead. He said that the house was in Salem, Massachusetts. It was perfectly legal to recover the unclaimed money.

At this time (August 6, 1836), the Church was having major financial difficulties. Debts were incurred to complete the building of the Kirtland Temple. Because of its debts, the Church was receiving much persecution from its enemies. Therefore, the brethren considered what Burgess told them.

The brethren met Burgess in Salem. Burgess told them he could not show them where the widow's house was. He said the city had changed too much since the last time he was there. Then he left. (See *CHC*, 1:411 for a more detailed account.)

Although the brethren were sincere in their efforts to help get the Church out of debt, the Lord described this journey as a folly (v. 1). A folly is a mistake. Although the brethren made an honest mistake, it was still a mistake. The Lord chastises the brethren in this section in the same loving way He chastised the saints in Section 95. The Lord does not "shame" the brethren (remember the material for 58:43). In fact, He comforts the brethren by telling them that people would not "discover your secret parts" (v. 4); in other words, they would not have to feel ashamed for their mistake.

Honest mistakes are made all the time. When we are in the position of chastiser, it is our responsibility to follow the pattern set by the Lord discussed in the material for Section 95: "Responsibilities of a Chastiser." When we are the ones who have committed the folly, it is our responsibility to admit that we made a mistake and take steps to correct it.

Instructions to the Brethren (111:3-11)

The Lord tells the brethren how to make the best of the situation. He tells them that there are treasures other than money in Salem (v. 10). He tells them that to find this treasure they would need to meet the people of the city and to "inquire diligently concerning the more ancient inhabitants and founders of this city" (v. 3, 9). Smith and Sjodahl wrote:

> "Ancient inhabitants" refers more particularly to the ancestors of the Prophet [Joseph Smith]. The Revelation was given at Salem, the county seat of Essex County, Massachusetts. It was in that county that Robert Smith, the first of the Smith family in America, settled. It was the residence of many more of the pioneer immigrants to America, whose descendants joined the Church. At Salem, the county seat, the records for all the towns in the county were kept, and the Smiths' record, among others, were there (*DCC*, p. 729).

Although Joseph Smith and the brethren committed a folly by trying to recover the hidden money in Salem, the Lord helped them find the treasure of their genealogy.

112

SOME DUTIES OF CHURCH LEADERS

Historical Context
At the time this section was given (July 23, 1837), Thomas B. Marsh was the president of the Quorum of the Twelve Apostles. The Lord instructs Elder Marsh in his duties as a leader. The Lord's counsel can be used by all Church leaders.

Some Duties of Church Leaders (112:1-12)
1. **Proclaim the gospel (112:5).** Refer to the material for 18:20, "Contending Against the Church of the Devil" for the use of the word "contend" in this verse.
2. **Be thou humble (112:10).** Church leaders are called to represent the Lord (remember the material for Section 99: "Who Receiveth You Receiveth Me"). To represent the Lord properly, a leader must be led by the Lord through prayer. To be led by the Lord, the leader must be humble (v. 10).
3. **Be not partial towards them (112:11).** Church leaders should not hold prejudices against any member of the group they lead. Each member should have the same chance to actively participate in the group.

4. **Let thy love be for them as for thyself (112:11).** Church leaders must love themselves. They must feel that they are worthy to represent the Lord. They must also treat each member of the group as equals to themselves.

5. **Pray for them (112:12).**

6. **Admonish them sharply for their sins (112:12).** Remember the material for Sections 95: "Responsibilities of a Chastiser" and 111: "Follies."

7. **"Preside over"** quorum members;

8. **"Sit in council with them;"** and

9. **"Teach them" (107:85-89).**

Gird up Your Loins (112:7, 14)

Remember the material for 36:8, "Gird Up Your Loins."

Let Thy Feet Be Shod (112:7)

Remember the material for 27:15-18, "Armor."

Take up Your Cross (112:14)

"And now for a man to take up his cross, is to deny himself all ungodliness, and every worldly lust, and keep my commandments" (*JST* Matt. 16:26).

The Churches (112:18)

Here, the term *churches* means stakes, wards, or branches.

I Come Quickly (112:34)

Remember the material for 33:18, "I Come Quickly."

113

ISAIAH

Historical Context

The night of September 21, 1823 the angel Moroni appeared to the young Joseph Smith three times (see J.S.—H. 1:27-54 for more detail). Each time, Moroni quoted the eleventh chapter of Isaiah and said it was about to be fulfilled (J.S.—H. 1:40. Obviously, it was important for the saints to understand the eleventh chapter of Isaiah. In the first six verses of Section 113, the Lord answers some of the saints' questions about the eleventh chapter of Isaiah.

The Servant in the Hands of Christ (113:3-6)

While the rest of this section is straight forward, the answers given in verses 4 and 6 are unclear. These verses do not name who they are talking about. Sidney B. Sperry said these verses probably referred to Joseph Smith. He said:

> By "stem of Jesse" Isaiah has reference to Christ, and by "rod" he has reference to a servant of Christ. But just who is the servant? A careful reading of verses 4 to 6 in the explanation convinces me that Joseph Smith is meant, for who fulfills the conditions of these verses, especially verse 6, better than he? Surely he had the lineage to which rightly belongs the priesthood (cf. *D&C* 86:8-11); he received the keys of the kingdom (*D&C* 65:2) for an ensign (standard; *D&C* 45:9) and for the gathering of the Lord's people in the last days (*D&C* 110:11). Moreover, the situation under which Moroni quoted the chapter from Isaiah favors Joseph Smith as being the "rod." He would logically be the "servant in the hands of Christ" who was to receive the instruction from Moroni and be prepared to understand the ancient prophecies concerning his mission in the latter days (*Book of Mormon Compendium*, p. 223).

114

DAVID W. PATTEN

David W. Patten (114:1)

David W. Patten was a member of the Quorum of the Twelve Apostles. In this section, he is called to serve a mission. He was killed by the mobs near Far West, Missouri before he could perform his mission in mortality. He was the first apostolic martyr of the latter-days. Wilford Woodruff said:

> David made known to the Prophet [Joseph Smith] that he had asked the Lord to let him die the death of a martyr, at which the Prophet, greatly moved, expressed extreme sorrow, "For," said he to David "when a man of your faith asks the Lord for anything, he generally gets it" (*Life of David Patten*, p. 53).

We can be sure that the Lord called Elder Patten to perform his mission on the other side of the veil. The Lord told Joseph Smith that Elder Patten was with Him

(*D&C* 124:19). On his deathbed, Elder Patten said to his wife, "Whatever you do else, Oh do not deny the faith" (*LHCK*, p. 214).

Others Shall Receive Their Bishopric (114:2)

In this verse, the Lord commands that unfaithful Church leaders be replaced. There were even unfaithful members in the Quorum of the Twelve Apostles who would have to be replaced (*D&C* 118:1). The term *bishopric*, here, means "any office or position of major responsibility in the Church" (*MD*, p. 89).

115

THUS SHALL MY CHURCH BE CALLED

Thus Shall My Church Be Called (115:1-4)

The saints knew that the Church must be called by the name of Christ (Eph. 5:22-24; 3 Ne. 27:3-10). Before the revelation in this section was given, the saints called the Church "The Church of Christ" (*D&C* 20:1), "The Church of Jesus Christ," "The Church of God," or "The Church of the Latter-day Saints" (*HC*, 3:23-24). In verses 1-4, the Lord standardizes the name of the Church.

B. H. Roberts explained the significance of the church's name. He said:

> The appropriateness of this title is self evident, and in it there is a beautiful recognition of the relationship both of the Lord Jesus Christ and of the Saints to the organization. It is "The Church of Jesus Christ." It is the Lord's; He owns it, He organized it. . . . But it is an institution which also belongs to the Saints. It is their refuge from the confusion and religious doubt of the word. It is their instructor in principle, doctrine, and righteousness. It is their guide in matters of faith and morals. They have a conjoint ownership in it with Jesus Christ, which ownership is beautiful recognized in the latter part of the title. "The Church of Jesus Christ of Latter-day Saints," is equivalent to "The Church of Jesus Christ," and "The Church of the Latter-day Saints" (*HC*, 3:24).

The apostle Paul referred to the members of the Church in his day as "saints" (1 Cor. 1:2). Thus, the Church in his day could be called "The Church of Jesus Christ of Saints." Because we are now living in the days just before the second coming, "latter-day" appropriately describes the saints of our day.

The Lord refers to worthy members of His church as "saints." *Saint* means holy or cleansed. Saints are "holy ones" or "cleansed ones." People can become holy and cleansed through obedience to the principles and ordinances of the Church of Jesus Christ.

Historical Context—Far West (115:5-19)

The Church at this time was centered in Kirtland and was receiving a great deal of persecution from people both in and out of the Church. 1837 is known as "The year of the Great Apostasy in Kirtland" (*ST*, 2:272). Wilford Woodruff said:

> There was a time when there were but two of the quorum of the Twelve Apostles then in . . . Kirtland who stood by Joseph Smith. . . . I was not a member of that quorum at that time; I was a Seventy. Several of these men called upon me in that time of this apostasy and asked me to join them against the Prophet; the Prophet was fallen, they said. . . . I saw that these men were yielding to the devil, and I told them so. Said I: "You will all go to hell unless you repent. . . ." A good many of them did fall. I will here name one instance. I saw one of these Apostles in the Kirtland Temple, while the Sacrament was being passed, stand in the aisle and curse the Prophet of God to his face while he was in the stand, and when the bread was passed he reached out his hand for a piece of bread and flung it into his mouth like a mad dog. He turned as black in the face almost as an African with rage and with the power of the devil. What did he do? He ate and drank damnation to himself. He did not go and hang himself, but he did go and drown himself, and the river went over his body while his spirit was cast into the pit where he ceased to have the power to curse either God or His Prophet in time or in eternity (see *Millennial Star* 57:339-340 in Doxey 4:214-15).

The Kirtland Temple became defiled and the Lord no longer accepted it as His house (see *D&C* 97:15-17 and 124:28). Joseph Smith was forced to flee Kirtland, Ohio. He went to Far West, Missouri. In verses 5-19, the Lord commands that His people gather to Far West and build a temple there. The saints began to build up Far West. In fulfillment of verse 10, they laid the corner stones of the temple on July 4, 1838. However, they did not complete the temple. Persecution forced the saints to flee from Far West.

Stakes (115:6, 18)

Remember the material for 82:13-14, "Stakes."

116

ADAM-ONDI-AHMAN

Bruce R. McConkie wrote:

Ahman is one of the names by which God was known to Adam. *Adam-ondi-Ahman*, a name carried over from the pure Adamic language into English, is one for which we have not been given a revealed, literal translation. As near as we can judge . . . *Adam-ondi-Ahman means the place or land of God where Adam dwelt* (*MD*, p. 19).

And Heber C. Kimball said:

The Prophet Joseph called upon Brother Brigham, myself and others, saying, "Brethren, come, go along with me, and I will show you something," He led us a short distance to a place where were the ruins of three altars built of stone, one above the other, and one standing a little back of the other, like unto the pulpits in the Kirtland Temple, representing the order of three grades of Priesthood; "There," said Joseph, "is the place where Adam offered up sacrifice after he was cast out of the garden." The altar stood at the highest point of the bluff. I went and examined the place several times while I remained there (*LHCK*, pp. 209-210).

Adam-ondi-Ahman is the place where Adam and Eve lived after they were cast out of the garden of Eden (*D&C* 117:8). It is also the place where Adam held a church conference. You can read about this conference in *D&C* 107:53-57.

117

THE MORE WEIGHTY MATTERS

Historical Context

In Section 115, the Lord commanded the Saints to gather and build a temple in Far West, Missouri. About 500 Saints left Kirtland, Ohio on July 6, 1838 and started out for Missouri (*DCC*, p. 744). Joseph Smith was in Far West at the time so he had no way of knowing who had stayed behind in Kirtland. But on July 8, 1838 Joseph Smith received the revelations in Sections 117-120. In Section 117, the Lord chastises William Marks and Newel K. Whitney for their unwillingness to sacrifice their property and come speedily to Missouri as they were commanded (v. 1-4). The Lord then tells William Marks and Newel K. Whitney what to do with the property under their stewardship and promises them that they will be blessed for their sacrifices (v. 5-11).

I, the Lord, Send Again the Snows (117:1)

Obviously, the Lord can control the weather.

Adam-ondi-Ahman and Olaha Shinehah (117:8)

Adam-ondi-Ahman and Olaha Shinehah are in Missouri north of Far West. (See the map on page 297 of the *D&C*.) Refer to the material for Section 116 for more information about Adam-ondi-Ahman.

Shinehah is the sun and *Olaha* might be from *Olea* which is the moon (Abr. 3:13). Smith and Sjodahl state:

> If so, the Plains of Olaha Shinehah would be the Plains of the Moon and the Sun, so called, perhaps because of astronomical observations there made (*DCC*, p. 745).

The More Weighty Matters (117:8)

"The more weighty matters" refers to the keeping of covenants. All the money or property in the world is but a drop (v. 8) when compared to the covenants we have made with the Lord to follow all His counsel. Read what the Lord has to say about "the weightier matters of the law" in Matt. 23:23-27.

The Nicolaitane Band (117:11)

The Nicolaitans mentioned in the New Testament (Rev. 2:6, 15) approved of immorality. Bruce R. McConkie wrote that the Nicolaitans of our day are

> members of the Church who [are] trying to maintain their church standing while continuing to live after the manner of the world. . . . [They] want their names on the records of the Church, but do not want to devote themselves to the gospel cause with full purpose of heart (*DNTC*, 3:446).

The Lord chastised Bishop Newel K. Whitney for not devoting himself fully to the cause of Zion. The Lord called on Bishop Whitney to "be a bishop not in name but in deed" (v. 11). Bishop Whitney needed to be concerned with "the more weighty matters" (v. 8).

Oliver Granger (117:12-15)

Oliver Granger was a man of faith and an excellent businessman. When Joseph Smith had to flee Kirtland, he appointed Oliver Granger as his business agent (*DCC*, p. 746). Oliver did such a good job that not only did other businessmen praise him (*DCC*, p. 746), but the Lord also commended him (v. 12, 15). The Lord told Brother Granger to continue to work to get the First Presidency of the Church out of debt (v. 13). The Lord also reminded Brother Granger that the sacrifices he made by keeping his covenants were "more weighty matters" than all the money he raised (v. 8, 13). About a year later, in fulfillment of verse 14, the Lord called Oliver Granger to be in charge of the temple and Church in Kirtland (*DCC*, p. 746).

118

VACANCIES IN THE QUORUM OF THE TWELVE FILLED

Vacancies in the Quorum of the Twelve Filled (118:1, 6)

In *D&C* 114:2, the Lord commanded that unfaithful Church leaders be replaced. William E. M'Lellin, Luke S. Johnson, John F. Boynton, and Lyman E. Johnson—all members of the first Quorum of the Twelve in this dispensation—had fallen away from the Church and were excommunicated (*HC*, 2:509; 3:31-32). Joseph Smith said:

> No quorum in the Church was entirely exempt from the influences of those false spirits who are striving against me for the mastery; even some of the Twelve were so far lost to their high and responsible calling, as to begin to take sides, secretly, with the enemy (*HC*, 2:487-489).

In verse 1 of this section, the Lord commands that these unfaithful men be replaced by the men named in verse 6. When the unfaithful leaders were replaced, their authority and priesthood were taken from them (114:2).

A Mission Call to the Twelve (118:2-5)

The Lord commanded all of the apostles, except for Thomas B. Marsh (v. 2), to meet the next year at the Far West Temple site. From there, they were to leave on missions. Wilford Woodruff said:

When the time came for the corner stone of the Temple to be laid, as directed in the revelation, the Church was in Illinois, having been expelled from Missouri by an edict from the Governor. Joseph and Hyrum Smith and Parley P. Pratt were in chains in Missouri for the testimony of Jesus. As the time drew nigh for the accomplishment of this work, the question arose, "What is to be done?" Here is a revelation commanding the Twelve to be in Far West on the 26th day of April, to lay the corner stone of the Temple there; it had to be fulfilled. The Missourians had sworn by all the gods of eternity that if every other revelation given through Joseph Smith were fulfilled, that should not be, for the day and date being given they declared that it should fail. . . . When President Young asked the question of the Twelve, "Brethren, what will you do about this?" the reply was, "The Lord has spoken and it is for us to obey." We felt that the Lord God had given the commandment and we had faith to go forward and accomplish it, feeling that it was His business whether we lived or died in its accomplishment. . . . We reached Far West and laid the corner stone according to the revelation that had been given to us. . . . We then returned, nobody having molested or made us afraid. We performed that work by faith, and the Lord blessed us in doing it (*JD*, 13:159-60).

119

THE LAW OF TITHING

Historical Context

Read the section heading.

Lyndon W. Cook states:

> There is no evidence that Mormon leaders or members perceived the economic plan embodied in section 119 to be an "inferior law" of Church economics. On the contrary, the 1838 program was viewed by the Saints simply as a new phase of consecration. Indeed, many hailed it as a markedly improved economic plan for obtaining donations and contributions (p. 77).

For information on how this section fits into the practice of the law of consecration and stewardship, refer to the material for Section 51, "The Law of Consecration and Stewardship."

Surplus Property (119:1-5)

The saints at this time were to give their surplus property to the Bishop in Zion (v. 1, 5). According to the apostle Franklin D. Richards, this meant that they were to give "that which was over and above a comfortable and necessary subsistence" (*JD*, 23:313). Although this was not necessarily a tenth of their property, it was called a tithe (v. 3-4) because the term "tithing" referred to any offering (see the section heading).

Brigham Young once asked Joseph Smith who should determine what "surplus" was under this plan. Brigham Young was told, "Let them be the judges themselves" (*JD*, 2:306). It was not until after the martyrdom of Joseph and Hyrum Smith, that a set amount of tithing the Saints were to give was established. In August 1844 (after the martyrdom of Joseph and Hyrum Smith), the Quorum of the Twelve wrote to the Church concerning tithing. Brigham Young, as the senior apostle and President of the Twelve Apostles, stated:

> Let every member proceed immediately to tithe himself or herself, a tenth of all their property and money. . . . And then let them continue to pay in a tenth of their income from that time forth, for this is a law unto this church as much binding on their conscience as any other law or ordinance" (*HC*, 7:251; also see 7:301, 358).

The immediate tithe of all property referred to by Brigham Young was the first part—the "beginning" (v. 3)—of the offering they were to make. Joseph Fielding Smith said:

> In more recent years the Church has not called upon the members to give all their surplus property to the Church, but it has been the requirement according to the covenant, that they pay the tenth (*CHMR*, 3:120).

They Shall Pay One-tenth of All Their Interest Annually (119:4)

After the saints had given the surplus that they had gained from living under the law of consecration to the bishop in Zion, they were commanded to "pay one-tenth of all their interest annually" (v. 4). Elder John A. Widtsoe stated:

> Tithing [now] means one-tenth of a person's income, interest, or increase. The merchant should pay tithing upon the net income of his business, the farmer upon the net income of his farming operations; the wage earner or salaried man upon the wage or salary earned by him. Out of the remaining nine-tenths he pays his current expenses, taxes, savings, etc. To deduct living costs, taxes, and similar expenses from the income and pay tithing upon the remainder does not conform to the Lord's commandment. Under such a system most people would show nothing on which to pay tithing. There is really no place for quibbling on this point. Tithing should be given upon the basis of our full earned income. If the nature of

a business requires special interpretation, the tithepayer should consult the father of his ward, the bishop (*Evidences and Reconciliations*, 2:86).

This tithe is to be paid in full each year (v. 4).

A Standing Law Forever (119:4)

Some question the "forever" part of this verse, worrying that it is incompatible with what they understand the law of consecration and stewardship to be. If, in the future, the Lord intends tithing His people other than having them offer the tenth of their increase, it is His prerogative to do so (*D&C* 56:4). He will make it known through His prophet (see the material for *D&C* 28:2, 12-13, "Revelation from the Lord").

Stakes (119:7)

Remember the material for 82:13-14, "Stakes."

120
DISTRIBUTION OF TITHING FUNDS

Historical Context

In *D&C* 119:2, the Lord told Joseph Smith how to use the funds collected from the tithing of the saints. Joseph desired further guidance from the Lord on how decisions should be made about the use and distribution of tithing funds. The Lord told him that the use and distribution of tithing funds would be the responsibility of a council composed of the First Presidency, the Presiding Bishopric, and the Quorum of the Twelve Apostles.

The following quotes explain how the revelation in this section is followed today:

> It [tithing funds] is not the property of the President [of the Church]. He does not claim it or collect it. Tithing is received by the local bishops in the respective wards, who are under the supervision of the local presidents of stakes. The whole income is accounted for to the presiding bishopric of the Church and is under their direction. Their office contains complete records of all the tithing paid during each year [remember the material for 85:1-5, 9-12, "The Book of the Law of God"]. Every tithepayer will find in that office his record. The entire receipts and

disbursements are there accounted for in the most complete detail. An auditing committee, composed of men well known in the community for their independence of character and business integrity, not of the leading authorities of the Church, chosen by the general conference, thoroughly inspect and report annually upon them. The funds thus received are not the property of the President of the Church or his associates, nor of the presiding bishopric, nor of the local bishops. They belong to the Church and are used for Church purposes (*Messages of the First Presidency*, 4:228-29).

Under the direction of the First Presidency a budget is drawn up, as nearly as may be at the first of the year, which includes all of the proposed expenditures of the tithing. This budget is the result of the careful consideration of the departments which are responsible for the expenditure of the funds.

This budget is then taken before the Council on the Expenditure of the Tithing, composed, as the revelation [Section 120] provides, of the First Presidency, the Council of the Twelve, and the Presiding Bishopric. This council considers and discusses the budget so submitted, approving or disapproving, as the case may be, individual items, but finally passing the budget.

The approved budget as it comes from that meeting is then turned over for its expenditures to a Committee on Expenditures. This committee then passes upon and authorizes the expenditures of the tithing. So that there is a complete check upon all of the tithing which is paid into the Church. None of it is expended except upon the approval and authorization of this committee (J. Reuben Clark, Jr., *CR*, Oct. 1943, p. 12).

121

THERE ARE MANY CALLED, BUT FEW ARE CHOSEN

Historical Context

Read the section heading.

In October of 1838, the governor of Missouri, Lilburn Boggs, issued the "extermination order." As Commander in Chief of the state militia, Boggs ordered his generals: "The Mormons must be treated as enemies and must be exterminated or driven from the state, if necessary for the public good" (*HC*, 3:175). Within the week:

the Prophet and several leaders of the Church were betrayed into the hands of the Missourians at Far West, Missouri. For the next several weeks Joseph Smith and his associates were abused and insulted, forced to march to Independence and then to Richmond, and on 30 November 1838 incarcerated in Liberty Jail in Missouri (see History of the Church, 3:188-89, 215). These men had not been convicted of any crime; nevertheless, they were held in the jail for several months (*DCSM*, p. 295).

While in jail, Joseph Smith wrote a letter to the saints. Sections 121-123 are from this letter. (For the full text of the letter, see *HC*, 3:289-305.)

Remember Thy Suffering Saints (121:1-6)

Note that Joseph Smith did not ask "Why?" or "Why me?" This was the cry of a prophet on behalf of his people. Compare this to 2 Ne. 33:3 and Alma 18:41. Trials and tribulations will be further discussed in the material for 122:5-8, "If Thou Art Called to Pass Through Tribulation."

Sheol (121:4)

See the Bible Dictionary.

Let Thine Anger Be Kindled Against Our Enemies (121:5)

Smith and Sjodahl comment:

> It is perfectly consistent with the gospel to ask God to execute justice in behalf of His people. It is contrary to the gospel for man to take vengeance into his own hands, but not to pour out his soul's bitterness under injustice and wrong, before God in prayer (*DCC*, p. 754).

Compare with 2 Sam. 22:32-43; Ps. 6:10; 7:6; 13:2; 2 Ne. 4:31; and Alma 33:10.

Peace Be unto Thy Soul (121:7-15)

The comforting words the Lord spoke to Joseph Smith and keys to overcoming trials will be discussed in the material for 122:5-8, "If Thou Art Called to Pass Through Tribulation."

The Lord's Anointed (121:11-25)

Verses 16-17 are a little unclear. Daniel H. Ludlow clarifies them by inserting the following words in brackets:

> Cursed are all those that shall lift up the heel against mine anointed, saith the Lord, and cry they [mine anointed] have sinned when they have not sinned before me. . . . But those who cry transgression [on the part of mine anointed] do it because they [those who lift up the heel against mine anointed] are the servants of sin (*Comp.*, 1:603).

Elder Harold B. Lee said: "Mark well those who speak evil of the Lord's anointed for they speak from impure hearts. Only the 'pure in heart' see the 'God' or the divine in man and accept our leaders and accept them as prophets of the Living God" (CR, Oct. 1947, p. 67).

Now is a good time to review the material for 21:5, "In Patience and Faith;" 43:7, "Our Duties;" 50:4-9, "Hypocrites in the Church;" and 50:23-36, 40-46, "Deciding What comes From God."

Not One of Them Is Left to Stand by the Wall (121:15)

When the scriptures speak of those that "stand by the wall," they refer to "every male." This phrase is used to speak of the destruction of a family down to the last man. The same phrase, slightly modified, is used with the same meaning in 1 Sam. 25:22, 34; 1 Kings 14:10; 16:11; 21:21; 2 Kings 9:8; and 18:27 (the language used in these verses is only offensive to modern readers).

From Generation to Generation (121:15, 21)

The punishment of the children for the sins of their ancestors will be discussed in the material for 124:50-52, "Unto the Third and Fourth Generation."

The Dispensation of the Fullness of Times (121:26-32)

Prophets throughout time have enjoyed the gift of the Holy Ghost; however, in the dispensation of the fullness of times "the keys, powers, and principles known in past dispensations individually are now enjoyed collectively" (DCSM, p. 298). By the power of the Holy Ghost, God sometimes reveals "unspeakable things" to certain people. 2 Ne. 4:25; 3 Ne. 26:16; and 28:25 are good examples. These unspeakable things are revealed to the rest of the world when the Lord commands it. Ether 4:1 is a good example of this. What were the unspeakable things the Holy Ghost revealed to Joseph Smith? Joseph Fielding Smith said, "We do not know, but it was far more than he was permitted to reveal to his fellows" at that time (CHMR, 2:177).

The Lord has revealed more about some of the topics spoken of in these verses. Concerning the time when "nothing shall be withheld" (v. 28), remember the material for 101:32-34, "The Lord shall reveal all things."

The Constitution of the Priesthood (121:34-46)

A country's constitution lays out the principles upon which the country governs and is governed. Verses 34-46 are referred to as the Constitution of the Priesthood. They lay out the principles upon which the priesthood governs and is governed.

The most important unit the priesthood can govern is the family. Elder Stephen L. Richards said:

Now may I just say a word about a man of the priesthood as the head of his household. . . . The difficulties that arise usually stem from an attempt on the part of the head of the household to exercise inconsiderate or autocratic authority. *There is no position in the Church in which the constitution and doctrine of the priesthood as revealed by the Lord has more direct application than to a husband and father in the home.* He must never cease to be guided by the divine direction that:

"No power or influence can or ought to be maintained . . . only by persuasion, by long-suffering, by gentleness and meekness, and by love unfeigned . . .

"Reproving betimes with sharpness, when moved upon by the Holy Ghost; and then showing forth afterwards an increase of love toward him whom thou hast reproved, lest he esteem thee to be his enemy." (*D&C* 121:41, 43.)

Every head of the household may win respect for his position if he will but truly follow these divine directions (*CR*, Oct. 1954, pp. 81-82; emphasis added).

There Are Many Called, but Few Are Chosen (121:34-40)

The *Doctrine and Covenants Student Manual* outlines the cause and effect relationship taught by these verses:

When the hearts of men—

1. Are set on the things of the world, or
2. Aspire to the honors of men,

They will act in ways detrimental to spiritual growth, including—

1. Covering their sins.
2. Gratifying their pride and vain ambitions.
3. Exercising unrighteous dominion over others.

These actions cause—

1. The heavens to withdraw themselves.
2. The Spirit of the Lord to be grieved.
3. A withdrawal of power and authority.
   The chain could be stated positively to answer the question, "How does one come to be chosen?"

When the hearts of men—

1. Are set on the things of God, and
2. Aspire for God's approval and honors,

They will act in ways beneficial to spiritual growth, including—

1. Repenting of their sins.
2. Humbling themselves.
3. Seeking the kingdom of God first.
4. Exercising love and charity toward others.

These actions cause—

1. The heavens to draw near.
2. The Spirit of the Lord to be near.
3. An increase in power and authority (p. 121).

Left To Kick Against the Pricks (121:38)

Just as the *rod* was used on sheep, the *prick* was a stick used to drive cattle. Good shepherds and ranchers did not need to use their rod or prick to beat the animals. They could lead their animals by gently tapping them to keep them from wandering away from the flock or herd. Thus, the rod and the prick were used to restrain the animals to set safe boundaries. So too, the commandments of the Lord set restraints—boundaries within which we can travel the path of life in safety. Elder Harold B. Lee examined this symbolism when he said the commandments of the Lord "are the restraints against which some people seem to rebel and are kicking constantly against—the 'pricks' of the gospel" (*CR*, Oct. 1947, p. 66).

What is the rod we are to guide our children with? Read 1 Ne. 11:25. Now read *JST* Rev. 2:26-27. Note the symbolism of ruling with a rod of iron. It is not ruling, as would a dictator, with an iron fist, but means ruling as would God, "with equity and justice." Spare the true "rod," or use it improperly, and, indeed, the child will spoil. Use the "rod" properly and the child will come to sing the psalm: "though I walk through the valley of the shadow of death, I will fear no evil: for thou art with me; thy rod and thy staff they *comfort* me" (Ps. 23:4; emphasis added).

Reproving Betimes with Sharpness (121:43-44)

When one is governed by the Constitution of the Priesthood, one gives feedback the way the Lord does. Review the material for 95:1-2, 9-17, "Responsibilities of a Chastiser."

Betimes means "early." The *Oxford English Dictionary* states that reproving betimes means to reprove "at an early time; in good time, in due time; while there is yet time, before it is too late; or in a short time, soon, speedily." Joseph Smith said, "I frequently rebuke and admonish my brethren, and that because I love them, not because I wish to incur their displeasure, or mar their happiness" (*HC*, 2:487). You can also see the Constitution of the Priesthood in action as you read about Nephi in 2 Ne. 1:25.

"With sharpness" is another key to good feedback. Sharp feedback is clear feedback. It tells the person exactly what the problem is and how to fix it. Also think of giving feedback as an operation on another's soul. The master physician knows to use clean, sharp tools.

Let Virtue Garnish Thy Thoughts Unceasingly (121:45)

To garnish means to beautify, decorate, adorn, embellish, or enhance. How do we let virtue garnish our thoughts *unceasingly*? The same way we *always* remember Christ (20:77) and pray *continuously without ceasing* (Alma 26:22; see also 2 Ne. 33:3; and 3 Ne. 18:15- 21). We must have a change of heart, a change of consciousness—we must be born again and become new creatures in Christ. Read 1 Pet. 1:22-23 and Mosiah 27:25-26 for further insight.

Then Shall Thy Confidence Wax Strong in the Presence of God (121:45)

How can we gain confidence that we stand worthy before the Lord, that He hears our prayers, and that we can feel at home in His presence? Review the material for 58:42-43, "I, the Lord, Remember them No More" and "By this Ye may Know if a Man Repenteth of his Sins."

The Doctrine of the Priesthood Shall Distill upon Thy Soul (121:45)

What is the doctrine of the priesthood? It is the things in verses 36-37 and 41-43. It is the "Constitution of the Priesthood." It is the knowledge and the characteristics that we need to gain to be like Christ and enter his presence. This "doctrine" must distill upon our soul in order that we may not only be called, but chosen. Just as with any other characteristic we may be trying to develop or change, gaining the attributes—the "doctrine"of the priesthood takes diligent effort. We receive the doctrine line upon line. As we do as instructed in verse 45, the doctrine of the priesthood shall distill (condense or concentrate little by little) upon our soul as the dews from heaven. Read Isa. 28:9-13 and 2 Ne. 28:30 for further insight.

Having the doctrine of the priesthood distill upon our soul also has reference to making our calling and election sure. This will be discussed in the material for 131:5, "The More Sure Word of Prophecy."

Promise of Righteous Dominion (121:46)

How does God exercise dominion? The opposite of verse 37. When the doctrine of the priesthood shall distill upon our souls, we will gain the promises of verse 46. We will rule and reign over our stewardship as God does over His—in righteousness. Our honor will be our glory and power (Moses 4:1-3). Because of our righteousness, our dominion will honor and respect us. In other words, we can become trustworthy enough that faith can be placed in us. Thus, our commands will be carried out "without compulsory means" (121:46).

122

IF THOU ART CALLED TO PASS THROUGH TRIBULATION

Historical Context

This section is a continuation of the epistle in Section 121 written to the saints by Joseph Smith while he was a prisoner in Liberty Jail.

Peace Be Unto Thy Soul (122:1-3, 9)

The Lord comforts His persecuted prophet with the following promises:

1. **"Thy friends . . . shall hail thee again" (121:9; 122:9).** Joseph could be comforted knowing that even though he was in prison with a death sentence hanging over him, he did not have to fear "what man can do" (122:9).

2. **"The ends of the earth shall inquire after thy name" (122:1-3).** The fulfillment of these verses is astonishing considering the humble and terrible circumstances Joseph Smith found himself in at that time.

3. **"Fools shall have thee in derision" (122:1).** To deride is to ridicule, mock, or scorn. Many people surrounding the prophet ridiculed and mocked him. However, Joseph Smith did not need to feel ashamed or lose his "confidence in the presence of God" (121:45). Those who speak evil of the Lord's anointed are fools (remember the material for 121:11-25, "The Lord's Anointed").

   What should we do about those that deride the Lord's prophet and Church? Wait until we get to Section 123: "Libelous Publications—Let Us Cheerfully Do All things that Lie in Our Power."

4. **"Thy voice shall be . . . terrible in the midst of thine enemies" (122:4).** Parley P. Pratt wrote:

   > Our guards . . . recounted to each other their deeds of rapine, murder, robbery, etc., which they had committed among the "Mormons" while at Far West and vicinity. They even boasted of defiling by force wives, daughters, and virgins, and of shooting or dashing out the brains of men, women and children.
   >
   > I had listened till I became so disgusted, shocked, horrified, and so filled with the Spirit of indignant justice, that I could scarcely refrain from

rising upon my feet and rebuking the guards, but I had said nothing to Joseph or anyone else, although I lay next to him, and knew he was awake. On a sudden he arose to his feet and spoke in a voice of thunder, or as the roaring lion, uttering, as near as I can recollect, the following words: "*Silence! Ye fiends of the infernal pit! In the name of Jesus Christ I rebuke you, and command you to be still; I will not live another minute and hear such language. Cease such talk, or you or I die this instant!*"

He ceased to speak. He stood erect in terrible majesty. Chained, and without a weapon, calm, unruffled, and dignified as an angel, he looked down upon his quailing guards, whose knees smote together, and who, shrinking into a corner, or crouching at his feet, begged his pardon, and remained quiet until an exchange of guards.

I have seen ministers of justice, clothed in ministerial robes, and criminals arraigned before them, while life was suspended upon a breath in the courts of England; I have witnessed a congress in solemn session to give laws to nations; I have tried to conceive of kings, of royal courts, of thrones and crowns; and of emperors assembled to decide the fate of kingdoms; but dignity and majesty have I seen but once, as it stood in chains, at midnight, in a dungeon in an obscure village of Missouri" (*Autobiography of Parley P. Pratt*, pp. 210-11).

If Thou Art Called To Pass Through Tribulation (122:5-8)

It is necessary that we "be chastened and tried" (review the material for 101:3-5, 35- 36, "They Must Needs be Chastened and Tried"). We must learn to cope with trials; after all, life is a trial (2 Ne. 2:21; Alma 42:4).

Joseph Smith said, "I feel, like Paul, to glory in tribulation" (127:2; Rom. 5:3). How did Joseph Smith and Paul avoid falling into despair because of their many afflictions? What did they do to "glory" in tribulation? Here are some of their "secrets:"

1. **Gain an eternal perspective (121:7; John 15:2; Rom. 5:3; 8:28; 2 Cor. 4:17).** When we do, we will feel the truth of the promise "that all these things shall give thee experience, and shall be for thy good" (121:7). We will be able to see the outcome of turning to the Lord in times of affliction. Read Rom. 5:3. To get this perspective we must let the Lord lift us up "on eagles wings" above the clouds of darkness. This will be discussed further in the material for 124:18, 99, "On Eagles Wings."

2. **Avoid becoming resentful and bitter (121:8 123:17).** We have no choice but to endure; however, we must choose to endure tribulation *well* (121:8). Who are they who "are arrayed in white robes" and stand "before the throne of God?" They are those who "came out of great tribulation" (Rev. 7:13-15). This will be discussed further in the

material for 123:17, "Let us cheerfully do all things that lie in our power; and then we may stand still."

3. **Put our suffering in perspective (121:10; 122:8; John 15:18).** No matter how bad off we are, there are others who have made it through worse. We can look to these heroes for strength. With the Lord's help, we will come off conqueror (10:5).

4. **Know and feel God is with us (62:1; 122:9; Alma 36:3).** We can take comfort in the fact that we are never left to suffer alone.

5. **Sorrow to repentance (2 Cor. 7:9-10).** Obviously, we bring some tribulation on ourselves through sin. However, even the most righteous are not spared from personal tribulations, disasters, and war (Alma 60:13; *D&C* 121:10; 122:8). In either case, we must learn to use our grief to make positive changes.

6. **Hope in Christ (122:9; 2 Cor. 12:9).** Joseph Fielding Smith wrote: "Did he [Joseph Smith] feel that he had been forsaken? This he alone can answer. Yet his trust was in the Lord, for all other help had failed him" (*CHMR*, 2:176). We can always trust in the Lord. No matter what trouble we are going through, the Lord's "hand is stretched out still" to hold us and lift us up (Isa. 5:25; 9:12, 17, 21; 10:4). We can believe what He says in Matthew 11:28-30. (Read it now.) Stephen E. Robinson wrote:

> The "easiness" of the Savior's yoke does not mean we can expect to be excused from the hard tasks of life or be immune to its hard realities. . . . Rather his yoke is easy (a) because it makes what was formerly impossible possible and (b) because he grants compensatory blessings and grace to help us through the hard times. The yoke of the law of Moses could not even be lifted, but the yoke of Christ can be lifted and carried because its weight is individually adapted to our abilities and strength. . . . But even beyond this, those who assume his yoke in humble obedience and consecrate their efforts to him soon learn that an unseen hand lightens the lead in the rough spots and leaves blessings out of all proportion to the required sacrifices (*Believing Christ*, pp. 102-103).

"If thou art called to pass through tribulation" may you come to feel like Joseph Smith and the apostle Paul, "to glory in tribulation" (122:5; 127:2).

If With a Sword
Thine Enemies Tear Thee from Thy Family (122:6)
Joseph Smith wrote:

> Myself and fellow prisoners were taken to the town, into the public square, and before our departure we, after much entreaty, were suffered to see our families,

being attended all the while by a strong guard. I found my wife and children in tears, who feared we had been shot by those who had sworn to take our lives, and that they would see me no more. When I entered my house, they clung to my garments, their eyes streaming with tears, while mingled emotions of joy and sorrow were manifested in their countenances. I requested to have a private interview with them a few minutes, but this privilege was denied me by the guard. I was then obliged to take my departure. Who can realize the feelings which I experienced at that time, to be thus torn from my companion, and leave her surrounded with monsters in the shape of men, and my children, too, not knowing how their wants would be supplied; while I was to be taken far from them in order that my enemies might destroy me when they thought proper to do so. My partner wept, my children clung to me, until they were thrust from me by the swords of the guards. I felt overwhelmed while I witnessed the scene, and could only recommend them to the care of that God whose kindness had followed me to the present time, and who alone could protect them, and deliver me from the hands of my enemies, and restore me to my family (*HC*, 3:193).

These events occurred just a few months before the revelation in section 122 was given. It must have been reassuring to Joseph Smith that the Lord knew exactly what he was going through and that it would all be for good (v. 7).

The Son of Man (122:8)
Remember the material for 45:39, "The Son of Man."

123

LIBELOUS PUBLICATIONS—LET US CHEERFULLY DO ALL THINGS THAT LIE IN OUR POWER

Historical Context
This section is a continuation of the epistle in sections 121 and 122 written to the saints by Joseph Smith while he was a prisoner in Liberty Jail.

Libelous Publications (123:1-16)
The saints are commanded to gather up the facts about their persecutions and any libelous (false) publications about the Lord's church. They are to do this:

1. that it may be published to the world and presented to the heads of government (v. 6);
2. that the whole nation may be left without excuse (v. 6);
3. that they will have the right to call upon the Lord to save them by His power (v. 6); and
4. that they can do their duty to God; angels; themselves; their wives; their children; the widows and fatherless, whose husbands have been murdered; the rising generation; and the pure in heart who are only kept from the truth because they know not where to find it (v. 7, 9, 11-12).

At this time, we do not know all the uses that the Lord has for this information. However, we do know that it is very important because the future of the Church depends on it (v. 15). In 1911, the First Presidency made the following statement:

> It is impossible to take up all the misrepresentations given to the world by anti "Mormon" preachers and writers. They have one merit. They stir up interest in what is called the "Mormon" question. People are led thus to investigate and many of them find out the truth, and unite with the people who are so greatly maligned (*CR*, Apr. 1911, 130).

Concatenation and Nefarious (123:5)

"*Concatenate* means 'to link together in a series or chain.' *Nefarious* means 'flagrantly wicked or impious'" (*Comp.*, 1:617).

Let Us Cheerfully Do All Things That Lie in Our Power; and Then We May Stand Still (123:17)

The first half of this commandment, "Let us cheerfully do all thing that lie in our power," is important. If Joseph Smith and the saints could follow this commandment while in jail and in the midst of persecution then so can we. However, the second half of this commandment, "and then may we stand still, with the utmost assurance," is equally important, and for some, harder to follow. Being a "worry-wart" is not healthy for us or for those around us. It shows a lack of faith in our power and in God's power. Our worrying and continually trying to fix things often interferes with the way that God wants to take care of the situation. To "let go and let God," the serenity prayer asks wisely: "God, grant me the serenity to accept the things I cannot change, the courage to change the things I can, and the wisdom to know the difference."

124
THE CHURCH IN NAUVOO—INTEGRITY

Historical Context
Read the section heading. Smith and Sjodahl add:

When this Revelation was given [Section 124], this beautiful city [Nauvoo] had about 3,000 inhabitants. A charter had been granted by the Illinois Legislature, by which Nauvoo was given a liberal municipal government, with authority to form a militia and erect a university. A Temple was about to be built. The scattered Saints were gathering, and the settlements in Illinois were growing rapidly. The mission in Great Britain was highly successful. . . . The Church had a moment's rest. There was calm before the next storm (*DCC*, p. 768).

Make a Solemn Proclamation (124:1-7, 9, 11-17, 107)
Joseph Smith and others began to prepare the proclamation but the prophet was killed before it was finished. The Quorum of Twelve Apostles finished the proclamation and published it on Apr. 6, 1845. As instructed in verse 3, they addressed the proclamation:

To all the Kings of the World;
To the President of the United States of America;
To the Governors of the several States;
And to the Rulers and People of all Nations (*Messages of the First Presidency*, 1:252).

They then wrote:

Know ye:
That the kingdom of God has come . . . even that kingdom which shall fill the whole earth, and shall stand for ever.
The great Elohim . . . has been pleased once more to speak from the heavens; and also to commune with man upon the earth, by means of open vision, and by the ministration of Holy Messengers.

* * * * *

And we now bear witness that his [the Son of Man's] coming is near at hand. . . .
In order to meet this great event there must needs be a preparation.

> Therefore we send unto you with authority from on high, and command you all to repent and humble yourselves as little children, before the majesty of the Holy One; and come unto Jesus [Christ] with a broken heart and a contrite spirit; and be baptized in his name, . . . and you shall receive the gift of the Holy Spirit (*Messages of the First Presidency*, 1:252-253.)

The proclamation goes on to testify of the restoration, the Book of Mormon, the establishment of Zion, and other subjects. You can read the rest of the proclamation in *Messages of the First Presidency*, Volume 1, pages 252-266.

Stakes (124:2, 36, 134, 142)

Remember the material for 82:13-14, "Stakes."

The Second Coming (124:8, 10)

Remember the material for Section 45: "The Second Coming."

I Love Him Because of the Integrity of His Heart (124:15, 20)

Spencer W. Kimball wrote: "No virtues in the perfection we strive for are more important than integrity and honesty. Let us then be complete, unbroken, pure, and sincere, to develop in ourselves that quality of soul we prize so highly in others" (*Faith Precedes the Miracle*, p. 248).

Integrity, like *perfect*, means true or whole. *Guile*, on the other hand, means deceitful or crafty. When we try to craftily deceive ourselves or others that we have no sins, we deny part of ourselves. Denying part of ourselves leaves us unwhole—we lose our integrity. To be whole, we cannot be deceitful. To be whole—to have integrity—we must confess and forsake our sins.

This is a good time to review the material for 58:43, "By This ye may Know if a Man Repenteth of his Sins."

On Eagles Wings (124:18, 99)

This phrase is used to express three ideas.
1. **Divine protection (124:18).** Review the material for 84:88, "Angels Shall Be Round About You, to Bear You Up."
2. **Personal revelation (124:99).** Cross reference this to 1 Ne. 11:1; 3 Ne. 28:13; Moses 1:1; 2 Cor. 12:2; and *D&C* 137:1.
3. **Physical, emotional, and spiritual strength (Isaiah 40:31).** Review the material for 89:20, "Shall Run and Not Be Weary—Physical and Emotional Strength."

David Patten (124:19, 130)

Remember the material for Section 114: "David W. Patten."

The Nauvoo House (124:22-24, 56-83, 111, 117, 119-122)

The "house" referred to was to be a hotel. Smith and Sjodahl wrote:

The erection of the hotel here referred to, generally known as the Nauvoo House, was commenced in the spring of 1841, and in 1846, when the Saints left Nauvoo, the walls were up above the windows of the second story. It fronted two streets, 120 feet on each. The estimated cost was $100,000. It was planned to be the most magnificent hotel in the West, at the time. When the Saints left the City, the unfinished building became the property of the Prophet's widow, and was subsequently claimed by her second husband, Mr. L. C. Bidamon. In 1872 he put part of it under roof and fitted it up as an hotel, known as the Bidamon House (*DCC*, p. 773).

The purpose of the hotel is given in verse 23. Otten and Caldwell comment:

The Nauvoo House made it possible for a stranger to visit the city of the saints and have a pleasant and positive experience with the church. This was a fellowshipping opportunity.

Latter-day Saints have an opportunity to provide a "Nauvoo House" experience with their own homes. The outward appearance of the grounds, the buildings, the fences, etc. as well as the spirit of the interior can provide an inviting atmosphere for others to have a pleasant experience while visiting a "Nauvoo House" of the saints (*ST*, 2:312-13).

The Nauvoo Temple (124:25-55)

Just as the saints began to settle in Nauvoo, the Lord commanded them to build a temple. This is hardly surprising (remember the material for 97:10-17, "Let the Temple be Built Speedily;" 101:1-8, 35-36, "Why the Saints were Cast Out of Zion;" and 101:43-62, "A Parable Concerning the Redemption of Zion"). This was the fifth temple the saints tried to build. Three of the others (Jackson County, Far West, and Adam-ondi-Ahman) were not completed. The only one completed before the Nauvoo Temple was the Kirtland Temple; however, the Kirtland Temple was desecrated by the enemy.

Otten and Caldwell note that:

the temple in Nauvoo was unique, in that it was the first "full-ordinance" temple built in this dispensation. Baptisms for the dead, as well as other priesthood ordinances for both the living and the dead, were to be performed in this temple (*ST*, 2:313).

Over a year after the revelation in section 124 was given, in May of 1842, some of the Church leaders became the first to receive the full endowment in the latter-days (*HC*, 5:1-2).

The Fullness of the Priesthood (124:28)

By the time the revelation in this section was given, both the Aaronic and Melchizedek priesthood had been restored. Why then, was a temple necessary to restore the fullness of the priesthood? Joseph Smith said: "If a man gets a fullness of the Priesthood of God, he has to get it in . . . obeying all the ordinances of the house of the Lord" (*HC*, 5:424). And Joseph Fielding Smith wrote:

> Let me put this in a little different way. I do not care what office you hold in this Church, you may be an apostle . . . or anything else, and you cannot receive the fullness of the Priesthood unless you go into the temple of the Lord and receive these ordinances (Elijah the Prophet, pp. 45-46).

Baptism for the Dead (124:29-33, 35)

This is the first time baptism for the dead is mentioned in latter-day scripture. Baptisms for the dead were being performed in the Mississippi River because of the special circumstances mentioned in verse 30 (*HC*, 7:261). There were also some problems with the way the baptisms were being recorded. The Lord revealed how to correct these problems in *D&C* 127 and 128. This will be further discussed in Section 128: "Baptism for the Dead."

The Temple in Jerusalem (124:36)

Just like all other authorized temples, the temple in Jerusalem will be built under the direction of the Lord's prophet—the leader of His church. Jews who have converted to The Church of Jesus Christ of Latter-day Saints will play a major role in the building of this temple (*The Millennial Messiah*, pp. 279-80; *Church News*, Aug. 7, 1971, p. 16).

The wording in verse 36 is interesting. Daniel H. Ludlow speculated that "this verse would seem to indicate that Jerusalem will not be part of an organized stake of Zion at the time the temple is built there in the last days" (*Comp.*, 1:622-23).

Oracles (124:39)

Remember the material for 90:1-5, "The Oracles."

Unto the Third and Fourth Generation (124:50-52)

Joseph Fielding Smith said:

> You have an idea that . . . when a man sins his children will be held responsible for his folly and be punished for it, for three or four generations. The commandment does not mean anything of this kind. The Lord never punishes a child for its parents' transgressions. . . . The real meaning . . . is that when a man transgresses he teaches his children to transgress, and they follow his teachings. . . . And by doing so suffer for the parent's iniquity which they have voluntarily brought upon themselves.
>
> There are numerous other passages of scripture showing the mercy and justice of the Lord and that they are not to be punished for the fathers' transgression [Deut. 24:16; Kings 14:6; 2 Chron. 25:4; Jer. 31:29-30; Ezek. 18:20] (*Improvement Era*, June 1955, p. 383).

The key to the punishment is: "so long as they repent not, and hate me" (124:52).

Almon Babbitt (124:84)

Almon Babbitt's "chief ambition was to make money, and . . . he advised the Saints to leave Nauvoo, contrary to the counsel of the Church leaders" (*DCC*, p. 784).

See footnote *a* for the golden calf reference.

William Law (124:97-90, 97-102)

In these verses, William Law was promised many blessings. He was appointed to the First Presidency. But even so, he would later reject the Lord and become a bitter enemy of the Church (*DCC*, p. 785).

Now is a good time to review the material for 50:4-9, "Hypocrites in the Church."

It Shall Redound to Your Glory (124:87)

This will make sense when you look up the scriptures given in footnote *b*.

The Joseph Smith Translation (124:89)

Remember the material for Section 91: "The Apocrypha."

Sidney Rigdon (124:103-110)

Remember Sidney Rigdon's background from the material for Section 35: "Elect Non-member Preachers." Verse 109 makes it clear that the Lord wanted Sidney Rigdon to heed the counsel we discussed in the material for 101:35-38, "Care Not for the Body."

Mine Only Begotten Son (124:123)

Review the material for 93:3-4, "Jesus Christ as the Father."

Church Officers and Offices (124:123-145)

Remember the material for 107:21-41, 58-67, 85-98, "Presiding Officers and Offices."

The Church Patriarch (124:124)

This verse does not mean the patriarch has greater authority than the president of the Church. Verse 125 and 107:91 make this clear.

At My General Conference (124:143-144)

Remember the material for 20:60-62, "General Conference."

125

GATHER UNTO THE PLACES
WHICH I SHALL APPOINT BY MY SERVANT

Historical Context

When the saints were forced to flee Missouri, some settled in Nauvoo, Illinois, and some settled on the other side of the Mississippi River in the territory of Iowa (see the map on page 297 of the *D&C*). In *D&C* 124:25-28, the saints were told to gather to Nauvoo, Illinois to build a temple there. The saints who had settled in the territory of Iowa asked if they should move to Nauvoo. In this section, the Lord told these saints what to do.

Gather Unto the Places
Which I Shall Appoint by My Servant (125:2)

In verse 2, the Lord says that those who desire to be called saints must gather to the places that He will appoint through His servant. Otten and Caldwell state:

> The places of gathering of the Lord's people are still being revealed by Him today through His living prophet. Every member of the church is assigned a place of membership within the geographical boundaries of the various church organizations. Every person is directed to gather with the saints [for Church activities] within an assigned ward or branch, stake or mission. The name and place of such designated gatherings is given by inspiration through those appointed to lead the Lord's church (*ST*, 2:320).

Zarahemla (125:3)

Daniel H. Ludlow wrote:

> The name *Zarahemla* was obviously taken from one of the major cities mentioned in the Book of Mormon. It has been suggested that the basic meaning of the word in Hebrew is "place of abundance"; thus, its meaning would be very similar to that of Bountiful, another Book of Mormon city. (*Ancient America and the Book of Mormon*, p. 152 in *Comp.*, 1:631).

Stakes (125:4)

Remember the material for 82:13-14, "Stakes."

126
BRIGHAM YOUNG'S FAMILY

Brigham Young was called to serve a mission in Europe (remember *D&C* 118:4-5). He returned two years later. He was also serving as the president of the Quorum of the Twelve Apostles for about six months prior to the revelation given in this section (124:127). The Lord not only recognized Brigham Young's sacrifices, but the sacrifices of his family also. It is comforting to know that the Lord is aware of sacrifices made by, and cares for the families of those that are serving in Church callings.

127
LET YOUR WORKS BE REDOUBLED

Historical Context—
An Epistle from the Prophet In Hiding (127:1-3, 10-12)

Joseph Smith, along with many of the saints who had been driven out of Missouri by Governor Boggs and the mobs (remember the historical context of Section 121), had moved to Nauvoo, Illinois. To get Joseph Smith back in the hands of the mobs of Missouri, the now ex-governor Boggs said Orrin Porter Rockwell shot at him and accused Joseph Smith as being an accessory to the shooting. Boggs and his gang convinced the Governor of Illinois, Thomas Carlin, to extradite Joseph Smith back to Missouri where they could get their hands on the prophet. Joseph Smith went into hiding. Verse 1 would later be proven right in a trial held in Springfield, Illinois (*HC*, 5:24).

Joseph wrote the epistles (letters) now known as sections 127 and 128 while he was in hiding. He said:

> I told them [the saints] it was likely I would have again to hide up in the woods, but they must not be discouraged, but build up the city, the Temple, &c.

When my enemies take away my rights, I will bear it and keep out of the way; but if they take away your rights, I will fight for you. I blessed them and departed (*HC*, 5:181).

I Feel, Like Paul, to Glory in Tribulation (127:2)

Remember the material for 122:5-8, "If Thou Art Called To Pass Through Tribulation."

Let Your Works be Redoubled (127:4)

Remember how important it was for the saints to build the temple (see the material for 97:10-17, "Let the Temple be Built Speedily;" 101:1-8, 35-36, "Why the Saints were Cast Out of Zion;" and 101:43-62, "A Parable Concerning the Redemption of Zion"). They needed to "redouble" their efforts.

The counsel to "let your diligence, and your perseverance, and patience, and your works be redoubled" is also important in the good works we are engaged in, whatever they may be. This is a good time to review the material for 53:7, "Endure to the End" and 123:17, "Let Us Cheerfully Do All Things That Lie In Our Power And Then We May Stand Still."

Baptism for the Dead (127:5-7, 9)

Wait until we come to Section 128: "Baptism for the Dead."

I Am About to Restore Many Things Pertaining to the Priesthood (127:8)

Remember from the material for 124:28, "The Fullness of the Priesthood" that the fullness of the priesthood can only be obtained by those who enter the temple. Also remember from the material for 124:25-55, "The Nauvoo Temple" that the endowment and other ordinances had not yet been fully restored.

The Prince of This World (127:11)

Who is this? See footnote *a* of this verse.

128

BAPTISM FOR THE DEAD

Historical Context (128:1)

Remember the material for 127:1-3, 10-12, "Historical Context—An Epistle from the Prophet In Hiding."

Baptism for the Dead is first taught (in latter-day scripture) in *D&C* 124:29-33, 35. Baptisms for the dead were being performed in the Mississippi River because of the special circumstances mentioned in *D&C* 124:30 (*HC*, 7:261). There were also some problems with the way the baptisms were being recorded. The Lord revealed how to correct these problems in sections 124, 127, and 128.

The Atonement—A Vicarious Ordinance

To better understand baptism and other ordinances done in behalf of the dead, it may be helpful to think of the atonement first. Jesus Christ was the only one who could atone for the sins of the world. However, all people, including people who lived and died before Christ, can be cleansed of their sins if they accept the atonement Christ preformed in their behalf. Similarly, only the living can perform certain gospel ordinances. However, those who have died can receive those ordinances if they accept the work preformed in their behalf.

Recorders and Witnesses (128:2-5)

Otten and Caldwell state:

> What are the functions of a witness? The following are included:
> 1. To verify that the ordinance was performed. This provides a protection for the recipient of the ordinance. He does not stand alone.
> 2. To verify that the ordinance was performed by an authorized priesthood holder. This is a protection against deception.
> 3. To verify that the ordinance was performed properly. This is a protection against error in performance.
> 4. To verify the time and the place that the ordinance was performed (*ST*, 2:330).

The Books Were Opened (128:6-14)

There are many books that we will be judged from. Some of these books are records "which are kept on the earth" (v. 7). We will be judged out of these books. These "books" include Church records of gospel ordinances we have received. We will also be judged by the standards set forth in other books, such as: the Book of Mormon, other books of scripture, "books" containing the things that we have been commanded to do by latter-day prophets, and "books" containing what is written about the time, place, and conditions in which we live (2 Ne. 25:22; 29:11; 3 Ne. 27:23-26).

We will also be judged from the "book of life" (v. 7). This book is kept in heaven. It, like Church records kept on earth, contains a record of the covenants we have made that have been sealed by the Spirit (v. 7, 14, and remember the material for 22:2, "Dead Works"). How is this possible? Through the sealing power explained in verses 8-10 and 14. What else will the Book of Life contain? Review the material for 62:3, "Your Testimony is Recorded in Heaven and Your Sins are Forgiven You."

The Symbolism of Baptism (128:12-14)

Water, depending on the context it is used in, can symbolize cleansing power (2 Kings 5:10), the source of life (John 4:7-14), or the place to which the river of life flows—the grave (Rom. 6:4; *D&C* 128:12). These meanings all come together in the ordinance of baptism. *D&C* 128:12-14; Romans 6:1-6; and Moses 6:59-60 further explain the symbolism of baptism.

Note that it is only through faith in Christ that we are saved from the grave. Jesus used an "object lesson" to teach this to His disciples. This object lesson is given in Matthew 14:22-33. Here, water is a symbol of the grave. Jesus walked on the water. This is a symbol of what He was about to do—conquer the grave. He taught that His disciples could also walk on the water, meaning they could conquer spiritual death if they would have faith in Him. Reread Matt. 14:22-33 with the symbolism of baptism in mind.

Paul (128:15-16)

Joseph Smith said the apostle Paul

is about five feet high; very dark hair; dark complexion; dark skin; large Roman nose; sharp face; small black eyes, penetrating as eternity; round shoulders; a whining voice, except when elevated, and then it almost resembled the roaring of a lion. He was a good orator, active and diligent, always employing himself in doing good to his fellow man (*TPJS*, p. 180).

We Without Them Cannot Be Made Perfect (128:15-18)

Why this is so is explained in verse 18. Links on a chain beyond a point where a "welding link" is broken are not part of the original chain. We must be sure all the links (children of God) are welded (sealed) to the chain (the family of God) so that our link (ourselves) will be part of that chain. If this is not done, the earth will "smitten with a curse." Why? Remember the material for 2:3, "The Earth would be Utterly Wasted."

The Gospel—A Psalm of Joy (128:19-23)

Gospel means "good news" What is the good news? The psalm of joy in these verses sings some of the good news of the latter-days.

The Dews of Carmel (128:19)

Daniel H. Ludlow wrote that this "has reference to the heavy dews that fall on Mount Carmel, which is located in the Holy Land alongside the Mediterranean Sea near the modern city of Haifa" (*Comp.*, p. 642). The "knowledge of God" that will "descend upon them" as the dews of Carmel will be discussed in the material for 131:5, "The More Sure Word of Prophecy."

The Chamber of Old Father Whitmer (128:21)

This is where the Church was first organized in the latter-days (*HC*, 1:60-61).

Michael, Gabriel, and Raphael (128:21)

Michael is Adam (v. 21). Gabriel is Noah (*HC*, 3:386). The identity of Raphael has not yet been revealed to the Church. According to the Book of Tobit in the Apocrypha, Raphael is "one of the seven holy angels, which present the prayers of the Saints, and which go in and out before the glory of the Holy One." (For more information on the Book of Tobit, see *Apocrypha* in the Bible Dictionary.)

Let the Mountains Shout for Joy (128:23)

Cross reference this verse with Helaman 12:7-13 (man is less than the dust because the dust obeys the voice of God) and Moses 7:48-49 (the earth mourns because of the wickedness of men).

The Great Day of the Lord (128:24)

Remember the material for Section 45: "The Second Coming."

Fuller's Soap (128:24)

A fuller is a person who washes clothes clean by putting them in a tub and treading on them. The fuller uses very strong lye or soap to get the clothes clean. Cross reference this verse to 76:107 and the symbolism will become clearer.

The Sons of Levi (128:24)

Remember the material for Section 13 under the heading "The Sons of Levi and Their Offering."

129

THREE KEYS BY WHICH MESSENGERS MAY BE KNOWN

Historical Context

Satan can appear as an angel of light (*D&C* 129:9; 2 Ne. 9:9; Alma 30:53; 2 Cor. 11:14). Satan had deceived members of the Church on several occasions. They believed that they were receiving revelation from the Lord when they were actually receiving revelation from Satan (remember the material for Sections 28 and 43). In this section, the Lord teaches us how we can protect ourselves from being deceived.

There Are Two Kinds of Beings in Heaven (129:1)

The statement in verse 1 does not mean that there are *only* two kinds of beings in heaven. And it does not mean that *all* beings referred to as angels are resurrected beings. Charles W. Penrose explained:

> The theme discoursed upon is the presence in heaven of two kinds or classes of beings, namely, first, resurrected beings and, second, spirits who are not resurrected. It is not asserted that there are no other kinds of persons in heaven than they, but the subject treated is of the two classes mentioned.
>
> Comparison with other texts of scripture, ancient and modern, makes clear the fact that there are other grades or classes of heavenly beings than the two spoken of in section 129. It is understood by ordinary students of modern religion that there are perfected beings called gods, who are higher than the angels (see *D&C* 132:16-39), and to whom the angels are servants. And even among the gods there are Presiding Personages, the Holy Trinity standing at the head. [*D&C* 121:32; 130:22-23.]
>
> There are angels of various appointments and stations. Michael is called an "archangel." (*D&C* 29:26; Dan. 10:13.) Some are resurrected beings like the angel that was sent to John the Revelator (Rev. 22:8, 9), and those already referred to in *D&C*, Section 132, while others are "ministering spirits sent forth to minister unto them who shall be heirs of salvation." (Heb. 1:14.) Some of these angels are described as "the spirits of just men made perfect" and are "not resurrected," and others were made ministering spirits before entering into mortality, serving among their fellows in their pre-existent state. Christ was a ministering spirit before his birth into this world. [Ether 3:14-16.] He was "anointed above

his fellows." The angel Gabriel was a ministering spirit after he had been a mortal man (Noah) and before his resurrection, for Jesus of Nazareth was . . . "the firstfruits of them that slept." (See Luke 1:11-30; Dan. 8:16; 9:21.)

Angels are God's messengers, whether used in that capacity as unembodied spirits, selected according to their capacities for the work required, or as disembodied spirits, or as translated men, or as resurrected beings.

*   *   *   *   *

The popular notion that angels are winged beings, because it is stated by some scripture writers that they saw them "flying though the heavens," is a fallacy. Cherubim and Seraphim spoken of by Ezekiel [10:3] and Isaiah [6:2, 6] are not to be classed with the angels, for the angels are of the same race and descent as man, whether in body or in spirit, and do not need wings for locomotion, nor do they appear in birdlike form. They are of the family of Deity in different degrees of progression and are "in the image and likeness" of the Most High.

There are fallen angels, too, who were cast down for transgression, as mentioned by Jude (verse 6), chief among whom on this earth is Lucifer or Satan, who has sought on many occasions to appear as an "angel of light" to deceive and lead astray. . . .That great spiritual personage was an angel of God in his "first estate," and yet never had a body of flesh, but "was in authority in the presence of God" as a spirit, before he rebelled. . . .

Thus it will be seen that all angels are not resurrected beings, nor is it so declared (see *IE*, Aug. 1912, pp. 949-52).

The Devil Will Offer You His Hand (129:8)

Why would the devil offer you his hand if he knows about this revelation? Because he has to obey when commanded by one holding priesthood authority. Joseph Smith said: "Wicked spirits have their bounds, limits and laws, by which they are governed; and it is very evident that they possess a power that none but those who have the priesthood can control" (*HC*, 4:576).

130

THE LAW OF BLESSINGS—THE GODHEAD

That Same Sociality Which Exists Here Will Exist There (130:2)

Orson Pratt said:

> A Saint, who is one in deed and in truth, does not look for an immaterial heaven but he expects a heaven with lands, houses, cities, vegetation, rivers, and animals; with thrones, temples, palaces, kings, princes, priests, and angels; with food, raiment, musical instruments, etc.; all of which are material. Indeed the Saints' heaven is a redeemed, glorified, celestial material creation, inhabited by glorified material beings, male and female, organized into families, embracing all the relationships of husbands and wives, parents and children, where sorrow, crying, pain, and death will be known no more. Or to speak still more definitely, this earth, when glorified, is the Saints' eternal heaven. On it they expect to live, with body parts, and holy passions: on it they expect to move and have their being; to eat, drink, converse, worship, sing, play on musical instruments, engage in joyful, innocent, social amusements, visit neighboring towns and neighboring worlds (*Millennial Star*, Nov. 17, 1886, p. 722).

Angels (130:5-7)

Otten and Caldwell expressed their personal view that

> God's house is a house of order. The Lord controls who comes to this earth. The world worries about invasions of people and forces foreign to this planet. How comforting to know that only those come here who are authorized by the Lord to minister to the inhabitants of this earth (*ST*, 2:343).

This Earth Will Be Made like unto Crystal (130:8-9)

Remember the material for Section 101 under the heading: "The End of the Millennium and of the Earth."

The United States' Civil War (130:12-13)

Remember the material for Section 87: "Prophecy on War."

The Law of Blessings (130:20-21)

See Appendix 3: "Blessings and Laws upon which they are Predicated."

The Godhead (130:22)

We refer to a mortal body as being "flesh and blood." Eternal, resurrected bodies are spiritual (*D&C* 88:27-28), made of flesh and bone. Joseph Smith said:

"Flesh and blood cannot go there [heaven]; but flesh and bones, quickened by the Spirit of God can" (*TPJS*, p. 326).

Joseph Fielding Smith said that the Holy Ghost "is a Spirit, in the form of a man" (*DS*, 1:38). He also said:

> The Holy Ghost is not a woman, as some have declared, and therefore is not the mother of Jesus Christ.
>
> It is a waste of time to speculate in relation to his jurisdiction. We know what has been revealed and that the Holy Ghost, sometimes spoken of as the Holy Spirit, and Comforter, is the third member of the godhead, and that he, being in perfect harmony with the Father and the Son, reveals to man by the spirit of revelation and prophecy the truths of the gospel of Jesus Christ. Our great duty is so to live that we may be led constantly in light and truth by this Comforter so that we may not be deceived by the many false spirits that are in the world.
>
> I have never troubled myself about the Holy Ghost whether he will sometime have a body or not because it is not in any way essential to my salvation. He is a member of the Godhead, with great power and authority, with a most wonderful mission which must be performed by a spirit. This has satisfied me without delving into mysteries that would be of no particular benefit (*DS*, 1:39).

131

THE MORE SURE WORD OF PROPHECY

The Celestial Glory (131:1)

See the material in Section 76 under the heading "Degrees Within the Kingdoms of Glory."

The New and Everlasting Covenant (131:2)

Review the material for 22:1, "A New and Everlasting Covenant."

An Increase (131:4)

"An increase," in this verse, means children. Joseph Smith said:

> Except a man and his wife enter into an everlasting covenant and be married for eternity, while in this probation, by the power and authority of the holy Priesthood, they will cease to increase when they die; that is, they will not have any children after the resurrection (*HC*, 5:391).

Only those who enter the highest degree of glory will receive the keys of eternal creation.

The More Sure Word of Prophecy (131:5)

The Lord defines "the more sure word of prophecy" in verse five. It is the same as having one's calling and election made sure. The Apostle Peter exhorted the saints of his day to "give diligence to make your calling and election sure" (2 Pet. 1:10). And to the saints in our day, Joseph Smith said: "Oh! I beseech you to go forward, go forward and make your calling and your election sure" (*TPJS*, p. 366).

Since we have been counseled to make our calling and election sure, it is important to understand this doctrine. To understand it, we must first define some terms.

1. **Calling.** In general, our calling is our church membership (Rom. 1:6-7; 1 Cor. 1:2). Through repentance and baptism we enter "the gate"—membership in the church.

2. **Election.** Like *calling*, *election* generally means church membership (Isa. 45:4; 65:9; Matt. 24:22; Mark 13:20; Luke 18:7; Col. 3:12; 2 Tim. 2:10; Titus 1:1).   However, our *calling* only puts us at the beginning of the "strait and narrow path which leads to eternal life" (2 Ne. 31:18). We must continue to "press forward with a steadfastness in Christ" (2 Ne. 31:17-20). This is what the elect do. The elect are those who hear the voice of the Lord and do as the Lord commands (*D&C* 29:7).

3. **Made Sure.** Our calling and election lead to many covenants. As we make these covenants we are promised blessings—among them, eternal life. But it is a conditional promise based on our obedience. This promise can be made (almost) unconditional. In other words, it can be made "sure." This is what making one's calling and election sure is.

4. **The Holy Spirit of Promise** is the sealing power of the Holy Ghost. Remember the material for 20:30-31, "Justification" and "Sanctification," and 22:2, "Dead Works."

5. **A person sealed by the Holy Spirit of Promise.** This is the same as a person being sealed up to eternal life, which is the same as making one's calling and election sure, which is the same as one having the more sure word of prophesy.

   It should be obvious that entering into the covenant of eternal marriage in the temple is not the same as being sealed by the Holy Spirit of Promise. Although the Holy Spirit of Promise seals the ordinance, the promised blessings are still conditional and based on obedience to the covenants made.

6. **The First Comforter** is the Holy Ghost (*TPJS*, p. 150—see quote below).

7. **The Second or Other Comforter** is Jesus Christ (*TPJS*, p. 150—see quote below and John 14:12-23).

The Prophet Joseph Smith taught how to receive all these things. He said:

> After a person has faith in Christ, repents of his sins, and is baptized for the remission of his sins and receives the Holy Ghost, (by the laying on of hands), which is the first Comforter, then let him continue to humble himself before God, hungering and thirsting after righteousness, and living by every word of God, and the Lord will soon say unto him, Son, thou shalt be exalted.

> When the Lord has thoroughly proved him, and finds that the man is determined to serve him at all hazards, then the man will find his calling and his election made sure, then it will be his privilege to receive the other Comforter.

*   *   *   *   *

> Now what is this other Comforter? It is no more nor less than the Lord Jesus Christ himself; and this is the sum and substance of the whole matter; that when any man obtains this last Comforter, he will have the personage of Jesus Christ to attend him, or appear unto him from time to time, and even he will manifest the Father unto him, and they will take up their abode with him, and the visions of the heavens will be opened unto him, and the Lord will teach him face to face, and he may have a perfect knowledge of the mysteries of the Kingdom of God; and this is the state and place the ancient saints arrived at when they had such glorious visions—Isaiah, Ezekiel, John upon the Isle of Patmos, St. Paul in the three heavens, and all the saints who held communion with the general assembly and Church of the Firstborn (*TPJS*, pp. 150-151).

As you "press forward with a steadfastness in Christ," your calling and election can be made sure and the knowledge spoken of in *D&C* 131:5 will "distill upon thy soul as the dews from heaven" (2 Ne. 31:17-20; *D&C* 121:45). Then you can receive the Second Comforter (*D&C* 88:3-4; John 14:16-23).

The conditional promise of eternal life can be made unconditional—almost. Bruce R. McConkie wrote:

> The prophets and apostles from Adam and Enoch down, and all men, whether cleansed and sanctified from sin or not, are yet subject to and do in fact commit sin. This is the case even after men have seen the visions of eternity and been sealed by that Holy Spirit of Promise which makes their calling and election sure. Since these chosen ones have the sure promise of eternal life, and since "no unclean thing can enter into" the Father's "kingdom" (3 Ne. 27:19), "or dwell in his presence" (Moses 6:57), what of sins committed after being sealed up into eternal life?

Obviously the laws of repentance still apply . . . .

And as a matter of fact, the added blessing of having one's calling and election made sure is itself an encouragement to avoid sin. . . .

But suppose such persons [who have their calling and election made sure] become disaffected and the spirit of repentance leaves them . . .? The answer is—and the revelations and teachings of the Prophet Joseph Smith so recite!—they must then pay the penalty of their own sins, for the blood of Christ will not cleanse them. Or if they commit murder or adultery, they lose their promised inheritance because these sins are exempt from the sealing promises. Or if they commit the unpardonable sin, they become sons of perdition (*DNTC*, 3:344).

The condition of murder is covered in 132:19. The condition of the unpardonable sin is covered in the material for 76:30-49, "A vision of sons of perdition." The condition of adultery was taught by Joseph Smith. Speaking of those having their calling and election made sure, he said: "If a man commit adultery, he cannot receive the celestial kingdom of God. Even if he is saved in any kingdom, it cannot be the celestial kingdom" (*HC*, 6:81). And Bruce R. McConkie wrote:

Thus, even though a man's calling and election has been sure, if he then commits adultery, all of the promises are of no effect, and he goes to a telestial kingdom, because when he was sealed up unto eternal life, it was with a reservation. The sealing was not to apply in the case of subsequent adultery. In other cases, through repentance, there is forgiveness for this sin which is second only to murder in the category of personal sins. (1 Cor. 6:9-11; 3 Ne. 30; *D&C* 42:24-26.) (*DNTC*, 3:348).

Just as people continue to sin after they are baptized, they may continue to sin after they make their calling and election sure. The key, as the quotes above emphasize, is the continuing spirit of repentance. Joseph Fielding Smith explained:

Verse 26, in section 132, is the most abused passage in any scripture. The Lord has never promised any soul that he may be taken into exaltation without the spirit of repentance. While repentance is not stated in this passage, yet it is, and must be, implied. It is strange to me that everyone knows about verse 26, but it seems that they have never read or heard of Matthew 12:31-32, where the Lord tells us the same thing in substance as we find in verse 26, section 132.

*   *   *   *   *

So we must conclude that those spoken of in verse 26 are those who, having sinned, have fully repented and are willing to pay the price of their sinning, else the blessings of exaltation will not follow. Repentance is absolutely necessary for the forgiveness, and the person having sinned must be cleansed (*DS*, 2:95-96).

For more information and examples of people who have made their calling and election sure, look under "Calling and Election Made Sure, Receive" in Appendix 3: "Blessings and Laws upon which they are Predicated."

It Is Impossible to Be Saved in Ignorance (131:6)

This does not refer to academic knowledge. It refers to knowledge of the saving ordinances and covenants of the gospel. It is impossible to be saved without a knowledge of these covenants because one must make and keep these covenants to be saved. (For example, see v. 2.)

132

THE LAW OF CELESTIAL MARRIAGE

Historical Context—You Have Inquired of My Hand (132:1)

Read verse 1.

In 1831 Joseph Smith was in the process of translating the Bible (remember the material for the *JST* in Section 91: "The Apocrypha"). Elder B. H. Roberts notes that Joseph Smith

> was doubtless struck with the favor in which the Lord held the several Bible Patriarchs of that period, notwithstanding they had a plurality of wives. What more natural than that he should inquire of the Lord at that time . . . "Why, O Lord, didst Thou justify Thy servants, Abraham, Isaac and Jacob; as also Moses, David, and Solomon, in the matter of their having many wives and concubines . . . ?" In answer to that inquiry came the revelation (*HC*, 5:xxix-xxx).

Even though the revelation was received in 1831, it was not committed to writing until 1843. The *History of the Church* (5:32) records the context of the writing of the revelation contained in this section. The following is from that record:

> In a sworn statement before John T. Caine, a notary public in Salt Lake City, on February 16th, 1874, William Clayton said:
> . . . . On the morning of the 12th of July, 1843, Joseph and Hyrum Smith came into the office in the upper story of the brick store, on the bank of the Mississippi

river. They were talking on the subject of plural marriage. Hyrum said to Joseph, "If you will write the revelation on celestial marriage, I will take it and read it to Emma, and I believe I can convince her of its truth, and you will hereafter have peace." Joseph smiled and remarked, "You do not know Emma as well as I do." Hyrum repeated his opinion, and further remarked, "The doctrine is so plain, I can convince any reasonable man or woman of its truth, purity and heavenly origin," or words to that effect. Joseph then said, "Well, I will write the revelation and we will see." He then requested me to get paper and prepare to write. Hyrum very urgently requested Joseph to write the revelation by means of the Urim and Thummim, but Joseph in reply, said he did not need to, for he knew the revelation perfectly from beginning to end.

Joseph and Hyrum then sat down and Joseph commenced to dictate the revelation on celestial marriage, and I wrote it, sentence by sentence, as he dictated. After the whole was written, Joseph asked me to read it through, slowly and carefully, which I did, and he pronounced it correct. He then remarked that there was much more that he could write on the same subject, but what was written was sufficient for the present.

While the revelation was written in 1843, it was not published until President Brigham Young directed Elder Orson Pratt to do so in 1852. It was included in the Doctrine and Covenants in 1876 (see *DCSM*, p. 327 and *JD*, 14:213-214).

The first half of the revelation mainly deals with the law of celestial marriage while the second half mainly deals with the doctrine of plural marriage.

The New and Everlasting Covenant (132:2-6)
Review 84:46-48 and the material for 22:1, "A New and Everlasting Covenant."

Conditions of the New and Everlasting Covenant (132:7-14)
Review the material for 22:2, "Dead Works."

The Law of Celestial Marriage (132:15-25)
The Law is clearly explained by these verses. It is that for a marriage sealing to be valid after death it must be done by the proper authority and be sealed by the Spirit. The details of these verses will be discussed below. First, I want to stress the importance of celestial—or temple—marriage. Heber J. Grant did this powerfully when he related the story of his temple marriage:

> I shall always be grateful, to the day of my death, that I did not listen to some of my friends when, as a young man not quite twenty-one years of age, I took the trouble to travel all the way from Utah County to St. George to be married in the St. George Temple. That was before the railroad went south of Utah County, and we had to travel the rest of the way by team. It was a long and difficult trip in those

times, over unimproved and uncertain roads, and the journey each way required several days.

Many advised me not to make the effort—not to go all the way down to St. George to be married. They reasoned that I could have the president of the stake or my bishop marry me, and then when the Salt Lake Temple was completed, I could go there with my wife and children and be sealed to her and have our children sealed to us for eternity.

Why did I not listen to them? Because I wanted to be married for time and eternity—because I wanted to start life right. Later I had cause to rejoice greatly because of my determination to be married in the temple at that time rather than to have waited until some later and seemingly more convenient time.

Some years ago the general board members of the Young Women's Mutual Improvement Association were traveling throughout the stakes of Zion speaking on the subject of marriage. They urged the young people to start their lives together in the right way by being married right, in the temples of the Lord.

I was out in one of the stakes attending a conference, and one of my daughters, who was the representative of the Young Women's general board at the conference, said: "I am very grateful to the Lord that I was properly born, born under the covenant, born of parents that had been properly married and sealed in the temple of the Lord."

Tears came into my eyes, because her mother died before the Salt Lake Temple was completed and I was grateful that I had not listened to the remarks of my friends who had tried to persuade me not to go to the St. George Temple to be married. I was very grateful for the inspiration and determination I had to start life right.

Why did it come to me? It came to me because my mother believed in the gospel, taught me the value of it, gave me a desire to get all of the benefits of starting life right and of doing things according to the teachings of the gospel.

I believe that no worthy young Latter-day Saint man or woman should spare any reasonable effort to come to the house of the Lord to begin life together. The marriage vows taken in these hallowed places and the sacred covenants entered into for time and all eternity are proof against many of the temptations of life that tend to break homes and destroy happiness (*Gospel Standards*, pp. 359-360).

Those Who Do Not Abide
the Law of Celestial Marriage (132:16-18)

Certain ordinances can only be done on earth. Celestial marriage is one of these ordinances. It is not done in heaven (v. 16). However, it can be performed here on earth on behalf of those who are already in "heaven" (the spirit world). It has been made abundantly clear that everyone will have the opportunity (in this life or the next) to receive all gospel ordinances—including celestial marriage (for example, see President Spencer W. Kimball, "The Importance of Celestial Marriage," *Ensign*, Oct. 1979, p. 5).

The Lamb's Book of Life (132:19)

Remember the material for 128:6-14, "The Books were Opened."

Sealed by the Holy Spirit of Promise (132:19, 26-27)

Review the material for 131:5, "The More Sure Word of Prophecy."

This is Eternal Lives (132:20-25)

While immortality is just living forever, eternal life is exaltation—God's life. Eternal life makes eternal lives—eternal posterity—possible. How do we receive eternal lives? See verse 24. How will we know God? We will be like Him (verses 20, 23-24 and see 1 John 3:2). How do we become like Him? Receive His law (v. 24).

Do The Works of Abraham (132:28-39)

What are the works of Abraham we are to do? Some are seeking for the priesthood and priesthood blessings (Abr. 1:2; 2:12), desiring to be righteous (Abr. 1:2), keeping covenants despite the costs (Abr. 1:11-12), presiding in righteousness (Abr. 2:6; Gen. 21:9- 14), sharing the gospel (Abr. 2:15), paying a full tithe (Gen. 4:18-19), becoming a peacemaker (Gen. 14), receiving revelation for our stewardship (Gen. 17:15-16), giving prompt obedience (Gen. 22:2-3), and teaching the gospel in word and deed (Gen. 22:7-8).

The Law of the Priesthood
as Pertaining to Plural Marriage (132:34-66)

The three questions that most often come up about these verses in the minds of members of the Church are:

1. Why did the Lord approve of some plural marriages and not others (see verses 34-39 and Gen. 25:1-6; 29; 30; 2 Sam. 12:7-8; and Jacob 2:27-30). What is the key to the answer? See verse 35.

2. Why have plural marriage at all? One reason the Lord has revealed is given in verses 40 and 45, Eph. 1:10, and Acts 3:20-21 (part of the restoration of *all* things). A second reason revealed by the Lord is given in verse 63 and Jacob 2:30 (to raise up seed).

3. What about plural marriage in the celestial kingdom? Will it be practiced in the celestial kingdom? Yes. Some men have been sealed to more than one wife for time and all eternity. Those who have kept their covenants (both physically and in their hearts) will remain sealed. Does one have to practice plural marriage to enter the celestial kingdom? No. Couples who remain faithful to their marriage covenant made in the temple are promised exaltation. As Otten and Caldwell state:

> When a worthy couple kneel at the sacred marriage altars of the temple, they
> are given the right to eternal companionship and are promised the same blessings

that were bestowed upon Abraham in ancient days. That is, they are assured of an eternal posterity, the rights and powers of the priesthood of God, and an eternal family relationship based upon the patriarchal order (*ST*, 2:360).

The Law of Sarah (132:34, 65)

Read Gen. 16:1-3. Smith and Sjodahl explain:

> Sarah gave Hagar to Abraham in accordance with law. It is known now that, according to the Code of Hammurabi, which, in many respects, resembles the later Mosaic law, if a man's wife was childless, he was allowed to take a concubine and bring her into his house . . . . This was the law in the country from which Abraham came. A concubine was a wife of inferior social rank (*DCC*, p. 831).

They Have Entered into Their Exaltation (132:37)

Elder Bruce R. McConkie noted: "What we say for Abraham, Isaac, and Jacob we say also for Sarah, Rebekah, and Rachel, the wives who stood at their sides and who with them were true and faithful in all things" ("Mothers in Israel and Daughters of Zion," *New Era*, May 1978, p. 37). Righteous earthly parents honor their Heavenly Parents by becoming heavenly parents themselves (remember the material for 38:1-8, "We Can Trust the Lord because He Knows Everything"). Obviously, then, just as there is a Heavenly Father, there is a Heavenly Mother. Elder McConkie further explains:

> This doctrine that there is a Mother in Heaven was affirmed in plainness by the First Presidency of the Church (Joseph F. Smith, John R. Winder, and Anthon H. Lund) when, in speaking of pre-existence and the origin of man, they said that "man, as a spirit, was begotten and born of heavenly parents, and reared to maturity in the eternal mansions of the Father," that man is the "offspring of celestial parentage," and that "all men and women are in the similitude of the universal Father and Mother and are literally the sons and daughters of Deity." (Man: Origin and Destiny, pp. 348-355.)

> This glorious truth of celestial parentage, including specifically both a Father and a Mother, is heralded forth by song in one of the greatest of Latter-day Saint hymns. *O My Father*, by Eliza R. Snow, written in 1843, during the lifetime of the Prophet, includes this teaching:

>> In the heavens are parents single? No; the thought makes reason stare! Truth is reason, truth eternal, Tells me I've a Mother there.

>> When I leave this frail existence, When I lay this mortal by, Father, Mother, may I meet you In your royal courts on high?

>> Then, at length, when I've completed All you sent me forth to do, With your mutual approbation, Let me come and dwell with you (*MD*, pp. 516-17).

By the Hand of Nathan (132:39)

Daniel H. Ludlow points out: "This statement clearly indicated that many of the prophets of ancient Israel held the sealing keys of the priesthood, even though the people as a whole did not hold the higher priesthood" (*Comp.*, 1:668).

Therefore He Hath Fallen (132:39)

The *Old Testament Student Manual* asks:

> Do we emphasize the David who killed Goliath, or the David who killed Uriah? Should we view him as the servant who refused to lift his hand against the Lord's anointed, or as the Lord's anointed who lifted his hand against a faithful and loyal servant? Was his life a tragedy, or a triumph?
>
> If a triumph, why, then, has "he fallen from his exaltation" (*D&C* 132:39) and lost "the greatest of all the gifts of God"? (*D&C* 6:13). If a tragedy, why is the Messiah prophesied to sit "upon the throne of David" (Isaiah 9:7), and be called "David their king"? (Jeremiah 30:9; see also 23:5-6; 30:15-17; Ezekiel 37:24-25) (p. 287).

This verse, anyway, emphasizes the fall of David. Joseph Smith said:

> David sought repentance at the hand of God carefully with tears, for the murder of Uriah; but he could only get it through hell: he got a promise that his soul should not be left in hell.
>
> Although David was a king, he never did obtain the spirit and power of Elijah and the fullness of the Priesthood; and the Priesthood that he received, and the throne and kingdom of David is to be taken from him and given to another by the name of David in the last days, raised up out of his lineage (*HC*, 6:253).

Whenever I start thinking that I have somehow reached the point where I would never give in to temptation to commit a major sin, I think of David. He was a most righteous youth, a brilliant soldier and leader, a poet and musician, a trusted servant of king Saul. But even he gave in to temptation. So, of course, I could too.

David's weeping of repentance and his desire for forgiveness can be felt as one reads his psalms. In Psalm 16:10, David realizes he has received a portion of forgiveness—he will not be left in hell or outer darkness, but will inherit the telestial kingdom.

Concerning Adultery (132:41-44)

Adultery and things like unto it were discussed in the material for 42:23-26, "Thou Shalt Not Commit Adultery."

Some misinterpret verse 44, concluding that the priesthood views women as property. A thoughtful reading of the Constitution of the Priesthood (see section 121) proves this mistaken concept to be repugnant to the priesthood. The terms "take" and "give" in this verse can easily be substituted with "divorce" and "marry." What is described in verse 44 is exactly what happens today. When a divorced woman decides to remarry in the temple, even if she has been divorced for years, it can be said that the priesthood holder preforming the ceremony "gives" her unto him that hath been faithful.

The Power To Bind and To Loose (132:46-48)

Elder Bruce R. McConkie taught:

> Properly speaking there is no such thing as a temple divorce; divorces in this day are civil matters handled by the courts of the land. But following a civil divorce of persons who have been married for eternity in the temples, if the circumstances are sufficiently serious to warrant it, the President of the Church has power to cancel the sealings involved. He holds the keys and power both to bind and loose on earth and in heaven. (Matt. 16:19; *D&C* 132:46; Doctrines of Salvation, vol. 2, p. 84.) (*MD*, pp. 110-11.)

For information on priesthood cursings see the material for 60:15, "Shake Off the Dust of Thy Feet." And for information on remitting sins see the material for Section 72 under the subheading "Be a Judge in Israel."

I Seal Upon You Your Exaltation, Joseph Smith (132:49-50)

Remember the material for 131:5, "The More Sure Word of Prophecy" and see *Calling and Election Made Sure, Receive* in Appendix 3: "Blessings and Laws upon which they are Predicated."

Instructions to Joseph and Emma Smith (132:51-57)

Concerning verse 51 the *Doctrine and Covenants Student Manual* states:

> No indication is given here or elsewhere about what the Lord had commanded the Prophet Joseph to offer to his wife, but the context seems to suggest that it was a special test of faith similar to the great test of Abraham's faith when the Lord commanded him to sacrifice Isaac (p. 334).

133

THE APPENDIX—LAST DAYS EVENTS

Historical Context

Joseph Smith received the revelation in this section at a special conference held to act on the publishing of the Doctrine and Covenants. Remember that sections 1 and 67-69 were also received at this conference. Now would be a good time to review the section headings and material for those sections.

The Lord gave the revelation in section 1 as the preface of the Doctrine and Covenants. Two days later, He gave the revelation in section 133. This revelation was placed in the book as an appendix (see the section heading). Elder John Widtsoe explained:

> The Appendix [section 133], supplements the introduction [section 1]. The two sections together encompass the contents of the book in a condensed form. An appendix is something which the writer thinks should be added to amplify that which is in the book, to emphasize it, to make it stronger or to explain the contents a little more completely" (*Message of the Doctrine and Covenants*, p. 17).

The Doctrine and Covenants Is for All (133:1, 16, 60-61)

As He did in section 1, the Lord again emphasizes that the Doctrine and Covenants is for all people (remember the material for 1:1-7, 34-36, "The Doctrine and Covenants is for All").

The Lord Shall Suddenly Come to His Temple (133:2)

This verse was partly fulfilled about four-and-a-half years later when the Lord appeared to Joseph Smith and Oliver Cowdery in the Kirtland Temple (remember the material for 110:1-8, "Appearance of the Savior in His House"). However, it will not be completely fulfilled until the Second Coming (remember the material for 45:44-54, 74-75, "Appearances of the Lord"). And when He comes, He will come suddenly. There will be no time to prepare. We must be prepared beforehand (remember the material for 33:18, "I Come Quickly").

He Shall Make Bare His Holy Arm (133:3)

The arm symbolizes strength. The Lord making His arm bare is the Lord revealing His strength to the world. An example of this is given in Exodus 15:1-18.

Sanctify Yourselves (133:4)

Remember the material for 20:31, "Sanctification."

Flee from Babylon to Zion (133:4-15)

Babylon symbolizes the worldly world we are to flee (v. 14). We do this by repenting. We get to Zion by being pure in heart. Once we get there, we should not go back to the worldly ways of Babylon (v. 15).

The Vessels of the Lord (133:5)

Remember the material for 38:42, "Be Ye Clean that Bear the Vessels of the Lord."

Stakes (133:9)

Remember the material for 82:13-14, "Stakes."

The Bridegroom Cometh (133:10-11)

Remember the material for Section 33: "Burning the Midnight Oil."

Let Judah Flee Unto the Mountains of the Lord's House (133:13, 35)

It is not enough for the Jews to just flee to Jerusalem; to escape spiritual Babylon, they must flee to the "mountains of the Lord's house." Many of the ancient prophets used mountains as places to be close to God—temples (Ex. 3:1-2; 1 Ne. 17:7; Ether 3:1; Abr. 2:20; etc.). The "mountains of the Lord's House" are temples (2 Ne. 12:2). Review the material for 124:36, "The Temple in Jerusalem."

The Angel Crying Through the Midst of Heaven (133:17, 36)

This can refer to all of the angels—one of whom is Moroni—who have participated and will participate in the restoration of the gospel and its keys.

The Second Coming (133:18-25)

Remember the material for Section 45: "The Second Coming."

The 144,000 (133:18)

The 144,000 high priests are not the only people who will be saved, nor are they the only people who have made their calling and election sure (77:1; Rev. 7:9).

The Restoration of the Ten Tribes (133:26-35)

There are twelve tribes of Israel. Two of them, Judah and Joseph, are "found," meaning we have their records (at least in part). The other ten tribes are said to be "lost."

The scattering of the ten tribes basically begins in 2 Kings 17:6 when the Assyrians defeated the Northern Kingdom of Israel. Where did the people of the ten tribes go?

1. **Some people remained in Israel** and were mixed with imported captives from other nations. They became Samaritans (2 Kings 17:24-41).

2. **Some people fled to the Southern Kingdom** of Judah for safety. This is why it can be explained that Lehi's family (descended from a tribe of the Northern Kingdom) was in the Southern Kingdom of Judah (Alma 10:3).

3. **Some people remained in Assyria** after their capture (*The Articles of Faith*, p. 325).

4. **Some people journeyed to the North.** One of the books of the Apocrypha tells about a group of Israelite captives that turned to the Lord and repented. They were led out of Assyria into the "north countries" (2 Esdras 13:41-46). This account is supported by 3 Ne. 15:15 (also see Jer. 3:18; *D&C* 110:11, and 133:26).

5. **As they traveled north, many people stopped and settled down** along the way (*The Articles of Faith*, p. 325-26).

6. **Certain groups of people** (such as Nephites and Mulekites) **were led elsewhere** (Jacob 5).

7. **Descendants from each tribe have since mingled and been scattered throughout the earth.**

Remember that in *D&C* 110:11, Moses restored the keys of the gathering of Israel and the leading of the ten tribes from the land of the north. Moses was in charge of the gathering and the leading of Israel in his day. He also predicted the scattering and eventual regathering of Israel (see Deut. 4). The keys that Moses restored are the authority to lead and gather all the people from the ten tribes of Israel (which includes all the people of the earth) into stakes of Zion. These keys are held by the president of the Church.

The gathering of Israel will be so marvelous and powerful that Jeremiah says God will no longer be called the Lord who led Israel out of Egypt, but will become known as the Lord who brought up the children of Israel from the land of the north (Jer. 16:14-15). The gathered ten tribes will receive their land inheritance with Judah and not with Ephraim (Ether 13:11). They will inherit Jerusalem, while Ephraim remains in Zion in the Western hemisphere (Jer. 3:18).

D&C 133:26-35 shows that part of the work of the gathering (directed by the president of the Church) will be done by "prophets" (remember the material for 35:3-6, "Elect Non-member Preachers") whom the Lord will call from among the scattered tribes. The "prophets" will begin the work of leading their people to freedom and the gospel. They will soften the "icy" hearts of their people. The gospel will spring up in lands where people once thirsted because they lived in a desert of knowledge. These people will come to "Ephraim" (members of the Church) to receive the entire truth and priesthood. They will bring their treasure of records which will tell of their escape from Assyria, their journey to the northern countries, their history and prophets, and the appearance of the Savior to them after his resurrection (2 Ne. 29:12-13; 3 Ne. 16:1-3). These records will become one with our other scriptures. In 1916, Elder Talmage said he believed that "there are those now living—aye, some here present—who shall live to read the records of the Lost Tribes of Israel" (*CR*, Oct. 1916, p. 76).

Of course, there is probably more to verses 26-35. Like the writings of Isaiah, these "are things pertaining to things both temporal and spiritual" (1 Ne. 22:3). Although there is much speculation about the temporal fulfillment of these scriptures, there is little more to be said about them doctrinally.

The Second Coming (133:41-51, 63-74)
Remember the material for 45:44-54, 56-57, 74-75, "Events at the Second Coming."

Thrash the Nations (133:59)
Remember the material for 35:13, "Thrashing the Nations."

They Sealed Up the Testimony (133:71-72)
At the time this revelation was given, the testament of the Doctrine and Covenants had not been "sealed up." However, it has been sealed since. This will be further discussed in the material for Section 135 under the heading "It was Necessary that Two Witnesses Seal their Testimony with Their Blood."

134

CHURCH AND STATE

Historical Context
This section was written by Oliver Cowdery and adopted as part of the standard works of the Church (*HC*, 2:247). It is a declaration of belief regarding governments and religions (read the section heading for more detail). At the time this declaration of belief was made, the Church was suffering severe persecution by

the government. Enemies of the Church were accusing the saints of being disloyal and rebellious against the government. J. Reuben Clark, Jr. said:

> They [the statements in Section 134] were given after the mobbings, plunderings, the assassinations of and part of our experiences in Missouri. They were uttered by a people, who, judged by human standards, had every reason to feel that their government had failed, and that they might not hopefully and successfully look thereto for their protection (*CR*, Apr. 1935, 90).

The fact that the saints made the statements in this section under such trying circumstances emphasizes the depth of their faith in God and that His hand is present in the establishment of governments and human laws.

Governments Are Instituted by God (134:1-8)

Governments are instituted of God but not all governments are of God. Citizens are "bound to sustain and uphold the respective government in which they reside" which meets the approval of God (v. 5). To be approved of God, a government cannot:

1. prescribe rules of worship (134:4);
2. control conscience or suppress the freedom of the soul (134:4); or
3. help or hinder any religion so long as the religion does not promote practices that violate the freedoms of others or encourage anarchy (134:4, 7, 9).

And it must secure to each individual:

1. the free exercise of conscience (134:2);
2. the right and control of property (134:2); and
3. the protection of life (134:2).

To secure these freedoms, governments must enact laws. Remember that the purpose of law is to make us free (see the material for Section 42 under the heading "Why the Lord Gives Laws"). A law is constitutional and justifiable before the Lord only if it supports the freedoms and rights mentioned above (*D&C* 98:5-7). Ezra Taft Benson wrote:

> The important thing to keep in mind is that the people who have created their government can give to that government only such powers as they, themselves, have in the first place. . . . So the question boils down to this: What powers properly belong to each and every person in the absence of and prior to the establishment of any organized form of government.

*   *   *   *   *

> [The government] cannot claim the power to redistribute money or property nor to force reluctant citizens to perform acts of charity against their will. . . . No individual possesses the power to take another's wealth or to force others to do

good, so no government has the right to do such things either (*The Constitution: A Heavenly Banner*, p. 7-9).

But it is not enough to be governed by constitutional laws that are justifiable before the Lord. It also takes a righteous people to uphold such laws. The words of John Adams were reiterated by President Benson:

> "Our Constitution," said John Adams (first vice-president and second president of the United States), "was made only for a moral and religious people. It is wholly inadequate to the government of any other" (*The Constitution . . .* , p. 23).

Joseph Smith also emphasized the requirement of a righteous people when he prophesied:

> This nation will be on the very verge of crumbling . . . and when the Constitution is upon the brink of ruin, this people will be the staff upon which the nation shall lean, and they shall bear the Constitution away from the very verge of destruction (July 19, 1840, Church Historian's Office, Salt Lake City; in *The Constitution . . .* , p. 28).

And Ezra Taft Benson wrote:

> Will we be prepared? Will we be among those who will "bear the Constitution away from the very verge of destruction?" If we desire to be numbered among those who will, here are some things we must do:
>
> 1. *We must be righteous and moral.* We must live the gospel principles—all of them. We have no right to expect a higher degree of morality from those who represent us than what we ourselves are. In the final analysis, people generally get the kind of government they deserve. . . .
>
> 2. *We must learn the principle of the Constitution and then abide by its precepts.* . . .
>
> 3. *We must become involved in civic affairs.* . . . "When the wicked rule the people mourn. Wherefore, honest men and wise men should be sought for diligently, and good men and wise men ye should observe to uphold . . ." (*D&C* 98:9-10).
>
> Note the qualities that the Lord demands in those who are to represent us. They must be good, wise, and honest. Some leaders may be honest and good but unwise in legislation they choose to support. Others may possess wisdom but be dishonest and unvirtuous. We must be concerted in our desires and efforts to see men and women represent us who possess all three of these qualities.
>
> 4. *We must make our influence felt by our vote, our letters, and our advice.* We must be wisely informed and let others know how we feel. We must take part in local precinct meetings and select delegates who will truly represent our feelings (*The Constitution . . .* , p. 28-30).

And:

> The devil knows that if the elders of Israel should ever wake up, they could step forth and help preserve freedom and extend the gospel. Therefore the devil has concentrated, and to a large extent successfully, in neutralizing much of the priesthood. He has reduced them to sleeping giants (*An Enemy* . . . , p. 275; in *TETB*, p. 619).

Does the Church counsel its members how to vote? Yes. The Church counsels its members to decide who is honest, good, and wise, and vote for that person. Does the Church counsel its members how to think on issues? Yes. The First Presidency stated:

> We encourage all members, as citizens of the nation, to be actively involved in the political process, and to support those measures which will strengthen the community, state, and nation—morally, economically, and culturally" (Letter from the First Presidency, Jun. 29, 1979; in *TETB*, p. 683).

Does the Church sometimes counsel its members how to support specific bills, referenda, and other legislation? Yes. For example, in 1994 the First Presidency stated:

> The principle of the gospel and the sacred responsibilities given us require that The Church of Jesus Christ of Latter-day Saints oppose any efforts to give legal authorization to marriages between persons of the same gender.
>
> *   *   *   *   *
>
> We encourage members to appeal to legislators, judges, and other government officials to preserve the purposes and sanctity of marriage. . . and to reject all efforts to give legal authorization or other official approval or support to marriages between persons of the same gender ("Same Gender Marriages," a statement by the First Presidency, 1 Feb. 1994, in *Ensign*, Apr. 1994, p. 80).

Is it right for the Church to be involved in government? Yes. Think about the roles of many Old Testament and Book of Mormon prophets (Isaiah, Moroni, etc.) as counselors or critics of their governments' policies. Now reread the material for *D&C* 21:4-5, "Obey All the Prophet's Words." Also see Appendix 5: "The Rock of Liberty."

The Constitutional Law of the Land (134:5-7)

The most pertinent passages to reread at this point are *D&C* 58:21-23; 101:76-95; 98:4-15; 134:5-7; and *AOF* 12. It is important to remember that these commandments were given in a time when the members of the Church were suffering severe discrimination and persecution by their government. At a time when it would be easy to justify rebelling against the laws of the land, the saints were admonished to honor them.

The saints are told to befriend "that law which is the constitutional law of the land" (190:6). The "law of the land which is constitutional" is defined as law that supports the "principle of freedom in maintaining rights and privileges," "that every man may act . . . according to the moral agency which I have given unto him" (98:5; 101:78). And who is to be granted these rights and privileges? The Lord says these constitutional laws of the land "should be maintained for the rights and protection of *all flesh*" (101:77; emphasis added). Besides not allowing people to dismiss the "protection of life" (134:2) granted to our posterity in utero, "all flesh" refers to people all over the world. In 1917, Elder Charles W. Penrose said:

> The principles of that great instrument [the U. S. Constitution] are to go forth to the nations, and the time will come when they will prevail, just as sure as the sun shines even when it appears to be in darkness and the clouds are over it (*CR*, Apr. 1917, p. 20).

And During World War II, the First Presidency of the Church delivered the following message:

> While by its terms this revealed word [*D&C* 98:4-7] related more especially to this land of America nevertheless the principles announced are worldwide in their application, and they are specifically addressed to "you" (Joseph Smith), "and your brethren of my church." When, therefore, *constitutional law obedient to these principles*, calls the manhood of the Church into the armed service of any country to which they owe allegiance, their highest civic duty requires that they meet that call. . . .
>
> The whole world is in the midst of a war that seems the worst of all time. This Church is a worldwide Church. Its devoted members are in both camps. . . . On each side they believe they are fighting for home, and country, and freedom. On each side, our brethren pray to the same God, in the same name, for victory. Both sides cannot be wholly right; perhaps neither is without wrong. God will work out in His own due time and in His own sovereign way the justice and right of the conflict, but He will not hold the innocent instrumentalities of the war, our brethren in arms, responsible for the conflict. . . . God is at the helm (see the full message in *CR*, Apr. 1942, pp. 90-95; emphasis added).

Are there times when we should break a law of the land which is not constitutional according to the Lord's definition? Elder Talmage noted:

> Occasions there are—and none knew this better than an apostle [Peter] who had himself set an example of splendid disobedience to unwarranted commands [Acts 4:18, 31; 5:28-32; 40-42]—when "we must obey God rather than men."

But those occasions are exceptional to the common rule of life. Normally, and as a whole, human law is on the side of divine order, and, by whomsoever administered, has a just claim to obedience and respect (Farrar, *Early Days of Christianity*, pp. 89-90; in *The Articles of Faith*, p. 524).

Elder Talmage again notes:

Pending the overruling by Providence in favor of religious liberty, it is the duty of the saints to submit themselves to the laws of their country. Nevertheless, they should use every proper method, as citizens or subjects of their several governments, to secure for themselves and for all men the boon of freedom in religious service. It is not required of them to suffer without protest imposition by lawless persecutors, or through the operation of unjust laws; but their protests should be offered in legal and proper order. The saints have practically demonstrated their acceptance of the doctrine that it is better to suffer evil than to do wrong by purely human opposition to unjust authority. And if by thus submitting themselves to the laws of the land, in the event of such laws being unjust and subversive of human freedom, the people be prevented from doing the work appointed them of God, they are not to be held accountable for the failure to act under the higher law (*The Articles of Faith*, p. 423).

And Joseph Fielding Smith wrote:

The Lord Almighty requires this people to observe the laws of the land, to be subject to "the powers that be," so far as they abide by the fundamental principles of good government, but he will hold them responsible if they will pass unconstitutional measures and frame unjust and proscriptive laws, as did Nebuchadnezzar and Darius, in relation to the three Hebrew children [Shadrach, Meshach, Abednego] and Daniel. If lawmakers have a mind to violate their oath, break their covenants and their faith with the people, and depart from the provisions of the constitution, where is the law, human or divine, which binds me, as an individual, to outwardly and openly proclaim my acceptance of their acts? (*GD*, p. 406.)

And even though many nations' governments use tax revenue in ways that are against the laws of God, and may even legislate *ex post facto* tax laws, the Church teaches:

Church members in any nation are obligated by the twelfth article of faith to obey the tax laws of that nation (see also *D&C* 134:5). If a member disapproves of tax laws, he may attempt to have them changed by legislation or constitutional amendment, or, if he has a well-founded legal objection, he may challenge them in the courts (Church Bulletin, 1993—2, in *Ensign*, Mar. 1994, p. 80).

Hopefully it is obvious by now that if God were ever to command His church to disobey the law of the land, He would do it through His prophet (remember the material for Section 28: "The Law of Revelation").

Religion Is Instituted of God

Religion is instituted of God, but not all religions are of God. Religious organizations have the right to:
1. establish rules and regulations for their organization (134:10);
2. excommunicate members who break the established rules and regulations (134:10); and
3. preach the gospel and warn the righteous to save themselves (134:12).

Religious organizations do not have the right to:
1. infringe upon the rights and liberties of others (134:4);
2. take people's property illegally (134:10); or
3. inflict any physical punishment (134:10).

In 1942, the First Presidency declared:

> The Church stands for the separation of church and State. The church has no civil political functions. As the church may not assume the functions of the state so the state may not assume the functions of the church. The church is responsible for and must carry on the work of the Lord directing the conduct of its members, one towards the other, as followers of the lowly Christ, not forgetting the humble, and poor and needy, and those in distress, leading them all to righteous living and a spiritual life that shall bring them to salvation exaltation, and eternal progression, in wisdom, knowledge, understanding, and power.
>
> The state is responsible for the civil control of its citizens or subjects, for their political welfare, and for the carrying forward of political policies, domestic and foreign, of the body politic. For these policies, their success or failure, the state is alone responsible, and it must carry its burdens. All these matters involve and directly affect Church members because they are part of the body politic, and members must give allegiance to their sovereign and render it loyal service when called thereto. But the Church, itself, as such, has no responsibility for these policies, as to which it has no means of doing more than urging its members fully to render that loyalty to their country and to free institutions which the loftiest patriotism calls for (see the full statement in *CR*, Apr. 1942, pp. 90-95).

We Do Not Believe It Right to Interfere with Bondservants (134:12)

Joseph Smith said:

> It should be the duty of an Elder, when he enters into a house, to salute the master of that house, and if he gain his consent, then he may preach to all that are in that house; but if he gain not his consent, let him not go unto his slaves, or servants, but let the responsibility be upon the head of the master of that house, and the consequences thereof (*HC*, 2:263-64).

135

MARTYRDOM OF JOSEPH AND HYRUM SMITH

Historical Context

Read the section heading.

It Was Necessary That Two Witnesses
Seal Their Testimony with Their Blood

At least two witnesses were present each time keys were restored in accordance with the divine law of witnesses (John 5:31 and 2 Cor. 13:1). The martyrdom of Joseph and Hyrum also fulfilled this law of witnesses. Joseph Fielding Smith said:

> Oliver Cowdery, through that place as the "Second President" [*D&C* 20:3], preceded the counselors in the Presidency—naturally so. Why shouldn't he? He had the same authority, had received the same keys with the Prophet Joseph Smith every time the heavens were opened, and he was an Assistant President of the Church and the second witness of the dispensation of the fullness of times, which is the greatest of all dispensations, for it was necessary that there be two Presidents, two witnesses standing at the head of this dispensation. . . .

> *   *   *   *   *

> Hyrum Smith became a president of the Church with Joseph Smith, which place Oliver Cowdery might have held had he not wavered and fallen from his exalted station. I am firmly of the opinion that had Oliver Cowdery remained true to his covenants and obligations as a witness with Joseph Smith, and retained his authority and place, he, and not Hyrum Smith, would have gone with Joseph Smith as a prisoner and to martyrdom at Carthage.

> The sealing of the testimony through the shedding of blood would not have been complete in the death of the Prophet Joseph Smith alone; it required the death of Hyrum Smith who jointly held the keys of this dispensation. It was needful that these martyrs seal their testimony with their blood, that they "might be honored and the wicked might be condemned" [*D&C* 136:39].

> *   *   *   *   *

> But here is another point. He had to die. Why? Because we read in the scriptures that the testimony is not of force without the death of the testator—that is, in his particular case, and in the case of Christ [Heb. 9:16]. It was just as necessary that Hyrum Smith lay down his life a martyr for this cause as a witness for

God as it was for Joseph Smith, so the Lord permitted them both to be taken in that way and both sealed their testimony with their blood (*DS*, 1:212, 219, 221).

Hyrum Smith

Hyrum Smith chose to join his brother in death. Hyrum was blessed by the First Presidency. He was told:

> [You will] have power to escape that hand of thine enemies. Thy life shall be sought with untiring zeal, but thou shalt escape. If it please thee, and thou desirest, thou shalt have the power voluntarily to lay down thy life to glorify God (Kirtland High Council Minutes, Dec. 1832-Nov. 1837, typescript, p. 186, LDS Church Archives; in M. Russell Ballard, "Brothers Bound by Love and Faith," *Ensign*, Sep. 1994, p. 65).

Hyrum was repeatedly warned not to go to Carthage. Joseph finally told Hyrum:

> "If you go back [to Carthage] I will go with you, but we shall be butchered." Hyrum said, ". . . let us go back and put our trust in God. . . . If we live or have to die, we will be reconciled to our fate" (*HC*, 6:549-50).

Hyrum was a great and humble older brother to Joseph. When the mob stormed the room in Carthage Jail where the brethren were held, Hyrum tried to hold the door closed to protect the others. But he was the first one killed. When he was shot, he fell to the floor and said, "I am a dead man!" Joseph went over to where his brother, Hyrum, lay and said, "Oh! my poor, dear brother Hyrum!" (*HC*, 7:102).

Their Innocent Blood Will Cry unto the Lord (135:7)

Remember the material for 87:1-4, 6-7, "Prophecy of the United States' Civil War."

136

CAMP OF ISRAEL

Historical Context

Read the section heading and verse 1.

Blessings Promised to the Camp of Israel

The Saints were being driven out of the United States. They were worried about having sufficient for their needs, being persecuted by their enemies, and having to flee Zion. The Lord comforted the Saints by promising that as they were obedient to the laws He would give them, they would be blessed with the following:

1. to have sufficient for their needs (136:10-11);
2. protection from enemies (136:17);
3. the eventual redemption of Zion (136:18); and
4. to behold the glory of God (136:37).

Note that the Lord promised these same blessings to the camp of Israel in the time of Moses (Ex. 16:1-17:6; Num. 14:1-10).

The Laws the Promised Blessings Are Predicated Upon

To receive the blessings that the Lord had promised the saints, they would have to obey the following laws:

1. be humble enough to seek the Lord's counsel (136:19);
2. keep all pledges (136:20);
3. do not covet (136:20);
4. do not take the name of the Lord in vain (136:21);
5. be kind and courteous (136:23-24);
6. obey the Word of Wisdom (136:24);
7. be honest in all doings (136:25-26);
8. be a wise steward (136:27);
9. praise the Lord with song, dancing, and prayer (136:28);
10. call on the Lord for comfort (136:29);
11. fear not enemies because of faith in the Lord (136:30); and
12. learn wisdom by calling on the Lord (136:32-33).

We can receive the same blessings as we obey these laws.

Stakes (136:10)

Remember the material for 82:13-14, "Stakes."

Praise the Lord with Dancing (136:28)

David O. McKay said:

> President Brigham Young . . . once said, in substance: "The atmosphere of the dance should be such that if any elder be called from the party to go to administer to a sick person, he could leave with the same spirit that he would go from his elder's quorum meeting" (*CR*, Apr. 1920, pp. 116-17).

Now Cometh the Day of Their Calamity (136:35-36)

Remember the material for 87:1-4, 6-7, "Prophecy of the United States' Civil War."

Joseph Smith's Death Was Needful (136:39)

Remember the material for Section 135: "Martyrdom of Joseph and Hyrum Smith."

137

THE CELESTIAL KINGDOM

Historical Context

Read the section heading.

Although Joseph Smith had previously received a vision of the celestial kingdom (remember Section 76: "The Vision"), he gains further understanding of the celestial kingdom in this section.

During the April 1976 conference of the Church, this vision and Joseph F. Smith's vision of the redemption of the dead (section 138) were accepted as scripture and included in the Pearl of Great Price. However, in June 1979 the First Presidency and the Quorum of the Twelve announced that they would be added to the Doctrine and Covenants as sections 137 and 138 (*Church News*, June 2, 1979, p. 3) instead of to the Pearl of Great Price.

The Glory of the Celestial Kingdom (137:1-4)

President David O. McKay received a vision of the celestial kingdom. He said:

I . . . beheld in a vision something infinitely sublime. In the distance I beheld a beautiful white city. Though far away, yet I seemed to realize that trees with luscious fruit, shrubbery with gorgeously-tinted leaves, and flowers in perfect bloom abounded everywhere. The clear sky above seemed to reflect these beautiful shades of color. I then saw a great concourse of people approaching the city. Each one wore a white flowing robe, and a white headdress. Instantly my attention seemed centered upon their Leader, and though I could see only the profile of his features and his body, I recognized him at once as my Saviour! The tint and radiance of his countenance were glorious to behold! There was a peace about him which seemed sublime—it was divine!

The city, I understood, was his. It was the City Eternal; and the people following him were to abide there in peace and eternal happiness.

But who were they?

As if the Savior read my thoughts, he answered by pointing to a semicircle that then appeared above them, and on which were written in gold the words:

"These Are They Who Have Overcome The World—Who Have Truly Been Born Again!" [D&C 137:2, 5] (Cherished Experiences, p. 102.)

Also remember what Orson Pratt said in the material for 130:2, "That Same Sociality which Exists Here will Exist There."

Heirs of the Celestial Kingdom (137:5-10)

Joseph Smith saw many heirs of the celestial kingdom (v. 5). All of them had received the gospel ordinances and been born again except for Joseph Smith's brother, Alvin (v. 6). When Joseph Smith could no longer understand the vision on his own, the Lord helped by giving Joseph Smith further understanding about two types of people who inherit the celestial kingdom despite not having received ordinances in mortality. These people are:

1. **All who have died without a knowledge of this gospel, who would have received it if they had been permitted to tarry (137:7-9).** These people will be judged "according to the desire of their hearts" (v. 9).

2. **All children who die before they arrive at the years of accountability.** *All* children who die before the age of eight will be saved in the celestial kingdom and will be reunited with their parents when their parents remain worthy (D&C 29:46-47; 68:25, 27; 137:10). Elder Wilford Woodruff said:

> Our children [who have died] will be restored to us as they are laid down if we, their parents, keep the faith and prove ourselves worthy to obtain eternal life (JD, 18:31-32).

And Elder Joseph Fielding Smith further explained:

> Boys and girls who die after baptism may have the endowment work done for them in the temple. Children who die in infancy do not have to be endowed. So far as the ordinance of sealing is concerned, this may wait until the millennium (*DS*, 2:55).

The same blessings that apply to little children apply to the mentally handicapped. Elder Joseph Fielding Smith said:

> Children born with retarded minds shall receive blessings just like little children who die in infancy. They are free from sin, because their minds are not capable of a correct understanding of right and wrong. . . . They do not require baptism. . . .
>
> For behold that all little children are alive in Christ, *and also all they that are without the law*. For the power of redemption cometh on all them that have no law; wherefore, he that is not condemned, or he that is under no condemnation, cannot repent; and unto such baptism availeth nothing (Moroni 8:22).
>
> Again the Lord has stated:
>
> And again, I say unto you, that whoso having knowledge, have I not commanded to repent?
>
> And he *that hath no understanding*, it remaineth in me to do according as it is written (*D&C* 29:49-50).
>
> Therefore the Church of Jesus Christ of Latter-day saints considers all deficient children with retarded capacity to understand, just the same as little children under the age of accountability. They are redeemed without baptism and will go to the celestial kingdom of God, there, we believe, to have their faculties or other deficiencies restored (*AGQ*, 3:20-21; emphasis added).

Children who die before the age of accountability and people who are mentally handicapped and cannot be accountable will come forth in the first resurrection to be reunited with their worthy parents (*D&C* 76:64-65). President Joseph F. Smith said:

> Joseph Smith taught the doctrine that the infant child that was laid away in death would come up in the resurrection as a child; and, pointing to the mother of a lifeless child, he said to her: "You will have the joy, the pleasure, and satisfaction of nurturing this child, after its resurrection, until it reaches the full stature of its spirit." There is restitution, there is growth, there is development, after the resurrection from death. I love this truth. It speaks volumes of happiness, of joy and gratitude to my soul (*GD*, pp. 455-456).

After their resurrection, those who died before the age of accountability will mature in a sinless state (*D&C* 45:58). They will receive all the blessings of exaltation including marriage (*D&C* 131:2).

Exactly when the spirit enters the body has never been revealed to the Church as doctrine. Therefore, there is no Church doctrine concerning miscarriages and stillbirths. In fact, it would be foolish to speculate when the spirit enters the body. In making the effort to "hit the mark," we would have already looked long "beyond the mark" (Jacob 4:14). The world, in the attempt to justify abortion, has already shown its desire to excuse the "most abominable above all sins save it be the shedding of innocent blood or denying the Holy Ghost" by rationalizing that not letting the body become habitable for the spirit by destroying the body is not like unto murder (Alma 39:5; and see the material for *D&C* 42:18-29, 42, "Laws on Moral Issues"). This dismissal of consequences leads to exactly what Satan had in mind from the beginning—the abolition of free agency (see Appendix 5: "The Rock of Liberty").

However, many of us have been deeply touched and saddened by occurrences of miscarriage or stillbirth. Although there is little to be said doctrinally, some general authorities have expressed their thoughts on the subject. Bruce R. McConkie wrote:

> When the fetus is born dead, it is said to be a stillbirth. Such an occurrence gives rise to anxiety on the part of mothers, in particular, as to whether the stillborn baby had in fact become a living soul, whether the partially or nearly formed body had become the home of a pre-existent spirit, and whether such a body will be resurrected. These are matters not clearly answered in the revelation so far available for the guidance of the saints in this dispensation. . . .
>
> That masterful document on the origin of man by the First Presidency of the Church (Joseph F. Smith, John R. Winder, and Anthon H. Lund) appears to bear out the concept that the eternal spirit enters the body prior to a normal birth, and therefore that stillborn children will be resurrected. It states: "The body of man enters upon its career as a tiny germ or embryo, which becomes an infant, quickened at a certain stage by the spirit whose tabernacle it is, and the child, after being born, develops into a man." (Man: His Origin and Destiny, p. 354.) This interpretation is in harmony with the general knowledge we have of the mercy and justice of that Infinite Being in whose divine economy nothing is ever lost. It would appear that we can look forward with hope and anticipation for the resurrection of stillborn children (*MD*, p. 768).

And Joseph Fielding Smith wrote:

> There is no information given by revelation in regard to the status of stillborn children. However, I will express my personal opinion that we should have hope that these little ones will receive a resurrection and then belong to us. I cannot help feeling that this will be the case.
>
> When a couple have a stillborn child, we give them all the comfort we can. We have good reasons to hope. Funeral services may be held for such children, if the parents so desire. Stillborn children should not be reported nor recorded as births and deaths on the records of the Church, but it is suggested that parents record in their own family records a name for each such stillborn child.

*   *   *   *   *

> President Young taught that we should have hope for the resurrection of stillborn children. "They are all right," he said, and nothing in the way of sealings or ordinances need be done for them (*DS*, 2:280-81).

138

THE SPIRIT WORLD

Historical Context—I Sat In My Room Pondering (138:1-11)

Read the section heading, verses 1-11, and the historical context of Section 137: "The Celestial Kingdom."

Where the Righteous and Wicked Were Gathered (138:12, 20-22)

Review the material for 76:73, 84, "The Spirit World: Paradise, Prison, and Hell" for information regarding the divisions of the spirit world and their geographical locations.

The Faithful Captives
Were Awaiting Their Redemption (138:16-18, 23, 50)

Why are the righteous spirits referred to as captives? First, because even the righteous are captives to death and hell (v. 23). No matter how righteous we are, we can only be delivered from death and hell by the grace of Jesus Christ. And second, because not having a body (even in paradise) is "bondage" (v. 50). Melvin J. Ballard Said:

> When we go out of this life, leave this body, we will desire to do many things that we cannot do at all without the body. We will be seriously handicapped, and we will long for the body; we will pray for that early reunion with our bodies. We will know then what advantage it is to have a body (*Crusader for Righteousness*, p. 213).

We cannot receive a fullness of joy until after the resurrection (remember 93:33).

Missionary Work in the Spirit World (138:30-37, 57-59)
1. **Who is taught?** See verses 30 and 32.
2. **What is taught?** See verses 33-35, and 57.
3. **Why is it done?** See verses 34, 37, and 58-59.

Faithful Daughters (138:39)
Remember the material for 132:37, "They Have Entered into Their Exaltation."

The Spirit of Elijah (138:46-48)
Review the material for Section 2: "Heart to Heart."

The Lord Gave Them Power to Come Forth from the Dead (138:51)
There are certain ordinances and priesthood keys that we cannot receive in this mortal life. Brigham Young said:

> It is supposed by this people that we have all the ordinances in our possession for life and salvation, and exaltation, and that we are administering in these ordinances. This is not the case. We are in possession of all the ordinances that can be administered in the flesh; but there are other ordinances and administrations that must be administered beyond this world. . . . We have not, neither can we receive here, the ordinance and the keys of the resurrection. They will be given to those who have passed off this stage of action and have received their bodies again, as many have already done and many more will. They will be ordained, by those who hold the keys of the resurrection, to go forth and resurrect the Saints, just as we receive the ordinance of baptism, then the keys of authority to baptize others for the remission of their sins. This is one of the ordinances we can not receive here, and there are many more. We hold the authority to dispose of, alter and change the elements; but we have not received authority to organize native element to even make a spear of grass grow. . . . We are organizing a kingdom here according to the pattern that the Lord has given for people in the flesh, but not for those who have received the resurrection, although it is a similitude. Another item: We have not the power in the flesh to create and bring forth or produce a

spirit; but we have the power to produce a temporal body. The germ of this, God has placed within us. And when our spirits receive our bodies, and through our faithfulness we are worthy to be crowned, we will then receive authority to produce both spirit and body [see *D&C* 131:4]. But these keys we cannot receive in the flesh. Herein, brethren, you can perceive that we have not finished, and cannot finish our work, while we live here, no more than Jesus did while he was in the flesh (*JD*, (Aug. 24, 1872), 15:136-137).

President Spencer W. Kimball quoted from the above teachings of Brigham Young and commented:

I buried my mother when I was eleven, my father when I was in my early twenties. I have missed my parents much. If I had the power of resurrection . . . I would have been tempted to try to have kept them longer (*Ensign*, (Report of General Conference), May 1977, p. 49).

Chosen in the Beginning (138:55-56)

Cross reference these verses with Jer. 1:5 and Abr. 3:22-23. Regarding the grand council Abraham saw, Joseph Smith said: "Every man who has a calling to minister to the inhabitants of the world was ordained to that very purpose in the Grand Council" (*TPJS*, p. 365).

OFFICIAL DECLARATION 1
THE MANIFESTO CONCERNING PLURAL MARRIAGE

For more information on the law of the priesthood as pertaining to plural marriage, review the material for Section 132: "The Law of Celestial Marriage."

Historical Context—
Inasmuch as Laws Have Been Enacted by Congress

Smith and Sjodahl wrote:

The doctrine of plural marriage was made known to the Prophet in 1831, or 1832, although the Revelation on the subject was not committed to writing until the year 1843. It should be noted that even then it was not given to the *Church*. This step was taken on the 29th of August, 1852, when the Revelation was read to a General Conference in the "Old Tabernacle," Salt Lake City, and accepted by the assemble as a revelation from God and part of the law of the Church. In voting for the Revelation, the Saints firmly believed that they were only exercising their legal right as American citizens. They believed that, as a majority, they had the indisputable constitutional right to regulate their domestic affairs, within the boundaries of their own territory, and that the Supreme Court of the United States would uphold this view, even if Congress should be of a different opinion. And they were strengthened in their position by the fact that not until ten years after the action taken by the Church in 1852 [of accepting plural marriage as part of the law of the Church] was any effort made by Congress to stamp plural marriage as illegal (*DCC*, p. 836).

However:

Stephen Harding, governor of the Territory of Utah, was able to get Justin R. Morril of Vermont to introduce a bill into Congress. The bill was signed into law 8 July 1862 by President Abraham Lincoln. The Anti-Polygamy Act of 1862 "defined plural marriage as bigamy, and made the contraction of such a marriage punishable by a fine of five hundred dollars and imprisonment for a term of five years" (Smith, *Essentials in Church History*, p. 432). This bill was the first of a flood of anti-Mormon legislation introduced during the next twenty-five years, most of which never passed (see Roberts, *Comprehensive History of the Church*, 5:433-41, 610-11) (*DCSM*, p. 361).

In 1874 the First Presidency asked George Reynolds to serve as a test case believing that the Supreme Court would rule the law unconstitutional since the First Amendment states: "Congress shall make no law respecting an establishment of religion, or prohibiting the free exercise thereof . . . ." However, in 1879 the Supreme Court ruled against George Reynolds.

After the Supreme Court declared the anti-polygamy laws constitutional, the federal government passed laws making it illegal for one who practiced plural marriage to hold public office. Then it passed a law that disincorporated the Church, giving the property to the government.[11] In July of 1887 President John Taylor died in hiding and Wilford Woodruff became the next president of the Church.

We Are Not Permitting Any Person To Enter Into Its Practice

For over a year-and-a-half before President Wilford Woodruff issued the Manifesto, he banned the practice of plural marriage (see the second and third paragraphs of the Manifesto). However, this was not made known to a great extent outside the Church. Elder George Q. Cannon said that "at no time has the Spirit seemed to indicate that this should be done. We have waited for the Lord

---

11. Respectively, these acts were the Edmunds Bill of March 1882 and the Edmunds-Tucker Law of March 1887.

to move in the matter" (*Millennial Star*, Nov. 24, 1890, p. 737). When the Lord did move in the matter, President Woodruff met with the Quorum of the Twelve and the First Presidency who sustained his proclamation concerning plural marriage in the latter part of September 1890.[12] The Manifesto was then proclaimed publicly.

Plural Marriage Was Banned for *All* People *Everywhere*

Despite President Woodruff's Manifesto concerning plural marriage, some members rationalized that plural marriage could still be preformed outside the U. S.—for example, in Mexico. This has led to several groups who have either left the Church or been excommunicated from The Church but still call themselves "Mormons." These people are not members of the Church of Jesus Christ of Latter-day Saints. In January of 1900, President Woodruff's successor, Lorenzo Snow, emphasized: "No member or officer [of the Church] has any authority whatever to perform a plural marriage or enter into such a relation" ("Slanders Are Refuted by First Presidency," *Millennial Star*, May 4, 1911, p. 275). Then in 1911, President Snow's successor, Joseph F. Smith, re-emphasized:

> There isn't a man today in this Church, or anywhere else, outside of it who has authority to solemnize a plural marriage—not one! There is no man or woman in the Church of Jesus Christ of Latter-day Saints who is authorized to contract a plural marriage. It is not permitted (*CR*, Apr. 1911, p. 8).

We Accept His Declaration As Binding

The Lord revoked the practice of plural marriage (see the excerpts from addresses by President Woodruff on p. 293 of the *D&C*). Review the material for 56:1-4, "I, the Lord, Command and Revoke."

The Lord Will Never Permit the President of the Church To Lead It Astray

Review the material for Section 21: "Follow the Prophet;" 28:2, 12-13, "Revelation From the Lord;" 43:1-7, "The Law of Revelation for the Church;" and 43:7, "The Gate."

---

12. See Clark, *Messages of the First Presidency*, 3:192 for more of the historical details regarding the issuing of the Manifesto.

OFFICIAL DECLARATION 2
EVERY BLESSING FOR EVERY WORTHY MEMBER

Historical Context

Read the heading and the first two paragraphs of the letter.

The Curse and the Mark of the Curse

The *curse* is being shut out from the people of God—being stripped of the high priesthood (Moses 5:35-41). The nature and purpose of the *mark* of the curse are discussed in Gen. 4:14-15; Moses 5:39-40; 2 Ne. 5:21; and Alma 3:7-8. A person who is cursed can still be righteous and blessed (Abr. 1:25-26). Note that the *curse* can be lifted without lifting the *mark* (Alma 23:18). In this Official Declaration, the Lord lifted the *curse* from all who are willing to repent.

Why?

Certain people and groups of people have been cursed as described in Abr. 1:26. For example, Jesus, before His resurrection, preached the gospel almost exclusively to the Israelites. He said, "I am not sent but unto the lost sheep of the house of Israel" (Matt. 15:24). And He commanded his apostles, "saying, Go not into the way of the Gentiles, and into any city of the Samaritans enter ye not: But go rather to the lost sheep of the house of Israel" (Matt. 10:5-6; see also Acts 13:42-49). But after His resurrection, He said, "Go ye into all the world, and preach the gospel to every creature" (Mark 16:15). He also gave the president of His church a revelation (and guided him in its interpretation) indicating that the Gentiles could also receive the full blessings of the gospel (Acts 11:1-18).

It seems to be human nature to seek a cause-and-effect relationship in things. Thus, some start speculating that our situation in life is due to our actions in the pre-existence. Even the disciples asked Jesus why a man was born blind. The Savior's answer applies to our topic: "that the works of God should be made manifest in him" (John 9:1-3). God knows our weaknesses and strengths. Certain people are sent to specific earthly homes at specific times (*D&C* 138:53; Acts 17:26; and read other scriptures listed under *foreordination* in the Topical Guide). This includes people who will not learn of the fullness of the gospel in mortality (Alma 29:8; and remember the material for 35:3-6, "Elect Non-member Preachers"). I may have been sent to a loving family in the United States which is active in the Church because of my weaknesses. You may have been sent to a very different family in a very different place with very different beliefs because of your strengths.

The Lord has not fully revealed why certain groups have been cursed. Joseph Smith wrote:

> "And he said, Cursed be Canaan; a servant of servants shall he be unto his brethren." "Blessed be the Lord God of Shem; and Canaan shall be his servant" (Gen. ix: 25, 26).
>
> Trace the history of the world from this notable event down to this day, and you will find the fulfillment of this singular prophecy. *What could have been the design of the Almighty in this singular occurrence is not for me to say*; but I can say, the curse is not yet taken off from the sons of Canaan, neither will be until it is affected by as great a power as caused it to come; and the people who interfere the least with the purposes of God in this matter, will come under the least condemnation before Him; and those who are determined to pursue a course, which shows an opposition, and a feverish restlessness against the decrees of the Lord, will learn, when perhaps it is too late for their own good, that God can do His own work, without the aid of those who are not dictated by His counsel (*HC*, 2:438; emphasis added; and review the material about steadying the ark of God for 50:4-9, "Hypocrites in the Church").

If it bothers you not knowing why, remember my suggestion given in the material for 101:32-34, "The Lord shall reveal all things." In any case, the Lord has now lifted the curse from all who are willing to repent.

CONCLUSION

I am glad you took on the Lord's challenge to search His book (1:37). I hope this guidebook helped you in your search.

The Lord gave five reasons to search the Doctrine and Covenants:

1. to bring us to an understanding (1:24);
2. to make known our errors (1:25);
3. to instruct and give us wisdom (1:26);
4. to chasten us that we might repent (1:27); and
5. to make us strong, bless us from on high, and give us knowledge from time to time (1:28).

And He promises that we can gain a testimony by the Spirit that the Doctrine and Covenants is true (1:39).

Did you feel these things happen to you as you searched the Lord's book? Have you felt blessed with greater understanding, knowledge, and wisdom? Have you felt the Lord urging you to change anything in your life? Have you felt blessed with greater strength to make those changes? Did you feel the Lord blessing you with greater faith in His word and in His prophets?

Yes? I hope you'll continue your search.

No? I hope you'll continue your search. Searching the scriptures takes some practice, just like most everything else in life that's worth doing. Your understanding probably increased more than you realize. It will probably be easier next time around.

I testify in the name of Jesus Christ that the Doctrine and Covenants is His word, revealed through His prophets, and that you can feel the blessings mentioned above flow into your life as you feast upon it.

Appendix 1
JESUS CHRIST IS JEHOVAH
See D&C 29:1

Comparing Biblical statements made about Jehovah (the LORD) with statements made about Jesus Christ clearly shows that Jesus is Jehovah. This chart shows a few of the many comparisons which give evidence of this important truth.

Title	Of Jehovah	Of Jesus Christ
Creator	Isa. 42:5*	John 1:1-3, 14*
		Col. 1:16-19
I Am	Ex. 3:13-15	John 8:56-59
		D&C 29:1
Judge	Jer. 25:31*	John 5:22*
	Isa. 33:22	2 Cor. 5:10
	1 Chron. 16:14	Acts 10:42
		2 Tim. 4:1
King	Isa. 33:22*	John 1:49*
	Ps. 96:10	
Law of Moses, Giver of	Ex. 20:1-17	3 Ne. 15:5
Rock	Ps. 18:31, 46	1 Cor. 10:1, 4
Savior	Isa. 12:2	John 14:6
	Isa. 33:22	Acts 4:12*
	Isa. 43:11*	2 Ne. 25:20
	Ps. 18:46	

*Shows Jesus Christ to be Jehovah in the *New World Translation* Bible also.

Appendix 2

INVITING IN THE SPIRIT

See D&C 42:13-14; 50:13-22

Elder Gene R. Cook of the First Quorum of the Seventy emphasized the importance of being directed by the Spirit in all we do. He said, "May I suggest seven scriptural performances (See Alma 31:10) that, *if humbly employed*, will immediately invite the Spirit into your heart and the hearts of others" (*Ensign*, Nov. 1988, 38, emphasis added). The following reviews some of what Elder Cook taught.

1. Prayer (3 Ne. 17:2-3; *D&C* 29:2; 136:29, 32). We may pray in our hearts and with people we are visiting. Always have less-active members and non-members pray. Review the material for *D&C* 29:2, "Three Steps to be Gathered."

2. Scripture (2 Ne. 32:3; Alma 31:5; *D&C* 18:33-36; 29:7). Scripture is the voice of the Lord and we can declare it as such. For example, instead of saying, "In Moroni 10:3-5 it says . . .," say, "Brother Jones, the Lord said. . . ." Scripture is even more effective when read with feeling and personalized if the situation is appropriate. For example, when reading Moroni 10:3-5 substitute a name for *you*:

> John, let's read Moroni 10:3-5. "Behold, I would exhort [John] that when [John] shall read these things . . . that [John] would remember. . . . And if [John] shall ask with a sincere heart. . . . And by the power of the Holy Ghost [John] may know the truth of all things.

Review the material for 18:33-36, "You have Heard the Voice of the Lord."

3. Testimony (See the material for *D&C* 100:5-8; 2 Ne. 33:1; and Alma 5:44-47). Testify boldly yet humbly as a representative or servant of Jesus Christ, using words everybody understands. For example, instead of, "I know Joseph Smith was a prophet beyond a shadow of a doubt because of the burning I feel in my bosom as I bear my testimony," the following may be more powerful: "I testify in the name of Jesus Christ that Joseph Smith is a prophet."

4. Express gratitude to God and man (*D&C* 59:7; John 13:34-35; 1 Ne. 11:21-23; and Moro. 7:47-48). Tell (as well as show) those you have stewardship over that you love and appreciate them. Express to them your love of God. Magnify the Lord and He will magnify you by his Spirit. Review the material for *D&C* 59:7, "Thank God in all Things."

5. Song (see the material for *D&C* 25:11-12). A smile and appropriate eye contact with those you are singing to are especially effective.

6. Priesthood ordinances (see the material for *D&C* 75:19; James 5:13-15; 3 Ne. 20:2-9; and *D&C* 84:20.)

7. Share spiritual experiences (Luke 10:25-37; Acts 26; *D&C* 50:21-22). Personal experiences, although they may not seem as miraculous as experiences of others, are almost always more effective. Sharing personal spiritual experiences is a good way to build trust with others because they feel *your* spirit as well as *the Spirit*. Spirit communicating with spirit is the heart of the gift of tongues.

Appendix 3
SOME BLESSINGS
AND LAWS UPON WHICH THEY ARE PREDICATED
See D&C 130:20-21

When I have noticed a fairly direct connection between a promised blessing which is based upon obedience to certain specified principles, I have noted it. The following list contains some of the interesting connections I have found. You can probably add many more.

All the Father has, Receive
Rev. 21:7 Overcome all things.

D&C 84:33-39 Magnify callings and receive the Lord's servants.

Born again, Be
Alma 22:16 Repent and call on God (see also Hela. 15:7).

John 3:5-8 Be baptized and receive the Holy Ghost.

Calling and election made sure, Receive (see also Eternal Life
and the material for 131:5, "The More Sure Word of Prophecy")

D&C 121:45 Let thy bowels be full of charity, and let virtue garnish thy thoughts unceasingly. (Having "the doctrine of the priesthood distill upon thy soul" is the process of receiving your calling and election made sure.)

Hela. 10:4-5 Declare the word of God with unwearyingness without fear, seeking the will of God and following it.

2 Pet. 1:5-10 Be diligent in gaining faith, virtue, knowledge, temperance, patience, godliness, brotherly kindness, and charity.

TPJS, p. 150 Have faith in Christ, repent of sins, be baptized, receive the Holy Ghost, hunger and thirst after righteousness, live by every word of God, and be determined to serve God at all hazards.

Follow the example of those who have received their calling and election made sure. For example:

Enos 1:5, 27	Enos
Moses 6:34	Enoch
Mosiah 26:20	Alma
Mosiah 28:7	The sons of Mosiah

3 Ne. 28:1-10	The Apostle John and the 12 disciples of Christ in the Americas.
Ether 12:37	Moroni
2 Tim. 4:6-8	The Apostle Paul
D&C 7:4-5	The Apostle Peter
D&C 90:3; 132:48-49	Joseph Smith

Charity

Mosiah 2:16 Serve.

Moroni 7:48 Pray for it.

Contentions, Have none

4 Ne. 1:15 Love God in your heart.

Convincing (Converting) Power

Alma 6:6; 17:9 Obey the true law of the fast as found in Isa. 58:3-12 and 3 Ne. 13:16-18.

Alma 26:22 Baptize thousands, repent, exercise faith, pray always, and do good works (see also Alma 7:24 must have faith, hope, and charity).

D&C 11:21 Seek to obtain the word of the Lord.

Dominion, Great

D&C 121:45-46 Be full of charity and virtuous thoughts.

Eternal life

(see also Sealing of Spirit and All that the Father has, Receive)

D&C 14:7 Eternal life is the greatest gift.

John 3:36 Believe on Christ.

John 17:3 Come to know Christ and the Father.

Rom. 2:7 Seek for it.

2 Ne. 31:19-20 Have faith, repent, be baptized, receive the Holy Ghost, be steadfast, have hope, love God, love all men, feast on the scriptures, and endure to the end.

Omni 1:26 Continue fasting and praying to the end.

D&C 20:14 (D&C 59:23) Do the works of righteousness.

Matt. 19:16 Note that there are also personal laws that must be obeyed.

Freedom

D&C 98:8 Live God's laws.

Gathered, Be

D&C 29:2 Be humble enough to listen and pray.

Glories of the kingdom, Receive

D&C 43:12 Sustain and pray for the prophet and other servants of the Lord.

Happiness
Ps. 146:5 Hope in the Lord.

Holy Ghost, The constant companionship of
D&C 121:45-46 Be full of charity and virtuous thoughts.

Instrument of God, Be an
Mosiah 23:10 Pray for it.
Alma 26:3 It is truly a blessing to be an instrument of God.

Joy
Alma 27:18 Be penitent and humble.

Judgement, righteous
D&C 121:45-46 Be full of charity and virtuous thoughts.

Knowledge (see also Wisdom)
Alma 17:2 Search the scriptures and pray and fast often.
D&C 89:19 Obey the Word of Wisdom.
D&C 93:28 Keep the commandments.
D&C 107:19 Receive the high priesthood.

Knowledge of the will of God and other mysteries
John 7:17 Obey the commandment to find out if it is a true commandment of God.
James 1:5 Ask God.
D&C 43:13 Provide whatever the prophet needs to accomplish his work.
D&C 76:5-10 Delight to serve God in righteousness to the end.
D&C 121:45-46 Be full of charity and virtuous thoughts to receive knowledge of doctrines.

Knowledge that Jesus is the Christ
D&C 93:1 Forsake sins, come unto Christ, obey His voice, and keep His commandments.

Mercy of God, The
Alma 9:17 Call on Him.

Ordinance of Honor and Glory, Receive
Rom. 2:7 Seek for them.
D&C 124:33-34 Go to the temple.

Peace
Ps. 119:65 Love the law.
John 16:33 Hope in the words of Christ (Moroni 7:41).

Philip. 4:8-9 Think on good things.

D&C 59:23 Do works of righteousness.

Prophecy, Spirit of

Alma 17:3 See Revelation, Spirit of.

Protection, Divine

Isa. 58:8 Obey the true law of the fast as found in Isa. 58:3-12 and 3 Ne. 13:16-18.

Remission of sins, Retain a

Mosiah 4:26 Feed, clothe, and administer to the needy.

Renewal of body

D&C 84:33 See Sanctification.

Revelation, Spirit of (see Knowledge and Wisdom)

Ex. 34:28; Deut. 9:9, 18; Isa. 58:9-11; Omni 1:26; 3 Ne. 27:1 Obey the true law of the fast as found in Isa. 58:3-12 and 3 Ne. 13:16-18.

Alma 13:28 Pray always (1 Ne. 4:6).

Alma 17:3 Fast, pray, and search scriptures.

Alma 26:22 To have revelation of things never before revealed. See Convincing (converting) Power

Ether 3:26 Believe that it is possible to be shown all things.

D&C 100:5-8 See Teach with power and authority of God.

Riches

Isa. 58:11-12 Be blessed with productivity by obeying the true law of the fast as found in Isa. 58:3-12 and 3 Ne. 13:16-18.

Jacob 2:18-19 Attain a hope in Christ and intend to do good with the riches.

3 Ne. 13:33 Seek first the kingdom of God.

Moroni 7:25 Attain them by faith.

D&C 6:7 Note that "riches" can mean "eternal life."

D&C 50:28 Attain them through purification.

D&C 136:10-11 Keep God's laws and have sufficient for needs.

Sanctification

D&C 84:33 Magnify callings.

Sealing of Spirit

Mosiah 5:15 Be steadfast, immovable, and do good works. (Alma 7:24 must have faith, hope, and charity to do this.)

See God (Note that this may be in this life or after.)

Matt. 5:8 Be pure in heart.

John 14:21, 23 Love God. To do this we must keep His commandments (John 14:15).

Heb. 12:14 Be holy.

D&C 67:10 Have no jealousies or fears and be humble.

D&C 88:42-50 Appreciate God's creations (see Alma 30:44).

D&C 88:68 Have an eye single to God's glory (see Moses 1:39), become sanctified (see Sanctification), be patient.

D&C 93:1 Forsake sins, come unto Christ, call on His name, obey His voice, and keep His commandments.

D&C 97:16 Enter temple.

D&C 136:37 Be obedient.

Spirit, Be magnified by

Isa. 58:8 Obey the true law of the fast as contained in Isaiah 58:3-12 and 3 Ne. 13:16-18.

Teach with power and authority of God

Alma 17:3 See Revelation, Spirit of.

3 Ne. 7:18 Have great faith.

D&C 100:5-8 Declare what the Lord puts in heart in His name sincerely and humbly.

Tempted, Not above that which you can bear

Alma 13:28 Be careful and pray continually.

War, Protection and help in time of

(Most of these laws apply to the nation as a whole.)

Deut. 20:19-20 Do not destroy the earth.

Deut. 23:9-14 Keep a clean camp.

Isa. 58:8 Obey the true law of the fast as found in Isa. 58:3-12 and 3 Ne. 13:16-18.

James 4:1 Have no lust (this is why there are wars).

Mosiah 7:33 Turn to the Lord with all your heart and serve Him (Ether 2:12).

Alma 46:12-13 Fight for God, religion, freedom, peace, wives and children.

Alma 60:21 Make good use of your means.

Alma 60:23 Clean the inner vessel.

3 Ne. 3:21 Fight only in defense (Mormon 4:4; *D&C* 98:33-37).

Morm. 7:4 Fight only if God commands it.

Ether 3:26 See Revelation, Spirit of.

D&C 76:5-10 See Knowledge.

D&C 98:5-6 Obey draft rules that support these other laws (Alma 51:14).

D&C 98:16, 33-38 Renounce war and follow the pattern given in these verses.

D&C 136:32 Be humble and prayerful.

Wisdom

Ether 3:26 See Revelation, Spirit of.

D&C 76:5-10 See Knowledge.

D&C 136:32 Be humble and prayerful.

Zion, Redemption of

D&C 103:5-8 Hearken unto the Lord's counsel.

D&C 103:36 Diligence, faithfulness, and prayers of faith.

D&C 105:4, 6, 10-12, 31 Be united, learn obedience, be taught more perfectly, gain experience in and knowledge of duties, be endowed with power in the temple, be faithful, humble, and become sanctified.

Appendix 4
A GUIDE TO THE BOOK OF REVELATION
See D&C 77

Keys To Understand the Book of Revelation

The Book of Revelation gets its name from the Greek *apo* (remove) and *kalypto* (covering). Put them together and you get *apocalypses*, or "unveiling." Therefore, in English, this book is called "Revelation" (the revealing or uncovering of).

Joseph Smith said, "The book of Revelation is one of the plainest books God ever caused to be written" (*TPJS*, p. 290). When the Apostle John wrote this book, he felt we should understand it (*JST* Rev. 1:3). In fact, Nephi tells us that when John wrote these things that they were plain "and easy to the understanding of all men," and that in the Lord's own due time they will come forth in their purity again (1 Ne. 14:19-27).

Why then is the Book of Revelation so hard to understand? Some of the plain and precious truths were taken from it, but we can still come to understand it. There are a four keys to understanding this book. They are:

1. **Study, ponder, pray.** We must study first. John mentions things in passing, assuming that we have enough gospel knowledge to understand. (For example, Rev. 19:13 Jesus comes in a robe dipped in blood). We must also be in tune with the Spirit. John says over and over again, "He that hath an ear, let him hear what the Spirit saith" (2:7; etc.). We should pray for the gift of prophecy (the gift by which the word of God is understood; remember the material for 46:22, "The Gift of Prophecy").

2. **Latter-day revelation.** The *JST*, *BOM*, *D&C*, and the writings of latter-day prophets serve as keys. They do not explain everything, but "as Champolion, by the key furnished in the brief text on the Rosetta stone, was able to open the secrets of Egyptian hieroglyphics, so the Bible student should be able to read the Apocalypse with a better understanding of it, by the aid of [latter-day revelation]" (*DCC*, p. 478).

3. **Explore symbols.** John came from an Eastern background. Eastern symbolism is concerned more with beauty than accuracy (for example, 1:16 a two-edged sword comes from the Lord's mouth), while Western

symbolism tends to be more concrete. While some of the symbolism of the Book of Revelation is self-explanatory or has been explained by the Lord, some of the symbolism is difficult to interpret. Joseph Smith said:

> Whenever God gives a vision of an image, or beast, or figure of any kind, He always holds Himself responsible to give a revelation or interpretation of the meaning thereof, otherwise we are not responsible or accountable for our belief in it (*TPJS*, p. 291).

He also said: "We may spiritualize and express opinions to all eternity; but that is no authority," and, "Never meddle with the visions of beasts and subjects you do not understand" (*TPJS*, p. 292). Therefore, in this guide to the Book of Revelation, there will be some verses that I will not attempt to explain.

   4. **Understand the chronology.** The Book of Revelation does not always follow a chronological order. John sometimes interrupts the flow of the revelation to teach us something important. I will refer to these interruptions as "teaching moments."

Historical Setting of the Book of Revelation

Daniel H. Ludlow wrote:

> Around A.D. 95, Roman authorities began to enforce a cult of emperor worship. Since true Christians would worship only the Lord, the Emperor Domitian banished many and confiscated their property. John was sentenced to confinement on the island of Patmos, where he remained at least a year (*Ensign*, Dec. 1991, p. 54).

According to tradition, by the time the Apostle John was writing the Book of Revelation:

> Peter had been crucified, Paul beheaded, Bartholomew skinned alive, Thomas and Matthew run through with spears. John was the only surviving apostle. . . . The history of the church included the lining of Nero's colonnade with crucified Christians and the savagery of the mobs screaming for blood in the Coliseum and the Circus Maximus (*Life and Teachings*, p. 449).

Organization of the Book of Revelation

The Book of Revelation is organized into seven basic parts. The number seven symbolizes wholeness or perfection. I will use the divisions and the basic names that Ludlow uses in "John: The Once and Future Witness" (*Ensign*, Dec. 1991, pp. 51-56).

Part 1: Introduction to the Book (*JST* 1:1-8)

1:1, 5. The revelation was given to John by an angel and by Jesus Christ Himself.

1:3. Remember that we are supposed to understand this book, and we will be blessed as we are obedient to its commandments.

1:4. Greeting to the seven churches (see Part 3 below). The seven "spirits" appear to be the seven servants of the seven churches (see *JST* Rev. 4:5).

1:6. There is more than one god. Jesus is a god and the Father is a god. See 1 Cor. 8:5-6 for greater understanding.

1:6-8. The doxology (praises to the Lord).

Part 2: Introduction to the Revelation (1:9-20)

1:10. It was Sunday. John was probably holding his own "sacrament meeting."

1:12, 20. The seven candle sticks are the seven churches to which John is writing. Candles do not make light, but hold it up. The Church holds up the light of Christ.

1:13-16. How does a mortal being describe an eternal being?

1:15. The sound of rushing waters is probably the loudest thing John had ever heard.

1:16. The sword coming out of God's mouth is His word (*D&C* 33:1). It gives life, but disobeying it brings death. See 1:20 for the meaning of the seven stars.

1:18. Spirits in hell will come out after the millennium and enter the telestial kingdom (*D&C* 76:81-85).

1:20. See the *JST* for the real meaning of the stars. The servants of the Lord are in His hand.

Part 3: Epistles to the Seven Churches (2:1-3:22)

Today we would refer to the seven "churches" mentioned in this part of the Book of Revelation as wards or stakes. John follows a four-part pattern in each of the letters he writes to the seven "churches." First, John addresses the saints. Second, John praises the saints for their good works, faithfulness in the face of opposition, rejection of false teachings, and clean garments (worthiness). Third, John tells the saints how to improve, and calls them to repent of their bad works, inadequate love for Christ, toleration of false priests, lack of commitment and faithfulness, and defiled garments (unworthiness). Fourth, John promises the saints celestial blessings for enduring to the end. These blessings include eating of the fruit of the tree of life (see 2:7); overcoming the second death (2:11); eating of the hidden manna (see 2:17); receiving a white stone with a new name (see 2:17); ruling nations (see 2:27); receiving the morning star (see 2:28); being clothed in white raiment (3:5); having name left in book of life (3:5); having name confessed by Jesus to the Father (3:5); having the names of God, New Jerusalem, and Christ written on them (see 3:12); and sitting down with Jesus and the Father on the throne of heaven (3:21).

1. **The Church in Ephesus (2:1-7).** This was one of the largest cities of the Roman empire. The temple of Diana is there (one of the seven wonders of the world). Selling silver idols of Diana was big business. The Christian doctrine of not worshipping idols was threatening this business. Therefore, the saints were being persecuted. Many of the saints did not stand up to the persecution and were failing to serve God with all their heart (2:4-5).

   2:1. Note the *JST.*

   2:6. The Nicolaitan doctrine approved of immorality (Bible Dictionary).

   2:7. This tree is the love of God and "the most desirable above all things" (1 Ne. 11:21-22).

2. **The Church in Smyrna (2:8-11).** Smyrna is present-day Izmir, the third-largest city in Turkey. It was and is an important port of trade. The "angel" (bishop) of this "church" (ward) is given encouragement. This encouragement helped him to not cave in under the persecution of the times. The bishop of Smyrna, Polycarp, would later be burned at the stake for refusing to deny Christ (*Life and Teachings*, p. 452).

3. **The Church in Pergamos (2:12-17).** This city was the provincial capital. The people who lived there worshiped a serpent god (*Life and Teachings*, p. 452). The saints were doing well but were beginning to be tolerant of secret combinations.

   2:14. The doctrine of Balaam is basically to "preach for money, or to gain personal power and influence" (*DNTC*, 3:450).

   2:17. After talking about the manna that the Israelites ate, Jesus said, "I am the living bread which came down from heaven: if any man eat of this bread, he shall live forever" (John 6:51).

4. **The Church in Thyatira (2:18-29).** This was the smallest of the cities but it received the longest letter.

   2:23. "Reins" means kidneys. Kidneys represent vitality. The Lord knows our inner self, our strengths, our weaknesses, and will judge us accordingly.

   2:26-27. The iron rod is the word of God (see the *JST* and 1 Ne. 11:25). The symbolism of ruling with a rod of iron, therefore, is not ruling, as would a dictator, with "an iron fist," but means ruling as would God, "with equity and justice" (*JST*).

2:28. "The morning star" refers to Jesus Christ (Rev. 22:16). Receiving "the morning star" means having one's calling and election made sure or receiving eternal life (2 Pet. 1:19).

5. **The Church in Sardis (3:1-6).** This was a wealthy inland trade center that had gained a reputation for its corruption (3:1). This city was spiritually dead (3:1).

    3:1. The seven spirits of God appear to be the servants of the seven churches (see *JST* Rev. 4:5).

6. **The Church in Philadelphia (3:7-13).** This "city of brotherly love" made lots of wine and worshiped Bacchus, the god of wine and party (*Life and Teachings*, p. 453).

    3:7-8. By the key of David (priesthood power), Christ can bring to pass His will. He can bless His saints and protect them from the persecution and evils of the world (open a door which no man can shut).

    3:12. To have the name of Christ, New Jerusalem, and God written on us means that we will be saved, live in the Celestial Kingdom, and be gods (see *DNTC*, 3:458).

7. **The Church in Laodicea (3:14-22).** There were hot springs just north of this city. The water that would flow from them was still lukewarm when it got to Laodicea. This city was known as "the City of Compromise" (see 3:15-16). There was also a medical school there that was known for healing eye irritations with its eye salve (*Life and Teachings*, p. 453).

    3:14. Amen signifies that something is valid and binding. Since it is through Christ that all things are sealed as valid and binding, Christ is the "Great Amen." The Laodicean saints were "lukewarm" like the water that flowed to their city. They needed to become more like the "Great Amen."

    3:15-16. Joseph Smith said, "I love that man better who swears a stream as long as my arm yet deals justice to his neighbors and mercifully deals his substance to the poor, than the long, smooth-faced hypocrite" (*TPJS*, p. 303).

    3:17-18. Even though this city was rich, well clothed, and known for its medical school that helped people to see; it was spiritually poor, naked, and blind. The Lord told the Laodicean saints to seek after spiritual wealth. To measure how pure gold is it is "tried in the fire." The purest riches that one can have are wisdom and eternal life (*D&C* 6:7).

3:19. There are three responsibilities of a righteous chastiser: (1) express love first, (2) chastise to build others up, not to tear down, and (3) help others know how to correct their mistakes (see the material for *D&C* 95:1-2, 9-17, "Responsibilities of a Chastiser").

3:20. We must open the door and invite the Lord in.

Part 4: The Vision of Heaven and Earth (4:1-16:21)

Part 4 contains a vision of heaven and earth. The vision of the earth gives highlights from the earth's history. But the main focus of this part is on the latter days and events just preceding the second coming of Jesus Christ.

4:4. The 24 Elders surrounding the throne of God are faithful Elders from the seven churches (stakes or wards of the Church of Jesus Christ). These Elders had previously died and were in paradise at the time (*D&C* 77:5).

4:6. Angels and God live on a globe like a sea of glass that is a Urim and Thummim where they can see the past, present, and future (*D&C* 130:6-9). The earth will become like this when it receives its paradisiacal glory and becomes celestialized. The sea of glass mentioned in this verse is the earth in its celestial state (D&C 77:1).

4:6-8. The beasts were shown to John to help us understand that all things will be saved and receive eternal joy as they remain obedient (*D&C* 77:2-3). Joseph Smith said:

> I suppose John saw beings there of a thousand forms, that had been saved from ten thousand times ten thousand earths like this, strange beasts of which we have no conception. . . . The grand secret was to show John what there was in heaven. John learned that God glorified Himself by saving all that His hands had made, whether beasts, fowls, fishes or men; and He will glorify Himself with them (*TPJS*, 291).

The eyes of the beasts represent their knowledge. The wings of the beast represent their power (*D&C* 77:4). Animals will resurrect, be able to communicate (Rev. 5:13-14; *TPJS*, 292), and may have a limited ability to act according to their agency during their mortal life (see *D&C* 101:24 beasts can become corruptible).

5:1. This book contained the history of the world as God had already seen it (*D&C* 77:6). Each seal represents 1,000 years (*D&C* 77:7). The earth has existed nearly 6,000 years since the fall. It is Friday night, and we will soon enter into the 1,000 years of the Sabbath, and then the earth will die, resurrect, be exalted, and enter into a new week and a new sphere of existence.

5:6. Note the *JST*.

6:1-21. The *First Seal*. Elder McConkie said that this is talking about Enoch as he led the army of the saints to victory (see Moses 7:13-17; *DNTC*, 3:476-78).

6:3-4. The *Second Seal*. Elder McConkie said that this is talking about the time of Noah when the earth was filled with violence (see Moses 8:22, 28, 29). The man on the red horse may represent the devil or other murderers of that time. (*DNTC*, 3:478).

6:5-6. The *Third Seal*. Elder McConkie said that the black horse represents hunger and famine (*DNTC*, 4:479-80). During the third thousand years of the earth's history since the fall, we read about famine in Abraham's day (see Abr. 2:17, 21). The famine was still going on in Jacob and Joseph's day (see Gen. 41:53- 57; and Gen. 42-44). Israelites were again perishing from hunger in the desert with Moses (see Ex. 16).

> *6:5.* The balances seem to show that food was so scarce that it had to be measured out exactly.

> *6:6.* An entire day's work could only feed one person, and barely was only eaten by humans in time of famine (*Life and Teachings*, 459). "Hurt not the oil and the wine" could mean that some food should be saved to make it through the famine (*DNTC*, 3:480).

6:7-8. The *Fourth Seal*. During these thousand years, the Israelites were overrun many times by other kingdoms. The Israelites were also constantly at war with themselves.

6:9-11. The *Fifth Seal*. These 1,000 years saw the restoration and apostasy of the Church and the martyrdom of all of its original prophets except John himself.

6:12-7:17. The *Sixth Seal*. We are now living during the last years of these 1,000 years.

> *7:1.* See *D&C* 77:8.

> *7:2-3.* See *D&C* 77:9. The angel is Elias (the name for a forerunner), and may refer to more than one person (*CHMR*, 1:301-2).

> *7:4-9.* See *D&C* 77:11. The 144,000 high priests are not the only people who will be saved, nor are they the only people who have made their calling and election sure (see v. 9).

> *7:9-17.* A "teaching moment." Before going into all the pains of the earth during the seventh seal, John tells us about the joy of being saved.

> *7:13-15.* Temple workers around the world included.

> *7:17.* One of my favorite promises: "God shall wipe away all tears from their eyes."

8:1-22:17. The *Seventh Seal*. John devotes most of his book to telling us about the events just before the second coming (11 chapters). During these thousand years there will be great judgements poured out upon the earth. The Battle of Armageddon (Rev. 8-9, 11, 16) will overthrow Babylon (17-18) and prepare the world for the second coming of Christ (19). Following the second coming, John sees Satan bound about a thousand years (20:1-6), the great last battle between good and evil (20:7-10), the final judgment (20:11-15), and the celestialization of the earth (21:1-22:5). Review the material for *D&C* 45: "The Second Coming" and 101:26-34, "The Millennium."

> **8:1.** Biblical scholars say that this time of silence symbolizes the great awe and respect for God's final judgements which are about to be poured out upon the earth. This may be a correct interpretation. Another interpretation is that the half hour is the Lord's time (about 21 years). After quoting *D&C* 38:11-12, Rodney Turner said, "The final labors of the Church and the 144,000 will be completed in this period of comparative heavenly calm before the "arm of the Lord" falls upon the nations (*D&C* 45:47)" (p. 331).

> **8:10.** See Isaiah 14:12 and *D&C* 76:25-27.

> **8:10.** "The wormwood associated with the star that fell from heaven is a symbol of the bitterness and awfulness which comes to all who follow the devil. Wormwood was a plant with an extremely bitter taste. To use it for food or drink was to eat that which brought about death" (*Life and Teachings*, p. 461).

> **9:3.** The locusts represent hoards of battle machinery (v. 7-10).

> **9:11.** *Abbaddon* (Hebrew) and *Apollyon* (Greek) mean destruction. Satan is the "destroyer" (section heading to *D&C* 61).

> **9:15.** I will not attempt to explain.

> **10:1-11.** A "teaching moment." The little book that John ate represents his calling to declare repentance to the world (*D&C* 77:14). A missionary call is sweet, but the work and rejection can be bitter. John has been called to live and prophesy before nations until the second coming. He is in a translated state. But John will die in order that he may receive a resurrected body (see the material for *D&C* 7: "John A Greater Work").

> **10:6.** Elder McConkie says that "time no longer," here, means "without delay" (*DNTC*, 3:507).

> **11:2.** I will not attempt to explain.

> **11:3-13.** See *D&C* 77:15. Olive trees (v. 4) provide oil for people's lamps. These witnesses will hold up the light of Christ as can-

dlesticks, and give others the Holy Ghost that those others might light their lamps. (See also Zechariah chapter 4.)

12-14. A "teaching moment." John teaches us about the kingdom of Christ and the kingdom of Satan. Some of the symbolism in these chapters is strange. But the most important thing that John does during these chapters is to compare and contrast the forces of good and evil. Here are some observations:

- Jesus *is* a morning star (2:24) *vs.* Satan was a star (8:10-11).
- Christ holds the key to *loose* people from hell (1:18; 20:13) *vs.* Satan's efforts to *imprison* people in hell (Rev. 9:1).
- Out of Christ's mouth comes a sword (Rev. 1:16) *vs.* out of Satan's mouth come frogs sent to deceive the world (16:13).
- Christ stands in the midst of candlesticks as the sun (2:1) *vs.* Satan stands in the midst of his army of locusts that darken the sun (9:3).
- The smoke that represents the prayers of the saints (8:3-4) *vs.* the smoke that comes up from hell (9:2).
- The lamb with twelve horns and eyes which represent Jesus and His disciples (*JST* 5:6) *vs.* the dragon with seven heads and ten horns which represent Satan and his disciples (12:3).
- Christ in red having conquered sin (19:13) *vs.* Satan in red glorying in sin (12:3).
- The bride (18:23; 21:2, 9; 22:17) *vs.* the harlot (17:5).
- The crowns of the 24 elders that they cast before the Lord (4:10-11) and the crowns that Christ wears (19:12) *vs.* the crowns that the heads of the dragon wear (12:3).
- The mark of God on the forehead of the righteous (22:4) *vs.* the mark of the beast on the forehead of the wicked (13:16-18).
- The New Jerusalem (3:12; 21:2) vs. Babylon (14:8; 16:19; 17:5; 18:2, 10, 21).

12:1. The church of Christ can clothe people in celestial glory (the sun). The church of Christ is above terrestrial churches (the moon).

JST 12:3. The woman is the Church of Christ and the man child she brings forth is the kingdom of Christ that He will rule during the millennium (see v. 7). The iron rod by which the kingdom of Christ will rule is the gospel. During the millennium, all people will be subjects in Christ's Kingdom, but not all will be members of His Church. (The man child is not Christ nor is it the priesthood because the Church did not bring these forth.)

JST 12:4, 6. The war in heaven is still going on; it has only moved to the earth.

JST 12:5. This is the apostasy (*D&C* 86:3). I will not attempt to explain the timing of the events* in v. 5, 14-17.

13:16. In the time of John, people would place a mark on their forehead to show that they were a disciple of a certain group. But what this verse refers to is only a symbolic mark. Note that servants of the Lord also receive a mark in their foreheads.

13:18. I will not attempt to explain.

14:6. This could represent other angels that restored gospel keys as well as Moroni.

14:20. Armageddon (a wine press) will be fought outside the city Jerusalem.

15. A "teaching moment." John again tells us of the joy of those who are saved.

16:9, 11, 21. Note that God sends plagues to help us to humble ourselves so that we will repent. But these people would not repent.

16:16. See *Armageddon* in the Bible Dictionary.

16:20. The earth will become one land again (see *D&C* 133:23-24 and Gen. 10:25). Some people say that there will be no more mountains or valleys. However, "the earth shall be like as it was in the days before it was divided." Therefore, there will be mountains and valleys. Besides, without mountains and valleys, where would we camp, ski, or go on picnics?

Part 5: "The Vision from the Wilderness" (17:1-21:8)

Ludlow states:

> In this vision, John views scenes of the earth's end. The scenes are arranged in a chiastic pattern:
> *A*. Babylon, the wicked world, is unveiled (17:1-18).
>   *B*. Babylon is judged (18:1-24).
>   *C*. Rejoicing takes place in heaven (19:1-10).
>   *D*. Christ's victory is completed (19:11-21).
>   *C*. The millennial era takes place (20:1-7).
>   *B*. Satan and his followers receive a final judgment (20:7-15).
> *A*. A new celestial world is unveiled (21:1-8) (*Ensign*, Dec. 1991, p. 56).

17:1. 2 Ne. 10:16 and 28:18 tell who the whore is.

19:10. Angels can be given divine investiture of authority, meaning they can speak as if they were the Lord (see also Rev. 22:8-9 and 3 Ne. 1:12-14). Moses wished that all of his people were prophets and had the testimony of Jesus (see *prophet* in the Bible Dictionary).

19:13. The red clothes that Christ will wear at His coming represent the atonement.

19:16. The thigh is one of the largest set of muscles in the body (note the symbolism).

20:1-3. During this time children will grow up without sin (*D&C* 45:58). Binding Satan limits his power. How and why will Satan be bound? See the material for *D&C* 101:28, "Satan shall not have power to tempt any man."

20:5. Spirits that are in hell and will be going to the telestial kingdom will not be resurrected until after the millennium (*D&C* 76:84-85).

20:8. See *D&C* 88:111-116 for a slightly more detailed description of this battle.

20:12. Joseph Smith clarifies this verse in *D&C* 128:6-7. There are many books that we will be judged from. Some of these books are records kept on earth (*D&C* 128:7). Some are books kept in heaven. Our actions are recorded in books in heaven that people there can look at (*D&C* 62:3; 128:7-8). We will also be judged by the standards set forth in the Book of Mormon, other books of scripture, the things that we have been commanded to do by latter-day prophets, and what is written about the time, place, and conditions in which we live (2 Ne. 25:22; 29:11; 3 Ne. 27:23-26).

20:13. Endless, Eternal, Everlasting, etc., are other names for God. So Endless punishment is just another name for God's punishment. The punishment that God gives does not mean that people will never come out of Hell. Elder James E. Talmage taught that Hell

> is a place prepared for the teaching, the disciplining of those who failed to learn here upon the earth what they would have learned. . . . No man will be kept in hell longer than is necessary to bring him to a fitness for something better (*CR*, April 1930, 97).

Revelation 20:13 shows that people will eventually come out of Hell.

Part 6: Vision from a Mountain (21:9-22:17)

In this part, John sees the celestialization of the earth.

21:16. Taking 606 feet, 9 inches to be a furlong, the city would be 1,400 miles wide, long and tall. These are cubic miles.

Part 7: The Conclusion (22:18-21)

22:8-9. See Rev. 19:10.

22:18-19. John warns scribes not to change his words. Note that John could only be referring to this book and not the entire Bible because the Bible had not yet been organized. This does not mean that there will not be any more scripture given. Bible scholars say that John wrote his other books after this one. Also, the Topical Guide lists at least 14 books that are supposed to be part of the Bible but are not. Also note the following scriptures: Deut. 4:2 (do not add or take away); John 21:25 (Jesus did many things that are not in the Bible); and Ezek. 37:15-17 (the stick of Joseph).

22:20. John testifies of Christ's coming. "I come quickly" refers to *how* the Lord will come, not *when* He will come (review the material for *D&C* 33:18, "I Come Quickly").

22:21. John leaves his apostolic blessing on the saints.

Appendix 5
THE ROCK OF LIBERTY

The purpose of this Appendix is to emphasize that the Lord's law is the foundation of a free society. The battle for freedom has been going on since the beginning. If it were easy to grasp the concepts of freedom and accountability, so many souls would not have been lost to the enemy. Therefore, the material that follows requires some effort to grasp. Before going on, please review the material for Section 42: "The Lord's Law" under the headings "The Lord's Law Affects Our Life" and "Why the Lord Gives Laws."

Freedom and Accountability

Read Moses 4:1-3. Satan wanted to overthrow God's power (Moses 4:3). But Satan could not because God is all-powerful. So Satan devised a plan to trick God into giving up His power (Moses 4:1). Of course, God, being much more intelligent than Satan, did not fall for the plot.

Satan knew that God's honor is His power (Moses 4:1, 3; *D&C* 29:36). If Satan could destroy God's honor, he would destroy God's power. Satan could destroy God's honor (and therefore His power) by tricking God into eliminating freedom. This would destroy God's honor (and power) because honor cannot be forced. Honoring is an active process that things must choose to do. Therefore, unless things can choose to honor God—unless things are free—God's honor (and power) are destroyed. Thus, Satan "sought to destroy the agency of man" (Moses 4:3).

So how could Satan destroy agency—the freedom to choose? The first way that most of us think of is by force. But this not only would be difficult, it would be impossible, for Satan cannot know and control our thoughts (*D&C* 6:16). However, there is another, easier, more seductive way to eliminate freedom: just don't hold people accountable for their actions. Instead of saving people from their sins (Matt. 1:21; Alma 7:14; 3 Ne. 9:21), propose to save people in their sins (Alma 11:32-37).

How does this destroy freedom? Read 2 Ne. 2:11-16; Alma 11:32-37; and Alma 42:17, 21. One of the lessons these verses teach is:

1. If personal responsibility for the consequences of our choices is removed, laws don't matter.
2. If laws don't matter, the law is destroyed and it does not matter what choices we make.

3. If it does not matter what choices we make, all choices are the same.

4. If all choices are the same, it does not matter if any choice is made at all.

5. If all choices (including making no choice) lead to the same consequence, there is no real choice to make—we have lost our freedom to choose.

In other words, if all choices lead to the same consequence, there is no real choice to begin with—the freedom to choose is destroyed. Being saved *in* sin sounds great because of the claim that we can choose to do whatever we want and still return to live in a free and prosperous celestial kingdom. It sounds so great that a third of Heavenly Father's children were seduced into believing this faulty philosophy of "freedom without consequence" (*D&C* 29:36). However, for those who search for and accept truth, it becomes clear that taking away accountability ultimately destroys freedom—thus destroying God's honor, thus destroying God's power, thus Satan thinks he gets his wish (but not really because we would not be free to give Satan the honor he wants).

To recap: if the consequences of choices are the same, then there is no choice to make—freedom is destroyed.

Read more about how law gives freedom in Prov. 6:23; John 8:32; 2 Cor. 3:17; Alma 61:15; and *D&C* 98:8. And read Gen. 3:4-5 and Moses 4:10-11 for another example of Satan using the seductive philosophy of eliminating the consequences of choices.

The Fall—A Lesson on Accountability

Read Gen. 2:16-17 and Moses 3:16-17. Cross reference those verses with Helaman 14:30-31. God stresses the fact that there must be accountability for one's choices if one is to truly have a free choice. He said: "Of every tree of the garden thou mayest freely eat, but of the tree of the knowledge of good and evil, thou shalt not [freely] eat" (Moses 3:16-17). In other words, "You can eat of the other trees without consequence, but you cannot eat of the tree of the knowledge of good and evil without consequence. Remember, if you choose to eat of it, I will forbid you to stay in the garden and you will surely die." Note how this follows the principles of freedom taught in 2 Ne. 2:13-16 and Alma 42:17. God affixed a consequence to eating the fruit. If he had not, as discussed above, Adam and Eve could not have chosen for themselves—could not have exercised freedom to eat it. Note that the consequence happened; Adam did die spiritually very soon after eating the fruit (was thrust out of the presence of the Lord) and physically in the same day (of the Lord's time—see Abr. 5:12-13). And, ultimately, Adam and Eve accepted responsibility for their actions, saying, "and *I* did eat" (Moses 4:18, 19; emphasis added).

Freedom and Accountability Versus Security

Freedom can be frightening because it requires accountability. It can be daunting to think that we are accountable for our lives. Thus, many seek security instead. People have been doing this from the beginning. One example occurred soon after the fall. Read Gen. 4:3-8 and Moses 5:18-33. Satan continued to use his "pro-choice/no fault" philosophy with Cain (and Lamech, see Moses 5:47-52). The Lord commanded that blood sacrifices should be offered in similitude of the Savior's future sacrifice (Moses 5:5-8). But Cain was seduced by Satan's doctrine of freedom without responsibility (note Moses 5:29-33). Cain was lulled into sacrificing his freedom for the security that Satan would provide (note Moses 5:33 again). Of course, Satan had no intention of providing Cain with the promised security (Alma 30:60).

Read Gen. 4:13-14 and Moses 5:38-39. Note that Cain did not show remorse (except for getting caught and punished). He did not accept responsibility for his actions. Instead, he blamed Satan, Abel, and the Lord for his situation. He did not understand that even if some things in our life are not our fault, we need to learn to stop blaming and take responsibility for changing our life for the better.

Another example of people trading freedom and accountability for security is found in Exodus. It was easier to get Israel out of Egypt that to get "Egypt" out of Israel. The Israelites' vacillation between accepting the laws on which freedom is based and rejecting freedom in their yearning for security is one of the main themes of the entire Old Testament. The problem they ran into again and again is that not only did they reject and lose their freedom, they never obtained the desired security.

Another example of a people avoiding accountability by trading their freedom for the promise of security is found in the fall of the Roman Empire:

> Sir Edward Gibbon (1737-1794), author of *The Decline and Fall of the Roman Empire*, wrote tellingly of the collapse of Athens, which was the birthplace of democracy. He judged that, in the end, more than they wanted freedom, the Athenians wanted security. Yet they lost everything—security, comfort, and freedom. This was because they wanted not to give to society, but for society to give to them. The freedom they were seeking was freedom from responsibility. It is no wonder, then, that they ceased to be free (Thatcher, *Imprimis*, March 1995, p. 3).

Ezra Taft Benson gave this warning:

> We must be careful that we do not trade freedom for security. Whenever that is attempted, usually we lose both. There is always a tendency when nations become mature for the people to become more interested in preserving their luxuries and their comforts than in safeguarding the ideals and principles which

made these comforts and luxuries possible ("Responsibilities of Citizenship," BYU Homecoming, Provo, Utah, 22 October 1954 in *TETB*, p. 600).

For further understanding of the principles of freedom and responsibility versus Satan's promise of security within his "no fault" philosophy, read Luke 12:16-21; 2 Ne. 1:13; 28:7-8, 20-23; Alma 11:34-35; and Moses 4:7-11.

The beauty of the plan of our Heavenly Father (which Satan cannot comprehend—see John 1:5; 2 Ne. 9:28; and Moses 4:6) is that as we are accountable, we not only gain greater freedom, we gain greater security within the arms of mercy (Alma 34:16). C. S. Lewis, writing from the perspective of a devil, poetically describes this concept which is so incomprehensible to those who stand in darkness (*D&C* 93:24-39). He wrote:

> The whole philosophy of Hell rests on recognition of the axiom that one thing is not another thing, and, specially, that one self is not another self. My good is my good, and your good is yours. What one gains another loses. Even an inanimate object is what it is by excluding all other objects from the space it occupies; if it expands, it does so by thrusting other objects aside or by absorbing them. A self does the same. With beasts the absorption takes the form of eating; for us, it means the sucking of will and freedom out of a weaker self into a stronger. "To be" *means* "to be in competition."
>
> Now, the Enemy's philosophy is nothing more nor less than one continued attempt to evade this very obvious truth. He aims at a contradiction. . . . The good of one self is to be the good of another. This impossibility He calls *Love*, and this same monotonous panacea can be detected under all He does and even all He is or claims to be.
>
> *   *   *   *   *
>
> All His talk about Love must be a disguise for something else. He must have some *real* motive for creating them and taking so much trouble about them. The reason one comes to talk as if He really had this impossible Love is our utter failure to find out that real motive. What does He stand to make out of them? That is the insoluble question. I do not see that it can do any harm to tell you that this very problem was a chief cause of Our Father's quarrel with the Enemy. When the creation of man was first mooted and when, even at that stage, the Enemy freely confessed that he foresaw a certain episode about a cross, Our Father very naturally sought an interview and asked for an explanation. The Enemy gave no reply except to produce the cock-and-bull story about disinterested Love which He has been circulating ever since. This Our Father naturally could not accept. He implored the Enemy to lay His cards on the table, and gave Him every opportunity. He admitted that he felt a real anxiety to know the secret; the Enemy replied, "I wish with all my heart that you did" (*The Screwtape Letters*, pp. 81, 86-87).

Not understanding that freedom rests on accountability and not security leads people to scorn the laws of God. They look upon those who insist we must live by God's precepts as foolish for believing such "cock-and-bull." With this in mind, I, perhaps foolishly, present some ideas on societal issues.

The Lord's Law—The Rock of Liberty

First, some review of the material for Section 42: "The Lord's Law." The Lord said: "Thus I grant unto this people a privilege of organizing themselves according to my laws" (*D&C* 51:15). It is indeed a privilege to live under the Lord's law. The Lord gives His true law in order to show us the path to freedom. God's law makes us free. Jesus said, "And ye shall know the truth, and the truth shall make you free," and "I, the Lord God, make you free, therefore ye are free indeed; and the law also maketh you free" (John 8:32; *D&C* 98:8).

The freedom that obedience to the laws of God brings is a societal, as well as personal issue. There are certain precepts that must be abided by for a nation to remain free. As Ezra Taft Benson said:

> The Ten Commandments came from God Himself to Moses, and form the foundation of civilized society. Designed by the Almighty, these laws plumb the depths of human motives and urges, and, if adhered to, will regulate the baser passions of mankind. No nation has ever perished that has kept the commandments of God.
>
> Neither permanent government nor civilization will long endure that violates these laws (*This Nation Shall Endure*, p. 105 in *TETB*, p. 577.)

And:

> The Ten Commandments and the Sermon on the Mount are the foundation principles upon which all civilized government and our present civilization are built (see Exodus 20:1-17; Matthew 5-7). . . . To disregard them as a nation inevitably will lead that nation to destruction. ("On My Honor," Explorer Presidents Conference, Ogden, Utah, 4 March 1978.) (*TETB*, pp. 677-678.)

The reason a free nation will be destroyed if it does not obey the Ten Commandments is not necessarily because God will send fire and brimstone from heaven, but because the precepts of the Lord's law are the guidelines to maintaining a free society. Referring to these fundamental guidelines for maintaining freedom, C. S. Lewis wrote:

> This thing which I have called the *Tao*, and which others may call Natural Law or Traditional Morality or the First Principles of Practical Reason or the First Platitudes, is not one among a series of possible systems of value. It is the sole source of all value judgements. If it is rejected, all value is rejected. If any value is retained, it is retained. The effort to refute it and raise a new system of value in

its place is self-contradictory. There never has been, and never will be, a radically new judgement of value in the history of the world. What purport to be new systems or (as they now call them) 'ideologies,' all consist of fragments from the *Tao* itself, arbitrarily wrenched from their context in the whole and then swollen to madness in their isolation, yet still owing to the *Tao* and to it alone such validity as they possess. . . . The rebellion of new ideologies against the *Tao* is a rebellion of the branches against the tree: if the rebels could succeed they would find that they had destroyed themselves" (*The Abolition of Man*, p. 56).

Cecil B. DeMille, producer of the movie *The Ten Commandments*, observed:

We sometimes think of law as the opposite of liberty. But that is a false conception. That is not the way that God's inspired prophets and lawgivers looked upon the law. Law has a twofold purpose. It is meant to govern. It is also meant to educate. . . .

God does not contradict himself. He did not create man and then, as an afterthought, impose upon him a set of arbitrary, irritating, restrictive rules. He made man free and then gave him the commandments to keep him free.

We cannot break the Ten Commandments. We can only break ourselves against them or else, by keeping them, rise through them to the fullness of freedom under God. God means us to be free (excerpts from the Commencement Address at Brigham Young University, May 31, 1957).

2 Nephi 2:27 expresses this same observation that choosing to obey the commandments leads to freedom while breaking them only leads to captivity.

Legislating Morality
Neal A. Maxwell, of the Twelve, wrote:

The notion of private morality is a great heresy. What goes on in our heads and our homes is clearly if subtly related to everything else in our lives. Sickness of spirit in a family is carried to the office or classroom just as surely as the flu.

There are no victimless crimes, no private wrongs. For every wrong act there is at least one victim, the doer, and secondary impacts that we just don't have the sophistication to measure. We can't have it both ways: extolling and exhorting over the interrelatedness of things in nature (with which we must truly be more concerned as stewards of this planet) while, at the same time, denying the ecology in human nature. Some inconsistently try to cover their face when sneezing to avoid infecting others, but are like a megaphone when telling a dirty joke.

Only a schizoid society could sanction the delusion that there is a private morality apart from public morality. There isn't an "indoor" and an "outdoor" set of Ten Commandments! (*Deposition of a Disciple*, p. 21.)

Some will say, "Well all that may be fine and good," and ask, "But how does this apply to society at large? After all, you can't legislate morality."

Not being able to legislate morality—meaning not being able to force people to think a certain way—has been well demonstrated by the failure to eliminate racial prejudice despite the enormous amount of legislation to enforce "fairness," and the failure to eliminate greed by legislating that the wealthy be taxed a higher percentage of their income. But legislating morality—meaning enforcing what somebody believes is good and right—is exactly what is done every time a law is made any law. For example, most people agree with a law against stealing. This law is based on the moral view that a person can own something. Some thieves, I'm sure, hold the moral view that everything is everybody's and therefore there is no such thing as stealing. Yet we have decided to legislate ownership laws because they are essential to maintain a free society (note *D&C* 134:2). The moral view that one can own something is enforced. Besides, if "you can't legislate morality," then the constitution most democracies are founded on is of no force because it is based on the moral view that people have certain rights and privileges (to life, liberty, etc.). Not only can you legislate morality, you can't help but legislate morality.

The Law of Chastity—Essential To Maintain a Free Society

Morality is constantly being legislated. However, certain issues—usually ones that promote the greatest freedom and prosperity but require the most personal accountability—get some shouting, "You can't legislate morality!" While most see (or take for granted) that lying and stealing cannot long be tolerated, many do not understand how the seventh commandment fits into their swing-your-fists-all-you-want-just-don't-hit-me morality. They may accept science's conclusion that the family unit evolved long before humans and was essential for the survival of higher species—that the family is the basic unit of society—but then do not make (or refuse to make) the connection between the concept and reality, and reject the seventh commandment that protects the basic unit of society. Yes, a society as large as most nations of the earth can be flexible enough to absorb the effects of a portion of its people not accepting accountability for protecting family, but when the masses do not, that society is on a downhill course to loosing its freedom. Destroy the basic unit of a free society, destroy the free society.

History demonstrates this fact. Societies that have tried to redefine the family structure may have benefitted (from the perspective of their leaders) in the short run, but the chaos of the basic unit soon led to a generation of chaos in which that society reaped the devastating social and economic consequences of its actions. Ezra Taft Benson wrote, "History reveals why the great Roman Empire fell." Referring to the work of the historian Will Durant, he continued:

> The first group of causes he lists as biological. These he considers the most fundamental. Mr. Durant claims they began with the educated classes, and started

with the breakdown of the home and the family, the limitation of children, the refusal to assume the obligations of honorable parenthood, the deferment and avoidance of marriage. . . . Sex ran riot and moral decay resulted (Benson, *The Red Carpet*, pp. 238-39; in *TETB* pp. 668-69).

What is it we're told? Those who fail to learn from history are bound to repeat it? Ezra Taft Benson taught:

> To the extent that citizens violate God's commandments, especially His laws of morality, to that degree they weaken the country's foundation. A rejection and repudiation of God's laws could well lead our nation to its destruction just as it has to Greece and Rome. It can happen to our country unless we repent. An eminent statesman once said: "Our very civilization itself is based upon chastity, the sanctity of marriage, and the holiness of the home. . . ." (J. Reuben Clark, Jr., *CR* October 1938, p. 137.) (*TETB*, p. 371.)

"When people proceed 'without principle,' erelong they will be 'without civilization,' 'without mercy,' and 'past feeling' (see Moro. 9:11-20)" (Neal A. Maxwell, of the Twelve, *Ensign*, May 1995, p. 68).

The U. S. currently exemplifies both sides of this lesson. It has rejected the accountability for the consequences of actions that some of its laws once proscribed. Some segments of its society have taken a harder blow. Over 70 percent of inner-city black children are being born to single mothers. This one fact alone is leading or has led to social and economic disaster. The soul of those that will bear the most burden is easily overlooked in the repetition of the sad statistics on education, crime, and poverty (so you can look them up on your own if you want). The other side of the lesson is currently being demonstrated by many inner-city Asian families. Many are first generation and do not speak the language. But they are maintaining more intact families. Although many start out living in the same inner-city environment, look up the statistics on their education, crime, and poverty after a few years of exercising their freedom.

Marriage—A Contract Concerning Family and Society

Since the basic unit of society is the family, harming the family unit harms society. If a free society is to protect itself—and its freedom—it must enact laws that protect and preserve families instead of being proud enough to think it can redefine families. Legislation that strengthens fathers and mothers helping their children strengthens liberty. Sexuality plays a tremendous role in all of this. The law of chastity is essential for the long-term preservation of a free society. The righteous Nephite and Israelite leaders understood this fact (Helaman 6:23; Alma 30:10-11).

The marriage contract serves (at least) two purposes. First, it is a contract that those who enter into it will be accountable for supporting each other and their children. Second, it grants authority to have sexual relations within that marriage. This can strengthen the couple's relationship, strengthening the family unit, strengthening society.

Sexual relations outside the marital contract harms one's present or future family. This harm can be emotional or physical (i.e., disease). It is within the right of a free society to mandate that its people not act on their desire to have sexual relationships that destroy the basic unit of that society. We license people who have the urge to drive to do so according to laws that protect us all. They may have the urge to run a red light because they feel it is a limit on their freedom to drive how they want. But that red light they have to sit at for a couple of minutes actually saves them time (Have you ever tried to get through a busy intersection when the traffic lights were not working?) and protects them and others from danger. Without good traffic and parking laws we would not have the freedom to drive at all because somebody could trap us in our parking space.

Laws on Procreation

The tremendous accountability that is required to maintain liberty and that intimidates some into opting for an elusive promise of security is brought to light in the sometimes fierce battle over laws regarding sex and reproduction. Satan knows that the (pro)creative process is at the very heart of things eternal. While Satan hides behind a facade of "You can eat the apple and not die," he knows that promoting security by relieving people from taking personal responsibility for the consequences of choosing to have sexual relations does not promote free agency at all. At the least, it promotes irresponsibility, and at the most, slavery. Then some wonder why with 93 percent of 1.5 million U. S. abortions a year for the last twenty years being performed for convenience it seems this society's up-and-coming citizens do not care about the consequences of their actions. "To claim that the solution to teenage sex and pregnancy is to merely acquaint youth with contraceptive devices and cleanliness procedures is not unlike a solution to the problem of shoplifting, which entails a course in how-not-to-get-caught" (Terrance D. Olson, Chair of the BYU Family Science Department, in an interview with *BYU Today* in 1985, quoted in *Brigham Young Magazine*, May 1995, p. 19). C. S. Lewis spoke to this:

> We remove the organ and demand the function. We make men without chests [hearts or souls] and expect of them virtue and enterprise. We laugh at honour and are shocked to find traitors in our midst (*The Abolition of Man*, p. 35).

Teen violent crime, the teen AIDS rate, and school dropout rates are increasing at a faster and faster pace. This is not what freedom is about. As Neal A. Maxwell, of the Twelve, said: "These and related consequences threaten to abort society's future" (*Ensign*, May 1995, p. 68).

Review the material for Section 134: "Church and State" for more about the Constitution and the requirement of a righteous and moral people to maintain its principles of protecting life and liberty.

Hate and Intolerance—Love and Forgiveness

Some are asking: "Can immorality or sin have a genetic basis?" If the fact that a behavior has a genetic link means that it is not immoral, then why do we discourage people's drunken behaviors and attempt to "reprogram" alcoholics? How could we be so prejudiced as to suggest that they suppress the urge to act on their genetically encoded instincts to drink themselves and others into slavery? Some cry that intolerance to immorality displays a lack of love and charity. (The people discussed in Alma 13:10-12 and 45:16 would be condemned.) But, can I not love my daughter with all my heart and also condemn her for not suppressing the urge to punch her little brother? While Jesus had an eternal love for the sinners he sat with, He condemned their sin.

The Saviour's love is for us all. We have all been given different weaknesses. God may give us these weaknesses by way of our genes or by way of our life situation. Our natural tendencies do not give us permission to break the laws of God. He knows our weaknesses and He will be our judge. He said:

> I give unto men weakness that they may be humble; and my grace is sufficient for all men that humble themselves before me; for if they humble themselves before me, and have faith in me, then will I make weak things become strong unto them (Ether 12:17).

With patience, faith in the Lord, and faith in ourselves, we can overcome our weaknesses. Jesus died for us to give us the chance to change ourselves. We can change our lives and be forgiven for any of these sins.

Zion—Prosperous, Strong, and Free

The Lord means for people to be free. The societies which have obeyed His law—His guidebook to freedom became prosperous, strong, and free. Why is Zion so powerful (see D&C 97:18-26 and Moses 7:17-21)? Because it promotes the accountability that is the requirement of liberty. It holds its people accountable to laws that promote and protect the family as its basic unit.

All people are invited to come to Zion. Although Zion even (and especially) loves those who wish to break its laws, they are not allowed to live in Zion. These outlaws use "flattering" words to destroy the foundation of liberty and convince others that Zion is a backwards, oppressive, bigoted, and prejudiced people (read Alma 46:10). But Zion terrifies the enemy because its people are so prosperous that they not only have the emotional and physical strength required to defend their families and their freedoms (read Alma 46:11-20), they also have the means necessary to support their defenses. Zion follows the Lord's guidebook to true, eternal freedom. Zion is built upon the rock of liberty.

BIBLIOGRAPHY

Andreoli, Thomas E., J. Claude Bennett, Charles C. J. Carpenter, Fred Plum, and Lloyd H. Smith, Jr. *Cecil Essentials of Medicine.* Third Edition. Philadelphia: W. B. Saunders Company, Harcourt Brace Jovanovich, Inc., 1993.

Benson, Ezra Taft. *The Constitution: A Heavenly Banner.* Salt Lake City: Deseret Book Co., 1986.

_____. *An Enemy Hath Done This.* Compiled by Jerreld L. Newquist. Salt Lake City: Parliament Publishers, 1969.

_____. *Teachings of Ezra Taft Benson.* Salt Lake City: Bookcraft, 1988.

_____. *A Witness and a Warning: A Modern-day Prophet Testifies of the Book of Mormon.* Salt Lake City: Deseret Book Co., 1988.

BYU Speeches of the Year. Provo: Brigham Young University Press.

Cannon, George Q. *Gospel Truth.* 2 vols. Compiled by Jerreld L. Newquist. Salt Lake City: Deseret Book Co., 1974.

Cassidy, Suzanne B. and David A. H. Whiteman. "Birth Defects and Genetic Disorders." *The National Medical Series for Independent Study: 2nd Edition: Pediatrics.* Edited by Paul H. Dworkin. Harwall, pp. 161-189).

Church News. Salt Lake City: Deseret News Press.

Clark, J. Reuben, Jr. *Behold the Lamb of God.* Salt Lake City: Deseret Book, 1962.

Clark, James Ratcliffe. *Messages of the First Presidency of the Church of Jesus Christ of Latter-day Saints.* 6 Vols. Salt Lake City: Bookcraft, 1965.

The Compact Edition of the Oxford English Dictionary. 2 vols. London: Oxford University Press, 1971.

Cook, Lyndon W. *Joseph Smith and the Law of Consecration,* Provo, UT: Grandin Book Co., 1985.

Cowley, Matthias F. *Wilford Woodruff, History of His Life and Labors,* Salt Lake City: Bookcraft, 1964.

The Doctrine and Covenants Student Manual: (Religion 324-325). Prepared by the Church Educational System. Salt Lake City: The Church of Jesus Christ of Latter-day Saints, 1981.

Doxey, Roy. *Latter-day Prophets and the Doctrine and Covenants.* 4 vols. Salt Lake City: Deseret Book Co., 1978.

The Ensign. Salt Lake City: The Church of Jesus Christ of Latter-day Saints.

"The Father and the Son: A Doctrinal Exposition by The First Presidency and The Twelve." In *The Articles of Faith.* 42d. ed. Salt Lake City: The Church of Jesus Christ of Latter-day Saints, 1982, pp. 466-473.

Garber, Ann, Michelle Fox, and Khalil Tabsh. "Genetic Evaluation and Teratology." *Essentials of Obstetrics and Gynecology.* 2d ed. Edited by Neville F. Hacker and J. George Moore. Philadelphia: W. B. Saunders Company, a division of Harcourt Brace and Company, 1992, pp. 93-108.

Grant, Heber J. *Gospel Standards: Selections from the Sermons and Writings of Heber J. Grant.* Compiled by G. Homer Durham under the direction of John A. Widtsoe and Richard L. Evans. Salt Lake City: Improvement Era, 1969.

Hymns of the Church of Jesus Christ of Latter-day Saints. Salt Lake City: The Church of Jesus Christ of Latter-day Saints, 1985.

Improvement Era. Salt Lake City: Mutual Improvement Association.

Journal of Discourses. 26 vols. Los Angeles: General Printing and Lithograph Co., 1961.

Kimball, Spencer W. *Faith Precedes the Miracle.* Salt Lake City: Deseret Book Co., 1972.

_____. *The Miracle of Forgiveness.* Salt Lake City: Bookcraft, 1969.

_____. *The Teaching of Spencer W. Kimball.* Edited by Edward L. Kimball. Salt Lake City: Bookcraft, 1982.

"Kirtland Revelation Book." Historical Department, The Church of Jesus Christ of Latter-day Saints, Salt Lake City.

The LDS Speaker's Sourcebook. Edited by Peggy Duckworth, Curtis Taylor, and Stan Zenk. Salt Lake City: Aspen Books, 1991.

Lee, Harold B. *Stand Ye in Holy Places.* Salt Lake City: Deseret Book Co., 1974.

Lewis, C. S. *The Abolition of Man, or, Reflections on Education with special reference to the teaching of English in the upper forms of Schools.* Paperback ed. New York: Macmillan Publishing Co., 1955.

_____. *The Great Divorce.* New York: Macmillan Publishing Co., 1960.

_____. *The Screwtape Letters.* Revised ed. New York: Macmillan Publishing Co., 1982.

The Life and Teachings of Jesus and His Apostles: Course Manual (Rel. 211-212). 2d ed. Prepared by the Church Educational System. Salt Lake City: The Church of Jesus Christ of Latter-day Saints, 1981.

Ludlow, Daniel H. *A Companion to Your Study of the Doctrine and Covenants.* 2 vols. Salt Lake City: Deseret Book Co., 1978.

Lundwall, Nels Benjamin, Comp. *Lectures On Faith by Joseph Smith.* Salt Lake City. n.d.

Maxwell, Neal A. *Deposition of a Disciple.* Salt Lake City: Deseret Book Co., 1976.

_____. *Men and Women of Christ.* Salt Lake City: Bookcraft, 1991.

_____. *Sermons Not Spoken.* Salt Lake City: Bookcraft, 1985.

_____. *That My Family Should Partake.* Salt Lake City: Deseret Book Co., 1974.

McKay, David O. *Gospel Ideals*. Salt Lake City: Improvement Era, 1954.

McConkie, Bruce R. *Doctrinal New Testament Commentary*. 3 vols. Salt Lake City: Bookcraft, 1965-73.

_____. *Mormon Doctrine*. 2d ed. Salt Lake City: Bookcraft, 1979.

Middlemiss, Clare. *Cherished Experiences from the Writings of David O. McKay*. Salt Lake City: Deseret Book Company. 1955.

Missionary Handbook published by The Church of Jesus Christ of Latter-day Saints, Salt Lake City, Utah copyright 1986 by Corporation of the President of The Church of Jesus Christ of Latter-day Saints.

Old Testament: Genesis - 2 Samuel (Religion 301) Student Manual. Prepared by the Church Educational System. Salt Lake City: The Church of Jesus Christ of Latter-day Saints.

Otten, L. G. and C. M. Caldwell. *Sacred Truths of the Doctrine and Covenants*. 2 Vols. 3d ed. Springville, Utah: LEMB, Inc., 1982.

Packer, Boyd K. *The Holy Temple*. Salt Lake City: Bookcraft, 1980.

Pearson, Glenn L. *The Book of Mormon: Key to Conversion*. Bookcraft, Salt Lake City, Utah, 1963.

Pratt, Parley P. *Autobiography of Parley P. Pratt*. 3d ed. Edited by Parley P. Pratt [son]. Salt Lake City: Deseret Book Co., 1966.

President's Commission on Model State Drug Laws. "Socioeconomic Evaluations of Addictions Treatment." Prepared by the Center of Alcohol Studies of Rutgers University, Piscataway, NJ. Dec. 1993.

Richards, LeGrand. *A Marvelous Work and a Wonder*. Rev. ed. Salt Lake City: Deseret Book Co., 1966.

Roberts, Brigham H. *A Comprehensive History of the Church*. 6 Vols. Salt Lake City: Deseret News Press, 1930.

Robinson, Stephen E. *Believing Christ: The Parable of the Bicycle and Other Good News*. Salt Lake City: Deseret Book Co., 1992.

Speeches of the Year, 1978. Provo: Brigham Young University Press, 1979.

Smith, Hyrum M., and Sjodahl, Janne M. *Doctrine and Covenants Commentary*. Rev. ed. Salt Lake City: Deseret Book Co., 1972.

Smith, Joseph. *History of The Church of Jesus Christ of Latter-day Saints*. 7 vols. 2d. ed. rev. Edited by B. H. Roberts. Salt Lake City: Deseret Book Co., 1978.

_____. *Teachings of the Prophet Joseph Smith*. Selected by Joseph Fielding Smith. Salt Lake City: Deseret Book Co., 1961.

Smith, Joseph F. *Gospel Doctrine*. 5th ed. Salt Lake City: Deseret Book Co., 1939.

Smith, Joseph Fielding. *Answers to Gospel Questions*. 5 vols. Compiled by Joseph Fielding Smith, Jr. Salt Lake City: Deseret Book Co., 1957-66.

_____. *Church History and Modern Revelation*. 2 vols. Salt Lake City: The Council of the Twelve Apostles, 1953.

_____. *Doctrines of Salvation*. 3 vols. Compiled by Bruce R. McConkie. Salt Lake City: Bookcraft, 1954-56.

_____. *Elijah the Prophet and his Mission*. Salt Lake City: Deseret Book Co., 1951.

_____. *The Progress of Man*. Salt Lake City: Deseret Book Co., 1964.

Sperry, Sidney B. *Book of Mormon Compendium*. Salt Lake City: Bookcraft, 1968.

Talmage, James E. *The Articles of Faith*. 42d. ed Salt Lake City: The Church of Jesus Christ of Latter-day Saints, 1982.

_____. *Jesus the Christ*. 33d ed. Salt Lake City: The Church of Jesus Christ of Latter-day Saints, 1981.

Taylor, John. *The Gospel Kingdom*. Selected by G. Homer Durham. Salt Lake City: Bookcraft, 1964.

Thatcher, Margaret. "The Moral Foundations of Society." An edited version of a lecture presented at a Hillsdale College seminar, "God and Man: Perspectives on Christianity in the 20th Century," in Nov. 1994. *Imprimis*. Hillsdale, Michigan: Hillsdale College, March 1995.

Times and Seasons. Nauvoo: The Church of Jesus Christ of Latter-day Saints, 1839-1846.

Turner, Rodney. "Joseph Smith and the Apocalypse of John." *The New Testament and the Latter-day Saints*. Edited by John K. Carmack et al. The Sidney B. Sperry Symposium (15th: 1987: Brigham Young University). Orem, Utah: Randall Book, 1987. pp. 319-345.

Widtsoe, John A. *Evidences and Reconciliations*. 3 vols. 2d ed. Salt Lake City: Bookcraft, 1951.

_____. *The Message of the Doctrine and Covenants*. Edited by G. Homer Durham. Salt Lake City: Bookcraft, 1969.

_____. comp. *Priesthood and Church Government*. Rev. ed. Salt Lake City: Deseret Book Co., 1954.

Wilson, Lycurgus A. *Life of David Patten*. Salt Lake City: The Deseret News, 1904.

Young, Brigham. *Discourses of Brigham Young*. Selected by John A. Widtsoe. Salt Lake City: Deseret Book Co., 1941.

INDEX

Bread (see *Jesus Christ*)

Brimstone, 334

Breastplate (see *Armor*)

Bridegroom (see *Jesus Christ*)

Buildings, church b. committee, 194-195; we dedicate ourselves to making them holy, 232

Burdens (see also, *Trials*), seek not to be cumbered, 134-5

Burgess, 236

C

Cain, seduced by Satan's pro-choice/no accountability philosophy, 332

Calamities (see *Persecution, Trials*)

Calling and election made sure, 274-277, 312-313; is not perfection, 276-277

Callings, cheerfully do, 258; foreordination in preexistence, 303; many called but few chosen, 251; magnify, 44, 164, 190; let your works be redoubled, 265-266; Lord blesses us our family for the sacrifice, 265; none too small 131-132; power in, 157; stand still and let God do His work, 258; work within boundaries, 156-157

Camp of Israel, 296-297; blessings promised to are same as in Old Testament times, 296

Capstone, The D&C is, 13

Carthage, Illinois, 294-295

Celestial Kingdom, characteristics of, 272, 298; heirs to, 298-299; three degrees in, 152; vision of, 297-298

Celestial Marriage (see *Marriage*)

Charity, gaining, 313; is not enduring abuse, 202-203

Chastise, keys for the chastiser, 196; purposes of, 207-208; reproving betimes with sharpness, 252; responsibilities of chastiser, 195-196, 236

Chastity (see also, *Sex*), key to personal and societal freedom, 73-75, 336-339; law of, 73-75; Lord warns of weaknesses, 134; Satan misguides, 134

Cherubim, 271

Children, are carnal, sensual, and devilish, 140; cannot be saved without atonement, 140; cannot sin, 140; instruction of, 139; have claim upon their parents, 161; of light, 225; in Millennium, 209; ordinances for those who have died, 298-301; parents to teach, 139; punishment of for sins of ancestors, 262-263; resurrect as a child, 299-300; salvation of, 139; turn to father, 15-16; unbaptized, 140; who die before age of accountability inherit celestial kingdom, 298-299; who die to be reunited with parents to be raised by them, 299-301

Choice, only through God's law, 330-335

Chosen (see *Calling*)

Church (see also, *Churches, Religion*), common consent in, 46-47; courts, 215-218; of devil 32, 53; government, 35; holds up light of Christ like a candle, 320; name of, 240-241; purpose of, 133, 197-198; records of, 89-90; separation of c. and state, 293

Churches (of the world), instituted by God, 293; pray for, 232; rights of, 293

Civil War, U. S., a curse for rejecting prophets, 171-172; prophesies and warnings of, 171-172

Cleansing of feet (see *Feet*)

Coffee (see *Word of Wisdom*)

Cola drinks (see *Word of Wisdom*)

Colesville, New York, branch of, 99; 106

Columbus, Christopher, ordained a high priest, 215

Comforter (see also, *Holy Ghost*), first, 275; second or other, 275-276

Commandments (see also, *Law of God*), are blessings, 113

Common consent, law of, 46-47

Common stock, plan of, 73

Concubines, 281

Conference, general c. of the church, 38-39

Confess sins for forgiveness, 110-112

Confidence in presence of God, 112, 253

Confounding the enemy, 143

Consecration, law of, definition of, 95; history of, 95-99; purposes of, 154-156; not replaced by tithing, 245; still in effect, 98; and United Order (see *United Order*), 153

Constitution (see also, *Government*), concerns all nations, 291; and constitutional laws, 288-293; disobedience of, 291-293; duty of citizens to support, 289; established by God, 215; of the priesthood, 250-251; protects all flesh, 215; on verge of crumbling, 289

Contending against evil, 32

Contention, avoiding, 313; not part of preaching, 32, 143

Converting power, 32

Convincing power, 19

Cook, Gene R., 310-311

Council, in heaven, 303; high (see *Courts*); standing, 216

Counselor (see also, *Leader*), duties of, 158; equal with president, 188

Courts, 215-218; bishop's, stake high council, first presidency, etc., 217; let accountability rest with, 218; purposes of church courts, 216; results of court actions, 217

Covenant, covenants are the "more weighty matters," 243-244; the new and everlasting, 41-42, 278; oath and, 165

Covill, James, 66-67

Cowdery, Oliver, Assistant President to the church, 294; entrusted with the Book of Commandments, 140-141; keeps history of the church, 90; "Lamanite" missionary, 57; one of Three Witnesses, 21; receives revelation, 25-26; upset with Joseph Smith, 50; to write and select books for church education system, 108; wrote D&C 134, 287

Cowdery, Warren, 225

Crime, cost of, 222-223

Cross, take up, 68

Curse, and mark of curse, 306; lifted from all who will repent, 307; by power of priesthood, 120, 283; purpose of, 306-307

D

Dancing, 297

Daniel, disobeys law, 292

Darkness, outer, (see *Perdition*)

David, fallen, 282; key of, 322

Daughters, of Sarah, 164

Fulness, of gospel in the Book of Mormon (see *Book of Mormon*); of times, 82, 250

G

Gabriel, is Noah, 269

Garments, clean, 320

Gate, is the senior apostle, 78-79

Gather, how to be gathered, 313; to places appointed by Lord's servants, 264; why gather, 80

Gathering (see *Tribes of Israel*)

Genealogy (see also, *Baptism for the dead*; *Temple work*), necessary for our salvation, 15-16; treasure of, 236-237

Generation, definition of, 163; of fullness of times (see *Fulness of times*)

Gentiles, 82, 106; cursed in the beginning, 306; vexed by "Lamanites," 173

Gibbon, Edward, 332

Gifts of the Spirit, the best, 87; seek earnestly, 87-88; what they are, 87-89; what they are for, 86; who has them, 86

Gilbert, Sidney, called to be an Elder, 101

Gilbert's store, destroyed, 220

Gird up loins, 63

Glory, 174-176; gaining, 313; ordinance of, 314

Godhead, oneness of, 37; characteristics of, 272-3

Godhood, 64-65, 281

Gospel, first principles of (see *Faith*); fulness of (see *Book of Mormon*); means good news, 269; parents to teach to children (see *Parents*); a psalm of joy, 269

Government, citizens generally get what they deserve, 289; citizens must be righteous, 289; civilized g. based on law of God, 334-335; duties of to be approved by God, 288; established by God, 288; leaders must be good, wise, and honest, 289; legislating morality, 335-336; pray for leaders, 232; separation of church and state, 289-290, 293

Grace, saved by after all we can do, 112

Granger, Oliver, 244

Gratitude, key to forgiveness and charity, 114

Grave (see *Baptism, symbolism of*)

H

Handicapped, mentally handicapped to inherit celestial kingdom, 299; physically handicapped and promises of Word of Wisdom, 185

Handshake, Satan will offer hand, 271

Happiness, gaining, 313

Harris, Martin, and lost manuscript, 16-17; witness of Book of Mormon, 21

Healing (see *Sickness, laws on*)

Hearing the voice of the Lord, 33

Heart, broken, 114-115; turning of to fathers (see *Genealogy*)

Heaven (see *Celestial Kingdom*; *Spirit world*)

Hell, a subdivision of spirit prison, 150-151; who enters, 151

Herbs (see *Medicine*)

High council (see *Courts*; *Stake High Council*)

High priests, the 144,000, 324

Holy Ghost, baptism of (see *Baptism of fire*); body of, 273; calling of, 273; characteristics of, 273;

Comforter (see also, *Comforter*), 45; enjoying companionship of, 314; gift of (see *Baptism of fire*); sin against (see *Perdition, sons of*)

Holy Spirit of Promise, 274

Home (see also, *House*), governed by the priesthood, 251; a home of . . . , 179; pattern after the Nauvoo House, 261

Homosexuality (see *Adultery*; *Chastity*)

Honor, ordinance of, 314

Hope, leads to faith, 26

Hosanna, definition of, 35

Hot drinks (see *Word of Wisdom*)

House (see also, *Home*), and building committee, 195; govern in meekness, 55-56; of God (see *Temple*); of learning, etc., 179; of the Lord, 195; of First Presidency, 195

Humility (see *Pride*)

Humor (see *Laughter*)

Hurlburt, Philastus, 220

Husband, duties of, 161, 251

Hypocrites in the church, 93-94

I

Idleness, 75-75

Immodesty (see *Adultery*; *Chastity*)

Immortality (see also, *Life*; *Lives*), 280

Independence, Missouri (see *Zion*)

Ingratitude (see *Gratitude*)

Isaiah, 238-239

Inspired version (see *Joseph Smith Translation*)

Instrument in the hands of God (see *Leaders*; *Missionary*)

Integrity, 260

Intelligence (see also, *Knowledge*; *Learning*; *Study*; *Wisdom*), 174-175; gaining, 193-194, 314; a being, 193; a property of a being, 193-194

Isaac, exaltation of, 281

Israel (see also, *Camp of Israel*; *Jerusalem*; *Tribes*)

J

Jackson County (see *Zion*)

Jacob, exaltation of, 281

Jehovah is Jesus Christ, 309

Jerusalem, temple of, 262; Judah to flee to, 285

Jesus Christ, Alpha and Omega, 34; the Amen, 322; as an angel, 271; appearance of, 234, 320; to appear in temple, 284; the bread of life, 321; Bridegroom, 58-59, 285; clothed in red, 328; comes quickly, 59; controls the elements, 121, 243; Creator, 191; eyes of fire, 234; is the Father 191-192; growth of, from grace to grace, 192; is Great I Am, 34; is Jehovah, 309; Judge, 152; King, 309; Law giver, 309; light of, 174-175, 320; Lord of Sabaoth, 173; the master physician, 252; millennial reign of (see *Millennium*); as a ministering spirit, 270-271; morning star, 322; omnipotent, 330; omniscient, 330; one with Father, 37; Other Comforter (see *Comforter*); received not of fullness at first, 192; savior of all Father's creations, 149, 191; second coming of, 59, 80-85; seeing (see *See God*); signs of coming, 81-85; Son of Man of Holiness, 84; stem of Jesse, 239; symbolism of walking on water, 268; taking name in vain of, 128-9

Jewels, are the righteous, 119

Jews (see also, *Judah*), Romans slaughter, 81-82; turn hearts to prophets, 202

John, the apostle, calling and election sure, 312; has a greater work to do, 28-29; has not died but will, 28-29

Johnson, John, to be a member of the United Firm, 198

John the Baptist restores Aaronic Priesthood, 29

Joseph (see *Tribes*)

Joseph Smith Translation of the Bible, 189-190

Journal (see also, *Book*; *Church, records of*)

Joy, gaining, 313

Judah (see also, *Jerusalem temple*; *Jews*), to flee to mountains of Lord's House, 285

Judge (see also, *Bishop*; *Jesus Christ, judge*), consequences of poor judgement, 216; judges in Israel, 144-5, 215-216; qualifications of, 215

Judgement, exercising righteous j., 314

Just (see *Resurrection, of just*)

Justice (see *Atonement*; *Forgiveness*; *Freedom*; *Mercy*)

Justification, 38

K

Keys, of Aaronic Priesthood (see *Aaronic Priesthood*); of David, 322; to discern spirits, 270-271; of dispensation of Abraham, 235; of Elijah, 235; of First Presidency, 158; of gathering and leading of ten tribes, 234-235; to kingdom, 158; of mysteries (see *Melchizedek priesthood*); and ordinances that cannot be received in mortality, 302-303; president holds all, 158; of resurrection, 150, 302-303; of sealing power, 235; of spirit creation, 150; three keys by which messengers may be known, 270-71

Kingdom (see also, *Celestial*; *Terrestrial*; *Telestial*), of God, 132-3; of heaven, 132-3; of the devil, 149-150

King James Version (see *Joseph Smith Translation*)

Kirtland, Ohio, gather to, 80; retain stronghold in, 131

Kirtland Temple, became defiled, 241; dedication of, 231-233; delay in building, 195; keys restored in, 234-235

Knight, Joseph, Sr., called to the work, 18

Knowledge (see also, *Learning, Study, Truth*; *Wisdom*); gaining, 314; gift of, 88; God's, 64-65; held back until the Millennium, 209-211; hidden, 184-185; learning of, 177; necessary to salvation, 277; only obtained through Spirit, 157; possibility of, 157; Satan's, 25-26; senses can be fooled, 157; of spiritual things, 157; that Jesus Christ is the Son of God, 87; treasures of, 184-185

L

Language, profanity 128-9; of scripture, 135-136

Lamanites, blossom as rose, 83-84; mission to, 57

Lamb (see *Jesus Christ*)

Last days (see *Second coming*)

Latter-day Saints (see *Church, name of*)

Laughter, cast away excess, 176-177; humor, 204-205; solemnity, 204-205

Law, blessings based on, 312-317; book of l. of God, 168; of chastity (see *Chastity*); of consecration (see *Consecration, law of*); and Constitution (see *Constitution*); disobedience of (see *Constitution*); freedom in (see *Freedom*; *Government*); of the land

(see *Constitution*; *Government*); of the Lord (see *Law of God*); purpose of, 70-71; of retaliation and retribution, 202-203; of sacrifice (see *Consecration*); shall go forth from Zion, 211; on sickness and death, 76-77; of tithing (see *Tithing*); of war, 200-201; on widows and orphans, 161-162

Law of God (see also, *Constitution*; *Government*; *Law*), basis for societal freedom, 334-335; the Lord's law, 69-78

Law, William, 263

Leaders (see also, *Counselor*; *Missionary work*; *Teach*), becoming instrument of God, 314; church leaders not perfect, 231; concentrate on the more weighty matters, 243; duties of, 237-238; gaining convincing power, 313; leaders of nations blessed, 232; let every man learn his duty, 230; Lord blesses family of church leaders, 265; speaking evil of church leaders, 249-250; strengthening church leaders, 230-231; strengthen your brethren, 230-231

Learning (see also, *Intelligence*; *Knowledge*; *Study*; *Truth*; *Wisdom*), gaining, 193-194, 314; house of, 179; impossible to be saved in ignorance, 277; let every man learn his duty, 230

Legislate (see also *Constitution*; *Government*; *Law*), morality, 335-336

Levi, sons of and their offering, 30-31

Levitical Priesthood (see *Aaronic priesthood*)

Levites (see *Levi*)

Lewis, C. S., 333-335, 338

Liberty (see *Freedom*)

Life (see also, *Lives*), eternal, 280, 313

Light, children of, 225; of Christ, 174-175; intelligence is, 174-175; of truth, 174-175, 192-193

Lincoln, Abraham, and Civil War, 171-172; and Joseph Smith, 171-172; signs anti-polygamy act of 1862, 304

Literary firm, 153

Lives, eternal, 280

Loins, armor for, 49; gird up, 63

Lord of Sabaoth (see *Jesus Christ, Lord of Sabaoth*)

Lord's day, the, 116

Lost tribes (see *Tribes, lost*)

Love, expressing invites Spirit, 310; is giving, 59-60

Loyalty (see *Smith, Hyrum*)

Lucifer (see *Satan*)

Lust (see also, *Adultery*; *Chastity*), causes war, 316

Lying, 73

M

McIlwaine's Bend, Satan disturbs water of, 121

Magnify, be magnified by the Spirit, 311, 316; m. your callings (see *Callings*)

Mammon, make friends with, 160

Man, sacrifice of natural m., 115; is spirit, 176

Manifesto concerning plural marriage, 303-305

Man of Holiness, 84

Manna, 321

Manuscript, lost m. of Book of Mormon, 16-17

Mark of the curse (see *Curse*)

Marriage, a contract concerning family and society, 337-338; in the Church, 147; law of celestial m., 277-279, 283; plural (see *Plural marriage*)